Ladies' COMPACTS

of the NINETEENTH & TWENTIETH CENTURIES

ROSELYN GERSON

WALLACE-HOMESTEAD BOOK COMPANY
RADNOR, PENNSYLVANIA

Published in Radnor, Pennsylvania 19089, by Wallace-Homestead Book Company

Designed by William E. Lickfield
Photographs by Arthur Field

Manufactured in the United States of America

Library of Congress Cataloging in Publication Data

Gerson, Roselyn.
Ladies' compacts of the nineteenth and twentieth centuries
Roselyn Gerson; photographs by Arthur Field.
p. cm.
Bibliography: p. 222
Includes index.
ISBN 0–87069–523–1
1. Compacts (Cosmetics)—History—19th century. 2. Compacts (Cosmetics)—History—20th century. 3. Compacts (Cosmetics)—Collectors and collecting. I. Title.
NK4890.C65G47 1989
730—dc19 88-51501
CIP

Current prices in the Value Guide are meant to be used as a guideline only and are not intended to determine prices. Dealer and auction prices are determined by condition, uniqueness, composition, age, and by supply and demand. Prices vary from one section of the country to another. The publisher and author assume no responsibility for any losses that may occur from the use of this value guide or from any other information in this publication.

1 2 3 4 5 6 7 8 9 0 8 7 6 5 4 3 2 1 0 9

In memory of our beloved firstborn grandchild
PAMELA BETH GERSON
1979–1981
Leukemia

I dedicate this book to my husband, Alvin, without whose encouragement, support, understanding, great patience, enthusiasm, and sense of humor this book would still be a dream and not a reality; to our children, Robin and Denis, Roy, Ira and Gayle, for their patience and understanding, and to our grandchildren, Ilyse, Sarah, Shayna, Katerina, and Andrew.

Contents

Foreword viii **Preface** x **Acknowledgments** xii

1 A History of Compacts 1

2 A Start-Off Guide for the Collector 18

Whiting & Davis Company Mesh Bags 18
The Famous Coty Powder Puffs 19
Chatelaines, Chatelettes, and Coach Chatelaines 25
Salvador Dali's "Bird-in-Hand" Compact 25
Minaudières, Carryalls, and Necessaires 27
A Vanity/Bracelet Compact 29
Tips from a Compact Collector 31
Newsworthy Compacts 33

3 Gallery of Compacts 37

4 Value Guide 171

Value Listing 172

5 Patents 180

Patent Numbers Issued by Year 180
A Sampling of Important Patents 181

6 Manufacturing Information 201

List of Materials 201
Compact Manufacturers and Trade Names 201
Landmark Ads from the Heyday of Compacts 206

Glossary 219 Bibliography 222 Index 225

Foreword

ANTIQUING—that's one word that always made me cringe. The weekend would begin with my wife's favorite request, "Let's go antiquing. It's fun!" I always begged off, saying that I had work to do. I finally found out what "fun" she had in the summer of 1976, the Bicentennial year, when we went to a July 4th celebration in Sparrowbush, New York. Suddenly I was surrounded by antique vendors and flea market booths offering all kinds of "bargains." Now, don't get me wrong, I like a bargain as well as the next guy, but spending $25 for an old cake plate was not my idea of fun—or a bargain either, for that matter.

As I wandered from table to table watching the excitement on my wife's face, I noticed a box with some small trinkets that were being sold as "collectibles." While my wife looked at the larger, big-ticket articles, I rummaged through the small items. That's when it happened! "Look at these great collectibles," I shouted. She put down the item she was ready to purchase and came to see the "specials" I had discovered.

They were two ladies' compacts. One was black enamel and the other was silver with a cloisonné center. The price was right: The enamel compact was 50 cents and the silver was 25 cents. Not only were they inexpensive, but they would need little space. I had to convince my wife to give up antiquing and take up collecting.

"Let me buy these for you as the start of your new collection and let's see if we can add to them at other markets," I pleaded. I was happy when she agreed. Look at how much money and room I saved just in that one trip alone. Little did I know! Here we are almost twelve years later and we now have compacts displayed on walls, in cases, and in trays. So much for space saving. I also defy anyone to find a silver or enamel compact today for 50 cents.

But I have to admit this small venture into the land of antiques and collectibles has changed our lives for the better. Now I look forward to spending my weekends with my wife searching for that one elusive different compact. In the past decade we have traveled to many parts of the country and have enjoyed each other's company and mutual interests. There are other benefits as well. I can honestly say I am now having "fun" and the work I saved for the weekend now gets done at the office.

Speaking of benefits, I have the sole distinction of being called "Mr. Compact Lady."

ALVIN GERSON

Preface

MOST of the manufacturers of ladies' vintage compacts are no longer in existence, and unfortunately, these manufacturers kept few or no records. Many firms moved, changed hands, or were absorbed by other companies. Any records that were maintained were lost in the shuffle. The information and data relating to compacts have been compiled from catalogs, magazines, advertisements, articles in antique papers, antique books, patents, and trademarks, and also from sources totally unrelated to compacts. I also did research in museums, libraries, auction houses, and at antique shows.

Many compacts have no identifying marks such as patent numbers, manufacturer's name, or place of origin. In order to determine the circa of these compacts, I compared their designs, mirrors, backs, clasps, powder sifters, puffs, composition, and motifs with similar examples. Many compact manufacturers spanned two or three decades, so rather than speculate on the exact date a specific compact was manufactured, only the name of the manufacturer, if known, is listed.

Vintage compacts and vanity cases are one of the most sought-after new collectibles today. They are especially desirable because their workmanship, design, technique, and the materials used would be expensive and virtually impossible to duplicate today. Vintage compacts are reminders of another era. They are a nostalgic, romantic link in miniature with the past. They were made of precious metals, base metals, fabrics, plastics, and in almost every conceivable natural or man-made material imaginable. Commemorative, premium, patriotic, figural, combination compacts, Art Deco, and enamel compacts are just a few of the myriad examples.

History once again repeats itself: The "old" compacts are the "new" collectibles. Vintage compacts are becoming more and more precious and are rapidly appreciating in value.

Acknowledgments

I wish to express my appreciation to the following people for their willingness to share resources and pictures and for allowing them to be included in this book: Manny Banayo, Manager, Archives, at Sears, Roebuck; Catherine Dike, "Cane Curiosa"; Cindy Fuener of the Illinois State Historical Library; Peggy Gilges, Art Nouveau and Art Deco at Christie's East; Joan Kropf, Curator of the Salvador Dali Museum; Linda Thomson, Public Relations at Whiting & Davis Co.; Charles H. Thorne, Media Relations Manager at Montgomery Ward; Ellen and Robert Yaseen of Stratton of London, Inc.; Janet Zapata, Tiffany Archivist. For their assistance I thank Arthur Ebbin, Interlibrary Loan Librarian at the Nassau County Library Service; Jim Huffman of the New York Library Patent Office; Lisa B. Mitchell, and Arthur Field. My thanks to the members of the Compact Collectors Club for offerings of new friendships and continued enthusiasm and encouragement. In addition, I am most grateful to Sandra Andacht who created the impetus needed to make this book a reality. I am also deeply appreciative to my editor, Kathy Conover, for her guidance and valuable input.

And a very special thank you to my dear friend, June Berliner, for her encouragement and for generously sharing her catalog resources with me.

A History of Compacts

THE use of cosmetics and cosmetic containers can be traced back to ancient civilization. The word "cosmetic" is derived from the Greek word *kosmein,* meaning to decorate or adorn. Cosmetics were used to enhance and embellish the natural beauty of both men and women. The oldest-known surviving cosmetic is powder which was originally made by pulverizing flowers and fragrant leaves.

The predecessors of the powder compact were the Oriental ointment containers, the Egyptian kohl-pot, the Etruscan cosmetic jar, the French unguent jar, and the English sweet coffer. Although cosmetics originated in the Orient, the Egyptian tombs yielded the first evidence of the use of cosmetics. In the days of antiquity, it was customary for kings and queens to be buried with their personal artifacts and most valued possessions. When Egyptian tombs were excavated, archaeologists discovered cosmetic spoons and containers known as kohl-pots (Fig. 1). Kohl-pots were found in various sizes and were made of onyx, glass, ivory, bone, alabaster, steatite, and wood. Kohl was a black mineral substance used to embellish eyelids and lashes. The kohl was applied with an elaborately carved ivory or wood cosmetic spoon or a kohl-stick (Fig. 2). In addition to being used as a cosmetic, kohl also shielded the eyes from the desert's glaring sun.

In ancient Greece, Rome, and China, carbonate of lead was used to whiten the face and alkanet was used for rouge. Queen Jezebel is believed to have introduced cosmetics to the Hebrews. In India, both men and women used cosmetics after the bath.

Cosmetics were used throughout the Middle Ages. The

Fig. 1 Egyptian kohl-pots, obsidian with gold mountings, Twelfth Dynasty. Courtesy of the Metropolitan Museum of Art, Purchase, Rogers Fund, and Henry Walters Gift, 1916 (16.1.33–35).

Crusaders returning to Britain brought back cosmetics from the harems in the East. Cosmetics were used extensively by men and women alike in Renaissance Italy and France. In Britain during Queen Elizabeth's reign, cosmetics were kept in sweet coffers that were restricted to the boudoir.

In late eighteenth-century England the use of cosmetics was so widespread that Parliament passed a law that made the use of cosmetics and other seductive ploys akin to witchcraft:

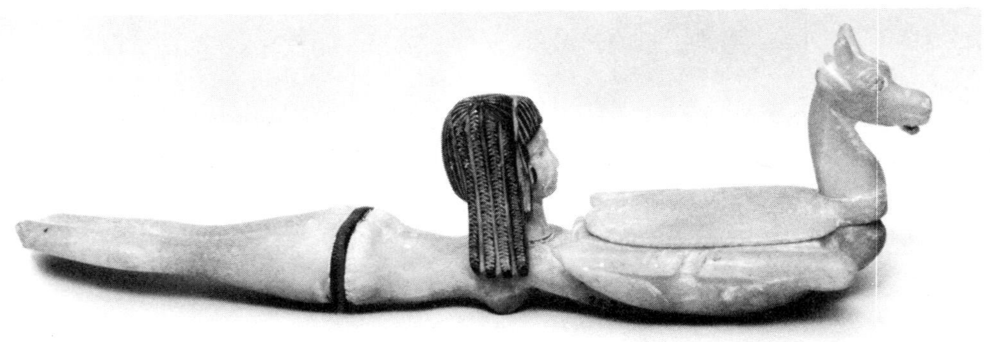

Fig. 2 Egyptian covered cosmetic spoon, alabaster and slate, c. Eighteenth Dynasty. Courtesy of the Metropolitan Museum of Art, Rogers Fund, 1926 (26.2.47).

That all women of whatever age, rank, profession, or degree, whether virgins, maids or widows, that shall, from and after such Act, impose upon, seduce, and betray into matrimony, any of His Majesty's subjects, by the scents, paints, cosmetic washes, artificial teeth, false hair, Spanish wool, iron stays, hoops, high heeled shoes, bolstered hips, shall incur the penalty of the law in force against witchcraft and like misdemeanors, and that the marriage, upon conviction, shall stand null and void.

Women who used cosmetics were suspected of being "ladies of the night," and it was suggested in *Eve's Glossary* by the Marquise de Fontenoy in 1897 that women, instead of using harmful artificial and poisionous substances, use only natural substances, such as the ingredients in the following three recipes. The first receipt, for *Baume des Sultanes,* a balm for the skin, was used in Oriental harems to mask imperfections. The recipe for powder was handed down from a celebrated beauty at the Court of Louis XIV of France. The third recipe is for rouge.

Baume Des Sultanes

Mix into 4 ounces of sweet almond oil
320 grains melted white virgin wax
320 grains whale white
100 grains finely powdered benzoin
60 grains tincture of ambergris
320 grains pulverized rice feculae
15 grains pure carmine

Poudre d'amour

Scrape six juicy raw carrots and half a pink beet-root. Squeeze the juice through a muslin bag and put it aside. Mix 3 ounces finely powdered cornstarch with the carrot and beet juice. Sit it in the sun and stir occasionally until the fluid evaporates, leaving the tinted starch dry. Sift through a piece of silk gauze and add:

300 grains Powdered Venetian talc
300 grains Powdered lycopodium
45 grains Powdered bergamot
7 grains Powdered bismuth

Sift again and keep in a sandalwood box.

Mousse de fraises (strawberry foam)

Put three quarts of fine ripe strawberries in a wide-mouthed, thick glass bottle together with a pint of distilled water. Place the bottle in a large saucepan of water on a slow fire and let it boil for two hours. Strain through an extra-fine hair-sieve and set aside. When cool, add:

4 drops attar of roses
2 drops attar of neroli
12 ounces deodorized spirit
15 grains pure carmine
30 grains best Russian isinglass, melted

Keep in a glass jar in a cool place. Apply with a fine sponge.

Fig. 3

1 Sterling-silver stylized floral engraved compact designed as hand mirror with coral cabochon thumbpiece, lipstick in handle, Italy, c. 1920s.

2 Antiqued sterling-silver enameled lipstick case; painted scene on lid lifts to reveal mirror, Italy, c. 1900s.

3 Antiqued sterling-silver enameled compact with painted scene on lid and gilded interior, Italy, late 19th century.

In the late nineteenth century, the use of cosmetics in Europe, particularly in France, Italy, and Austria, experienced a revival. The most precious, stunning, and exquisitely executed compacts were made in Europe at the turn of the century. Italy produced sterling-silver compacts with gilt overlay and colorful painted enamel scenes on the lids, and also engraved sterling-silver compacts resembling hand mirrors with a lipstick concealed in the handle (Fig. 3). French compacts or vanity cases

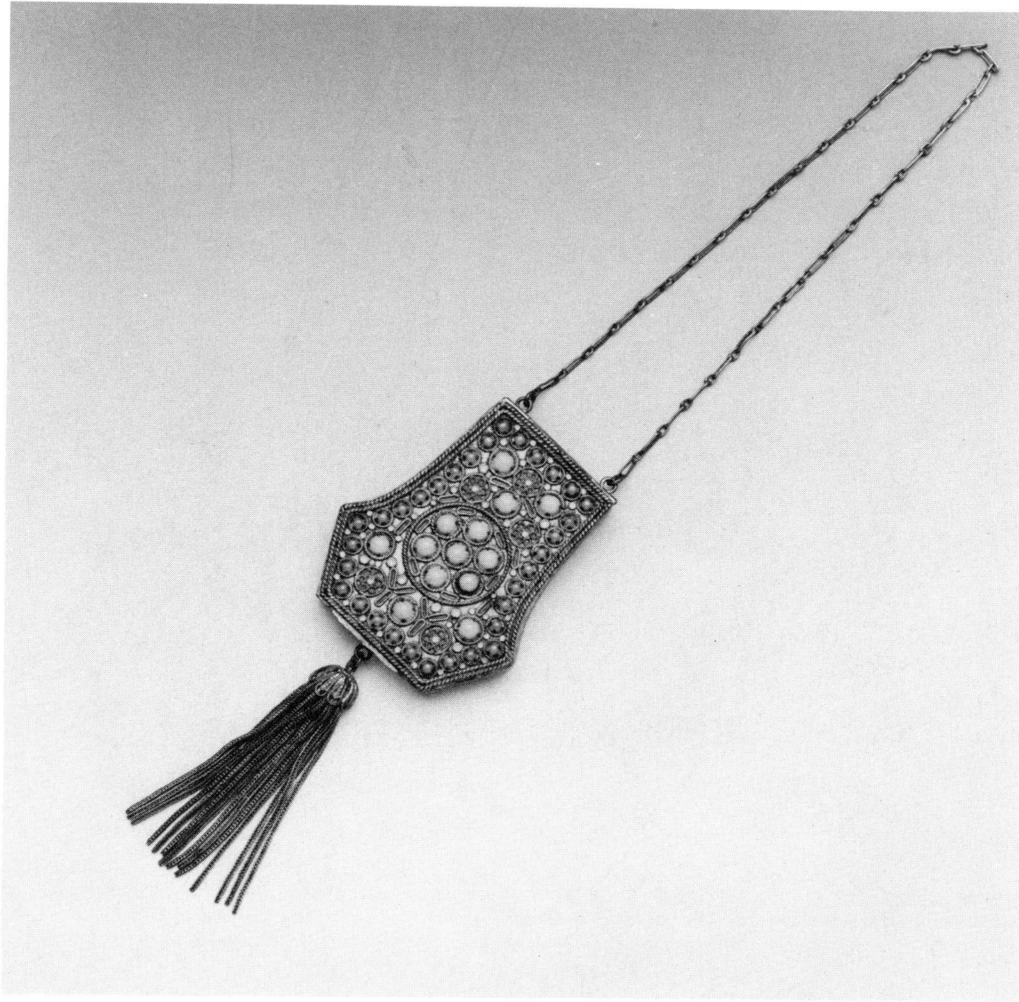

Fig. 4 Matte goldtone-finish vanity case with enameled lid encrusted with pronged blue and pink cabochon stones; carrying chain and tassel, goldtone interior, and compartments for powder, lipstick, and eye makeup, France, turn of the century.

were finished in a matte gilt and encrusted with gems or stones set in prongs, with either a wrist chain or finger-ring chain attached (Fig. 4). The ladies' cane/compact was popular in France and was sold in the early 1900s by prestigious jewelry houses such as Hermès of Paris. Austrian compacts were elaborately enameled with a ring, chain, or lipstick attached.

During the Victorian Era the use of artificial beauty aids was frowned upon in polite society, a conservative attitude that was also adopted in America. Before World War I the use of makeup was considered immoral. Instead, proper diet, fresh air, and exercise were recommended as the only way to improve on nature. In the early twentieth century, women were advised to pinch their cheeks to obtain a natural, rosy glow. In 1923 the Dorothy Gray cosmetic firm introduced the face patter to stimulate circulation and thereby make the cheeks naturally pink (Fig. 5).

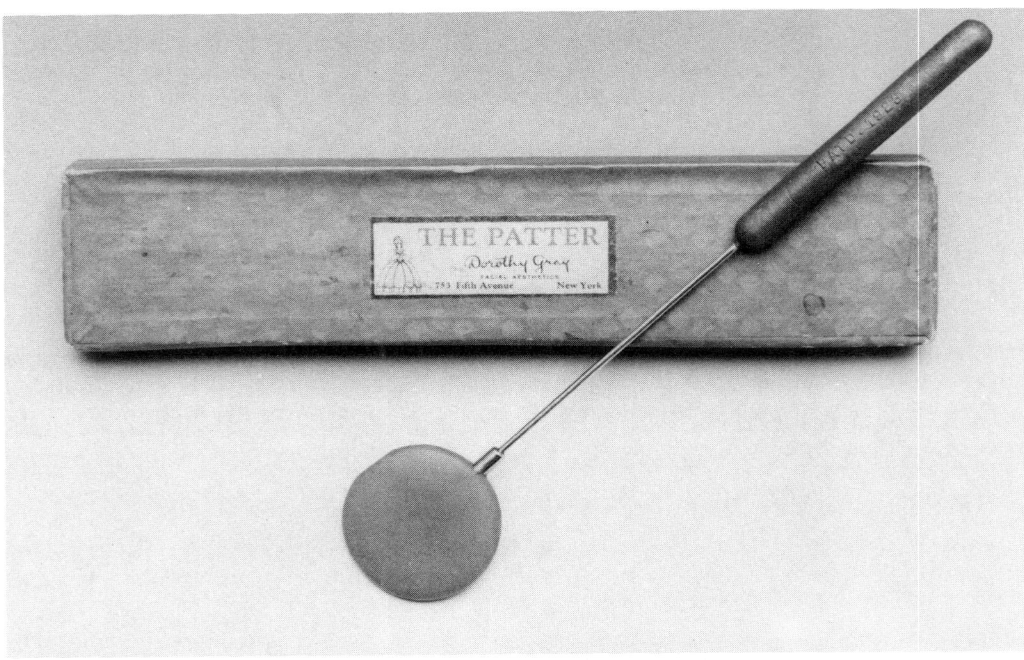

Fig. 5 Dorothy Gray "Patter" with description on lid: "A specially contrived instrument for applying stimulation to the facial muscles without irritating the skin"; original Patter box, patented 1923.

New Cert. under Sec. 7(c) issued July 20, 1948, to Lehn & Fink Products Corporation, Bloomfield, N. J.
For Amendment under Sec. 7(d) of the Act of July 5, 1946, see other side.

Registered June 2, 1931

Trade-Mark 283,555

RENEWED

UNITED STATES PATENT OFFICE

DOROTHY GRAY, OF BLOOMFIELD, NEW JERSEY, AND NEW YORK, N. Y.

ACT OF FEBRUARY 20, 1905

Application filed December 17, 1930. Serial No. 309,068.

Dorothy Gray

STATEMENT

To the Commissioner of Patents:

Dorothy Gray, a corporation organized under the laws of the State of New Jersey, located at Bloomfield, New Jersey, and having an office at No. 683 Fifth Avenue, New York, New York, has adopted and used the trade-mark shown in the accompanying drawing, for PATTERS FOR THE SKIN AND TISSUE AND REDUCING CHIN STRAP, in Class 44, Dental, medical, and surgical appliances, and presents herewith five specimens showing the trade-mark as actually used by the applicant upon the goods, and requests that the same be registered in the United States Patent Office in accordance with the act of Februry 20, 1905, as amended.

The trade-mark has been continuously used and applied to said goods in applicant's business since July 15, 1928.

The trade-mark is a facsimile of the signature of applicant's predecessor in business.

Applicant is the owner of registration No. 200,419, June 30, 1925, assigned by applicant's predecessor, together with the right to use her facsimile signature, by assignment recorded January 22, 1927, in liber I 129, page 110.

The trade-mark is applied or affixed to the goods by placing a printed or other appropriate label, displaying the mark, on receptacles containing the goods, and in divers other ways.

The undersigned hereby appoints Edward S. Rogers, Allen M. Reed and William T. Woodson, 843 Peoples Gas Building, Chicago, Illinois, and Francis L. Browne, Dudley Browne, and Thomas L. Mead, Jr., suite 605, Shoreham Building, 15th and H Streets, N. W., Washington, D. C., its attorneys, to prosecute this application for registration, with full power of substitution and revocation, to make alterations and amendments therein, to receive the certificate of registration and to transact all business in the Patent Office connected therewith.

DOROTHY GRAY,
By EDWARD PLANT,
Pres.

Dorothy Gray trademark 283,555 registered on June 2, 1931, for Patters of the Skin.

Attitudes regarding cosmetics changed drastically in the first quarter of the twentieth century. The use of makeup during the day became accepted and was no longer looked upon with disdain. The trend-setting silver screen stars played an important part in the acceptance of makeup. The word "makeup" in fact originated with stage and screen stars. Women began to recognize the importance of personal beauty and adopted a "modern" image aided by the use of cosmetics. As women became "liberated" and as more women entered the business world, the use of cosmetics became a routine part of a woman's grooming. Subsequently, the compact became a necessity.

Before World War I, women smoking in public was universally frowned upon. In fact, an Italian composer, Ermanno Wolf-Ferrari, wrote an opera in 1909 called "Il Segreto di Susanna" (The Secret of Susanna). Susanna's secret was not that she was unfaithful to her husband, but rather that she smoked cigarettes without her husband's knowledge. After the war, when it became acceptable and fashionable for women to smoke, accessories that accommodated both makeup and cigarettes emerged. Ronson, Elgin American, Evans, Volupté, and Richard Hudnut made compact/cigarette cases in a variety of combinations, designs, and materials. These cases not only conserved space in a purse but also allowed a woman to light a cigarette and at the same time have access to her compact.

The nomenclature soon broadened for the various styles of cosmetic containers in addition to the "compact":

Compact: A small portable makeup box (Fig. 6) containing a mirror, puff, and powder with either a screw-top, slip-cover, or piano-hinge lid.

Vanity case: A powder compact that also contains rouge and/or lipstick (Fig. 7).

Vanity bag: A dainty evening bag, usually made of mesh, incorporating a compact as an integral part of the bag (Fig. 8).

Vanity purse: A leather, fabric, metal, or beaded purse that contains a vanity case as part of the purse.

Vanity clutch: A small clutch bag with specific compartments for a

Fig. 6 Elgin American satin and gilt hand-engraved compact with plastic beading around edge and center monogram, c. 1950s.

Fig. 7 Black plastic vanity case with rhinestone geometric design on lid; front opens to reveal mirror and powder and rouge compartments, back contains coin pocket; black carrying cord with lipstick concealed in tassel, c. 1920s.

Fig. 8 Sterling-silver hallmarked octagonal mesh vanity bag with goldtone interior and finger-ring chain.

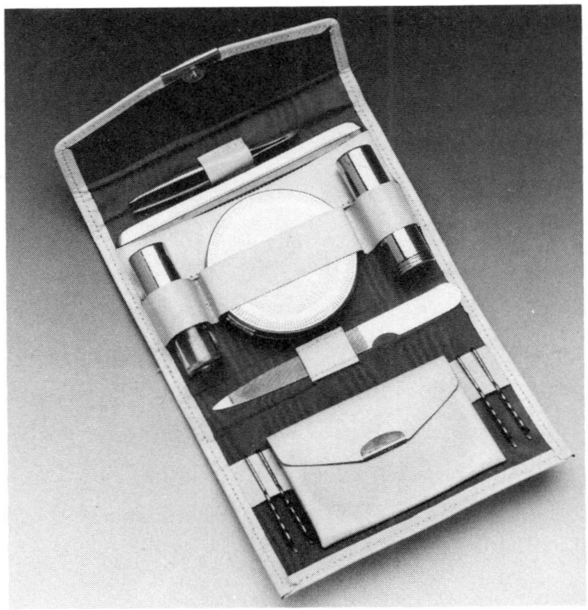

Fig. 9 Rumpp beige cowhide vanity clutch lined in red moiré; compartments for compact, lipstick, perfume, tweezers, nail file, bobby pins, and change purse.

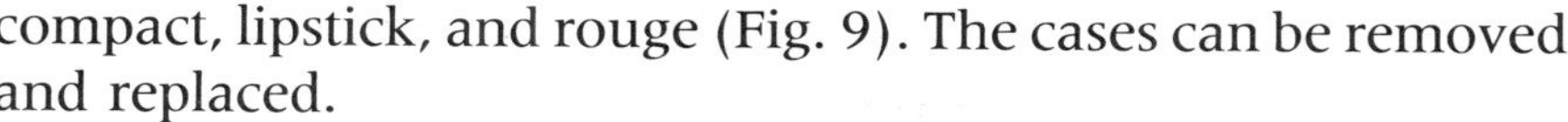

compact, lipstick, and rouge (Fig. 9). The cases can be removed and replaced.

Vanity reticule: A bag with compartments for a compact and lipstick and rouge cases, which can be removed and replaced.

Vanity box: A fitted traveling cosmetic case.

Vanity pochette: A drawstring powder pouch with a mirror located on the outside base.

Vanity pouch: A compact with a shallow powder pouch.

Minaudière: A rigid box-shaped evening bag made of precious metals, some set with precious or semiprecious gems, with compartments for powder, lipstick, rouge, mirror, coin holder, comb, and cigarettes or any combination.

Necessaire: A smaller version of the minaudière, cylindrical in shape and made of precious metal, base metal, or a synthetic material.

Carryall: A mass-produced, inexpensive version of the minaudière.

Pli: A makeup tube containing powder at one end and a push puff at the other end.

Powderette: A pencil-shaped powder container that releases powder when the tip is pressed and sometimes contains a lipstick at the other end.

Puff-kase: A tubular powder container with a sliding, removable puff.

Tango-chain: A lipstick or rouge container attached to a compact or vanity case by a short chain.

Flapjack: A slim, flat, round compact resembling a "flapjack" pancake.

Portable containers for cosmetics enjoyed immense popularity and became an indispensable fashion accessory. Fashion-setters dictated that a woman have a different compact or vanity case for each outfit in her wardrobe.

Compacts were made to suit every taste and price range. The prices of compacts varied depending on the manufacturer and on the materials used. The famous jewelry houses—Cartier; Hermès; Boucheron; Tiffany; Van Cleef & Arpels; Asprey's; Maubousson; Chaumet; Fabergé; Black, Starr, and Frost—were often commissioned to manufacture exquisite compacts in precious metals, many encrusted with precious gems. Some of these compacts were so elegantly made that they were considered a form of jewelry (Fig. 10).

Fig. 10 Tiffany & Co. owl-and-pussycat compacts in textured 18-karat gold; cat with diamond, emerald, and sapphire eyes; owl with diamond and emerald eyes. Reproduced with permission from Tiffany & Co.

Cosmetic houses such as Coty, Evening in Paris, Tre-Jur, Charles of the Ritz, Colleen Moore, Dorothy Gray, Helena Rubinstein, Jonteel, Lady Esther, Richard Hudnut, Princess Pat, Ritz, Tangee, Woodbury, Yardley, and Elizabeth Arden jumped on the bandwagon and began to mass-produce affordable compacts in many styles. Even though they were made of less expensive materials, these compacts could equal the beauty of the most expensive compacts. These compacts came complete with powder, either pressed or loose, which could be refilled.

Many cosmetic houses contracted with metal and paper firms to manufacture empty compact cases to be filled with their own cosmetics. The most popular compact manufacturers in the twentieth century were Elgin American, Volupté, Evans, Whiting & Davis, and Stratton of London. The Elgin National Watch Company, the Wadsworth Watch Case Company, and the Illinois Watch Company were all subsidiaries of Elgin American in Elgin, Illinois. Elgin American manufactured compacts, compact/watches, and compact/music boxes and was the forerunner in the manufacture of the affordable "carryall."

The Volupté Company in Elizabeth, New Jersey, was one

MANUFACTURERS

ROUGE and FACE POWDER COMPACTS

LIP ROUGE, LIP POMADE NAIL POLISH

(Cake form)

ONE QUALITY ONLY

IN METAL and PAPER BOXES

CENTRALLY LOCATED FOR QUICK SHIPMENTS

ABONITA COMPANY, Inc.

134 S. CLINTON ST. CHICAGO

Private-brand compact advertisement from the December 1920 issue of *The American Perfumer.*

of the most prolific manufacturers of ladies' compacts in the late 1930s and 1940s. Volupté manufactured compacts in every conceivable style, design, and shape.

The Evans Company in North Attleboro, Massachusetts, manufactured cigarette cases, compacts, vanity pouches, mesh vanity bags, and vanity purses. Stratton of London and Whiting & Davis still manufacture compacts today. Stratton of London has been manufacturing compacts, mirrors, and lipstick cases for almost fifty years. Today, the company produces several different styles of beautifully painted and decorated compacts, some with a matching mirror, comb, and lipstick case.

The Whiting & Davis Company in Plainville, Massachusetts, has been the leader in the manufacture of mesh bags and vanity bags since the latter part of the nineteenth century. The company's exquisite mesh evening bags and compacts are still being manufactured today.

It is unusual that an article that was essentially utilitarian be produced in such a diversity of materials, styles, shapes, decoration, and motifs, and with such painstaking detail. Cosmetic containers were executed in almost every natural or man-made material, from precious metals and gemstones to paper, damascene, enamel, and plastics.

The kaleidoscope of shapes and motifs used in the manufacture of compacts reflected the mood and spirit of the times. Compacts came in a variety of shapes: square, rectangular, round, triangular, oblong, oval, and hexagonal. Some were shaped as hand mirrors with a lipstick or perfume vial concealed in the handle, round balls, bells (to be used as holiday tree ornaments), hearts, walnuts or acorns, baskets, animals, and birds.

Tutankhamen's tomb, unearthed in 1922, set off an Egyptian revival, with the emergence of many souvenirs. One of them was a Cleopatra's needle compact with hieroglyphics inscribed on the obelisk (Fig. 11).

During World Wars I and II, compacts displayed patriotic motifs. Compacts made in the shape of the Army, Navy, and Marine hats were popular. The flag, inscribed messages from loved ones, and emblems of the Armed Forces were also part of the design on the patriotic compacts. The compact was one of the most popular gifts a serviceman could give to his loved ones waiting at home. President Jimmy Carter as an ensign at the Naval Academy in Annapolis gave Rosalynn Smith, his future wife, a beautiful compact for the holidays. The compact was engraved "ILYTG," a Carter family endearment that stands for "I love you the goodest."

Famous fictional and cartoon characters also appeared on the lids of the compacts. Charlie McCarthy, Mickey and Minnie Mouse, Alice in Wonderland, Popeye, and Little Orphan Annie were just a few. The original movie press book for the epic film *Gone with the Wind,* made in 1940, advertised Volupté's "Scarlett O'Hara compact—$2.00 at all department, novelty, etc. stores. Three styles—Southern scenes—inspired by the picture."

Fig. 11 Silvered-metal compact with Cleopatra's needle motif; hieroglyphics inscribed on obelisk.

In 1940 Volupté also manufactured four different versions of a hand-shaped compact: lace glove, a hand with manicured nails, one with an engagement ring, and an unadorned hand. Henriette, Kigu, and K & K made several types of basket-shaped and ball compacts: an eight ball, a ball with a pair of dice on the lid, a roulette ball, and floral baskets with handles.

The designs and decoration of compacts became more and more ingenious. Some were shaped as musical instruments—drums, guitars, pianos—or as miniature suitcases and cameras, such as the Kamra-Pak. A silver triple-tiered compact was manufactured in the 1920s that swivels open to reveal multiple makeup compartments. Some compacts in the 1930s even had windshield wipers attached to clean the mirror. And then there were miniature vanity tables and a grand piano with collapsible legs that fold flat on the underside of the compact (Fig. 12). Also in demand were souvenir compacts of the states and foreign countries, scenic spots, historical areas, and commemo-

Fig. 12 Volupté goldtone compact designed to resemble vanity table; collapsible cabriole legs (silvered metal shown open, goldtone shown closed).

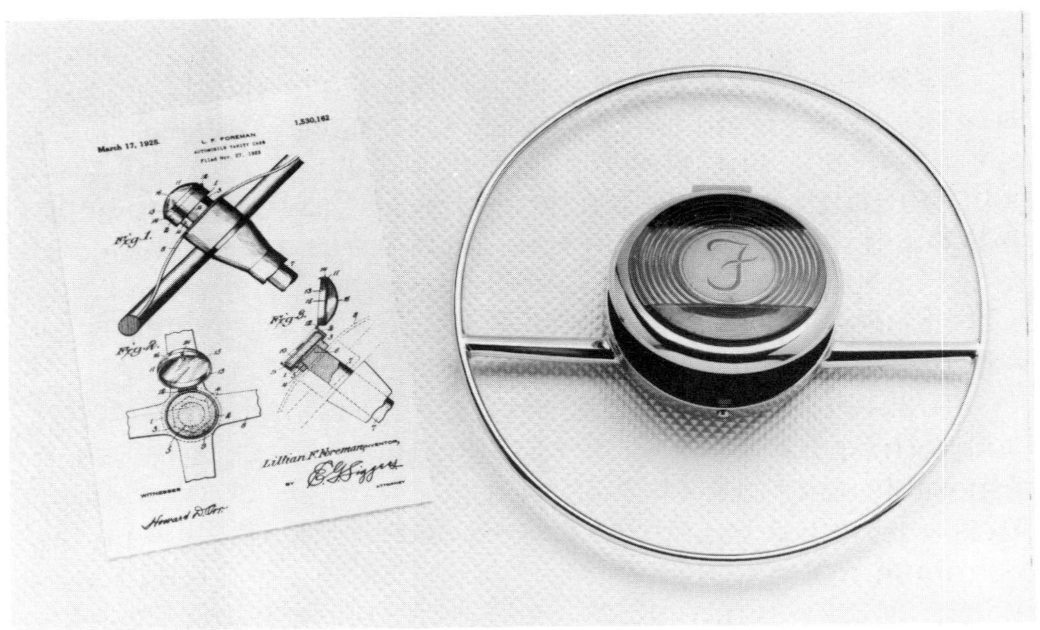

Fig. 13 Automobile steering-wheel compact; compact designed as the horn; silvered-metal red and white letter *F* on compartment lid; interior has mirror and lights (patent shown not necessarily one for compact/wheel shown), c. 1920s.

rative events. Some of the most stylized and colorful compacts were made during the heydays of Art Nouveau and Art Deco.

These affordable compacts could be purchased over the counter at any novelty, five-and-dime, drug store, or department store. Women who did not live in an urban area could buy compacts through the mail-order catalogs of Sears Roebuck, Montgomery Ward, Baird-North, Pohlson, and the Boston Shepard Store.

Multipurpose, combination, and gadgetry compacts such as watch/compacts, music box/compacts, compass/compacts, and barometer/compacts were popular. Some compacts concealed manicure sets, sewing kits, ivory slates and slim pencils for jotting down notes, dance programs, combs, coin holders for "mad money," and compartments for calling cards and pills. The Segal Key Company made a compact with a concealed blank key that slides out by pressing a button. Ladies' fans had a hidden compact on the base so that makeup could be applied discreetly. Compacts made for automobiles (Fig. 13) were incorporated in the visor, steering wheel, or on the gear-shift handle for easy access and an impromptu and hasty "touchup."

The vanity hatpin, popular in 1910, was considered a lethal weapon because of its long steel shank.

During prohibition, many necessaires concealed whiskey flasks, and some compacts could even be attached to a woman's garter underneath her dress. There was even a waterproof compact/bracelet that could be worn on the beach and into the water.

Today, the pendulum is swinging back to the time when ladies' compacts were all the rage. Compacts now are usually disposable and made of plastic—a far cry from the vintage compacts whose intricate and exacting workmanship, design and technique made them works of art in themselves, some even worthy of a museum display. For the collector today, they are miniature treasures with an elegant history, no less than small jewels of the past.

A Start-Off Guide for the Collector

THREE terms you need to be familiar with when discussing antiques or collectibles are "nomenclature," "provenance," and "attribution."

Nomenclature is the defining word for an article within a category. For example, in the overall category of jewelry, the nomenclature for a specific item of jewelry would be ring, bracelet, brooch, pendant, etc.

Provenance is the history or background of an article. Authenticated proof of the manufacturer, country of origin, date of manufacture, and a receipt showing date and place of purchase would be evidence of an item's provenance. Having the original presentation box or pouch enhances the provenance. Knowing the provenance of an article allows you to command a greater price.

Attribution denotes the previous owner of item, either a family, museum, gallery, or corporation. An item has greater value if a famous—or infamous—person or celebrity previously owned the object. Items belonging to Andy Warhol and the Duchess of Windsor were recently sold at auctions far above the actual value of the items simply because of their attribution. The attribution of an article is usually included in its provenance.

Whiting & Davis Company Mesh Bags

The Whiting & Davis Co., originally known as Wade Davis, was founded in 1876 in Plainville, Massachusetts, and is the oldest handbag manufacturer in North America. The vanity-bags created by Whiting & Davis between 1896 and 1935 have

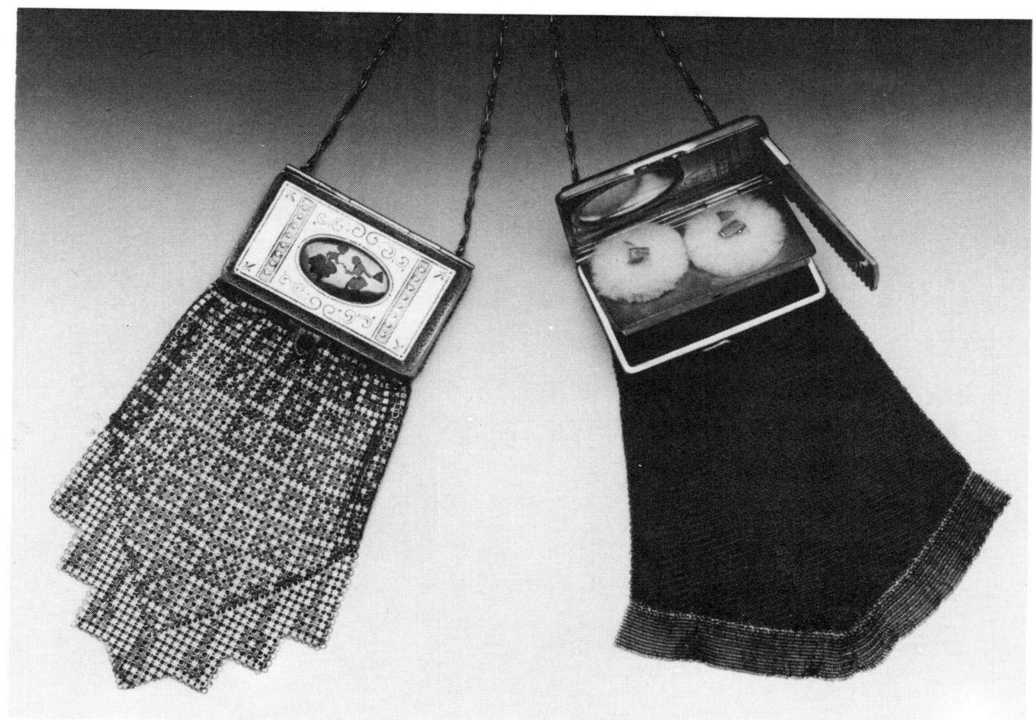

Fig. 14 Whiting & Davis "Elsa" vanity with compartments for powder, rouge, and comb (multicolored mesh shown closed, soldered baby mesh shown open).

become sought-after collectors' items because of their intricate craftsmanship, beautiful colors, and delicate patterns.

The mesh bags were handcrafted from 1892 to 1912, when the first automatic mesh machine was made. Whiting and Davis manufactured two popular types of mesh ring designs: star-shaped mesh (1900–1915) and tiny mesh (1910–25). Metal tags with the familiar Whiting & Davis Co. trademark were attached to the mesh bags from 1908 until 1925. After 1926 the trademark was imprinted on the frame of the mesh bag.

The Famous Coty Powder Puffs

The Coty trademark No. 158,435 was registered in France on September 15, 1914, by François Joseph de Spoturno Coty.

RENEWED

Whiting & Davis Co, Inc.,
Plainville, Mass.

M??KS

?ORDS

SECOND RENEWAL

UNITED STATES PATENT OFFICE.

WHITING & DAVIS COMPANY, OF PLAINVILLE, MASSACHUSETTS.

TRADE-MARK FOR MESH BAGS COMPRISED WHOLLY OR IN PART OF PRECIOUS METAL.

ACT OF FEBRUARY 20, 1905.

155,562. Registered May 30, 1922.

Application filed August 25, 1921. Serial No. 152,195.

STATEMENT.

To all whom it may concern:

Be it known that WHITING & DAVIS COMPANY, a corporation organized and existing under the laws of the State of Massachusetts, located and doing business at Plainville, Norfolk County, in the State of Massachusetts, has adopted and used the trade mark shown in the accompanying drawing, for mesh bags comprised wholly or in part of precious metal, in Class No. 3, Jewelry and precious-metal ware.

Applicant does not claim the right to the exclusive use of the words "Mesh Bags" apart from the mark as shown.

The trade-mark has been continuously used in the business of the applicant since July 29th, 1921.

The trade-mark is "affixed" to the goods by tag and stamped on frame.

[L. S.] WHITING & DAVIS COMPANY,
By CHARLES A. WHITING,
Treasurer.

DECLARATION.

State of Massachusetts county of Norfolk ss:

CHARLES A. WHITING, being duly sworn, deposes and says that he is treasurer of WHITING & DAVIS COMPANY the applicant named in the foregoing statement; that he believes the foregoing statement to be true; that he believes the applicant to be the owner of the trade-mark sought to be registered; that no other person, firm, corporation, or association, to the best of his knowledge and belief, has the right to use said trade-mark in the United States of America, either in the identical form or in any such near resemblance thereto as might be calculated to deceive; that said trade-mark has been used by applicant in commerce among the several States of the United States; that the description and drawing presented truly represent the trade-mark sought to be registered; and that the specimens show the trade-mark as actually used upon the goods.

CHARLES A. WHITING.

Subscribed and sworn to before me, a notary public this 9th day of August, 1921.

[L. S.] BYRON S. GARDINER,
Notary Public.

Whiting & Davis Company trademark 155,562 registered on May 30, 1922, for mesh bags.

They all want it

Women who have seen the "Delysia" universally declare that it is the handiest, most compact and appealing purse-mesh bag they have ever seen. This reflects the attitude of the women of your neighborhood. They will want the "Delysia" Vanity Mesh Bag. Why not profit by pleasing them?

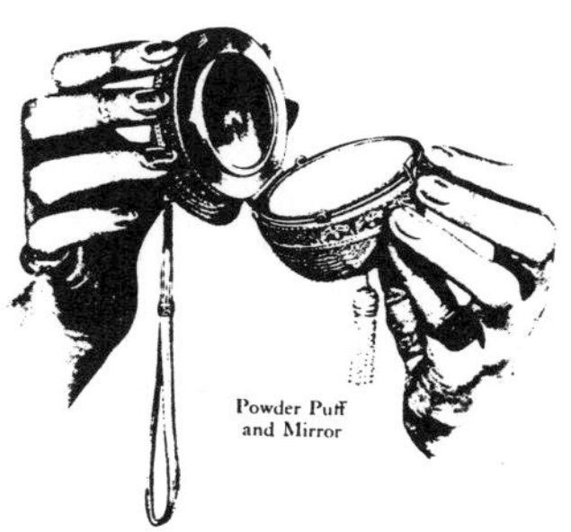

Powder Puff and Mirror

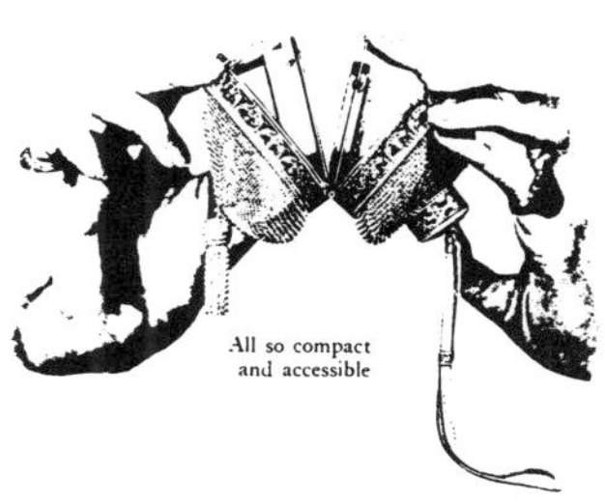

All so compact and accessible

Helping you sell

Whiting & Davis' continent-wide advertising continually working for you, featuring the Mesh Bags you carry, helps to increase your volume of business. The new bags will help the *jeweler* hold the Vanity Bag business. You can get an even quicker turnover if you will make a direct hook-up with this advertising by using our attractive display cards in your windows and on your counters. Dealer helps sent on request. *Use the mailing card to your wholesaler herewith.*

WHITING & DAVIS COMPANY
PLAINVILLE (NORFOLK COUNTY)
MASSACHUSETTS
In Canada, SHERBROOKE, QUEBEC

For Money, Keys, Handkerchief, etc.

Easy selling beauty and utility

In the light of cold, practical dealer consideration you can at once see that outside the appealing beauty and utility of the "Delysia" Vanity Mesh Bag, it is an article that will afford *immediate* sales—*and sales that will be easy to make.*

Approbation from Paris

The most charming of French actresses writes of the "Delysia": "Not only is it more practical than all others which I have seen or used but it also is so artistic and so new that everybody is envious of it."

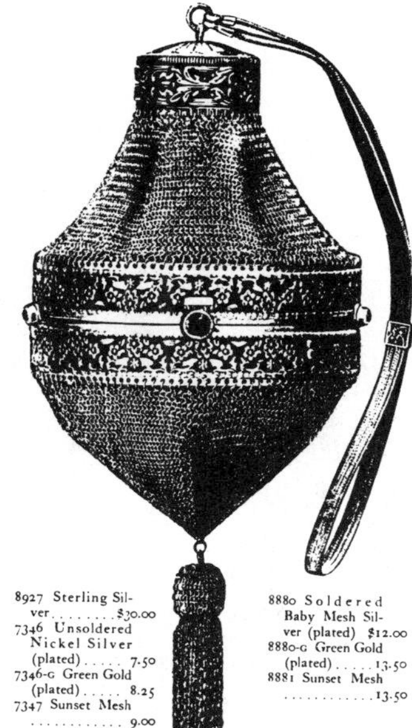

8927 Sterling Silver $30.00
7346 Unsoldered Nickel Silver (plated) 7.50
7346-G Green Gold (plated) 8.25
7347 Sunset Mesh 9.00

8880 Soldered Baby Mesh Silver (plated) $12.00
8880-G Green Gold (plated) 13.50
8881 Sunset Mesh 13.50

Above prices to the retailer—order through your wholesaler

Note the compartments

The illustrations picture graphically the usefulness of this beautiful creation:

(1) For Money, Keys, Handkerchief, etc.

(2) Powder Puff and Mirror.

(3) Rouge Puff and Mirror.

(4) Note the *two* mirrors—one with the powder and one with the rouge—all so compact and accessible. Change and handkerchief are always get-at-able. When Milady does not want to wear the "Delysia" Vanity Mesh Bag as a wrist bag it fits easily into her pocket or hand bag, holding just the things she continually wants at her finger tips.

Rouge Puff and Mirror

The Whiting & Davis "Delysia" mesh vanity-bag advertisement, c. 1920s. Reproduced with permission of the Whiting & Davis Co.

RENEWED

Coty, Inc.,
423 West 55th. St.,
New York, N. Y.

SECOND RENEWAL

UNITED STATES PATENT OFFICE.

FRANCOIS JOSEPH DE SPOTURNO COTY, OF SURESNES, FRANCE.

TRADE-MARK FOR FACE POWDERS.

ACT OF FEBRUARY 20, 1905.

151,463. Registered Feb. 7, 1922.

Application filed October 27, 1920. Serial No. 138,842.

STATEMENT.

To all whom it may concern:

Be it known that I, FRANCOIS JOSEPH DE SPOTURNO COTY, a citizen of France, residing at Paris, France, and doing business at 13 Boulevard de Versailles, Suresnes, France, have adopted for my use the trade-mark shown in the accompanying drawing.

The trade mark has been continuously used in my business since the year 1914.

The particular description of goods to which the trade mark is appropriated is face powders, comprised in Class 6, Chemicals, medicines, and pharmaceutical preparations.

The trade mark is usually displayed by printing same on labels which are attached to packages containing the goods.

FRANCOIS JOSEPH de SPOTURNO COTY.

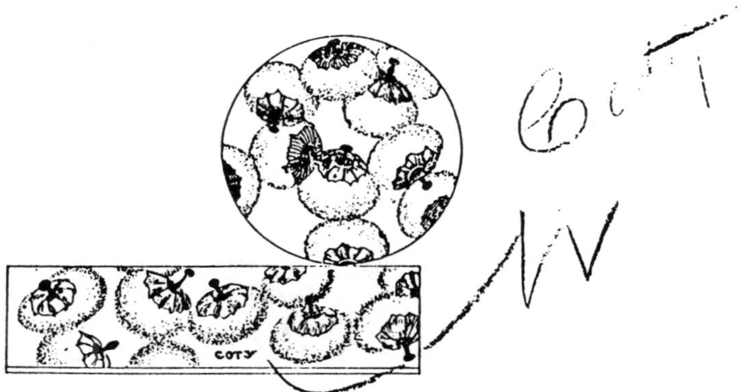

DECLARATION.

United States consulate general, city of Paris, Republic of France ss

FRANCOIS JOSEPH DE SPOTURNO COTY, being duly sworn, deposes and says that he is the applicant named in the foregoing statement; that he believes that the foregoing statement is true; that he believes himself to be the owner of the trade mark sought to be registered; that no other person, firm, corporation or association, to the best of his knowledge and belief, has the right to use said trade mark in the United States, either in the identical form, or in any such near resemblance thereto as might be calculated to deceive; that said trade mark has been registered in France on September 15, 1914 No. 158,435; that the description and drawing presented truly represent the trade mark as actually used upon the goods.

FRANCOIS JOSEPH de SPOTURNO COTY.

Subscribed and sworn to before me, this 22 day of Sept., 1920.

[L. S.] CLEMENT S. EDWARDS,
Consul of the United States of America at Paris, France.

François Joseph de Spoturno Coty trademark 151,463 registered on February 7, 1922, for face powders.

Coty powder and powder-compact advertisement from a 1926 issue of *Theatre Magazine*.

This trademark (page 22) is for Airspun Face Powder and Compact container with white and gold powder puffs on an orange background. René Lalique, the famous French glassmaker, and Léon Bakst, the renowned designer of stage settings and costumes for the Ballet Russe, collaborated on this creation. The powder-puff trademark has been used since 1914 on Coty's cosmetic products.

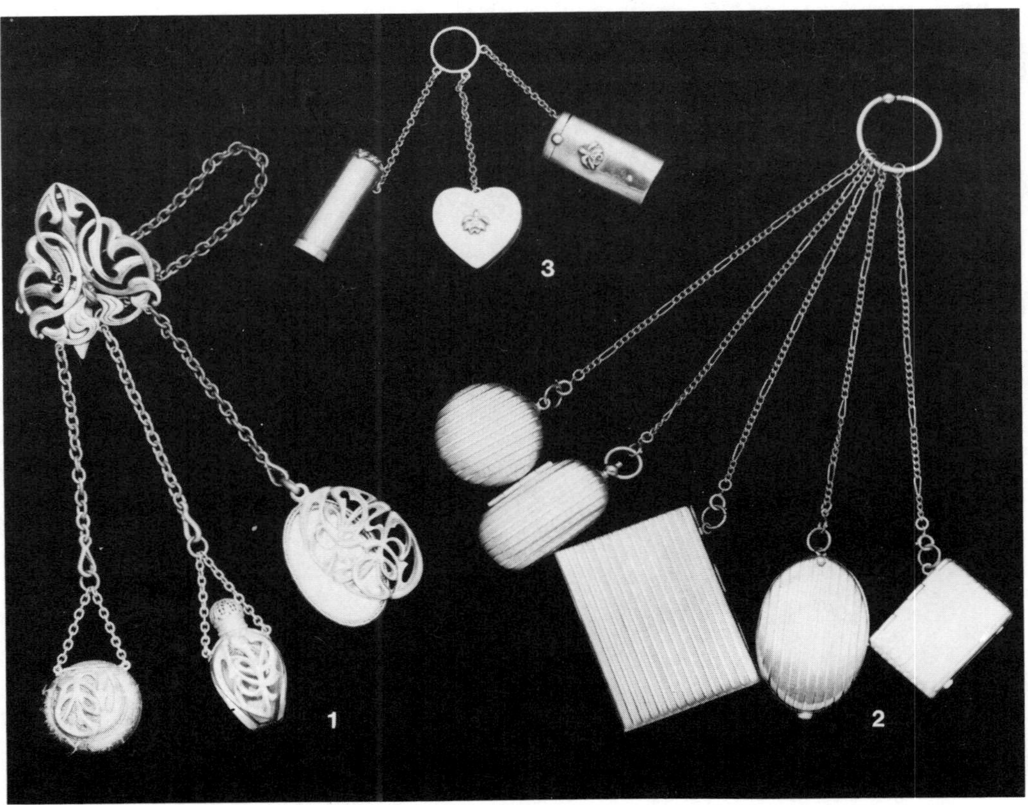

Fig. 15
1 Antiqued, silvered filigree coach-chatelette with compact, perfume bottle and swivel mirror suspended from chain filigree hook, Continental, 19th century.
2 Fluted German silver chatelaine with compact, coin holder, memo book, locket/pin container, and stamp holder.
3 Georg Jensen sterling-silver mini chatelette with heart-shaped compact; lipstick container and pin carrier decorated with raised silver orchid.

Chatelaines, Chatelettes, and Coach Chatelaines

In medieval times, when the Crusaders were away fighting the wars, they entrusted the keys to the many rooms of their castles to their ladies. The ladies carried the keys on chains attached to their belts and became known as Chatelaines. Eventually the name Chatelaine became associated with an article of jewelry.

Chatelaines were popular during the Victorian era as a decorative, utilitarian piece of jewelry. They were made in a variety of shapes, materials, and sizes and consisted of several chains suspended from a hook or clasp attached to the belt. The vanity chatelaine usually had a powder compact, lipstick holder, writing slate, slim pencil, coin holder, and vinaigrette or perfume container suspended from the chains.

Chatelettes are chatelaines with shorter and fewer chains.

Coach chatelaines were made with hooks that could be hung inside a coach so the ladies could avail themselves of this portable vanity while traveling.

Salvador Dali's "Bird-in-Hand" Compact

Salvador Dali, the Spanish surrealist painter, sculptor, and illustrator (May 11, 1904–January 23, 1989), was born in Figueras, Catalonia, Spain, and studied in Barcelona and Madrid. He became known as the *enfant terrible* of surrealism, as well as its best-known exponent. Since 1932 Dali's works have been shown throughout Europe, the United States, and the Orient.

Dali designed many commercial works of art as well in the 1940s and 1950s. In 1950 he was commissioned to design a compact for Elgin American, which became known as the "Bird-in-Hand."

The Bird-in-Hand compact is $4\frac{1}{2}''$ by $2\frac{1}{2}''$ with ruby red eyes and was manufactured in three different finishes—satin bronze, silver, and sterling silver—with a 14-karat gold overlay effect on the wings. The compact contains a powder compartment, pillbox, and lipstick. The bird's head holds the slide-out lipstick

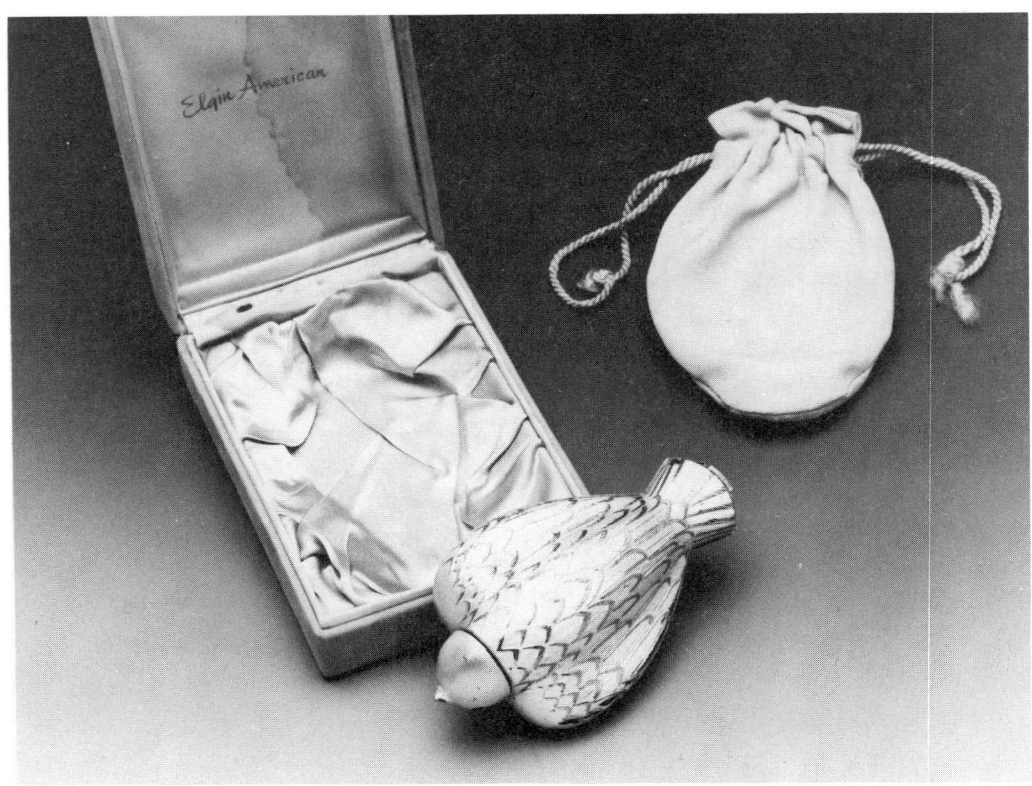

Fig. 16 Elgin American Dali "Bird-in-Hand" compact with turquoise drawstring carrying case and turquoise suede fitted presentation box.

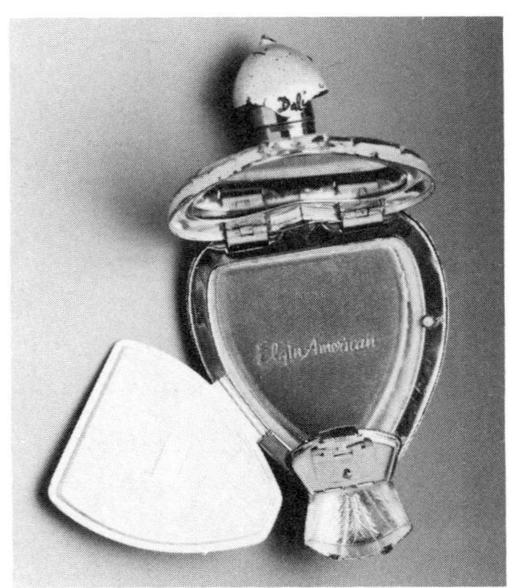

Fig. 17 Elgin American Dali "Bird-in-Hand" compact opened to reveal lipstick holder; powder and pillbox compartments.

Fig. 18 Elgin American Dali "Bird-in-Hand" compact; underside reveals Dali signature.

and the body contains the powder box, which is revealed when the wings are spread apart. The tailpiece conceals the pillbox. Dali's signature appears on the underside of the bird's head. The compact comes with a turquoise drawstring carrying case and a suede turquoise Elgin American fitted, hinged presentation box.

The minimum prices for the Bird-in-Hand compact were listed in Elgin American's 1952–53 catalog:

Satin bronze finish	Dealer $ 7.50	Retail $ 15.00
Silver finish	Dealer $12.50	Retail $ 25.00
Sterling silver	Dealer $50.00	Retail $100.00

A Bird-in-Hand compact is on display in the Salvador Dali Museum, 1000 3rd Avenue South, St. Petersburg, FL 33701.

Minaudières, Carryalls, and Necessaires

In the 1930s women customarily wore evening gowns to dinner parties and the theater. Since women often traveled in the same social circles, the well-dressed woman needed several different gowns with matching bags. To resolve the problem of changing evening bags to match each costume, Van Cleef & Arpels invented the minaudière, the one evening bag that could harmonize and complement each dress. The minaudière is a rigid metal box-shaped evening bag, really a supercompact, with compartments for cosmetic and personal necessities—powder, lipstick, coins, a watch, cigarettes, and comb. It was Estelle Arpels, co-founder with her husband Alfred Cleef of Van Cleef and Arpels, who inspired the name for the firm's jeweled evening bags. Her brothers, Julien, Charles, and Louis, who were also partners, used to say that no one could "minauder," or charm, in society as their sister Estelle. Thus, the name minaudière. The original minaudières were sold at fashionable, expensive jewelry houses. They were usually made of gold or silver and sometimes encrusted with precious gems.

The carryall, an affordable, mass-produced version of the

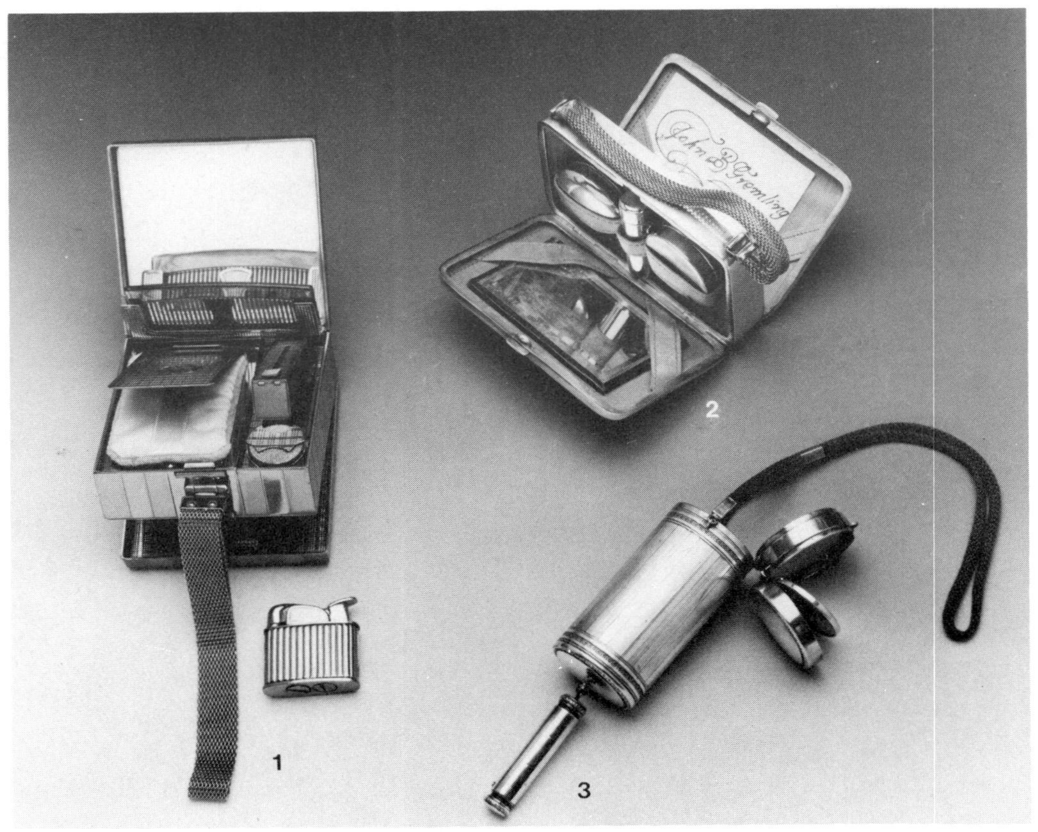

Fig. 19

1 Evans goldtone swirl-design carryall with mesh wrist chain; dual openings (one side reveals mirror and compartments for powder, lipstick, coins, and comb; the other side has compartment for cigarettes and lighter), c. 1940–50s.

2 Silver minaudière engraved with a lighthouse and sailboat on one side and the monogrammed letter *G* on the reverse, gray grosgrain interior, dual openings (one with mirror, fitted sleeves with powder, rouge, and lipstick containers; the other with fitted sleeves for calling cards, perfume container, and memo case with slim pencil), probably England, late 19th century.

3 Webster Company sterling-silver cylindrical necessaire with lipstick suspended from bottom and gilded interior; mirror separates powder and rouge compartments; second opening reveals cigarette, flask, or money compartment, c. 1920–30s.

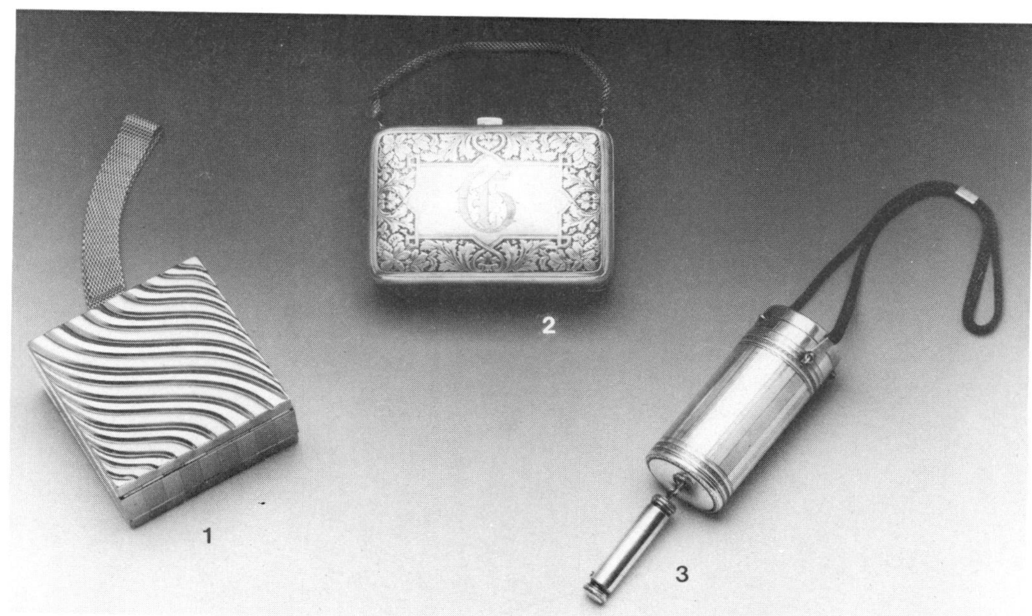

Fig. 20 Carryall, minaudière, and necessaire in Figure 19 shown closed.

minaudière, was manufactured in a variety of beautiful finishes by many popular compact manufacturers.

The necessaire, a cylindrical or bolster-shaped, smaller version of the minaudière with fewer compartments, was made in either precious metals or inexpensive finishes.

A Vanity/Bracelet Compact

On November 23, 1926, Elijah L. Johnson was granted a patent for a wrist cosmetic holder #1,607,985. His justification for the product:

> Modern usage of cosmetics by the feminine sex demands that certain necessary cosmetics be carried on the person so that they may be conveniently and promptly applied whenever the situation demands it. Cosmetics are usually kept in a vanity case, but places are often frequented by the feminine sex where cases cannot be conveniently carried. One example of this is in a ballroom where a vanity case would be very much in the way. Another example

Nov. 23, 1926. **1,607,985**

E. L. JOHNSON

COSMETIC HOLDER

Filed Jan. 16, 1926

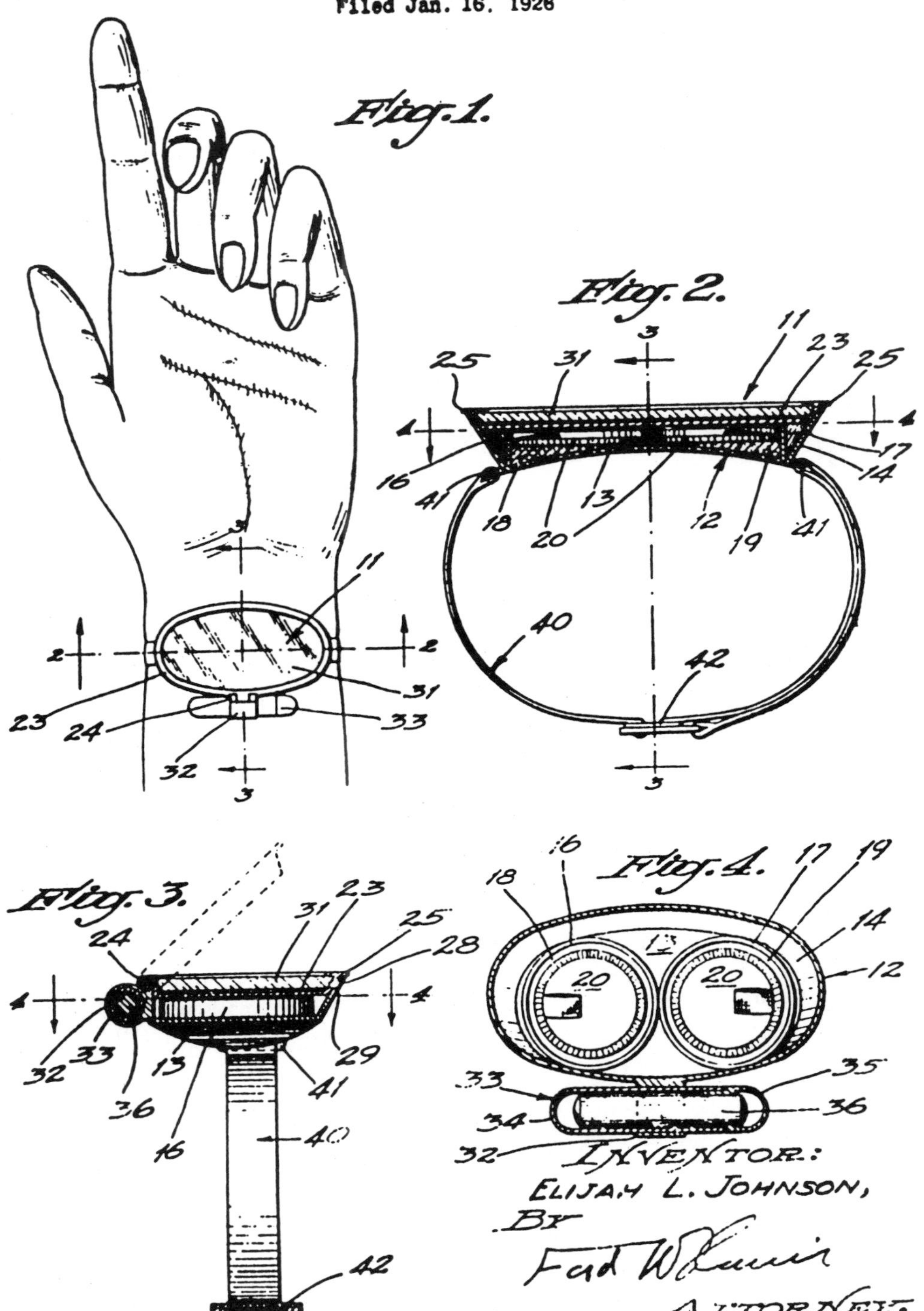

of its utilities is automobile driving where a lady driver's attention is detracted from her driving while searching for cosmetics in a vanity case. With my invention the cosmetics are handy and may be readily applied with little distraction and little danger of accidents which might occur from inattention to driving. It is the object of this invention to provide a cosmetic holder which is adapted to be secured to the wrist. The cosmetic holder of my invention is in the form of a bracelet which will be very convenient for use and will in no manner interfere with a person's activity. It is quite essential to a lady's appearance and particularly to her self-satisfaction that she be able to inspect her countenance at various intervals. A lady, however, is often constrained from such an inspection, since considerable attention might be attracted by opening a vanity case and she might suffer considerable embarrassment. It is another object of my invention to provide a cosmetic holder which is adapted to be secured to the wrist and which has a mirror, by means of which a person's appearance may be very readily inspected without attracting attention.

Tips from a Compact Collector

Compacts can be found at flea markets, tag and garage sales, thrift stores, vintage clothing stores, and consignments shops. But the best source, if you are looking for a specific collectible, is still an antique shop or antique show. Quality vintage compacts may now be found at many auction houses as well, and many antique papers advertise compacts for sale.

When you travel, check the Antiques section in the Yellow Pages of the local telephone directory for antiques shops and the local paper's daily-event section for flea markets, tag sales, and street fairs.

The International Compact Collectors Club, P.O. Box Letter S, Lynbrook, N.Y. 11563, publishes the newsletter "Powder Puff," which features a Seekers, Sellers, and Swappers column.

When purchasing a compact by mail, always inquire as to the condition and age, and request a complete description, including price. Ask whether you can return the compact if you are not satisfied. Always request a receipt when making a purchase. The receipt should describe the compact in as much detail as possible. The price, condition, composition, and name, and address or phone number of vendor should also be included.

If a compact comes in the original box or pouch, do not destroy or discard it. The value of the compact is increased if it has its original box. Original parts of a collectible should always be left intact. Missing, broken, or torn parts, such as colored stones, tassels, mirrors, or carrying cords, may be replaced with parts that will adhere to and not alter the style or original design. Check to see whether there has been a "marriage" between two compacts—one part of a compact attached or inserted in a compact of like design. Lipsticks are sometimes removed from an inexpensive compact and inserted in a more expensive compact. A reputable dealer will tell you if this has been done.

Enameled compacts purchased for investment purposes should be in mint condition. Minor flaws in a compact purchased for your collection and not for resale may be repaired. Repairing chipped or scratched enamels may be costly and decrease the value of the compact.

Only mirrors that are broken should be removed and replaced in a vintage compact. Do not replace a mirror that is discolored, flawed, or in need of resilvering. The original mirror enhances the value of the compact.

Remove loose and solid powder, rouge, lipstick, and perfume from vintage compacts before adding them to your collection. The loose powder will spill when the compact is opened, and the solid powder, rouge, lipstick, and perfume will probably be rancid.

Never apply a sticker directly to the surface of a compact. The acids from the glue may discolor or irreparably damage the finish, especially an enamel finish. Apply a price or identification sticker to the metal or mirror inside the compact, better, attach a string-tag to the compact.

Parts of a vintage compact are sometimes fragile and should be handled as little as possible. The best way to display, share, and enjoy your collection is in a glass-enclosed cabinet or case. Compacts may be displayed in a revolving, lighted curio cabinet or in a showcase such as those used to display watches. Another way to display compacts is in a viewing table that can also serve as a coffee or cocktail table, or in a 3″ to 5″ deep shadowbox. The compacts can be suspended from hooks or placed on shelves inside the framed box. Several shadowboxes mounted on the wall create an interesting and unusual wall arrangement.

Keep a running inventory of your collection. List the items on index cards and keep them in a file box. Note the date, price, and place of purchase and the name of the seller. Also include any information on the history, previous owner, or background that you can obtain from the seller. Include a full description, including size, finish, and condition, and a photograph of the compact.

Photograph or videotape your collection so that you will have a complete and accurate record of your collection for insurance purposes. Keep the photos in a safe place in your home and a duplicate set in a friend's home or in a safety deposit box.

Always use a *certified* appraiser when you have your collection appraised. The appraisal should be typewritten, dated, and signed and contain a complete, accurate description of the collection (not a "laundry list" description such as "round," "small" "red," or "compact."

Keep your appraisal up to date. If you should sustain a loss, your insurance company will pay only the latest amount listed by the appraiser.

Newsworthy Compacts

Classic vintage and contemporary compacts are making the news. On June 16, 1988, Christie's East Auction House featured a collection of "compacts" dating from the 1920s and 30s. The auction catalogue describes them as "Designed for both function and flash, no bigger than a lady's palm, but large enough for the essentials: a powder puff, loose or pressed powder and a mirror. Many ingeniously incorporate places for rouge and lipstick. Overall they display a colorful sampling of design applied to the everyday, a glimpse of period style.'' They were offered in lots of five with the estimated catalogue price for each lot $200–$250. Souvenir, silver, enameled, tango-chain, plastic and combination vanities were just a few of the styles offered. Some of the compact manufacturers represented were Elgin, Volupté, Girey, Coty, Mondaine, Houbigant, Evans, La Mode, Yardley and Richard Hudnut.

A vintage ''Charlie McCarthy'' compact, manufactured by Evans, sold in 1988 for $400 at the ''Screen Smart Set'' auction. The compact was donated by Mrs. Edgar Bergen, widow of the renowned ventriloquist and ''voice'' of Charlie McCarthy. The proceeds from the auction were donated to the Motion Picture Actors' Home.

Nancy Reagan, wife of then-President Reagan, received a Lifetime Achievement Award ''for the outstanding contributions she has made to American fashion'' from The Council of Fashion Designers of America. This item was reported in the Daily News section of the November 18, 1988 *Chicago Tribune.* The accompanying photograph showed the fashionable Mrs. Reagan using a compact mirror to adjust her makeup.

Raisa Gorbachev and other high-powered guests were invited by Esteé Lauder to visit the cosmetic firm in December, 1988. The guests received ''golden'' compacts from Esteé Lauder. One of the guests, newswoman Barbara Walters, showed her television audience the compact she received, the ''Golden Alligator'' compact.

The August, 1988, issue of the Kiplinger Magazine *Changing Times* featured ''What to Do with a Little Bit of Money'' (how to invest $1,000 or less), with sensible suggestions that range from savings bonds to undiscovered collectibles. Highlighted is a column on the new collectible—vintage compacts—entitled ''Take A Powder.'' Many collectible vintage compacts were described.

Ten thousand of Andy Warhol's favorite treasures were auctioned off in the Spring of 1988 at Sotheby's. Due to the Warhol provenance, the prices averaged about twice the amount that was estimated by Sotheby's. The auction began with the collectibles. There were twenty-four compacts sold singly or along with other items for a total of more than $53,000. Tiffany & Co., Cartier, Van Cleef & Arpels, Boucheron and Jean Fouquet were some of the prestigious jewelry houses represented. Shagreen, 14 carat, 18 carat, silver, gilt metal, enameled, Art Deco, Art Nouveau, combination compacts, and a silver chatelaine hung with a compact were among the offerings. The highest price was $9,075 for a rectangular Jean Fouquet black-and-coral enameled silver vanity-case. The lipstick separates two pop-up panels which open to reveal two mirrored cosmetic compartments, c. 1925, France. The *Maine Antique Digest* (June, 1988) reported that Paloma Picasso, jewelry designer for Tiffany & Co., bought one lot which consisted of two compacts and one lipstick case, silver and silver gilt with tiny cabochon rubies by Boucheron, Paris, c. 1940 for $1,650.

Gallery of Compacts

Fig. 21

1 Stratton goldtone compact with scenic transfer on lid, c. 1950s.

2 Rex Fifth Avenue painted, enameled compact with two pink flamingoes on a turquoise background.

3 Schildkraut goldtone cloisonné compact with two blue peacocks on a white background.

4 Marhill mother-of-pearl carryall with painted peacock and glitter on lid.

5 Gwenda goldtone enameled painted foil compact, England.

6 Goldtone compact with two pink and gray simulated feathered birds enclosed in a plastic dome.

7 Blue enameled silvertone mini-flapjack compact, c. 1930s.

8 Goldtone triangular enameled compact with two green birds in flight on a light blue background and finger-ring chain.

9 Wadsworth goldtone hand-painted yellow enamel fan-shaped compact, c. 1940s.

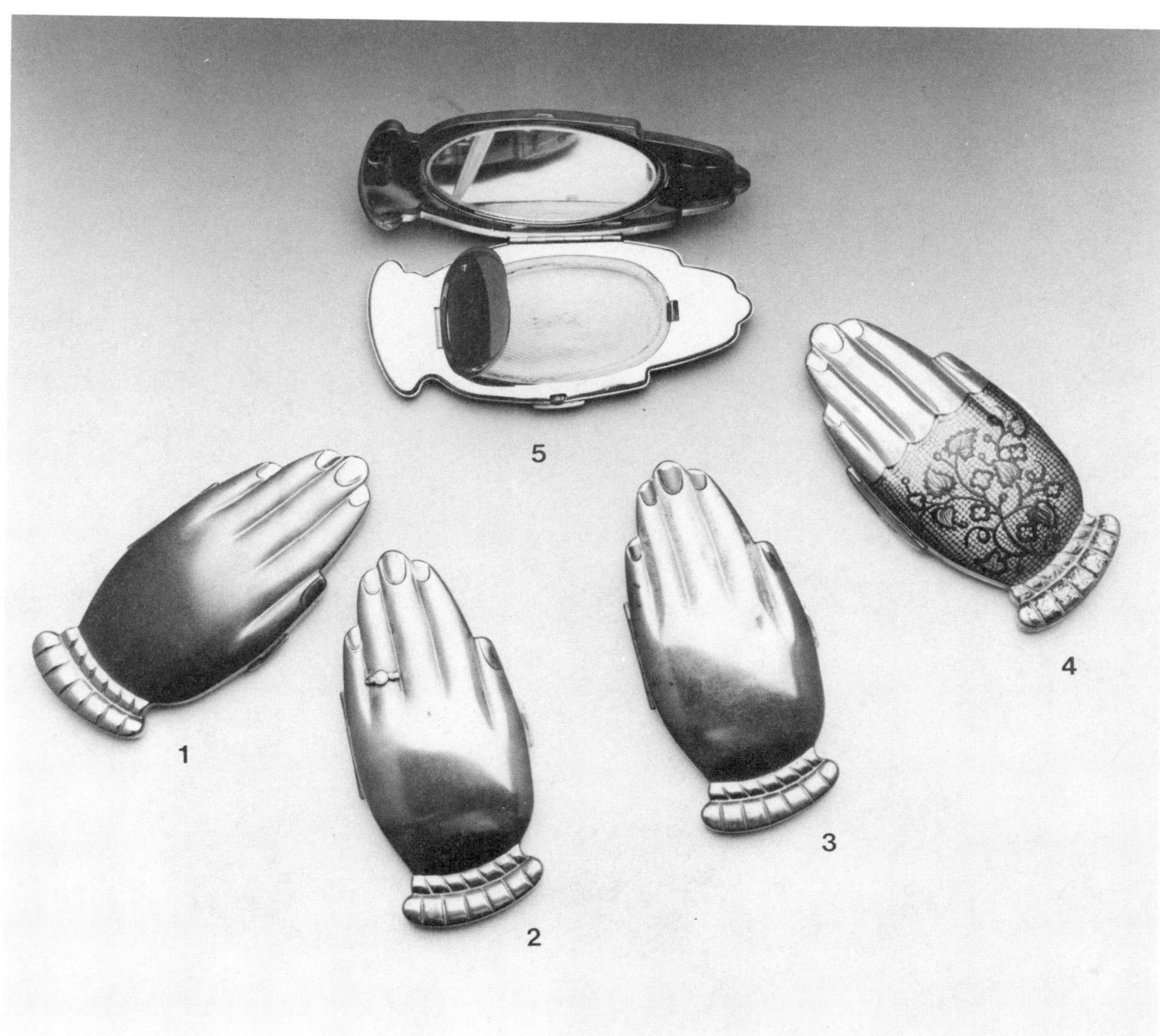

Fig. 22

1 Volupté goldtone hand-shaped compact, c. 1940s.

2 Volupté goldtone "faux diamond engagement ring" hand-shaped compact, c. 1940s.

3 Volupté goldtone "manicured" hand-shaped compact, c. 1940s.

4 Volupté goldtone "lace gloved" hand-shaped compact, c. 1940s.

5 Volupté goldtone hand-shaped compact, c. 1940s (shown open).

Fig. 23

1 Kigu "Cherie" goldtone heart-shaped compact with jeweled crown on lid, England, c. 1940–50.

2 Elgin American stylized heart-shaped enameled compact with "Give me your answer do!" on lid, c. 1940–50.

3 Kigu goldtone blue enamel compact with heart-shaped enameled flower on lid, England, c. 1940–50.

4 Marathon goldtone compact with heart on lid; lid opens to reveal a locket; compact opens by pressing the plastic side panels.

5 Evans pink and yellow goldtone basketweave compact, c. 1946.

Fig. 24

1 Goldtone heart-shaped compact with brocade lid, c. 1930s.

2 American Maid goldtone heart-shaped compact with engraved lid (shown open).

3 La Mode silver-plated heart-shaped compact.

4 Enameled goldtone heart-shaped lock-motif compact.

5 Engraved silver-plated heart-shaped compact with carrying chain.

6 Matte goldtone mini compact.

7 Goldtone heart-shaped compact with purple orchid inlaid in black plastic on lid.

8 Evans goldtone heart-shaped compact with lipstick concealed in black tassel and black carrying cord, c. 1940s.

Fig. 25

1 Amita damascene compact inlaid with gold and silver view of Mt. Fuji capped in silver on black matte-finish lid, Japan c. 1920s.

2 Gilt inlaid vanity case with carrying-chain mirror, coin holder, and powder compartment, Japan, c. 1920 (shown open).

3 Damascene compact inlaid with gold and silver view of Mt. Fuji capped in silver on black matte-finish lid; complete with hinged, fitted presentation box, K24.

4 Damascene compact black matte finish inlaid with gilt Egyptian scene.

5 Damascene vanity case, with gold and silver view of Mt. Fuji capped in silver on black matte-finish lid; carrying chain and compartments for powder, lipstick, and rouge, K24.

6 Damascene compact with elaborate gold inlaid pagoda scene on front lid, bamboo inlaid on back lid, loop for chain, c. 1920s.

7 Amita damascene compact, with gold and silver floral motif on black matte-finish lid, Japan, c. 1920s.

8 Damascene-style gilt compact with scene of man and horse on lid, c. 1930s.

Fig. 26

1 Silver-plated vanity case with white pearlized miniature of woman walking a dog on black background mounted on the front lid; carrying chain, compartments for powder, lipstick, rouge, and compartment that "May be used for either Cigarettes, Money, Calling Card or Rosary," c. 1920s.

2 Black enamel silvered-metal tango-chain vanity case with silvered Scottie dogs; compartment for powder, metal mirror opens to reveal rouge, lipstick attached with a chain, c. 1920–30s.

3 Sabor gilt and plastic compact with Lucite dome enclosing two kissing poodles made of thread, France, c. 1930s.

4 Small blue enamel vanity case with Scottie dog transfer; powder compartment and metal mirror opens to reveal rouge compartment, c. 1920–30s.

5 Zell Fifth Avenue goldtone compact with poodle motif set with red cabochon stones and a lipstick in a fitted black grosgrain case, c. 1940–50s.

6 Sterling $\frac{3}{4}$″-square compact with chain attached to a ring mounted with a hunting dog, c. 1920s.

7 Sterling black enamel compact with small plastic dome enclosing a three-dimensional head of a Scottie, Germany, c. 1920–30s.

8 Black enamel compact with painted poodle on a white enamel disk on lid, c. 1930s.

9 Black enamel gilt vanity case with gilt Scottie on lid; powder compartment, metal mirror lifts to reveal rouge compartment, c. 1920–30s.

10 Plastic cigarette/compact combination with metal cutout Scottie on lid, c. 1940s.

11 Tooled leather bulldog-motif compact with beaded eyes and bell at base.

Fig. 27

1 Girey "Kamra-Pak" sparkling confetti plastic vanity case resembling camera; mirror, powder and rouge compartments, and slide-out lipstick, c. 1930–40s.

2 Wadsworth "Compakit" black plastic vanity case resembling camera with carrying case; powder compartment in front of case, lipstick and cigarette lighter on top, opening for cigarettes at bottom of case, c. 1940 (shown open).

3 Same as **2** (shown in carrying case).

4 Kamra-Pak-style blue checkerboard enamel vanity case with compartments for powder and lipstick; reverse side opens to reveal manicure kit, c. 1940.

5 Kamra-Pak-style lizard vanity case for powder and lipstick; reverse side opens to sewing kit, c. 1940s (shown open).

6 Snakeskin Kamra-Pak-style vanity purse with carrying handle; compartments for lipstick, powder, rouge, comb, and coins; other side reveals manicure kit, c. 1940–50s (shown open).

7 Black suede Kamra-Pak-style vanity purse with carrying handle; compartments for lipstick, powder, rouge, comb, and coins; other side has cigarette compartment and lighter, c. 1940–50s.

8 Kamra-Pak-style black enamel vanity case with powder compartment, lipstick, and perfume bottle.

9 Girey "Kamra-Pak" vanity case in blue leather with pink plastic top resembling camera; mirror, powder and rouge compartments, and slide-out lipstick, c. 1930–40s.

10 Multicolored tooled leather-covered Persian-design compact.

11 Kamra-Pak-style blue painted enamel vanity case with girl leaning against lamppost mounted on front lid; compartments for powder, lipstick, and cigarettes, c. 1940s.

12 Mireve black enamel vanity case with powder compartment, sliding lipstick, and perfume bottle, France.

13 Kamra-Pak-style green painted enamel vanity case with Oriental scene on front lid; compartments for powder, lipstick, and cigarettes, c. 1940s.

Fig. 28

1 Black and white mother-of-pearl vanity case with attached lipstick, c. 1930s.

2 Mother-of-pearl fan-shaped miniature compact with rhinestones, Japan.

3 Miniature 1″-round mother-of-pearl compact with faux ruby surrounded by rhinestones.

4 Volupté mother-of-pearl "Swinglok" carry-all, c. 1940–50s.

5, 6, 7 Marhill mother-of-pearl set with compact, comb, and lipstick/mirror.

8 Stylized mother-of-pearl checkerboard compact designed as a book.

9 Petit-point-bordered mother-of-pearl compact.

10 Max Factor mother-of-pearl lipstick case.

11 K & K gray mother-of-pearl compact with faux sapphires and rhinestones, c. 1930–40s.

12 Pierced mother-of-pearl light blue and white compact with a dove mounted in center.

13 Round mother-of-pearl checkerboard compact, c. 1930s.

14 Volupté "Pocketwatch" mother-of-pearl compact, c. 1940–50s.

15 Mother-of-pearl 5″-round checkerboard compact, c. 1940s.

16 Maxley mother-of-pearl compact with inlaid black diagonal stripes and mother-of-pearl cameo, c. 1930s.

Fig. 29

1 Evans petit-point goldtone mesh vanity bag with metal mirror and powder and rouge compartments, c. 1940–50s.

2 Evans rhinestone and white velvet vanity bag with carrying chain, metal mirror, and powder and rouge compartments, c. 1940–50s.

3 Gilt mesh vanity bag with multicolored synthetic stones; metal mirror and powder compartment, c. 1930–40s.

4 Tapestry vanity pouch with floral pattern on lid, c. 1920–30s.

5 Rex gilt mesh vanity pouch with mini white plastic beads, c. 1930s.

6 Pink satin vanity pochette with pink and green trim, mirror on outside base, c. 1920s.

7 Gilt mesh vanity bag with blue synthetic stone; finger-ring chain, metal mirror, and powder compartment, c. 1930–40s.

8 Evans rhinestone and black velvet vanity bag with mirror and powder and rouge compartments, c. 1940–50s (shown open).

Fig. 30

1 Rex Fifth Avenue multicolor-striped taffeta vanity pochette with mirror on outside base, c. 1940s.

2 Pale blue satin vanity pochette with a border of lace and colored beads, possibly handmade; mirror on outside base, c. 1920s.

3 Silvered mesh vanity pouch with silvered repoussé disk on black enamel lid, c. 1930s.

4 Beaded vanity pouch with silvered lid, c. 1930s.

5 Evans oval gilt mesh, red enamel vanity pouch.

6 Square leather vanity pouch with gilded lid.

7 Rex Fifth Avenue navy blue taffeta vanity pochette with green polkadots; mirror on outside base, c. 1940s.

8 Pink satin vanity pochette with lace and pink and green trim; mirror on outside base, c. 1920s.

9 Brown fur vanity pouch with collapsible bottom.

Fig. 31

1 Evans black velvet vanity purse with transfer picture of apple; metal mirror and powder and rouge compartments, c. 1940–50s.

2 Evans gilt mesh, white enamel vanity purse with metal mirror and powder and rouge compartments, c. 1940–50s.

3, 4 Evans gilt mesh vanity pouch with painted flowers on white enamel lid, c. 1930s (front and back view).

5 Rex Fifth Avenue pink fabric vanity pochette; mirror at base of compact, c. 1940s.

6 Volupté light blue collapsible leather vanity pouch, c. 1930s.

7 Evans silvered-metal mesh vanity pouch with black enamel lid, c. 1930s.

8 Gilt-mesh vanity pouch with picture of butterfly on lid, c. 1930s.

9 Brown suede vanity pochette, c. 1930s.

10 Blue cloissoné enameled silvered mesh vanity pouch with painted roses on lid, c. 1930s.

11 Evans gilt-mesh white cloissoné vanity pouch, c. 1930s.

12 Evans miniature gilt-mesh white cloissoné vanity pouch, c. 1930s.

13 Evans black rhinestone vanity pouch made of bead-like material, c. 1930s (shown open).

Fig. 32

1 Blue leather one-piece horseshoe-shaped compact.

2 Zell Fifth Avenue blue leather compact; sides open to reveal billfold and coin purse, c. 1940s.

3 Maroon gold-tooled leather-covered horseshoe-shaped compact, possibly Spain.

4 Mondaine white leather-covered book-motif compact, c. 1930s.

5 Mondaine blue gold-tooled leather compact, c. 1930s.

6 Alligator compact with pull-out mirror, possibly Spain.

7 Square gold-tooled leather compact, possibly Italy.

8 Mondaine maroon gold-tooled leather compact, c. 1930s (shown open).

9 Square leather-buckle compact, c. 1950s.

10 Lesco Bond Street small green alligator compact.

Fig. 33

1 Lin-Bren green leather compact with envelope-motif coin holder on lid, c. 1940s.

2 Gold-tooled leather compact with Venice canal scene on lid, possibly Italy.

3 Lin-Bren green leather compact/cigarette holder combination (shown with open cigarette case), U.S. Patent No. 2,471,963, c. 1940s.

4 Same as **3** in black leather (shown closed).

5 Same as **3** in red leather (shown open).

6 Maroon leather compact with sleeve for lipstick, c. 1930s.

7 Dorette small snakeskin vanity purse with zippered compartments for powder and purse; lipstick concealed in front lid.

8 Lady Vanity oval blue leather compact with snap closing.

9 Square alligator compact with goldtone lipstick attached to side.

Fig. 34

1 Green lizard compact with lipstick hinged on top of lid, probably Argentina.

2 Gold-tooled brown leather horseshoe-shaped compact, Argentina.

3 Persian gold and black compact with padded lid.

4 Larue green-gold tooled leather compact designed as a book; lid contains sliding mirror (shown open).

5 Brown gold-tooled leather compact, Italy.

6 Mondaine green leather vanity case with carrying cord and miniature portrait of a woman within a gold-tooled border; mirror, powder, rouge, and lipstick compartments, c. 1930–40s.

7 Light brown lizard horseshoe-shaped purse-motif compact, Argentina.

8 Round brown leather compact.

9 Marcee handmade horseshoe-shaped gold-tooled leather compact.

10 Persian gold and navy blue compact with padded lid and back.

Fig. 35

1 Croco square white leather zippered compact with decorative multicolored cord inset on lid, Israel.

2 Navy blue horseshoe-shaped leather compact with gold-tooled fleur-de-lis on lid.

3 Horseshoe-shaped gilt-metal compact with decoratively tooled leather inserts on lid and back, probably Argentina.

4,5 Mondaine tooled leather-covered case designed as a book, c. 1930–40s (shown open and closed).

6 Horseshoe-shaped red leather zippered compact with attached sleeve for lipstick.

7 Croco round light blue zippered compact with decorative multicolored cord inset on lid, Israel.

8 Fur compact with coin-purse snap closure, Argentina.

9 Square gold-tooled leather compact with Venice canal scene, possibly Italy.

10 Nan Co-ed zippered horseshoe-shaped compact with scene of cowboy on a horse with branding-iron marks.

11 Leather compact with colorful Persian scene.

12 Wadsworth cobra envelope-shaped compact.

Plate 1

1 Lampl light blue enamel compact with five colorful three-dimensional scenes from "Alice in Wonderland" encased in plastic domes on lid.

2 Sterling-silver white cloisonné mini bell-shaped compact decorated with painted holly; diminishing mirror and loop for chain.

3 Kigu "Flying Saucer" metal compact with blue celestial scene on both sides (shown open).

4 Square goldtone compact with sailor steering ship and copper steering wheel mounted on lid.

5 Volupté "Collector's Item" metal compact with grand piano on lid and raised keys on keyboard.

6 Samaral brown leather and brass compact designed to resemble guitar with strings, Spain.

7, 8 Pygmalion textured-brass compact designed to resemble grand piano; collapsible legs, England (**7** shown open, **8** shown closed).

9 Charbert red, white, and blue enamel "Drumstick" compact, c. 1930s.

10 Elgin American silvered-metal compact designed to resemble coin.

11 Avon copper-colored metal lip-gloss container designed to resemble Lincoln penny.

12 Red, white, and blue compact designed to resemble telephone dial with slogan "I Like Ike" imprinted on lid; red map of the United States on lid.

13 Evans "Charlie McCarthy" mesh vanity pouch with raised Charlie McCarthy head on black enamel lid.

14 Orange, blue, and white lusterware compact with colorful Oriental figure mounted upright on screw-top lid.

15 French ivory mini compact with raised Bobby's head mounted upright on screw-top lid.

16 Djer-Kiss silvered-metal vanity case with raised nymphs on lid; powder and rouge compartments, c. 1920s.

17 Orange enamel mini compact with painted intaglio figures of Mickey and Minnie Mouse; powder sifter.

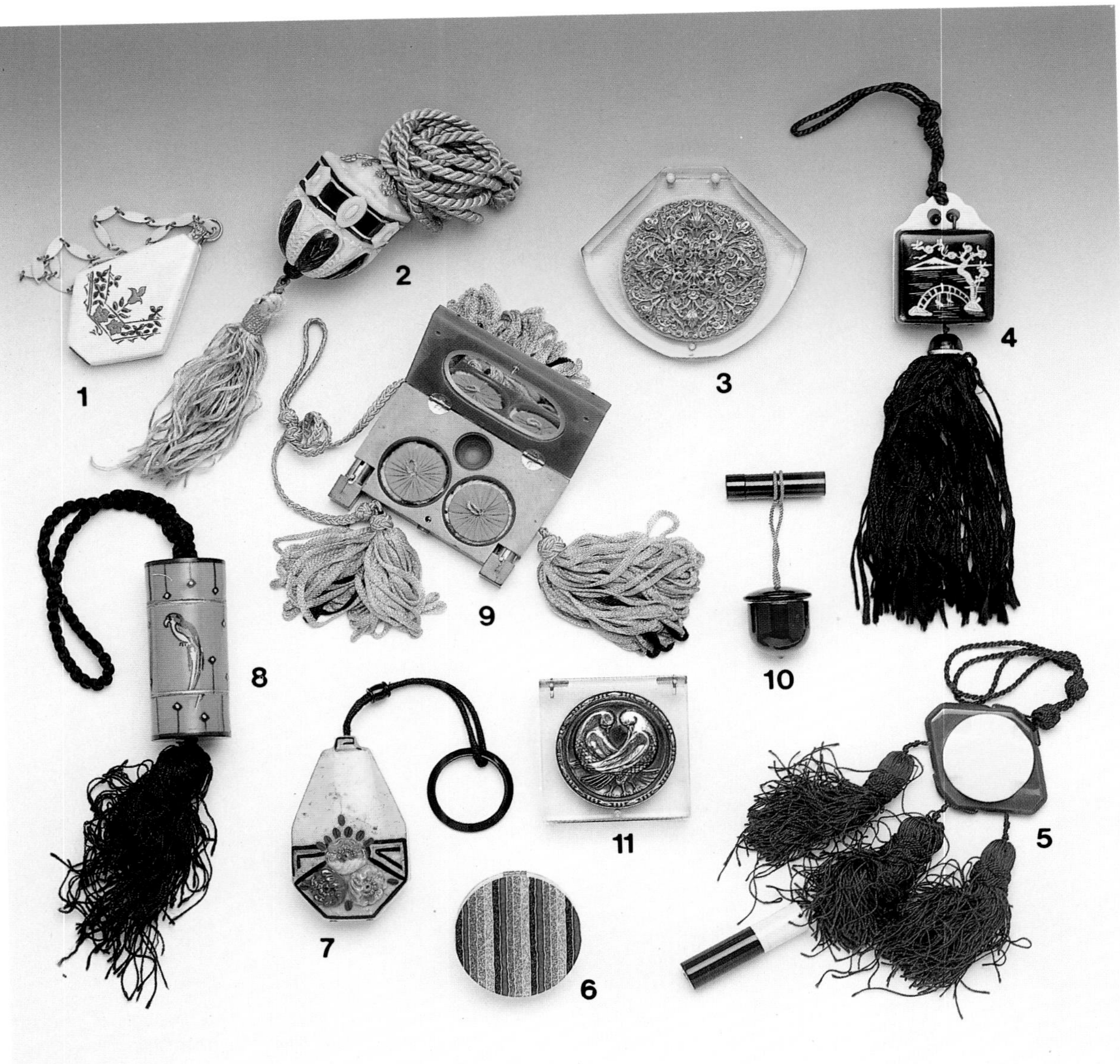

Plate 2

1 French ivory compact with painted red and green flowers; carrying chain made of plastic links, c. 1920s.

2 French ivory and green molded plastic dual-opening vanity case with carrying chain and tassel; powder and rouge compartments, c. 1920s.

3 Yellow Lucite compact with filigree metal lid, c. 1920s.

4 Ebony and French ivory dual-opening vanity case with Oriental scene on lid; powder and rouge compartments; carrying cord with lipstick concealed in tassel, c. 1920s.

5 Blue and ivory plastic screw-top compact; carrying cord with lipstick concealed in tassel, c. 1920s.

6 Multicolor striped glitter plastic compact, c. 1920s.

7 Marbleized yellow plastic vanity case with raised multicolored flower on lid; ring carrying cord with ojime button, c. 1920s.

8 Pink bolster-shaped vanity case decorated with painted parrot; carrying cord with lipstick concealed in tassel, c. 1920s.

9 Oblong green plastic vanity case striped with ebony; compartments for powder, rouge, and slide-out lipsticks; tassel and tasseled carrying cord, c. 1920s (shown open).

10 Brown plastic tango-chain screw-top compact designed as an acorn; lipstick attached by gold cord.

11 Blue Lucite compact with sterling repoussé medallion of two doves on lid.

Plate 3

1 Gilded-metal embossed vanity case with multicolored intaglio decoration; prong set with red stones and pearls; compartments for powder and lipsticks, France, turn of the century (shown open).

2 Oblong gilded-metal embossed vanity case with multicolored intaglio decoration; prong set with red stones and painted cloisonné inserts; powder and rouge compartments and sliding lipstick, France, turn of the century.

3 Goldtone embossed compact with multicolored intaglio decoration; prong set with green stones; loop for chain, France, turn of the century.

4 Gilded-metal embossed mini compact with multicolored intaglio decoration and lid set with blue stones and pearls, France, turn of the century.

5 Gilded-metal embossed compact with multicolored intaglio decoration and enameled painted lid set with blue cabochon stones, France, turn of the century.

6 Horseshoe-shaped gilded-metal embossed vanity case with multicolored intaglio decoration; prong set with purple stones; carrying chain and compartments for powder and lipsticks, France, turn of the century.

7, 8 Oblong gilded-metal embossed vanity case with multicolored intaglio decoration; prong set with blue stones and painted disk; powder and rouge compartments, France, turn of the century. (**7** shown closed, **8** shown open).

9 Goldtone mini compact with multicolored intaglio decoration; prong set with purple stones, France, turn of the century.

10 Gilded-metal embossed vanity case with multicolored intaglio decoration with cameo-like disk on lid; prong set with pink stones, France, turn of the century.

11 Gilded-metal compact with multicolored intaglio decoration; prong set with blue stones and pearls; loop for chain, France, turn of the century.

12 Goldtone embossed vanity case with multicolored intaglio decoration; prong set with red and turquois stones; tassel and carrying chain, France, turn of the century.

13 Goldtone filigree miniature compact; prong set with turquois stones, Continental, 19th century.

14 Goldtone enameled compact with red, green, and goldtone enamel back and painted enamel scene on lid, Continental, turn of the century.

15 Horseshoe-shaped gilded-metal embossed vanity case with multicolored intaglio decoration; openings for powder and rouge, prong set with blue stones, pearls, and painted disk; France, turn of the century.

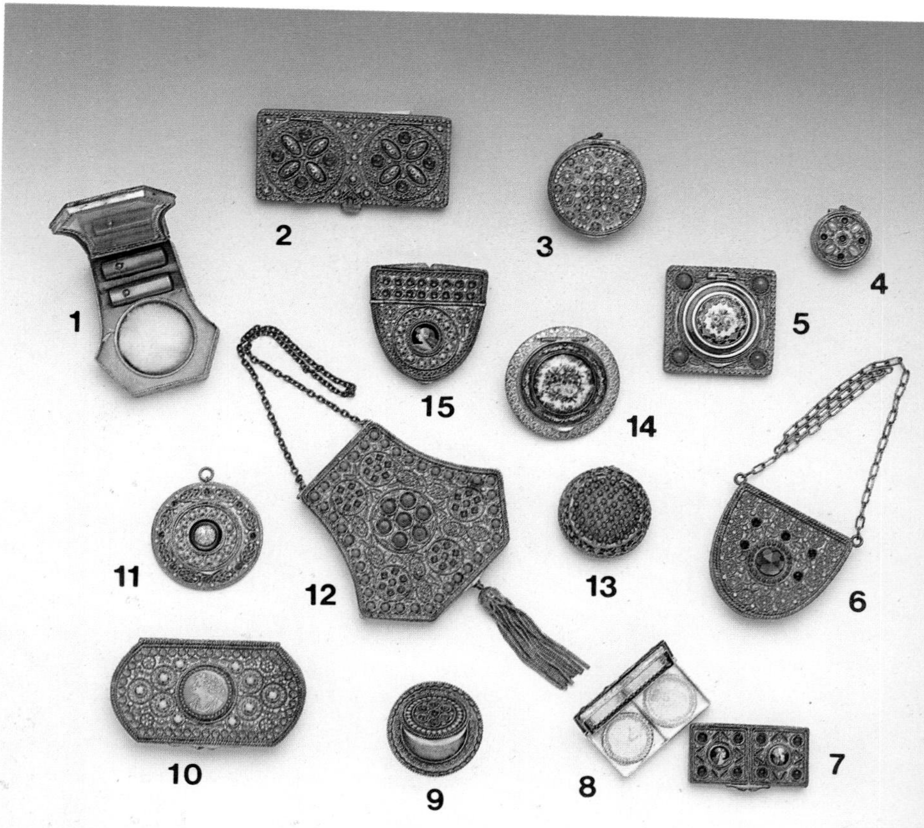

Plate 4

1 Ebony wooden compact shaped as castanets with metal Paris insignia on lid and orange tasseled carrying cord, France.

2 Yellow bolster-shaped vanity case with silhouette and black polka dots; carrying cord with lipstick concealed in tassel, c. 1920s.

3 Platé "Trio-ette" rose cameo molded-plastic vanity case shaped as hand mirror; powder on one side, rouge on the other; lipstick concealed in handle, c. 1940s.

4 Crystal Lucite compact with polished metal cutout of man taking siesta next to cactus plant, c. 1940s.

5 Ebony plastic rhinestone-studded compact with screw top, c. 1920s.

6 Red beetle-shaped novelty plastic compact.

7 Oval red plastic compact set with rhinestones; carrying cord and tassel, c. 1920s.

8 Pink Lucite-rimmed sterling-silver compact with sterling hinge and catch.

9 Venine blue plastic vanity case with goldtone filigree lid; compartments for powder and rouge.

10 A. Bourjois & Co. "Novita" ebony plastic compact with canal scene painted on lid; fancy braided carrying cord with two lipsticks and perfume containers concealed in tassels, France.

Plate 5

1 Green and goldtone embossed oblong compact with painting of two girls in disk on lid, Italy, turn of the century.

2 Vermeil etched silver and blue enamel compact, Italy, turn of the century.

3 Silver etched compact with colorful enamel design on lid and French ivory cutout, Continental, turn of the century.

4 Octagonal champlevé, gilded and embossed compact with two shades of blue, Italy, turn of the century.

5 Red and goldtone champlevé compact shaped as hand mirror; lipstick concealed in handle; red cabochon lipstick thumbpiece, Italy, turn of the century.

6 Shaded red and green enamel goldtone compact designed to resemble purse, Italy, turn of the century.

7 Gilded embossed compact with colorful enameled coats-of-arms on lid, Italy, turn of the century.

8 Shaded red enamel goldtone compact with painted flowers on lid, Italy, turn of the century.

9 Antiqued goldtone envelope compact with blue stone thumbpiece, Italy, turn of the century.

10 Scalloped antique goldtone compact with blue enamel encircling French ivory miniature on lid, Italy, turn of the century.

11, 12, 13 Vermeil engraved silver compact, lipstick, and comb set decorated with blue enamel and multicolored painted scenes; red cabochon lipstick thumbpiece, Italy, turn of the century.

14 Goldtone embossed compact designed to resemble pocketwatch; lid with Roman numerals and painted country scene, Italy, turn of the century.

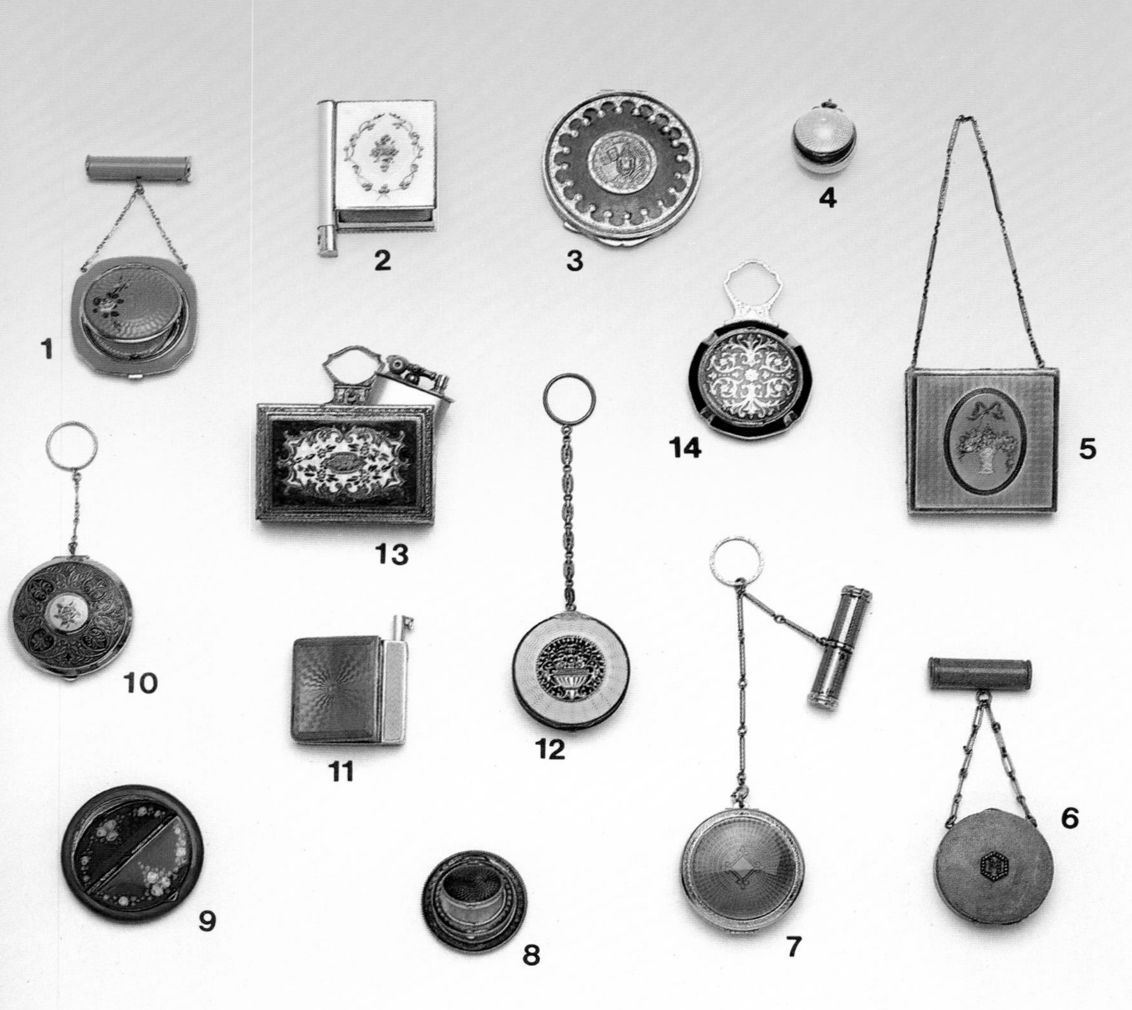

Plate 6

1 Evans blue enamel tango-chain vanity with painted cloisonné lid; powder and rouge compartments (shown open).

2 La Mode gilded metal cloisonné compact with painted flowers on lid; sliding lipstick.

3 Gilded-metal engraved compact with blue enamel lid and rhinestones on outer edge; metal "Saint Genesius, Guide My Destiny" medallion on lid, Continental.

4 Sterling-silver hallmarked light blue cloisonné ball-shaped compact; loop for chain, Germany.

5 Square, embossed silver, lavender cloisonné vanity case with painted basket of flowers on lid; goldtone interior with compartments for powder, rouge, and lipsticks; carrying chain.

6 Shagreen tango-chain compact with initial set with marcasites, c. 1930s.

7 Richard Hudnut "Deauville" blue cloisonné tango-chain vanity; metal mirror and powder and rouge compartments; lipstick attached to finger-ring chain, c. 1920s.

8 Green cloisonné goldtone vanity case with openings for powder and rouge, Austria, 19th century (shown open).

9 Sterling-silver hallmarked blue enamel vanity case with painted roses; adjacent openings for powder and rouge.

10 Round nickel-silver red and black enamel compact; metal mirror and compartments for powder sifter and rouge; finger-ring carrying chain, c. 1920s.

11 Sterling-silver hallmarked green cloisonné compact; lipstick in upper section, Germany.

12 Sterling-silver hallmarked yellow cloisonné compact with cutout silver medallion on lid; finger-ring chain, Austria.

13 Engine-turned nickel-silver compact/cigarette-case/lighter combination with green enamel lid.

14 Red and black champlevé and gilded vanity case with powder and rouge compartments and through handle.

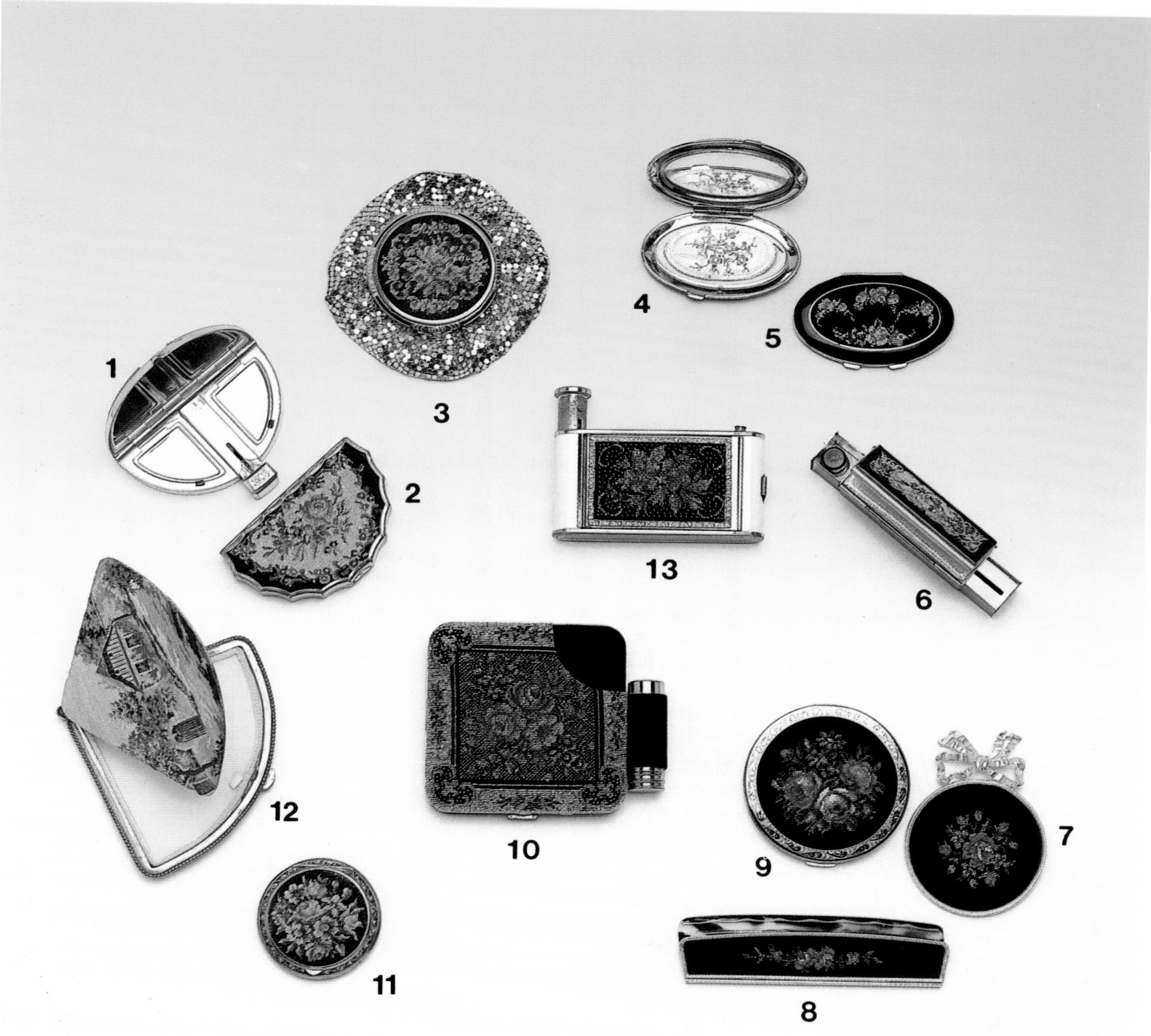

Plate 7

1 Petit-point halfmoon-shaped goldtone vanity case with powder and rouge compartments and sliding lipstick, c. 1930s (shown open).

2 Petit-point scalloped halfmoon-shaped goldtone vanity case, c. 1930s.

3 Evans petit-point goldtone mesh vanity bag with metal mirror and powder and rouge compartments in lid, c. 1940–50s.

4, 5 Rowenta oval enameled petit-point compacts (**4**, brown enamel, shown opened; **5**, black enamel, shown closed).

6 Quinto petit-point compact with sliding lipstick and perfume container (shown open).

7, 8, 9 Petit-point gilt mirror, comb, and compact set, Austria.

10 Petit-point goldtone compact backed in black faille with tandem lipstick.

11 Petit-point lid, rim, and back of round compact with powder sifter.

12 Triangular petit-point compact with swivel mirror.

13 White enamel metal petit-point compact with petit-point lid designed to resemble camera; lipstick at top, cigarette case in back, West Germany.

Plate 8

Foster & Bailey sterling-silver necessaire with mirror, writing slate, and compartments for powder and rouge; removable bolster-shaped flask/cigarette container concealed by multicolored fringed skirt.

Plate 9

Beauty-Full black chinoiserie minaudière with raised enamel Oriental scene; mirror and compartments for powder, rouge, pills, comb, cigarettes, and bill-clip; lipstick on top opens minaudière when pushed back, France.

Plate 10

Black silk damask and goldtone vanity purse, exterior oval filigree compact set with cabochon jade, pearls, green and blue stones; thumbpiece set with gems; silk-lined interior; powder and rouge compartments and carrying chain.

Plate 11

1 Whiting & Davis black and white double-mesh vanity bag with two separate mesh bags joined at top; powder and rouge compartments; engraved frame, blue stone cabochon thumbpiece, and carrying chain, c. 1920s.

2 Whiting & Davis pale green mesh vanity bag with pink roses; dual openings with embossed lids (one side monogrammed, the other side dated 1925); powder and rouge compartments and carrying chain, c. 1920s.

3 Whiting & Davis purple, black, and silver mesh vanity bag with purple enamel vanity case on outside of frame, lined interior; powder sifter, metal mirror, and compartment for rouge in lid; carrying chain, c. 1920s.

4 Goldtone mesh vanity bag with micro-mosaic cover; lined interior with metal mirror and powder and rouge compartments in lid; carrying chain.

5 Whiting & Davis multicolored mesh vanity bag with rigid mesh lid set with multicolored stones; carrying chain and compartments for powder, rouge, comb, and bills, c. 1920s.

6 Whiting & Davis "El-sah" (imprint on attached interior metal tag) multicolored mesh vanity bag with embossed silvered-metal lid, carrying chain and compartments for powder, rouge, and comb, c. 1920s.

7 Whiting & Davis multicolored baby-mesh vanity bag with light blue enameled frame and carrying chain; light blue silvered vanity case incorporated on frame; compartments for powder sifter; metal mirror and rouge compartments in lid; lined interior, c. 1920s.

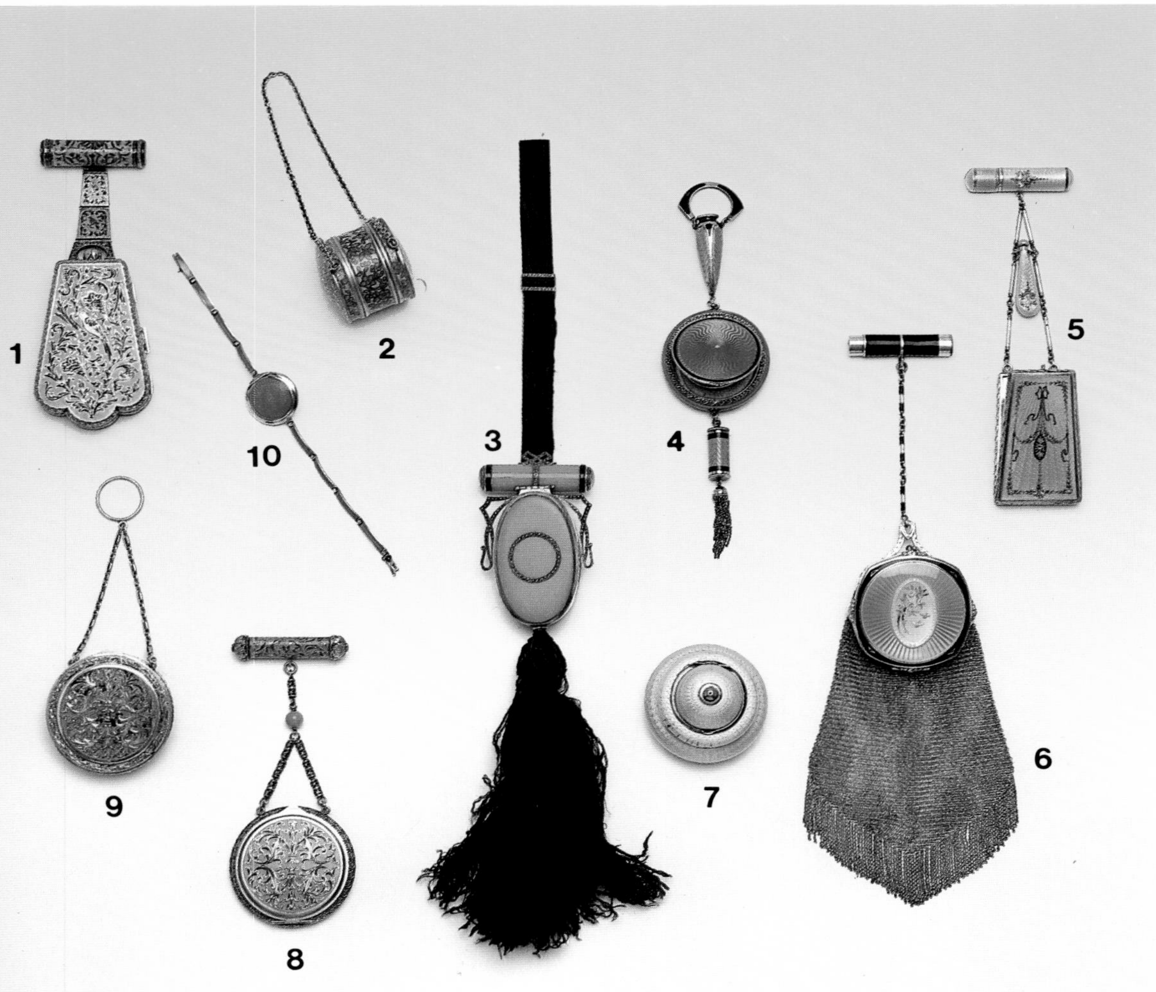

Plate 12

1 Sterling-silver hallmarked green enamel vanity case with goldtone interior, lipstick attached to vanity by enameled links; embossed perfume knob at base of links; partitions for powder, rouge, and cigarettes, Austria, turn of the century.

2 Blue-flowered enamel two-sided vanity case with powder on one side and rouge on the other; wrist chain, Continental, turn of the century.

3 Sterling-silver hallmarked salmon-colored plastic vanity case with marcasite trim; tandem lipstick and powder and rouge compartments; tassel and marcasite-decorated carrying cord, Continental.

4 Foster & Bailey blue cloisonné vanity case suspended from enameled perfume container; powder and rouge compartments; lipstick attached at base; tassel and black enameled finger-ring chain.

5 Green cloisonné silver tango-chain vanity with pink roses; powder and rouge compartments; lipstick attached by two enameled link chains with perfume suspended between the two chains.

6 Foster & Bailey sterling-silver mesh tango-chain vanity bag with light blue cloisonné lid with painted flowers; powder and rouge compartments; lipstick attached by enamel chain, turn of the century.

7 Peach copper and cloisonné vanity case with two-tier openings for powder and rouge, Germany, 19th century.

8 Sterling-silver hallmarked green champlevé tango-chain with bar-brooch lipstick, Austria, turn of the century.

9 Sterling-silver hallmarked green champlevé compact with finger-ring chain, Austria, turn of the century.

10 Sterling-silver hallmarked blue cloisonné compact/bracelet with enameled links, Germany, 19th century.

Plate 13

1 Coty goldtone compact with Coty trademark (stylized white puffs on an orange background) on lid.

2 Elgin American goldtone compact with colorful enamel swirls and "G.E. Color T.V." logo on lid.

3 Segal red enamel nickel-silver compact with sliding key blank in lid, c. 1930s.

4 Turquoise plastic screw-top perfume container with lipstick and eye makeup containers suspended from gold cord.

5 Brown lizard zippered compact designed to resemble suitcase with carrying handles.

6 Vantine's blue silk compact decorated with embroidery and gold thread; beaded tassel and carrying cord with ojime bead, c. 1920s.

7, 8 Molded orange plastic round clip-on compact (**7** shown closed, **8** shown open).

9 Yellow marbleized plastic ball compact decorated with faux pearls; tassel and carrying cord.

10 Wadsworth compact with "Simplicity Printed Pattern 25 cents" on lid.

11 Pink satin vanity case with gold braid; powder and rouge compartments; carrying cord with ojime bead and beaded tassel, c. 1920s.

12 Volupté black enamel goldtone compact designed to resemble artist's palette with raised paint tube, brushes, and colors on lid.

Plate 14

1 White enamel tango-chain vanity case with country scene on lid; lipstick attached by two link chains; powder sifter and rouge compartments; original fitted presentation box.

2, 3 Embossed vermeil compact and lipstick set with enameled country scene on lid, Italy, turn of the century.

4 Octagonal silvered-metal blue cloisonné vanity case with roses; powder sifter and rouge compartment and through handle, c. 1920s.

5, 6 Antiqued goldtone oval embossed vanity case with cloisonné lid, carrying chain and compartments for powder sifter, rouge, lipstick, and coins (**5** shown open, **6** shown closed).

7 Lavender cloisonné silvered-metal vanity case with blue flowers; powder sifter and rouge compartment; swivel handle.

8 Green enamel tango-chain vanity case with flowers on lid and lipstick; powder sifter and rouge compartment; double-link chain, c. 1920s.

9 La Mode blue cloisonné goldtone vanity case with metal mirror, compartments for powder and rouge, and two sliding lipsticks on either side.

10 La Mode green cloisonné goldtone vanity case with picture locket in lid; and metal mirror, compartment for powder and two sliding lipsticks on either side (shown open).

11 Silvered-metal and enameled vanity case with painted raised tree and house on lid; engine-turned link chain; compartments for powder, rouge, and lipsticks, c. 1930s.

12 Sterling-silver blue cloisonné vanity case with pink flowers; openings on either side for powder and rouge; two loops for chain.

13 Black enamel goldtone vanity case with pink rose; two sides open (one for powder, the other for rouge); carrying cord with lipstick concealed in tassel.

Plate 15

1, 2 Richard Hudnut "Deauville" vanity case with red and black enamel profiles on lid; powder and rouge compartments; lipstick holder attached to compact and finger ring, c. 1920s (**1** shown open, **2** shown closed).

3 Richard Hudnut "Deauville" vanity case with white and green enamel profiles on lid; powder and rouge compartments; original fitted presentation box; c. 1920s.

4 Evans "Tap Sift" white cloisonné vanity case with black stylized "skyscraper" motif and key pattern around rim; powder sifter and rouge compartment, c. 1920s.

5 Evans "Tap Sift" green cloisonné tango-chain vanity case with black stylized "skyscraper" motif; powder sifter and rouge compartment; lipstick attached by double chain, c. 1920s.

6 Richard Hudnut "Le Debut" silvered-metal vanity case with powder and rouge compartments; lipstick attached to compact and finger ring, c. 1920s.

7 Art Deco abstract cloisonné vanity case with link carrying chain; compartments for powder, rouge, and lipstick.

8 Silvaray Art Nouveau red enamel metal compact.

9 Bree green enamel vanity case with metal profile on lid; powder slide and compartments for rouge and lipstick, c. 1930s.

10 Art Nouveau silvered halfmoon-shaped enameled vanity case with multicolored swirls; goldtone interior, link carrying chain, and compartments for powder, rouge, and lipstick.

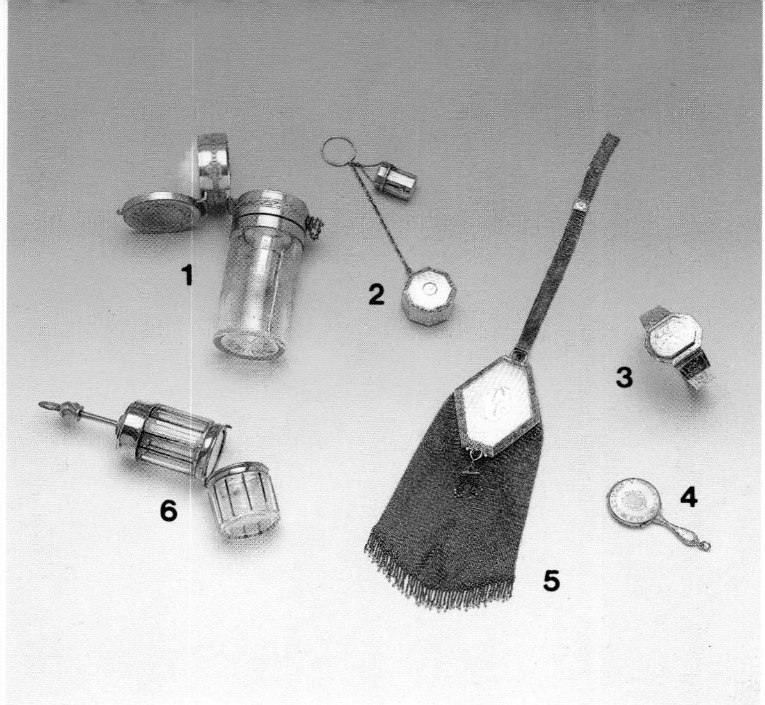

Plate 16

1 Cylindrical etched-glass compact/perfume container with goldtone compact on top, probably France (shown open).

2 Tiffany & Co. gold octagonal two-sided tango-chain mini compact with floral design around rim, turn of the century.

3 Octagonal gold compact/bracelet with engraved lid and band.

4 Gold engraved mini compact shaped as hand mirror; loop for chain.

5 Gold mesh vanity bag with sapphire cabochon thumbpieces and fringes set with pearls; carrying chain, c. 1920s.

6 Etched-glass compact/perfume container with goldtone lids, glass striped with blue enamel; carrying ring (shown open).

Plate 17

Compact with three enameled shields on screw-top lid, suspended from dance-program book; "Bal Kolejowy, Stanislawowie, 8 lutego, 1908" in goldtone on cover; white velvet fringed belt hook, Poland.

Plate 18

Embossed brass vanity/hatpin, $1\frac{1}{2}''$ round, with raised fleur-de-lis on lid, $11\frac{1}{2}''$ steel pin.

Plate 19

1, 2, 3 Enameled compact shaped as hand mirror; interior and exterior mirrors and matching comb (**1** shown closed, **2** shown open, **3** matching comb)

4 Sterling-silver hallmarked white cloisonné miniature oval compact shaped as hand mirror with painted roses on lid; loop for chain, Continental.

5 Sterling-silver hallmarked pink cloisonné enameled miniature compact shaped as hand mirror with painted flowers on lid; loop for chain, Continental.

6 Brass miniature compact shaped as hand mirror with orange cloisonné enamel lid; interior and exterior mirrors and loop for chain, Continental.

7 Sterling-silver blue cloisonné miniature oval compact shaped as hand mirror; interior and exterior mirrors and loop for chain, Continental.

8 Sterling-silver hallmarked yellow cloisonné miniature compact shaped as hand mirror; loop for chain, Continental.

9 Octagonal silvered-filigree metal vanity case

shaped as hand mirror; interior reveals powder sifter; two-sided mirror and rouge compartment decorated with red stones; lipstick in handle.

10 Sterling-silver oval miniature compact shaped as hand mirror; handle unscrews to reveal lipstick and perfume containers; loop for chain, Continental.

11 Petit-point compact shaped as hand mirror; filigree handle and interior and exterior mirrors, Austria.

12 Sterling-silver miniature oval compact shaped as hand mirror; exterior diminishing mirror and loop for chain, Continental.

13 Vermeil sterling-silver hallmarked compact shaped as hand mirror with pink cloisonné lid and exterior mirror; interior lid incorporates writing slate; loop for chain.

14 White cloisonné compact shaped as hand mirror with painted flowers on lid; fold-over handle contains compartments for lipstick and eye makeup; interior and exterior mirrors.

15 Goldtone compact shaped as hand mirror decorated with colored cabochon stones; interior and exterior mirrors, France.

16 Blue and white champlevé goldtone compact shaped as hand mirror with painting of man and woman on lid; lipstick in handle and blue cabochon thumbpiece, Italy.

17 Red and white champlevé octagonal goldtone compact shaped as hand mirror with painting of girl on swing on lid; lipstick in handle and red cabochon thumbpiece, Italy.

18 Goldtone compact shaped as hand mirror with green enamel-decorated lid; interior and exterior mirrors, France.

19 Art Deco miniature compact shaped as hand mirror with rhinestones on lid; interior and exterior mirrors.

20 Sterling-silver, hexagonal mini compact shaped as hand mirror with coat-of-arms on lid; loop for chain, Continental.

Plate 20

1 Antique goldtone vanity case with faux baroque pearls and blue stones on filigree lids; opening on either side for powder and rouge; pearl-decorated tassel and braided finger-ring chain.

2 Antique goldtone chatelette; compact with lipstick case, coin holder, and belt hanger decorated on both sides with filigree overlay set with aquamarine-colored stones, Continental.

3 Pierced silvered-metal bolster-shaped necessaire with onyx filigree disk set with blue stones and marcasites on lid; tassel and carrying chain (shown open).

4 Pattie Duette "Vivaudou" antique goldtone-filigree vanity bag set with blue stones; vanity case on inside hinge; lined interior; carrying chain with lipstick concealed in tassel, Continental, turn of the century (shown open).

5 Antique goldtone-filigree vanity case with multicolored stones on lid; opening on either side for powder and rouge, sliding lipsticks at sides, and perfume vial at top; tassel and carrying cord, Continental, turn of the century.

6 Antique goldtone filigree oval vanity case with stones and center cabochon stone; braid carrying chain with lipstick concealed in tassel, Austria, turn of the century.

7 Antique goldtone vanity bag with blue stones and pearls; cover incorporates compact with onyx disk set with blue stones; tassel and carrying chain; silk back, Continental, turn of the century.

8 Antique goldtone tango-chain vanity-bag compact with green stones; tassel and filigree lipstick holder; silk back, Continental, turn of the century.

9 Gilded filigree compact with turquoise stones; butterflies suspended from neck chain.

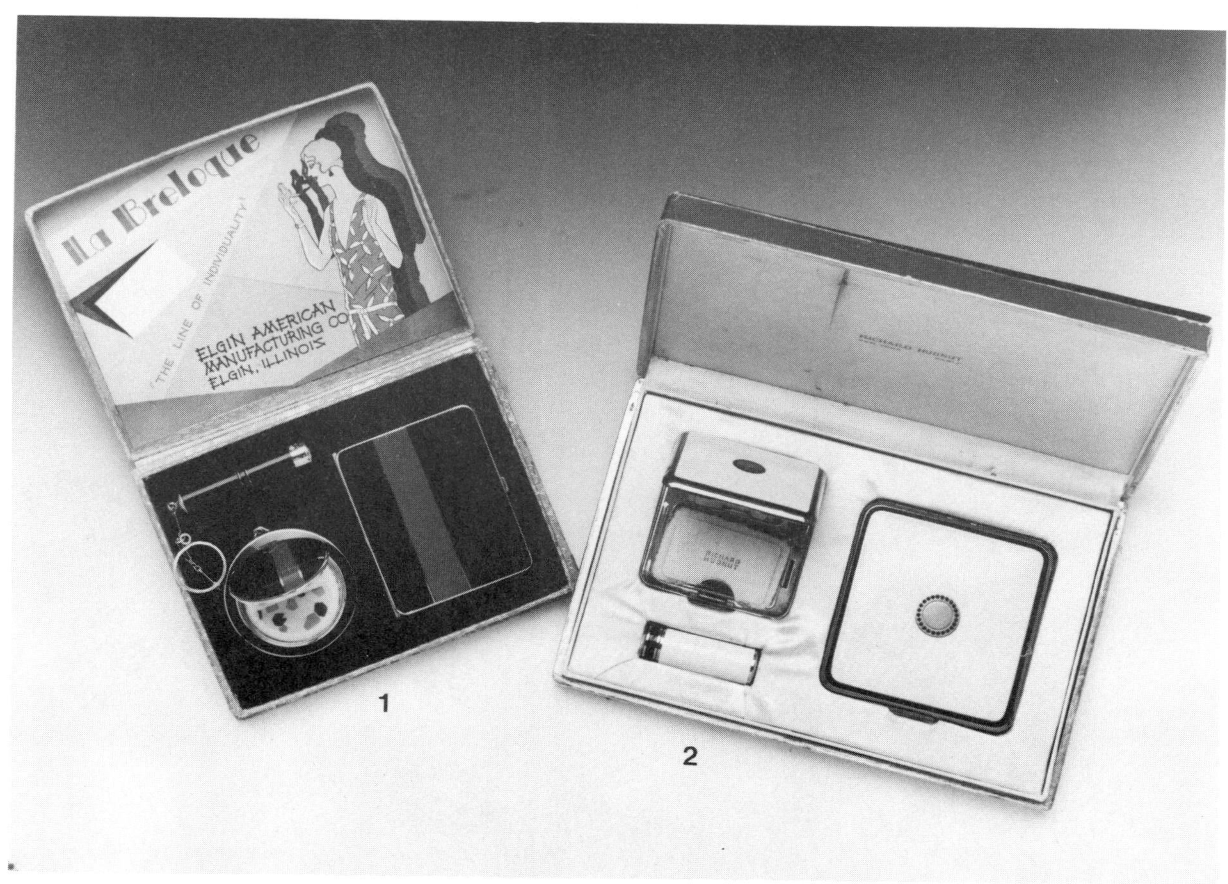

Fig. 36

1 Elgin American "La Breloque" tango-chain red and black enameled compact; lipstick with matching cigarette case in original presentation box.

2 Richard Hudnut compact in white with black enamel border; lipstick and matching cigarette case in original presentation box, c. 1920–30s.

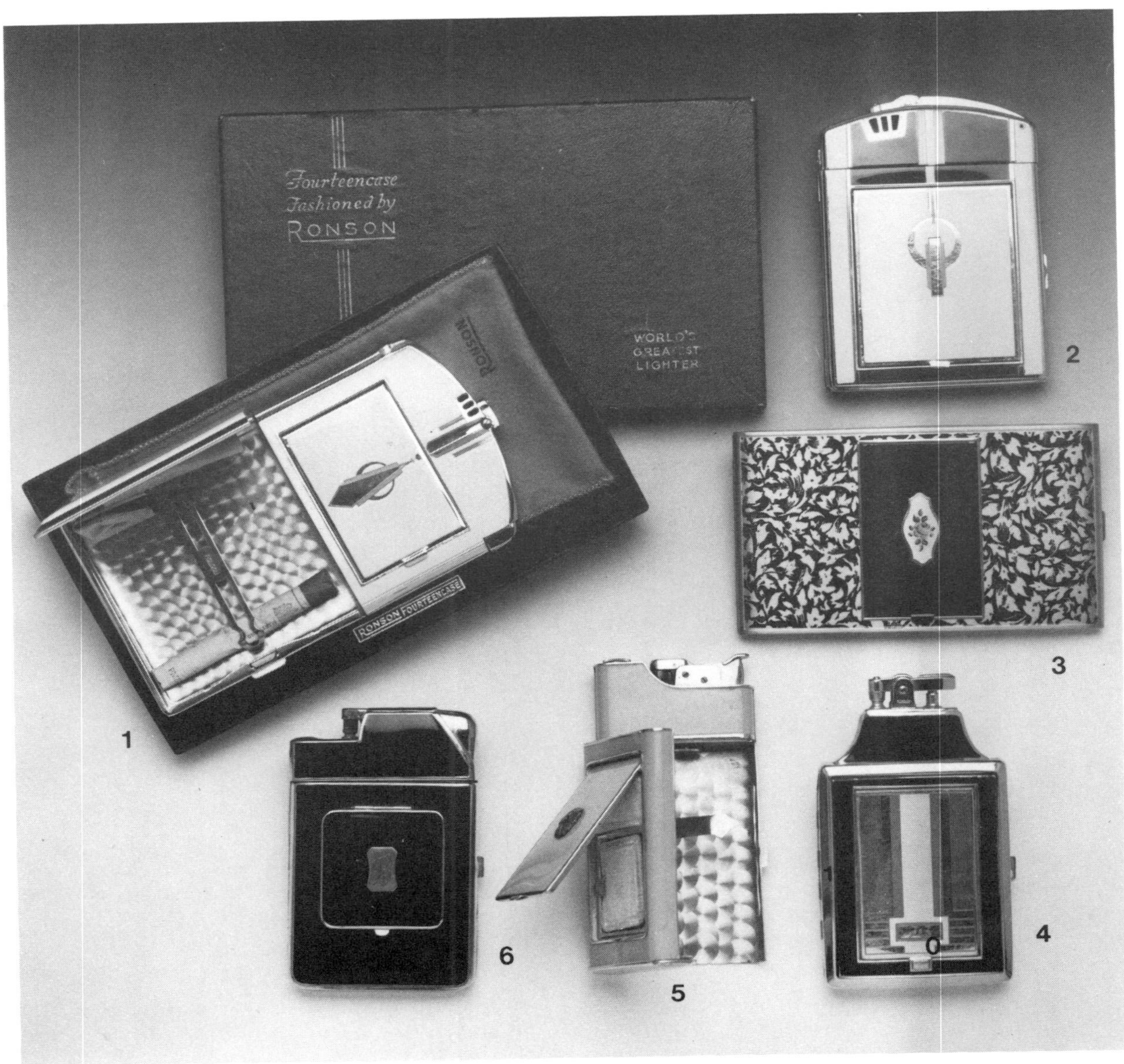

Fig. 37

1 Ronson "Fourteencase" white Art Deco enamel combination compact/lighter/cigarette case with flannel pouch and original presentation box.

2 Ronson white and brown marbleized Art-Deco enamel combination compact/lighter/cigarette case, c. 1930–40s.

3 Black enamel gilt-decorated combination compact/cigarette case, black enamel compact with white flower cloisonné disk on lid, c. 1930s.

4 Ronson brown marbleized Art-Deco enamel combination compact/lighter/cigarette case, c. 1930–40s.

5 Evans light blue enamel combination compact/lighter/cigarette case with marcasite decoration on lid of compact, c. 1930s.

6 Marathon black-enamel silvered-metal combination compact/lighter/cigarette case with initialed medallion on compact lid, c. 1930–40s.

Fig. 38

1 Evans bronzed metal combination compact/cigarette case with engine-turned design and white cloisonné disk on front lid, c. 1930s.

2 Richard Hudnut green and black enamel metal compact and cigarette case, 1930s.

3 Ronson silvered-metal compact/cigarette-case combination, c. 1930–40s.

4 Enameled white cloisonné side-by-side compact/cigarette case/calling-card combination, c. 1930–40s (shown open).

5 Enameled blue cloisonné side-by-side compact/cigarette case/calling-card combination, c. 1930–40s.

6 Marathon white enamel and silvered combination compact/lighter/cigarette case with enameled scene on lid of compact, c. 1930–40s.

7 Lampl black enamel goldtone compact/cigarette-case combination with rhinestone and green faux gemstones on lid; compact in center flanked by compartments for cigarettes, c. 1930s.

8 La Mode light and dark blue enamel compact/cigarette case with pearl-beaded removable compact centered on lid of cigarette case.

Fig. 39

1 Dunhill Vanity silvered vanity case designed to resemble cigarette lighter; powder and rouge compartments, top reveals sliding lipstick, c. 1920s.

2 Dunhill Vanity goldtone vanity case designed to resemble cigarette lighter; powder and rouge compartments, top reveals sliding lipstick, U.S. Patent No. 1,639,628, c. 1920s (shown open).

3 Green and black enamel metal compact/cigarette-case combination (shown open).

4 Maroon marbleized plastic-covered goldtone two-sided compact/cigarette-case combination.

5 Mascot brick-design engine-turned goldtone two-sided compact/cigarette-case combination, England.

6 Tan and brown enamel metal compact/cigarette-case combination with white cloissoné flowered disk on lid.

7 Evans silvered green enamel Art Deco miniature compact designed to resemble cigarette lighter; top releases powder, bottom slides out to reveal lipstick.

8 Ronson brown enamel goldtone compact/cigarette-case combination, c. 1930–40s.

9 Lampl goldtone compact/cigarette-case combination with rhinestones and green faux gemstones on lid of compact; compact in center flanked by compartments for cigarettes, c. 1930s.

10 Black enamel combination compact/lighter/cigarette case with yellow cloissoné and painted rose on lid of compact.

Fig. 40

1 Illinois Watch Case Co. square goldtone compact/watch combination with three initials monogrammed on lid, c. 1930s.

2 Evans oblong silvered-metal compact/watch combination, c. 1950s.

3 Illinois Watch Case Co. round goldtone compact/watch combination with engraved design on lid, c. 1930–40s.

4 Evans square goldtone compact/watch; lid designed to resemble trunk with straps, c. 1940s.

5 Goldtone oblong compact/watch/coin-holder combination with carrying chain, Germany.

6 Black enamel silvered-metal vanity-case/watch combination with powder and rouge compartments (shown open).

7 Evans square goldtone engine-turned checkerboard compact/watch combination, c. 1940s.

8 Elgin American round goldtone compact/watch combination with black grosgrain carrying case; lid engraved to resemble pocketwatch, c. 1950s.

9 Illinois Watch Case Co. yellow enameled bronze clamshell vanity-case/watch combination with gold-plated interior and compartments for powder and rouge, c. 1930s.

Fig. 41

1 Elgin American silvered compact/music-box combination with three gilded deer on lid; melody is "Anniversary Waltz," black carrying case, c. 1950s.

2 Pale yellow enamel goldtone vanity-case/compass combination with powder and rouge compartments; lid contains compass and pictures of ships and their destinations, France.

3 Elgin American gilt and satin-finish compact/compass combination with engraved scene on lid depicting the continents, c. 1950s.

4 Marbleized brown enamel and goldtone decorated compact/thermometer combination, France.

5 Goldtone compact with silvered music score of "Stardust" mounted on lid, c. 1920s.

6 Black matte enamel goldtone compact/music-box combination with slide-out lipstick; lid designed as piano keyboard, French melody, c. 1930s.

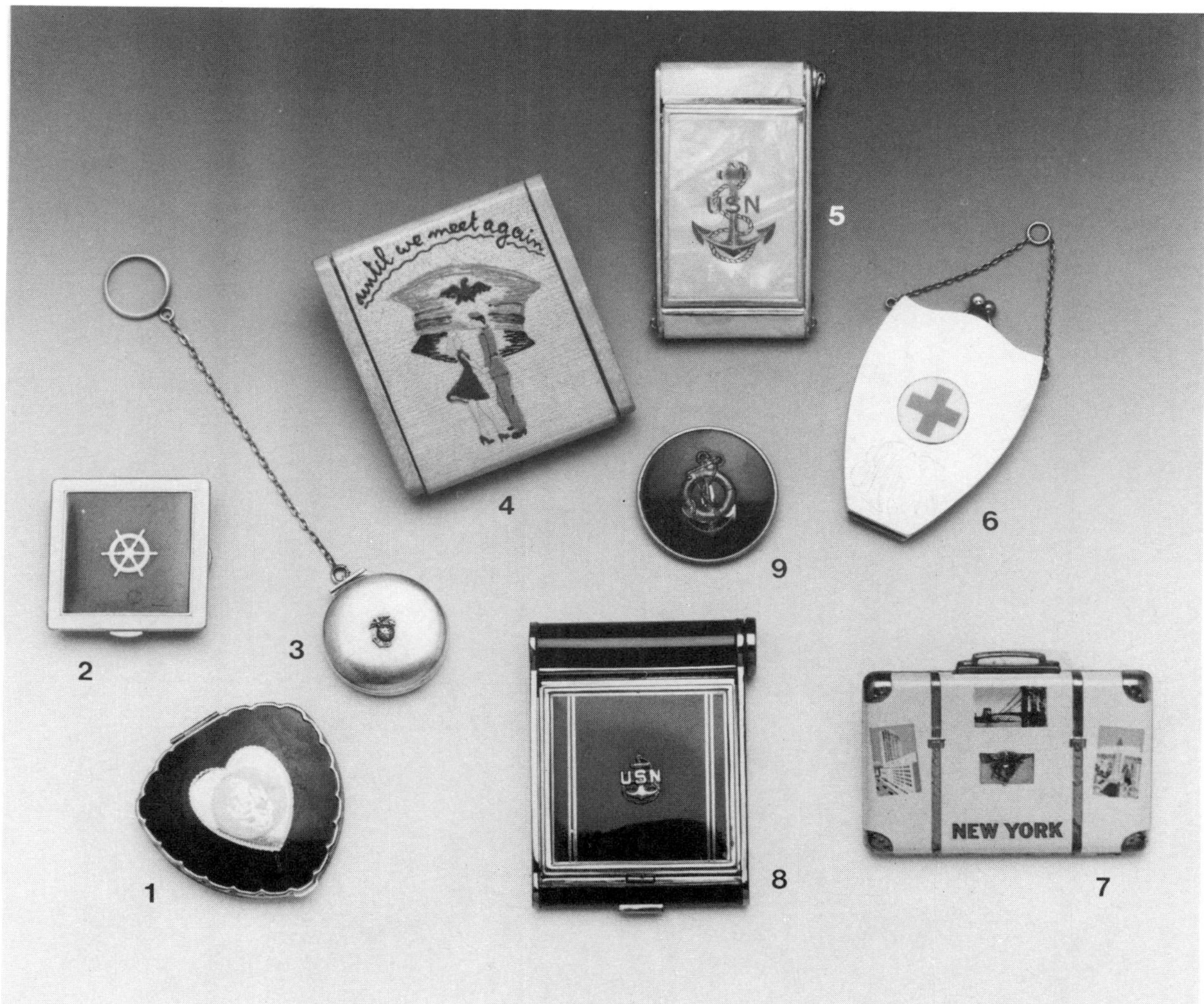

Fig. 42

1 Black enamel goldtone vanity case with U.S.N. insignia in gilt heart on lid; powder and rouge compartments, c. World War II.

2 Navy blue and white small vanity case with nautical motif on lid; powder and rouge compartments, c. World War II.

3 Sterling-silver compact with Marine Corps insignia on lid; gilded interior with diminishing mirror in lid and finger-ring chain, c. World War I.

4 Wood compact with painted serviceman and girl, "Until We Meet Again" painted on lid, c. 1940s.

5 Zell yellow marbleized plastic Kamra-Pak-style vanity case with Navy insignia on lid; powder and rouge compartments and slide-out lipstick, c. 1940s.

6 Sterling-silver shield-shaped compact with carrying chain, Red Cross enameled insignia disk on lid, monogrammed, c. World War I.

7 Yellow enameled suitcase-motif vanity case with stickers depicting New York's points of interest; metal Marine Corps insignia on lid, powder and rouge compartments, c. 1940s.

8 Brown marbleized enamel Kamra-Pak-style compact with U.S. Navy insignia on lid and sliding lipstick, Germany c. 1940s.

9 Black enamel round clip-on compact with U.S. Navy insignia on lid, c. World War II.

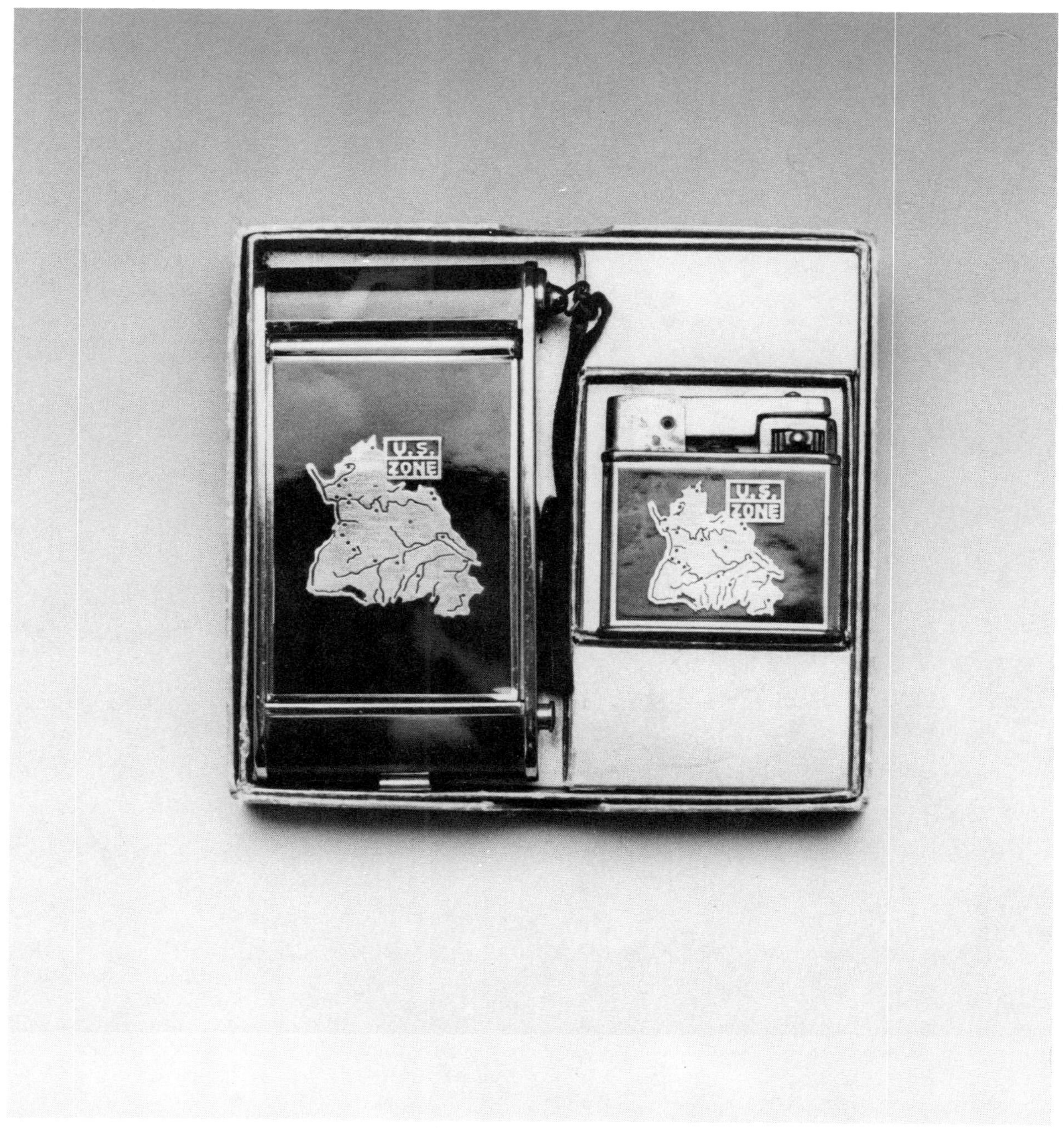

Fig. 43 Weltzunder blue marbleized enamel Kamra-Pak-style vanity case and matching cigarette lighter with silvered metal cutout map of U.S. Zone on lid; original presentation box, Germany, c. 1940s.

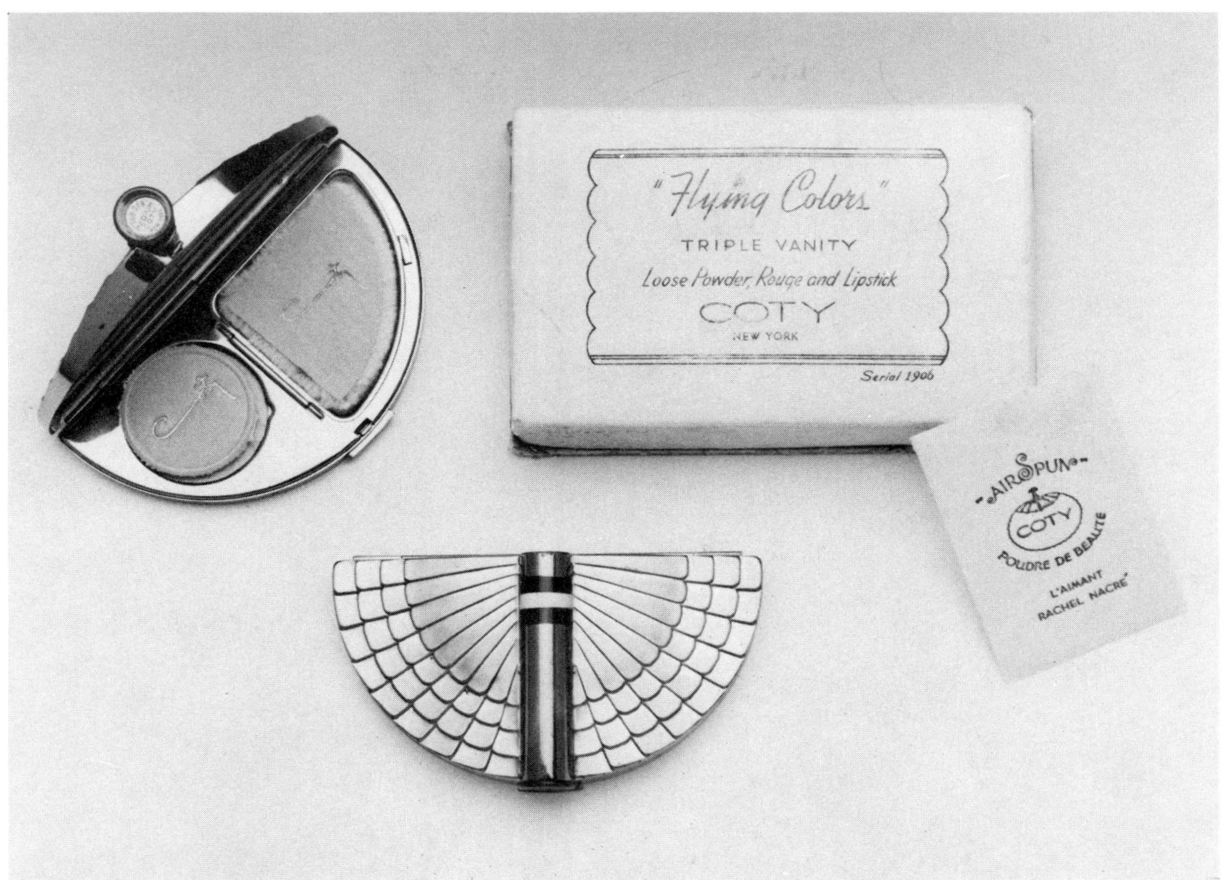

Fig. 44 Coty "Flying Colors" gilt-metal triple vanity case designed to resemble spread eagle wings with red, white, and blue lipstick tube in center; original presentation box and packet of Coty Airspun face powder, c. 1940s.

Fig. 45

1 Bronzed-metal compact designed as Air Force officer's cap with jeweled Armed Forces disk on top, c. 1940s.

2 Khaki plastic compact designed as Army officer's cap, c. 1940s.

3 Red, white, and blue plastic compact designed as Navy officer's cap, c. 1940s.

4 Goldtone compact with copper Armed Forces cap mounted on lid, c. 1940s.

5 Navy blue and white plastic compact designed as Navy officer's cap, c. 1940s.

6 Red, white, and blue plastic compact designed as Navy officer's cap, c. 1940s (shown open).

7 Black enamel goldtone heart-shaped vanity case with Armed Forces emblem on lid; powder and rouge compartments, arrow slides out to reveal lipstick, c. 1940s.

8 Rex Fifth Avenue red enamel oval compact, mother-of-pearl army hat mounted on lid, inscribed "Mother Love Son," U.S. Army, c. 1940s.

9 Satin goldtone compact with copper replica of Army officer's hat mounted on lid, c. 1930s.

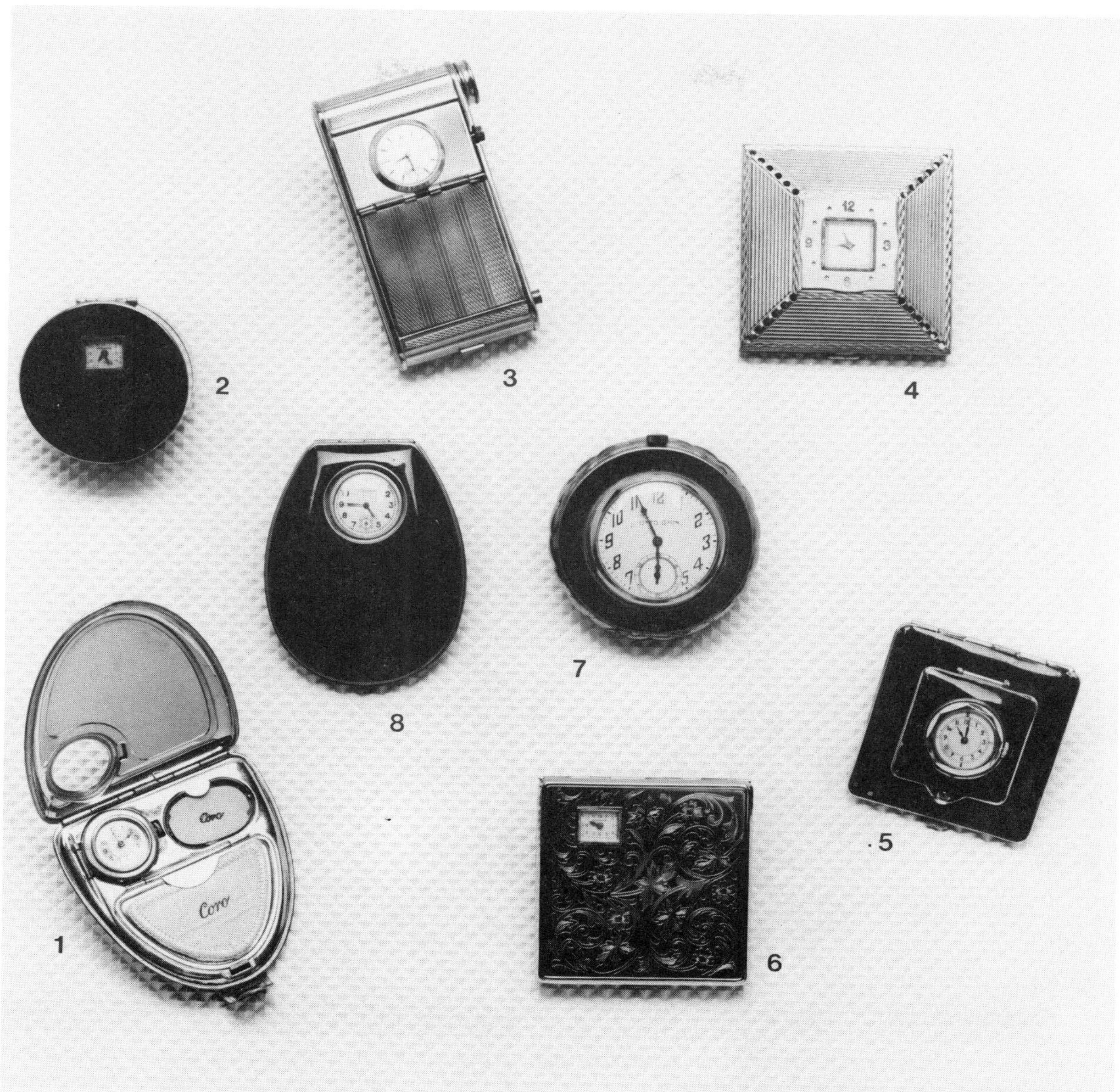

Fig. 46

1 Coro black enamel horseshoe-shaped vanity-case/watch combination with snap closing; powder and rouge compartments, c. 1920s.

2 Illinois Watch Case Co. compact/watch combination, c. 1930s.

3 Medana goldtone engine-turned Kamra-Pak-style compact/watch combination; back contains cigarette compartment, sliding lipstick case, West Germany, c. 1940–50s.

4 Ameré goldtone engine-turned compact, Switzerland.

5 Brown enamel compact/watch combination, Germany.

6 American Beauty goldtone engraved vanity-case/watch combination with powder and rouge compartments, c. 1940s–50s.

7 Goldtone compact/watch combination, Germany.

8 Timepact black enamel elongated horseshoe-shaped vanity-case/watch combination with powder and rouge compartments.

Fig. 47

1 Volupté goldtone compact with Cub Scout, Den Mother emblem.

2 Satin goldtone Girl Scout compact.

3 Sterling-silver octagonal miniature compact with Harvard University emblem on lid; loop for chain.

4 Stork Club goldtone compact and lipstick.

5 Arthur Murray presentation goldtone compact with picture of Arthur Murray Dancers on front lid.

6 Satin-finish goldtone compact with silvered shovel mounted on lid, souvenir of ground-breaking for office in Worcester, Massachusetts, presentation box.

7 Enameled "Eastern Star" jeweled compact.

8 Silvered "Veterans of Foreign War" vanity case with powder and rouge compartments.

Fig. 48

1 Goldtone compact designed as suitcase decorated with travel stickers.

2 Silver octagonal compact with cutout map of India on lid.

3 Goldtone compact with scenes of Paris mounted on lid.

4 Painted brown enamel compact, Paris.

5 Satin-finish goldtone vanity case designed as suitcase decorated with travel stickers, c. 1930s.

6 Green enamel goldtone compact with scenes of Ireland on lid, England.

7 Goldtone compact with scenes of Scotland on black plastic lid, England.

8 Miref goldtone compact with "Paris, 1412" enclosed in plastic dome on lid.

Fig. 49

1 Silvered-metal compact with gilt design of the State of Alaska on lid.

2 Agme goldtone compact with scenes of North America on satin-finish lid, Switzerland.

3 Green painted enamel compact depicting the Empire State Building, New York.

4 Compact with scene of Pennsylvania Turnpike on lid.

5 Elgin American compact with Georgia state flag and flower on lid, c. 1940–50s.

6 Oblong wood compact with map, state flower, and scenes of California on lid.

7 Silvered-metal vanity case with "Souvenir of Washington, D.C." printed on lid.

Fig. 50

1 White plastic-covered metal compact with "The Woman's Shop, Springfield, Mass." printed on slip-cover lid.

2 Engine-turned goldtone compact with "Compliments of The Rainbow Inn" printed on yellow marbleized plastic disk decorated with simulated sapphires, c. 1920s.

3 Silvered-metal repoussé floral-decorated compact with shield with scene of the White House mounted on lid; loop for chain.

4 Silvered-metal horseshoe-shaped compact with shield of "Battle Bennington Vt." mounted on lid.

5 Artcraft round blue enamel compact with "Indian and Mohawk Trail" painted on lid.

6 Goldtone engine-turned compact with "Summit Pikes Peak" on white plastic disk set with red stones mounted on lid.

7 Silvered-metal compact with photograph of "Old Orchard Beach, Maine" on lid, c. 1930s.

8 Engine-turned silvered-metal vanity case with shield of "The Pier, Old Orchard Beach, Maine" mounted on lid; powder and rouge compartments.

9 Black enamel compact with photograph of "Bellingrath Gardens, Mobile, Ala." printed on lid, c. 1920s.

Fig. 51

1 Engine-turned goldtone compact with "Sesquicentennial 1776–1926, Philadelphia, Pa." printed on plastic disk on lid.

2 Wooden compact with tapestry design of 1939 New York World's Fair on lid.

3 White enamel miniature flapjack compact with "A Century of Progress, 1833–1933" on silver disk mounted on lid.

4 Columbia Fifth Avenue mesh vanity pouch with orange and blue scene of 1939 New York World's Fair on lid.

5 Octagonal silvered-metal vanity case with copper coin inset in lid, inscribed "Sesquicentennial International Exposition, Philadelphia, 1926."

6 Columbia Fifth Avenue navy blue moiré vanity pouch with orange and blue scene of 1939 New York World's Fair on lid.

7 Light blue enamel metal compact with "Trylon & Perisphere 1939" disk mounted on lid.

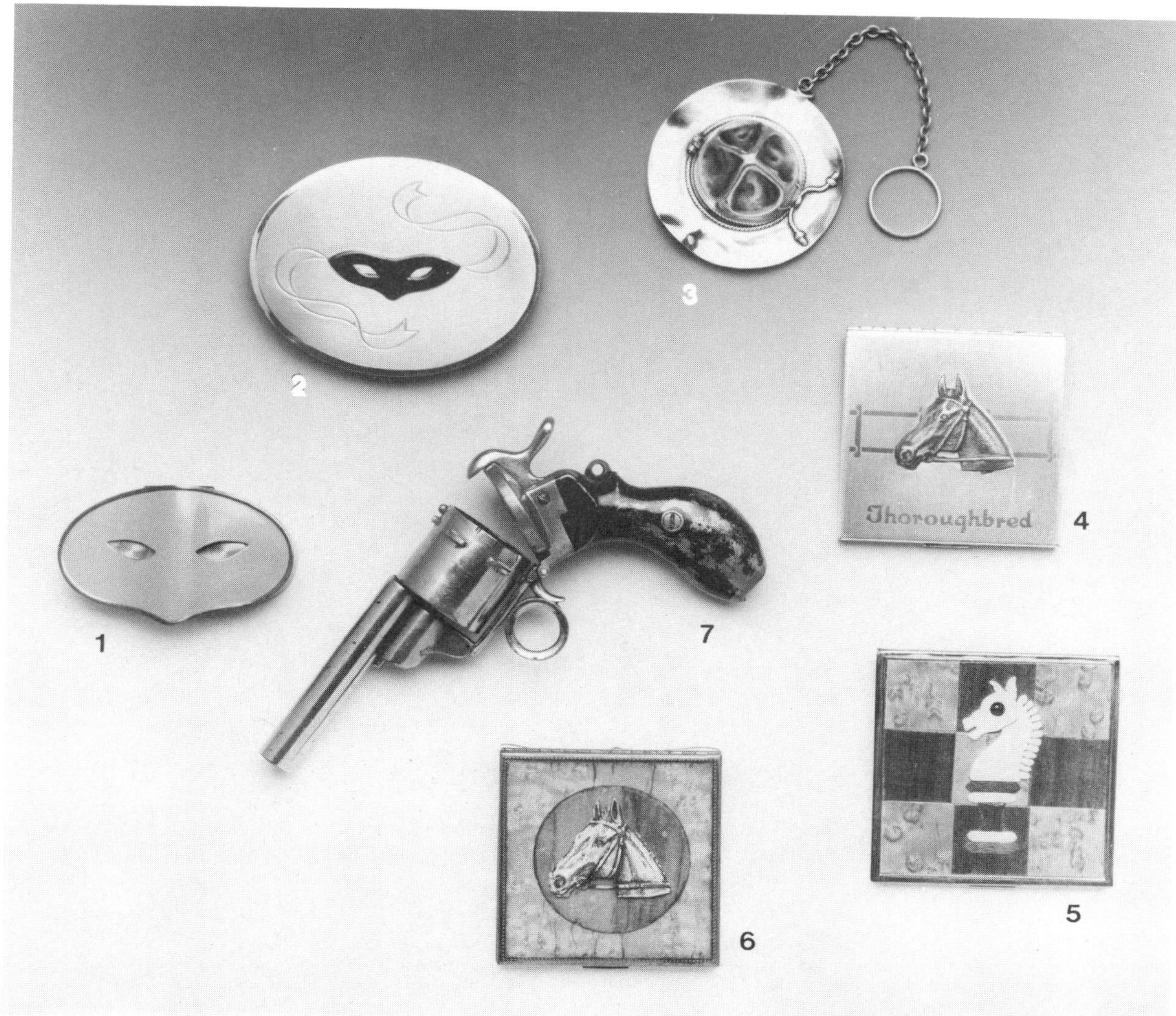

Fig. 52

1 Elizabeth Arden light blue harlequin-shaped compact, c. 1940s.

2 Dorothy Gray oval goldtone compact with black enamel harlequin mask on lid, c. 1940s.

3 Silver cowboy-hat compact with finger ring and metal mirror.

4 Pilcher silvered compact with horse's head mounted on lid, "Thoroughbred" printed below, Kentucky Derby, 1953.

5 Pilcher "Slimpact" wood compact with chess knight set on inlaid checkerboard lid, c. 1940–50s.

6 Pilcher wood compact with horse's head mounted on lid, c. 1940–50s.

7 Lady's silvered and black metal pistol/compact, c. 1950s.

Fig. 53 Antiqued gilt parure designed with a Fede-type decoration applied to the mesh vanity pouch; locket, pillbox, screw-back earrings, necklace, and two bracelets, one with secret opening, c. 1930s.

Fig. 54

1 Goldtone compact designed as hand mirror with decorated, engraved lid.

2 Engine-turned decorated goldtone compact designed as hand mirror; ring for chain, Germany, c. 1920s.

3 Engine-turned decorated goldtone compact designed as hand mirror, Germany, c. 1920s (shown open).

4 Silver engraved scalloped-edged compact formed as hand mirror with lipstick in handle.

5 Sterling-silver compact formed as hand mirror with bloodstone cabochon thumbpiece; lipstick in bolster-shaped handle, Italy, c. 1920s.

6 Sterling-silver compact formed as hand mirror with coral cabochon thumbpiece; lipstick in cylindrical handle, Italy, c. 1920s.

7 Blue enamel compact formed as hand mirror with painted scene on lid.

8 Silvered miniature Limoges compact formed as hand mirror with painted scene on lid, France.

9 Goldtone Limoges compact formed as hand mirror with painted scene on lid, France.

10 Miref gilt compact formed as hand mirror with lipstick in handle; beveled mirror on both sides of compact, France.

11 Antique silver-plated triangular compact designed as hand mirror with turquoise cabochon thumbpiece; lipstick in handle.

12 Hoechst silver-plated compact designed as hand mirror with lipstick in handle; flannel case, probably Germany.

Fig. 55

1 Pewter-colored metal compact shaped like hand mirror; lid decorated with stylized cutout flowers, France.

2 Ivory-colored plastic miniature compact shaped like hand mirror, Germany, c. 1920s.

3 Silvered miniature compact shaped like hand mirror, lid decorated with petit-point, France.

4 Coty plastic compact designed as hand mirror; lid decorated with Coty trademark powder puffs, lipstick in handle.

5, 6 Platé "Trio-ette" plastic vanity case designed as hand mirror; powder and puff on one side, rouge on other side; lipstick in handle, c. 1940s (black case shown open, white case shown closed).

7 Black and gilt enameled compact formed as hand mirror with lipstick in handle.

8 Satin-finish goldtone compact shaped like hand mirror with cupid centered on lid.

9 Goldtone compact shaped like hand mirror with plastic floral decoration on lid.

10, 11 Blumpak plastic compact shaped like hand mirror (amber compact shown open, yellow compact shown closed).

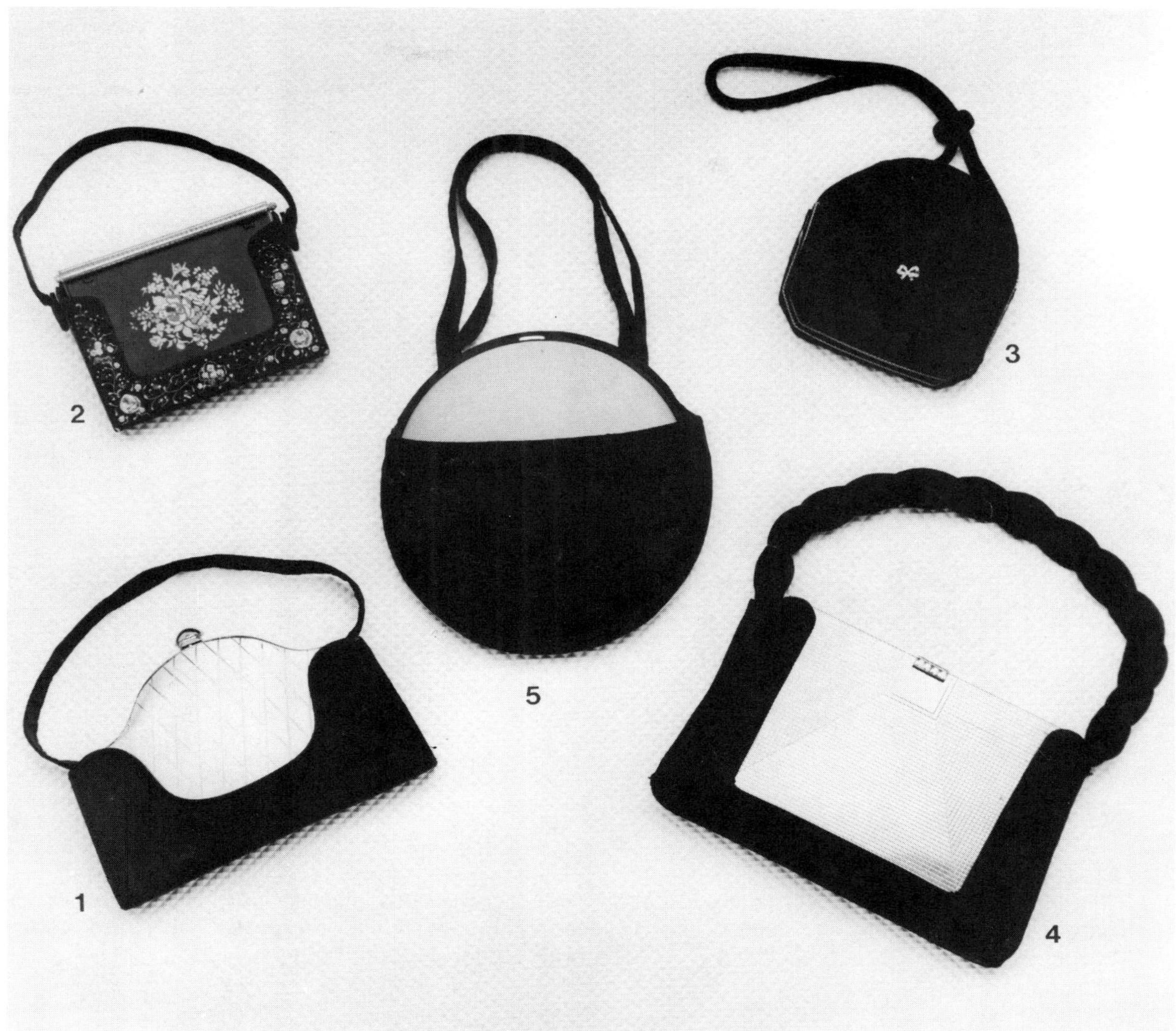

Fig. 56

1 Volupté silvered-metal, criss-cross gilt-decorated carryall, interior reveals mirror; compartments for powder, puff, lipstick, and personal items; black faille carrying case.

2 Volupté black matte painted floral "Swinglok" carryall with painted floral black faille carrying case; compartments for lipstick, powder, and cigarettes, c. 1940–50s.

3 Goldtone compact with black suede carrying case decorated with gold trim; snap openings on both sides.

4 Engine-turned geometric-design gilt carryall with compartments for powder, rouge, comb, and cigarettes; lipstick has rhinestone trim; black faille carrying case with twisted handle, c. 1940–50s.

5 Blue enamel super compact with zippered compartment and navy blue faille carrying case, c. 1940–50s.

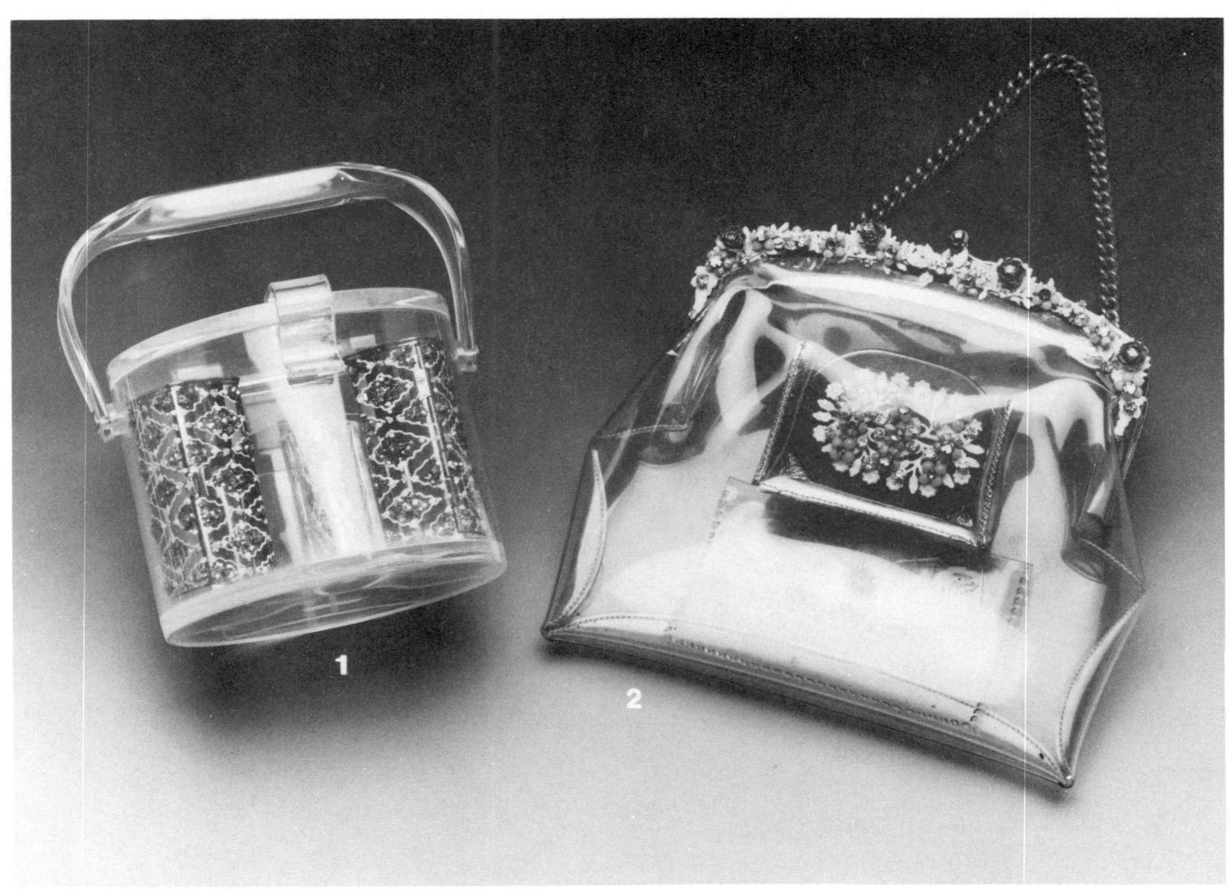

Fig. 57

1 Clear Lucite vanity reticule with painted, sparkle-decorated goldtone compact, lipstick, and cigarette case.

2 Maxim clear plastic vanity reticule; compact and frame of reticule decorated with rhinestones and white, pink, and blue flowers.

Fig. 58

1 Oval rose-colored velvet vanity case with cameo medallion on lid; compartments for powder, rouge, and lipstick; carrying cord with ring and ojime bead, c. 1920s.

2 Black velvet vanity case with embroidered butterfly and edged with gold trim; compartments for powder, rouge, and lipstick; carrying cord with ring and ojime bead, c. 1920s.

3 Fuller plastic compact with sleeve for comb mounted on lid.

4 Elgin American red, white, and blue enamel "Drumstick Set"; compact and lipstick in drum-and-drumstick motif; original presentation box.

5 Ivory-colored marbleized plastic compact with red trim around edge and sailing ship picture on lid, snap closure, c. 1920s.

6 Evening in Paris wood compact with decorated lid, c. 1940s.

7 Plastic compact with copper-etched lid depicting scene of lady and lamb, signed Biscay, France.

8 La Faveur de Paris "Sifta-Pak" blue tooled-leather powder bag with mirrored lid and drawstring powder puff, France, c. 1920s.

9 Elmo navy blue moiré vanity powder bag with mirror and drawstring powder puff, snap closing, c. 1920s.

10 Pink silk double compact box with lace and gold braid trim and compartments for powder and rouge, snap closing, c. 1920s (shown open).

11 Blue silk compact with netting and ribbon with slip-cover lid, c. 1920s.

12 Rose silk compact with lace and braid trim and slip-cover lid, c. 1920s.

13 Delettrez "Wildflower" pale blue paper compact with colorful floral spray on lid, c. 1940s.

14 Harmony of Boston tan box-shaped compact with snap closing, c. 1920s (shown open).

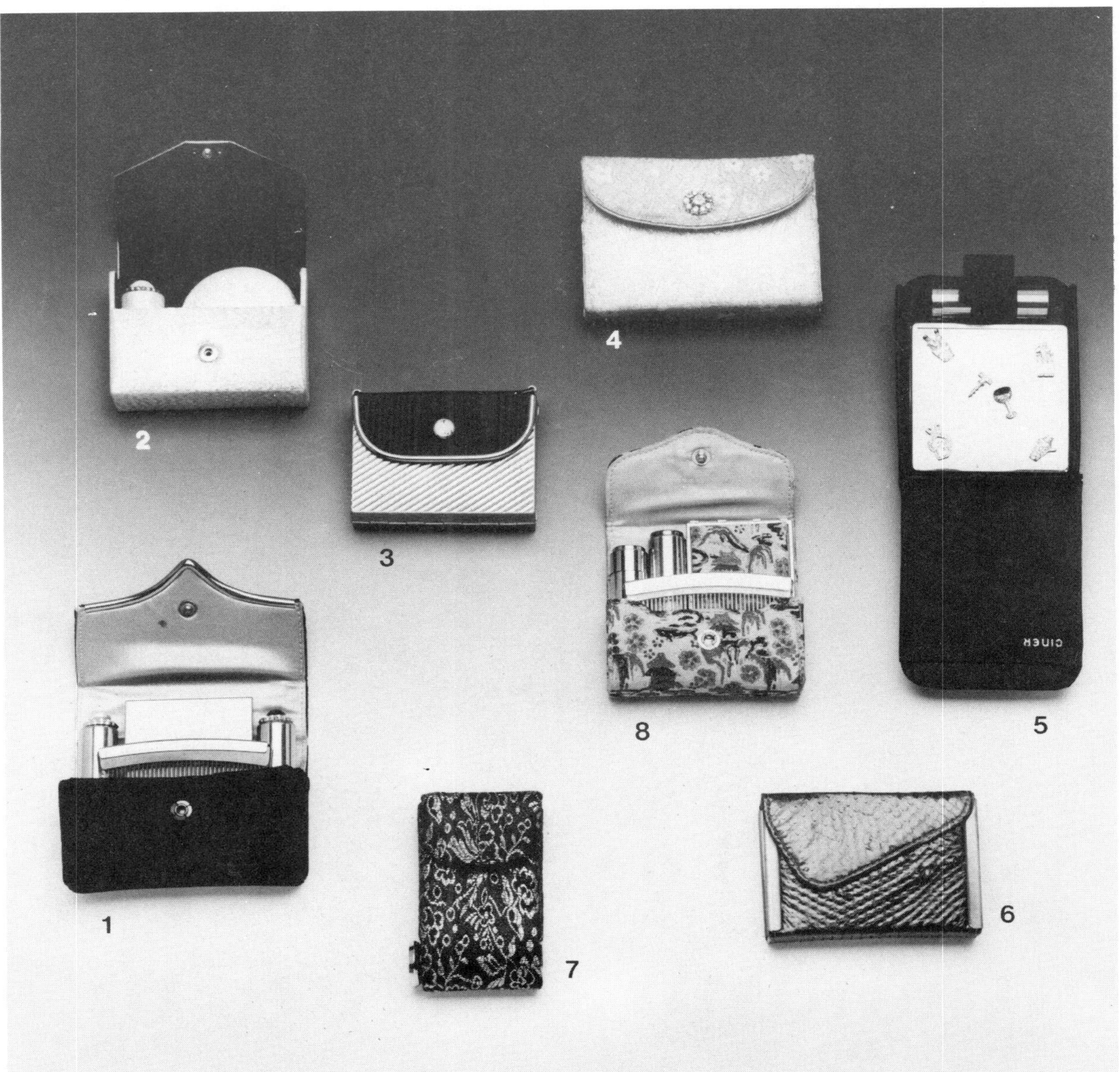

Fig. 59

1 Zell Fifth Avenue black suede vanity clutch with compact, two lipstick tubes, and comb; metal trim on outer lid and snap closing, c. 1940s.

2 Silver lamé vanity clutch with silver-lamé-covered compact and lipstick, c. 1940s.

3 Navy blue moiré and gilt vanity clutch with gilt compact, lipstick, and comb, c. 1940s.

4 Richard Hudnut white and gold fabric vanity clutch with compact and lipstick, decorated with "Tree of Life" motif set with green stones, c. 1940s.

5 Ciner black satin vanity clutch with rhinestone-decorated compact and lipstick, c. 1940s.

6 Lin-Bren red lizard vanity clutch with compact and lipstick, c. 1940s.

7 Renard black and gold fabric vanity clutch with pull-up compact and lipstick in sleeve at bottom of clutch, c. 1940.

8 Majestic floral vanity clutch with compact, two lipstick tubes, and comb, c. 1940s.

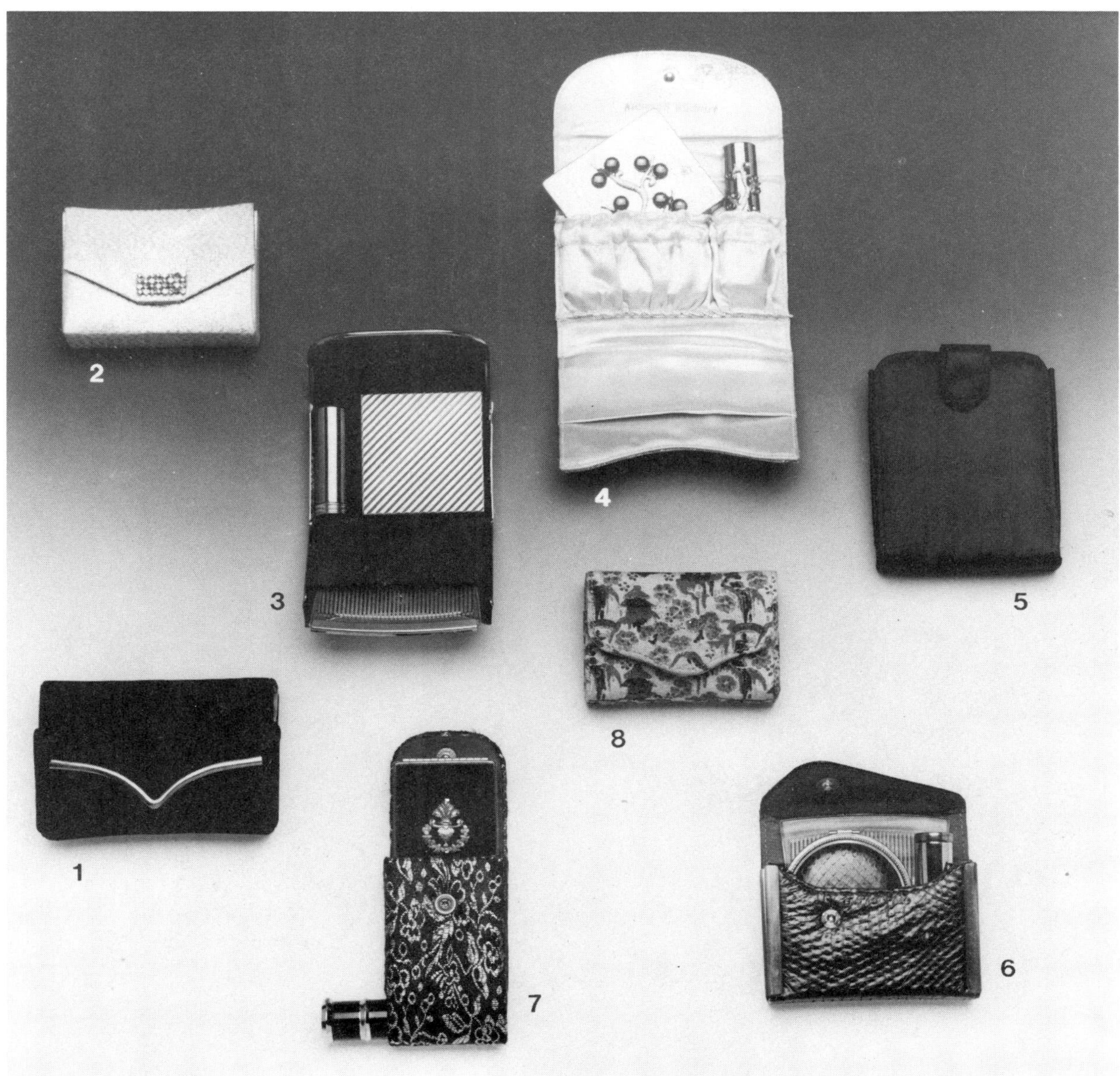

Fig. 60 Vanity clutches in Figure 59, with several shown open.

Fig. 61

1 Black suede and brass vanity purse with rhinestones on lid and around center; top opens to reveal compact, France.

2 Brown suede smaller version of **1** (shown open).

3 Britemode rigid black velvet vanity purse; lid lifts to reveal compact, France.

4 Black suede cylindrical vanity purse; top lifts to reveal compact, opening beneath compact reveals partition for comb, handkerchief, etc., France (shown open).

5 La Vedelte black suede cylindrical vanity purse; top lifts to reveal compact, opening beneath compact reveals partition for comb, lipstick, matches, etc.; bottom swivels and raises vanity to eye level, France (shown open).

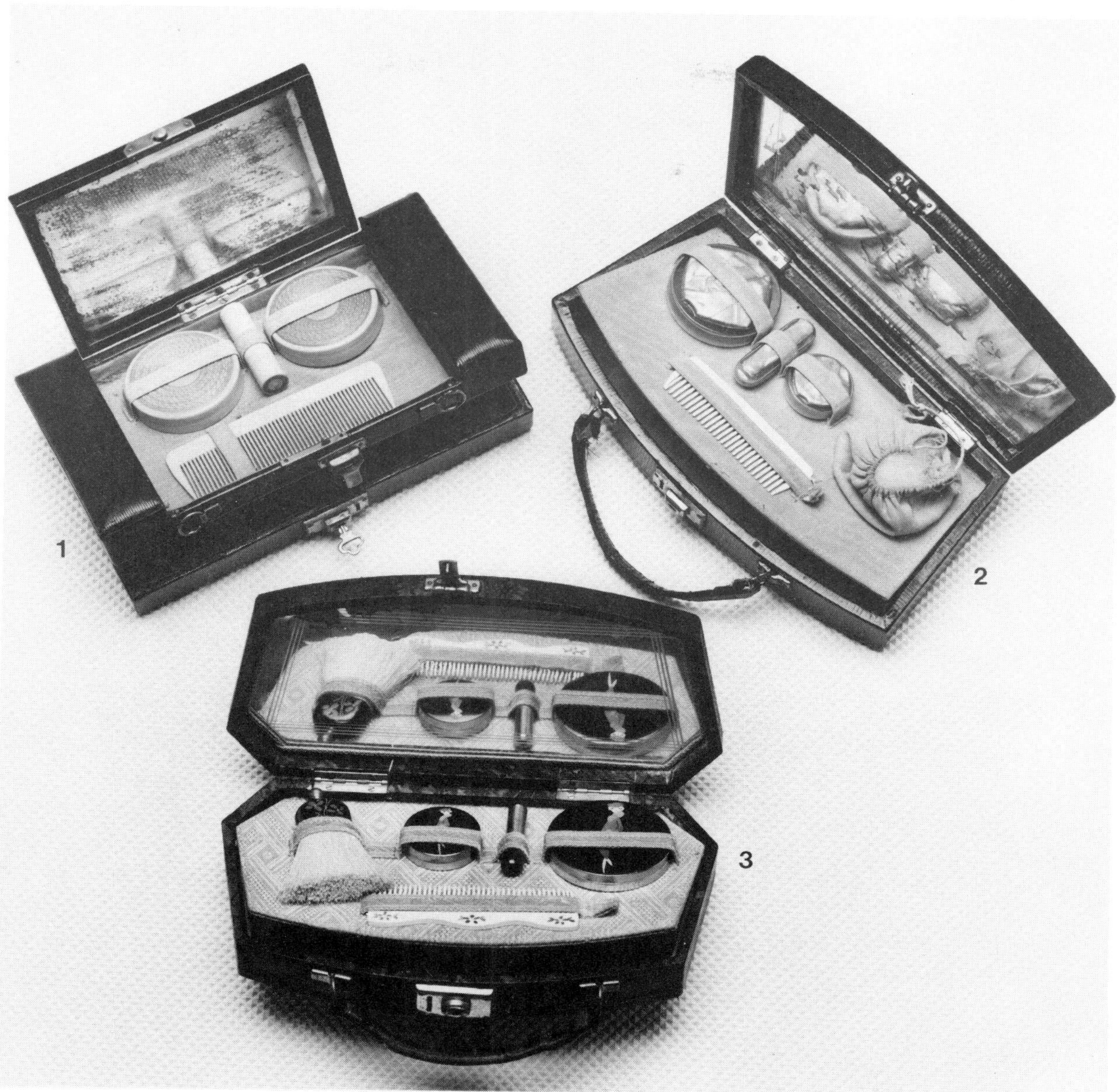

Fig. 62

1 Black leather oblong vanity box fitted with mirror, comb, powder, rouge, and lipstick containers; lower half opens for personal articles; lock and key, c. 1920s.

2 Black leather vanity box fitted with mirror, comb, drawstring puff holder, pearl-like compact, and rouge and lipstick containers, c. 1920s.

3 Black leather hexagonal vanity box fitted with small round mirrors on outside and interior lids; comb, powder, rouge, and lipstick containers and small whisk broom; lower half opens for personal articles; lock and key, c. 1920s.

Fig. 63
1 Black suede vanity purse with brass star-shaped studs; top opens to reveal compact, sides snap open, France.
2 Black suede basket-shaped vanity purse with gold braid and removable compact in lid, France.
3 Black suede and brass bolster-shaped vanity purse; lid opens to reveal compact, France.
4 Black suede and brass vanity purse with rhinestone-shaped bows connected by brass chains, France.

Fig. 64 Vanity purses in Figure 63 shown open.

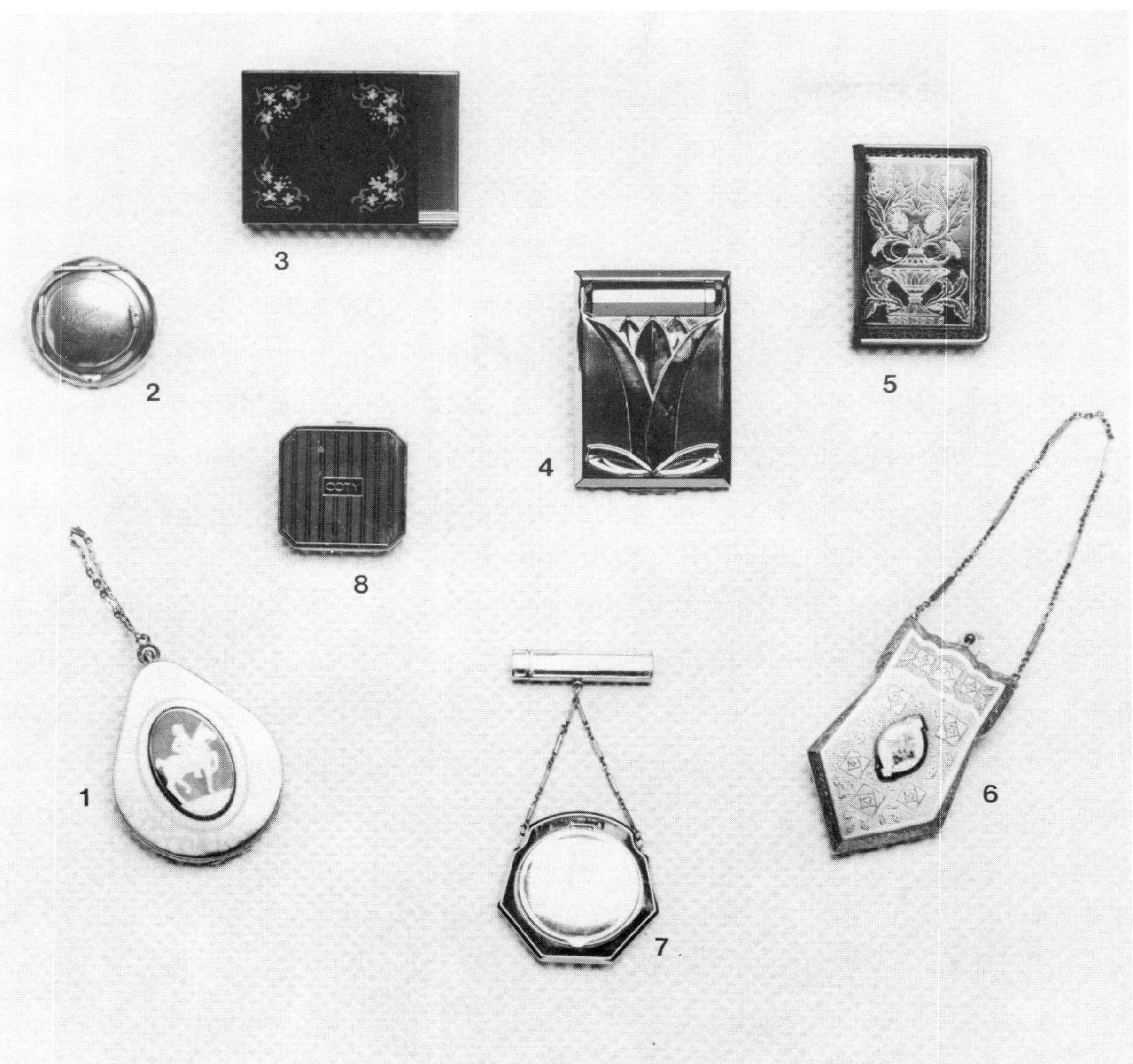

Fig. 65

1 Tear-shaped gilt and silvered vanity case with silvered man and horse encased in plastic dome; gilt interior, carrying chain, and compartments for powder, rouge, and lipstick.

2 Sterling-silver hallmarked double-tier compact; upper lid reveals locket; compartment for powder in lower lid, c. 1915.

3 Volupté black enamel gilt compact with sliding lipstick; black enamel inner and outer lids decorated with flowers.

4 Richard Hudnut gilt compact with raised tulip design: lipstick encased in lid cover.

5 Mondaine multicolored tooled leather vanity case designed to resemble book; compartments for powder, rouge, and cigarettes.

6 Marathon gilt and silvered engraved vanity case with enameled disk on lid; gilt interior, carrying chain, and compartments for powder, rouge, and lipstick.

7 E.A.M. nickel-finish tango-chain vanity; lid holds metal mirror and rouge compartment, lower half contains powder compartment.

8 Coty octagonal polished nickel-finish vanity case; upper lid for rouge, lower opening for powder.

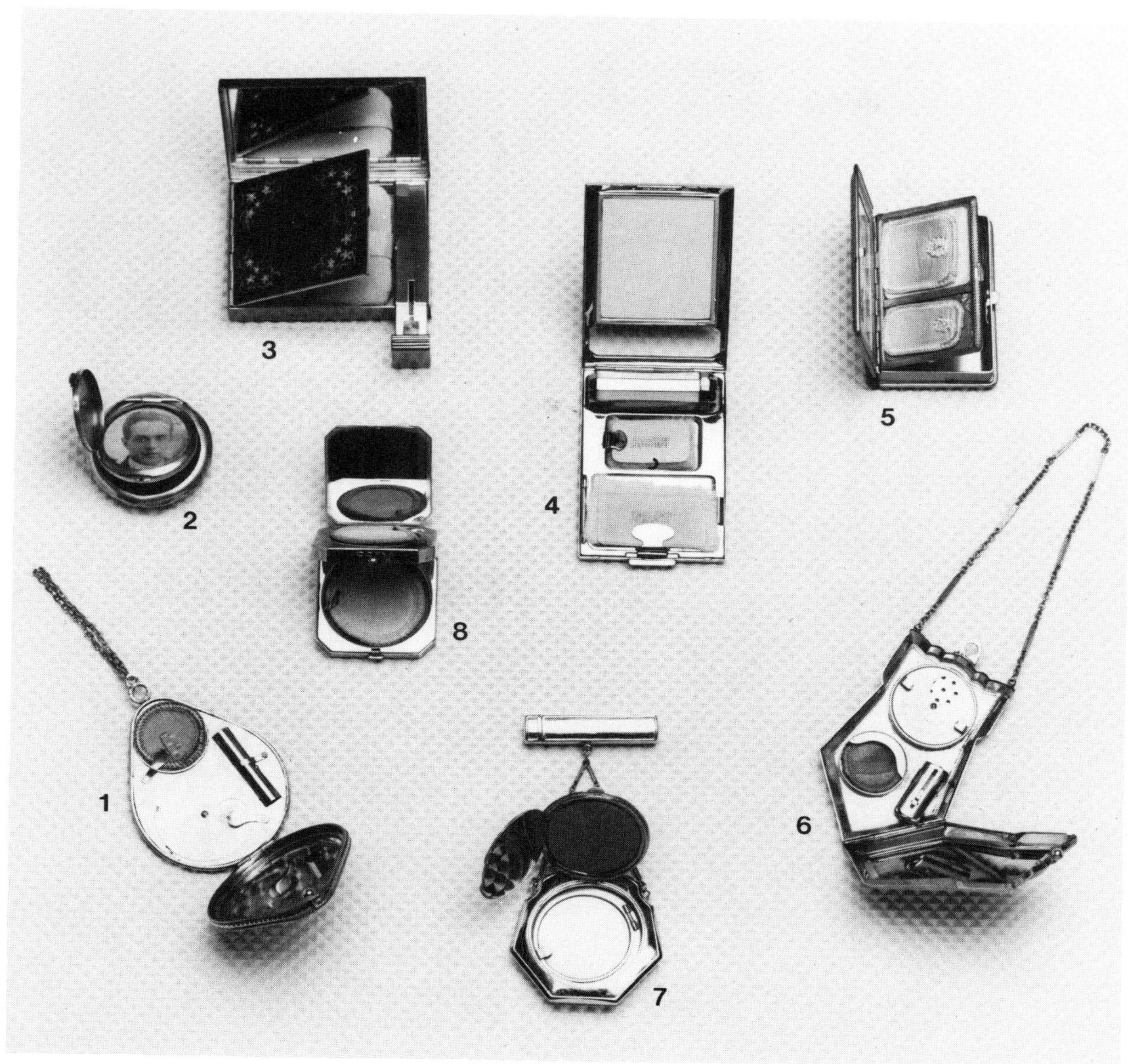

Fig. 66 Vanity cases and compacts in Figure 65 shown open.

Fig. 67

1 Brown suede vanity purse with brass, green stones, and rhinestones; mirror and powder, rouge, lipstick, cigarette, and comb compartments, Argentina.

2 Brown antelope suede vanity purse with Lucite and brass trim; mirror and powder, rouge, and cigarette compartments, Argentina.

3 Brown alligator vanity purse with marcasite decoration on lid; mirror and powder, rouge, and lipstick compartments, Argentina.

4 Ostrich-skin vanity reticule with mirror, fitted powder, rouge, and hairpin containers, c. 1900s.

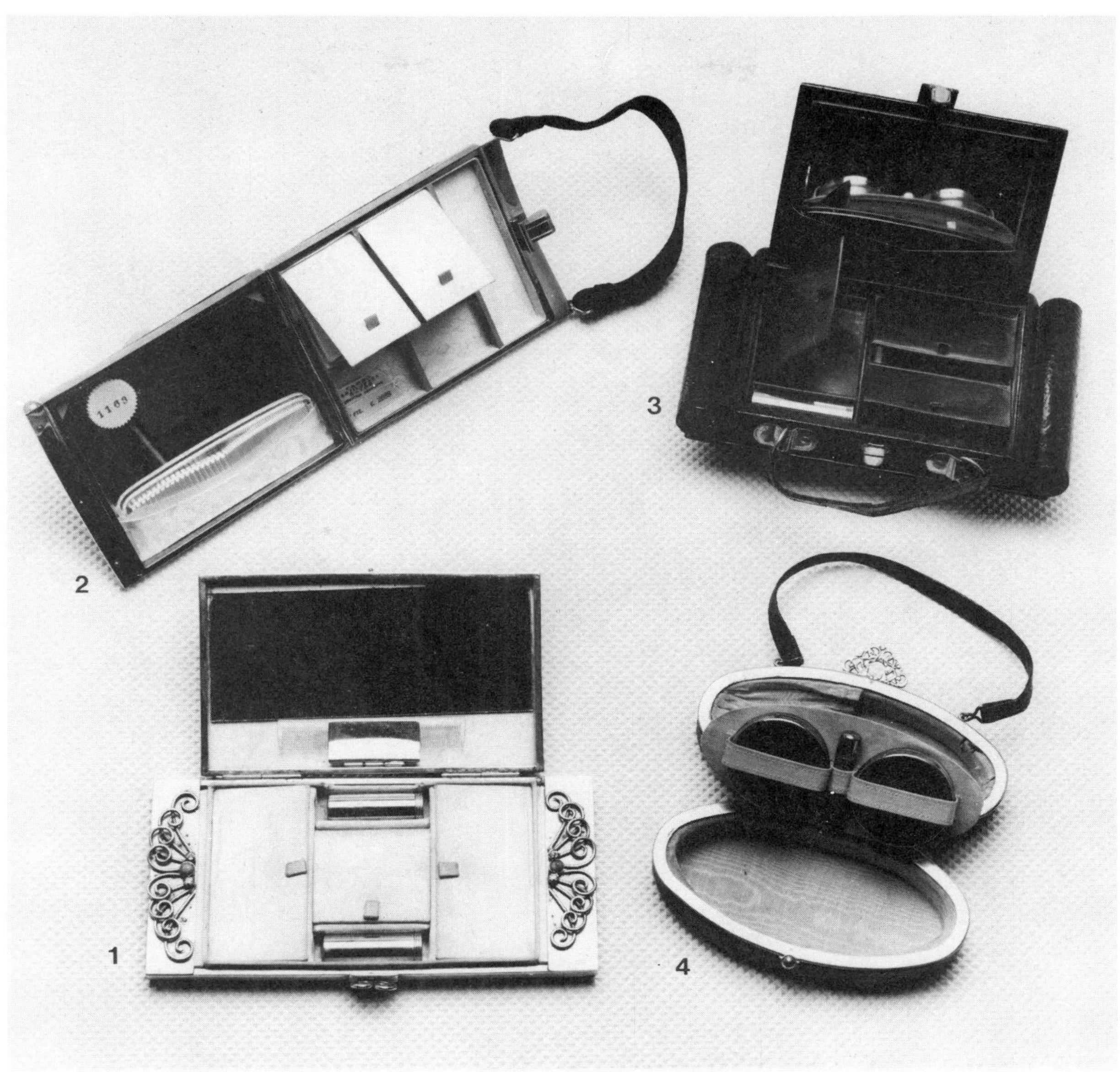

Fig. 68 Vanity purses and reticule in Figure 67 shown open.

Fig. 69 Lucien Lelong "Evening Passport" black satin velvet-trimmed vanity reticule with gold satin-lined compartments for "powder compact, rouge, lipstick, perfume, cigarettes, matches, currency, mirror and everything else"; comes complete with Lucien Lelong powder and rouge compacts, mirror, perfume, and lipstick.

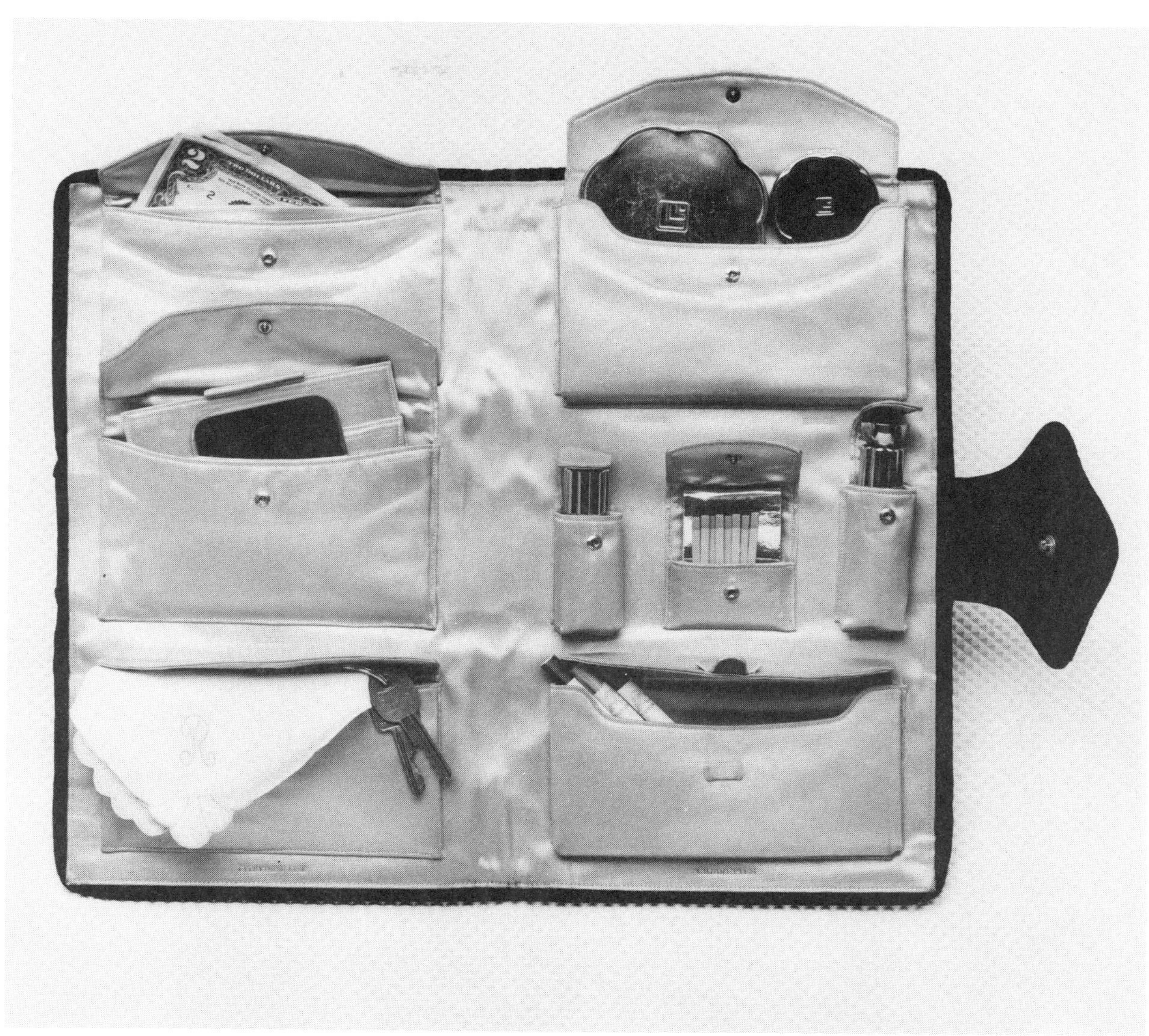

Fig. 70 Vanity reticule in Figure 69 shown open.

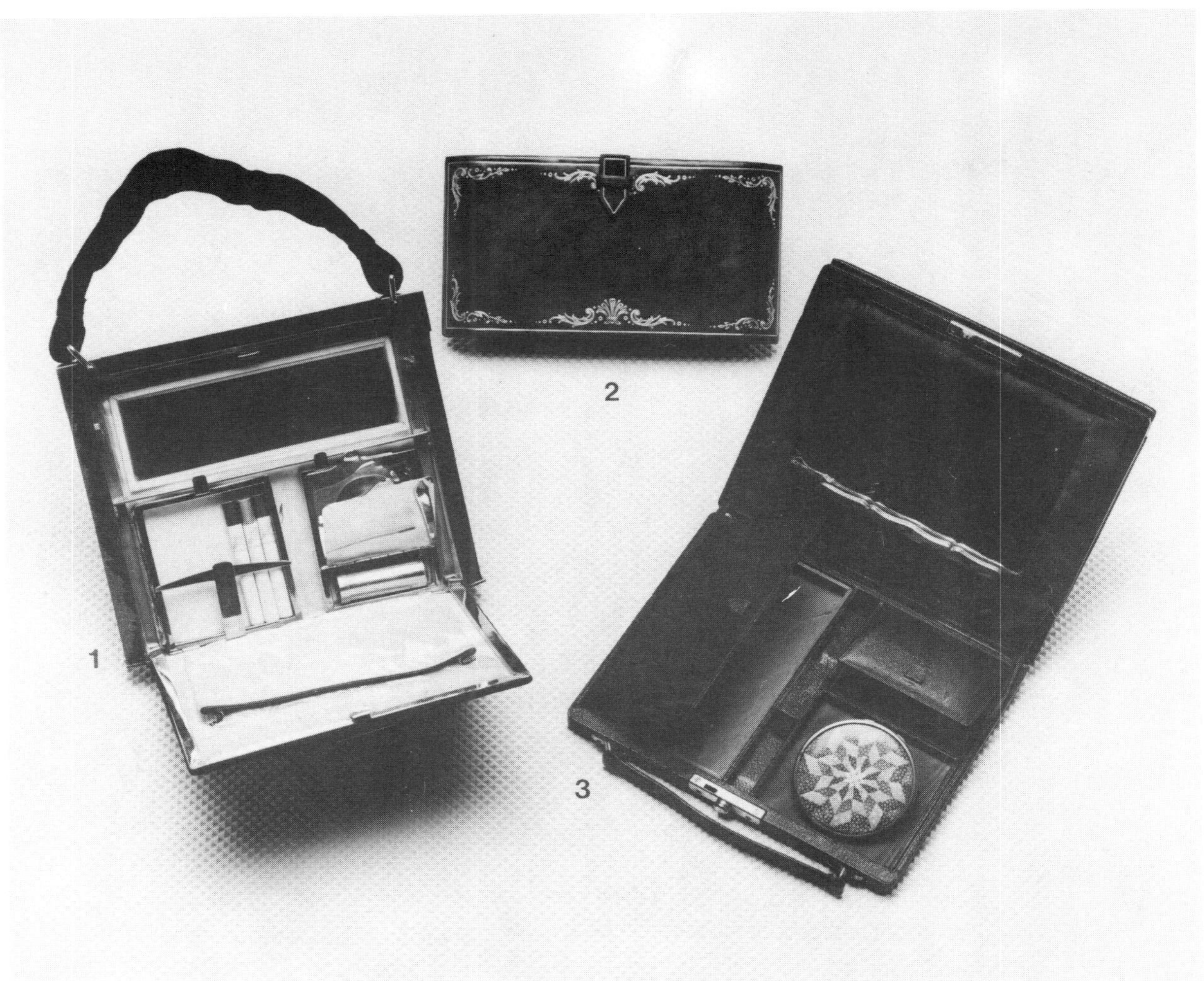

Fig. 71

1 Black quilted suede vanity purse lined in pink moiré; goldtone compartments for powder, rouge, lipstick, and cigarettes, Argentina (shown open).

2 Gold-tooled leather vanity purse; leather-lined with compartments for powder, lipstick, and cigarettes.

3 Coty brown leather vanity purse; leather-lined with compartment for powder compact, lipstick, perfume, and cigarettes, France (shown open).

Fig. 72

1 Minois black vanity purse with compartments for powder, lipstick, comb, and perfume, France (suede shown closed, faille shown open).

2 Ma Poudre black suede and gilt carryall designed to resemble book; compartments for powder, rouge, lipstick, and perfume, France.

3 Evans black suede and gilt vanity purse with watch on carrying strap; compartments for powder, lipstick, coins, and comb, c. 1940s.

4 Minois black suede carryall with suede and gilt covered compartments for powder, cigarettes, and lipstick, France (shown open).

5 Monois black suede carryall with compartments for powder, cigarettes, and lipstick, France.

6 Black suede carryall decorated with mother-of-pearl; wrist carrying handle and compartments for powder, comb, and lipstick.

Fig. 73

1 Wilardy box-shaped Lucite vanity purse enclosing sparkling gold-star-shaped confetti; lid lifts to reveal compartments for powder, comb, and lipstick.

2 Lin-Bren gold and silver damask bolster-shaped vanity purse; openings reveal compact and purse at opposite ends.

3 Oblong Lucite vanity purse enclosing sparkling silver confetti; compartments for powder, comb, and perfume.

Fig. 74 Vanity purses in Figure 73 shown open.

Fig. 75

1 Volupté "Swinglok" goldtone carryall with rhinestones; black faille carrying case and compartments for powder, lipstick, cigarettes, and comb, c. 1940–50s.

2 Volupté chrome and copper super carryall with copper rose on lid; compartments for powder, folding comb, lipstick, and cigarettes, c. 1940–50s.

3 Volupté engine-turned silvered-metal carryall with red faux gemstones; compartments for powder, lipstick, and cigarettes, c. 1940–50s.

4 Volupté engine-turned silvered-metal super carryall with compartments for powder and cigarettes, c. 1940–50s (shown open).

5 Elgin American satin silver-finish carryall with bronze fawns; black moiré carrying case; compartments for powder, rouge, lipstick, and cigarettes, c. 1950s.

6 Yellow cloisonné carryall with painted roses on lid; lipstick slides out and opens lid; compartments for powder, rouge, and comb, c. 1940–50s.

7 Volupté gilt super carryall with enameled horses; compartments for powder and cigarettes, c. 1940–50s.

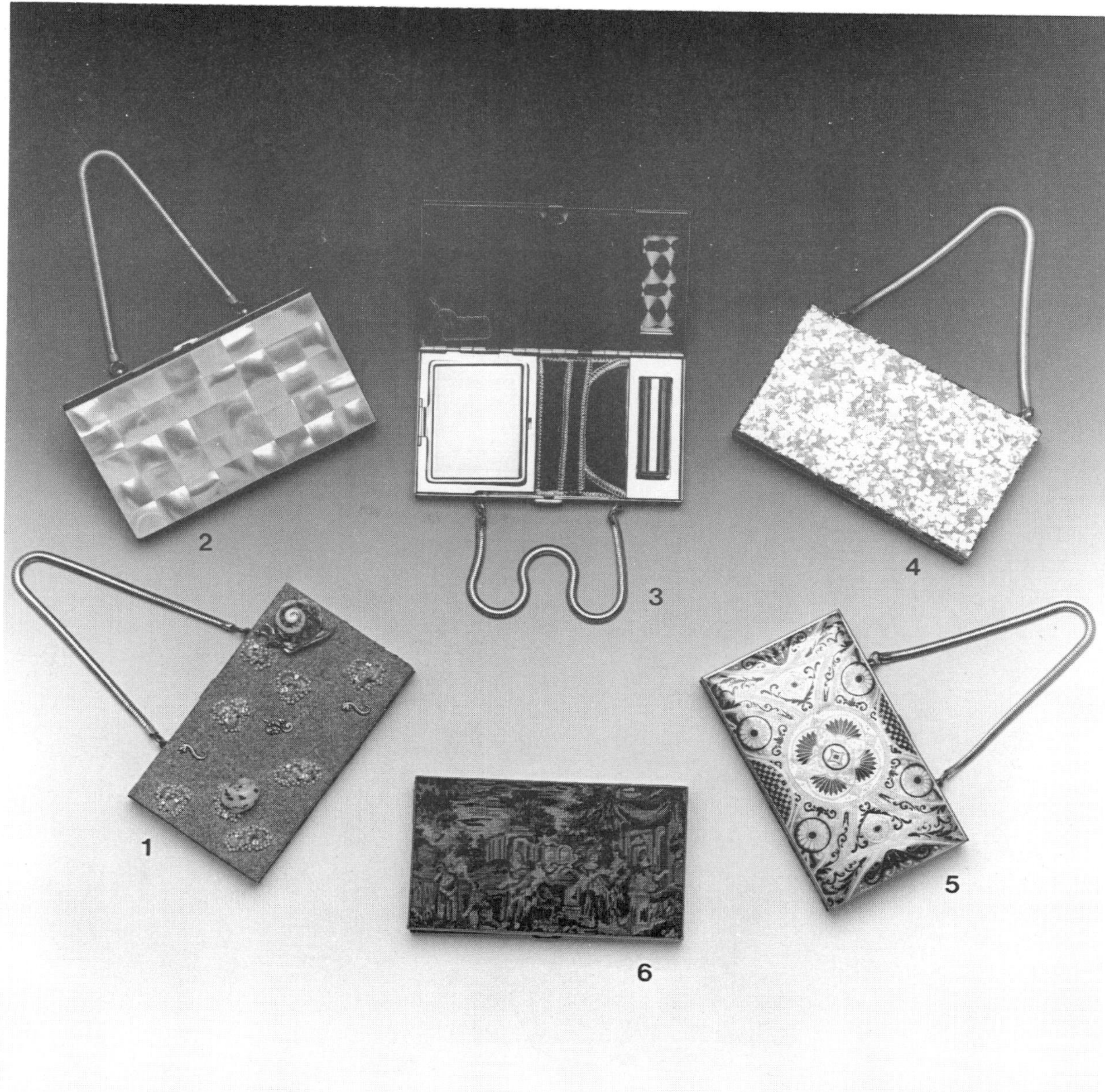

Fig. 76

1 Cork carryall decorated with shells, sea serpents, and faux mini pearls; snake chain and compartments for powder, lipstick, comb, and cigarettes, c. 1940–50s.

2 Mother-of-pearl carryall with snake chain and compartments for powder, lipstick, comb, and cigarettes, c. 1940–50s.

3 Carryall in **2** shown open.

4 Lucite and goldtone carryall, lid enclosing sparkling, multicolored confetti; snake chain and compartments for powder, lipstick, comb, and cigarettes, c. 1940–50s.

5 Padded leather carryall with Persian design; snake chain and compartments for powder, lipstick, comb, and cigarettes, c. 1940–50s.

6 Petit-point carryall with colorful scenes; compartments for powder, lipstick, comb, and cigarettes, c. 1940–50s.

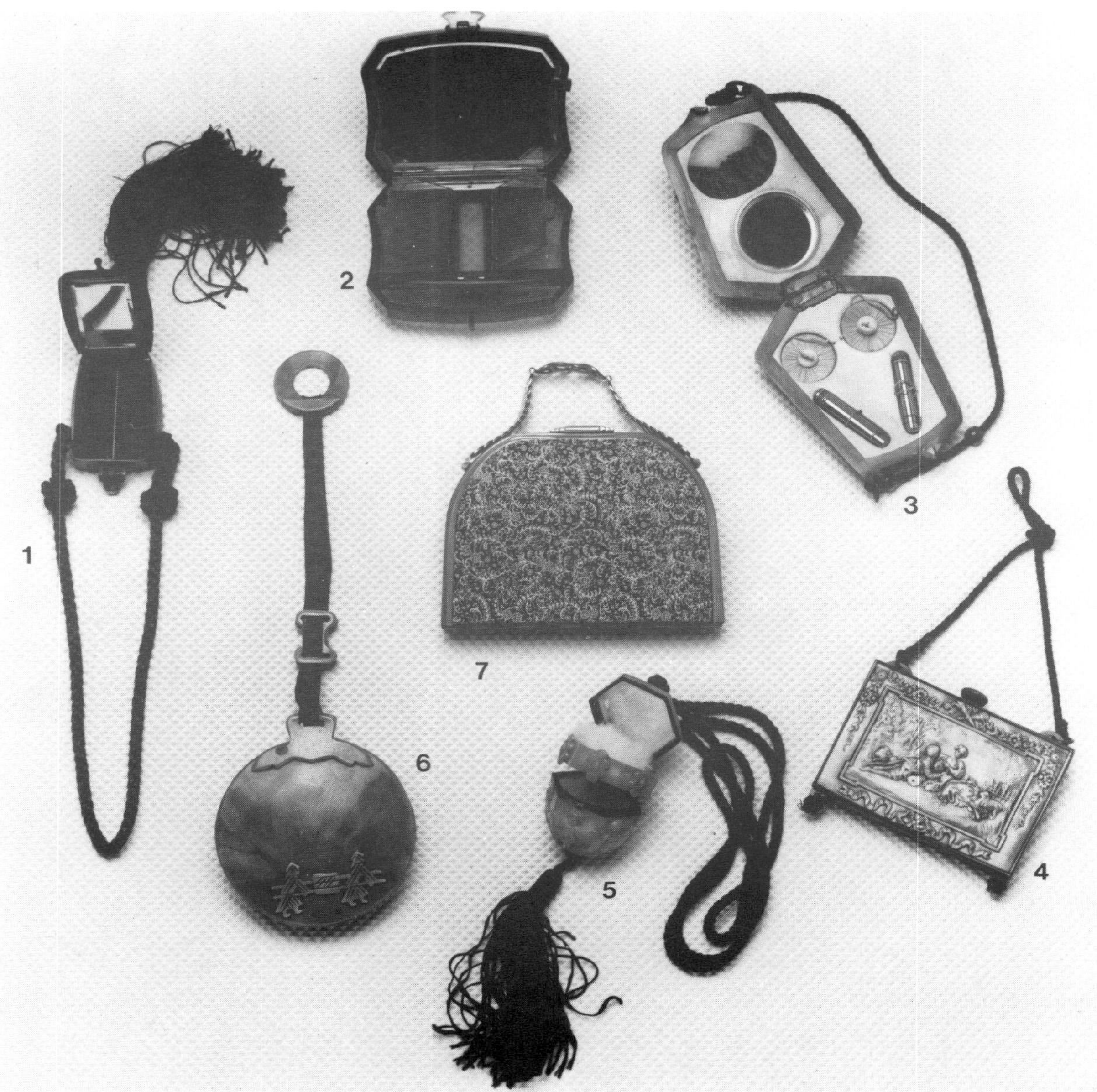

Fig. 77

1 Brown plastic vanity case with carrying cord and tassel; powder and rouge compartments, c. 1920s (shown open).

2 Butterscotch-colored plastic vanity case; writing slate on back of mirror and compartments for powder, rouge, lipstick, and comb, c. 1920s (shown open).

3 Tan plastic vanity case with maroon flowers; carrying cord and compartments for powder, rouge, two lipsticks, mirror, and pocket for puff, c. 1920s (shown open).

4 Tan and brown vanity case with country scene on lid; carrying cord and compartments for powder, lipstick, and perfume, c. 1920s.

5 Egg-shaped yellow plastic vanity purse with cherubs; black tassel and carrying cord; powder and rouge compartments, c. 1920s.

6 Gold-colored plastic vanity reticule with Oriental motif; black and gold carrying cord with ring and buckle ojime; compartment for powder and puff, c. 1920s.

7 Stratton black and gold floral-decorated metal vanity reticule with fancy metal carrying chain; compartments for compact, coin purse, and comb, c. 1950s.

Fig. 78

1 Tyrolean black suede vanity purse edged with brass filigree; compact and cigarette compartment, c. 1940–50s (shown open).

2 Edward's Bags, Ltd., pouch-shaped black faille vanity purse with engraved gilt compact lid.

3 Lee Fran rigid black corduroy vanity purse with gilt compact mounted on silvered lid, c. 1940s.

4 Zell Fifth Avenue black faille vanity purse with powder compact and cigarette compartments, c. 1940s (shown open).

5 Navy blue leather vanity purse trimmed with brass filigree; compartments for powder, cigarettes, and comb, c. 1940–50s.

Fig. 79

1 Antique silvered carryall with gilt engraved flowers and mesh wrist loop; compartments for powder, comb, and cigarettes with lipstick holder at side, c. 1950s.

2 Satin-finish and polished gilt vanity purse with compartments for powder, comb, lipstick, and cigarettes, c. 1940s.

3 Satin-finish and polished gilt vanity reticule with compartments for compact, lipstick holder, perfume, and comb, c. 1940s.

4 German silver vanity purse with repoussé floral design around edges; interior has coin holders, powder compartment, writing slate, nail file, shoe-button hook, and pencil with retrievable point.

5 Red marbleized enamel and gilt carryall with compartments for powder, rouge, lipstick, comb, cigarettes, and calling cards.

6 Silvered and gilt striped metal-mesh carryall with compartments for powder, lipstick, comb, and cigarettes, France.

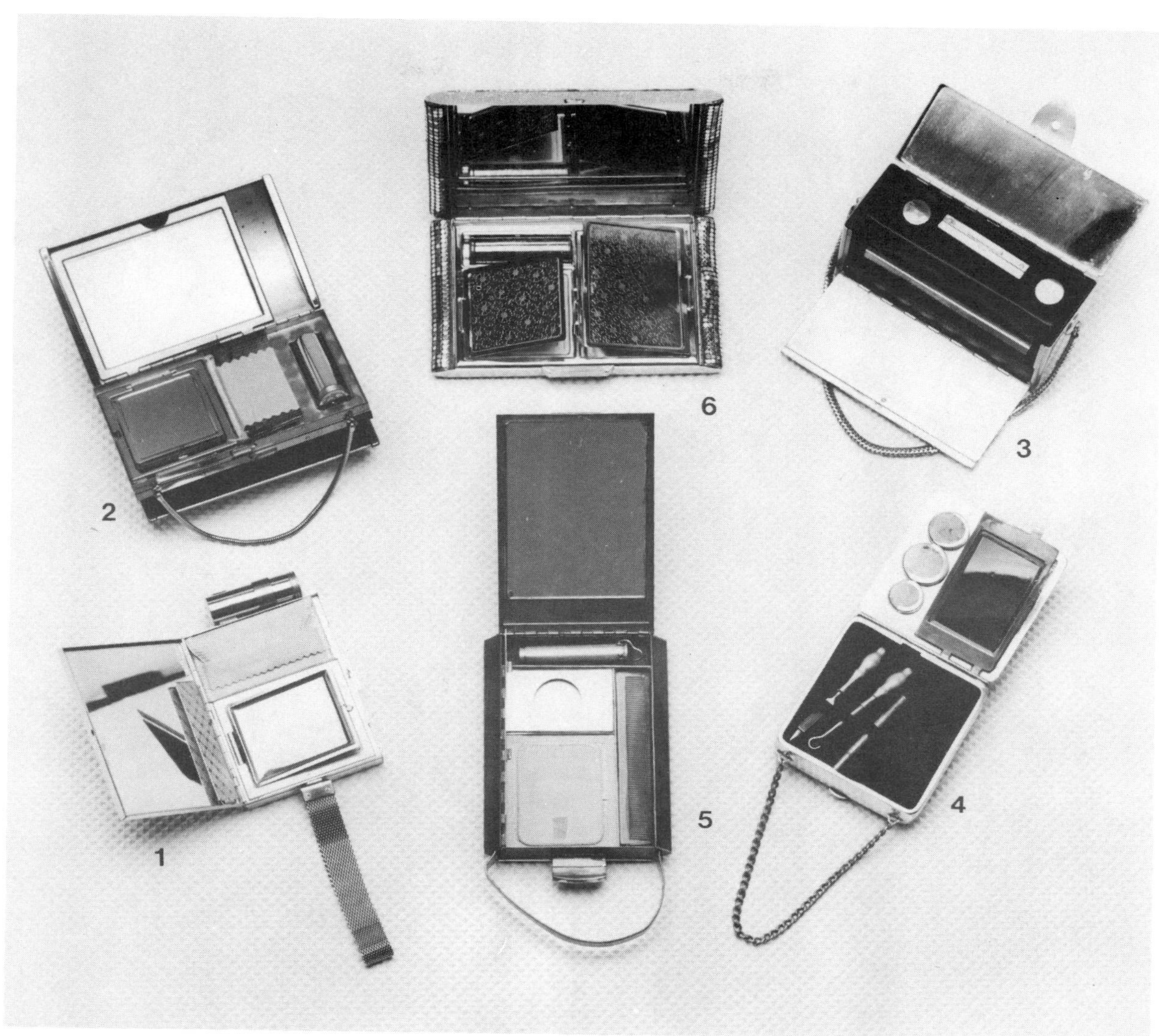

Fig. 80 Carryalls and vanity purses in Figure 79 shown open.

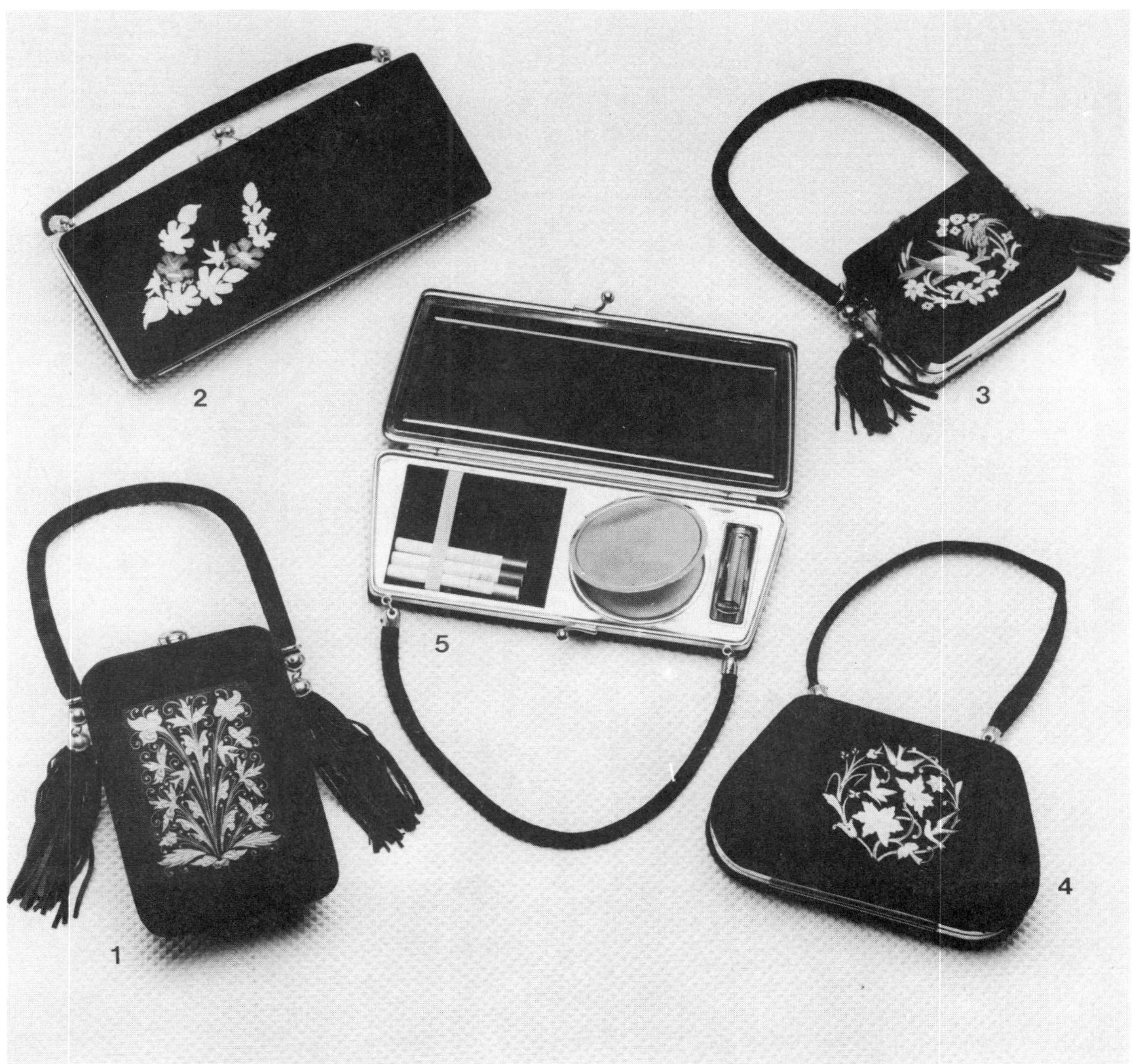

Fig. 81

1 Black suede vanity purse with gilt engraved floral decoration on black matte background; compartments for powder, lipstick, and cigarettes, Argentina.

2 Black satin oblong vanity purse with gilt and silver flowers; compartments for powder, lipstick, and cigarettes, Argentina.

3 Small black suede vanity purse with gilt flowers and bird; compartments for powder, lipstick, and cigarettes, Argentina.

4 Black satin vanity purse with gilt flowers; compartments for powder, cigarettes, and lipstick, Argentina.

5 Black suede vanity purse with gilt flowers; compartments for powder, lipstick, and cigarettes, Argentina (shown open).

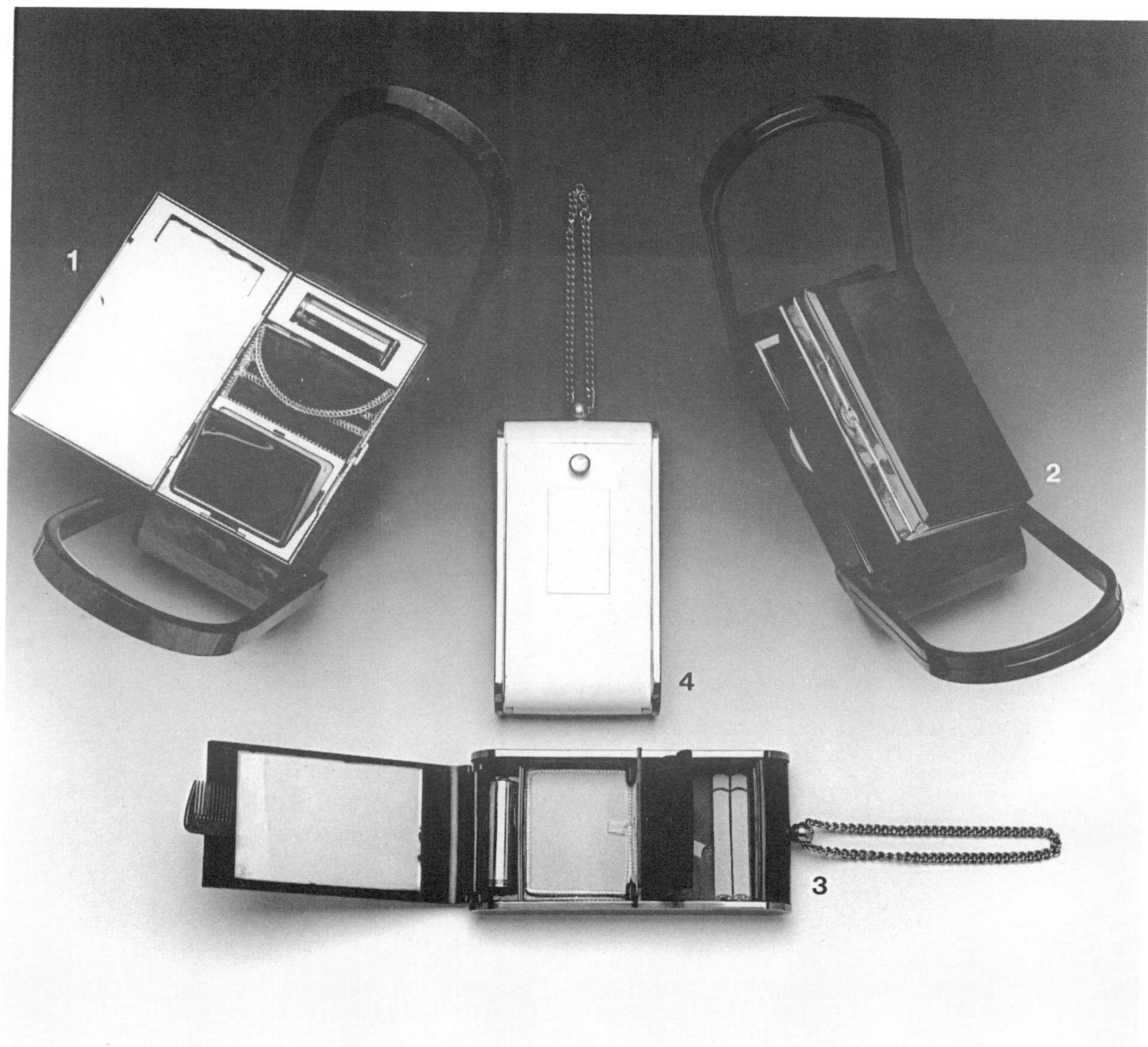

Fig. 82

1, 2 Wilardy plastic vanity purse; top opens to reveal compartments for powder, lipstick, comb, and cigarettes, c. 1940s (**1**, gray, shown open; **2**, brown, shown closed).

3, 4 Plastic carryall with brass carrying chain and compartments for powder, lipstick, cigarettes, and comb, c. 1940s (**3**, black, shown open; **4**, white, shown closed).

Fig. 83

1 Black silk beaded minaudière with pink embroidered flowers on handle, front and back; gilded interior and compartments for powder, lipstick, comb, and cigarettes, France.

2 Douane white silk vanity purse with varicolored stones; compartments for powder, lipstick, perfume, and comb, France.

3 Taupe Oriental-pattern silk vanity purse with Oriental-motif clasps; pink silk-lined interior; compartments for powder, rouge, comb, coins, cigarettes, and match holder, France.

Fig. 84 Minaudière and vanity purses in Figure 83 shown open.

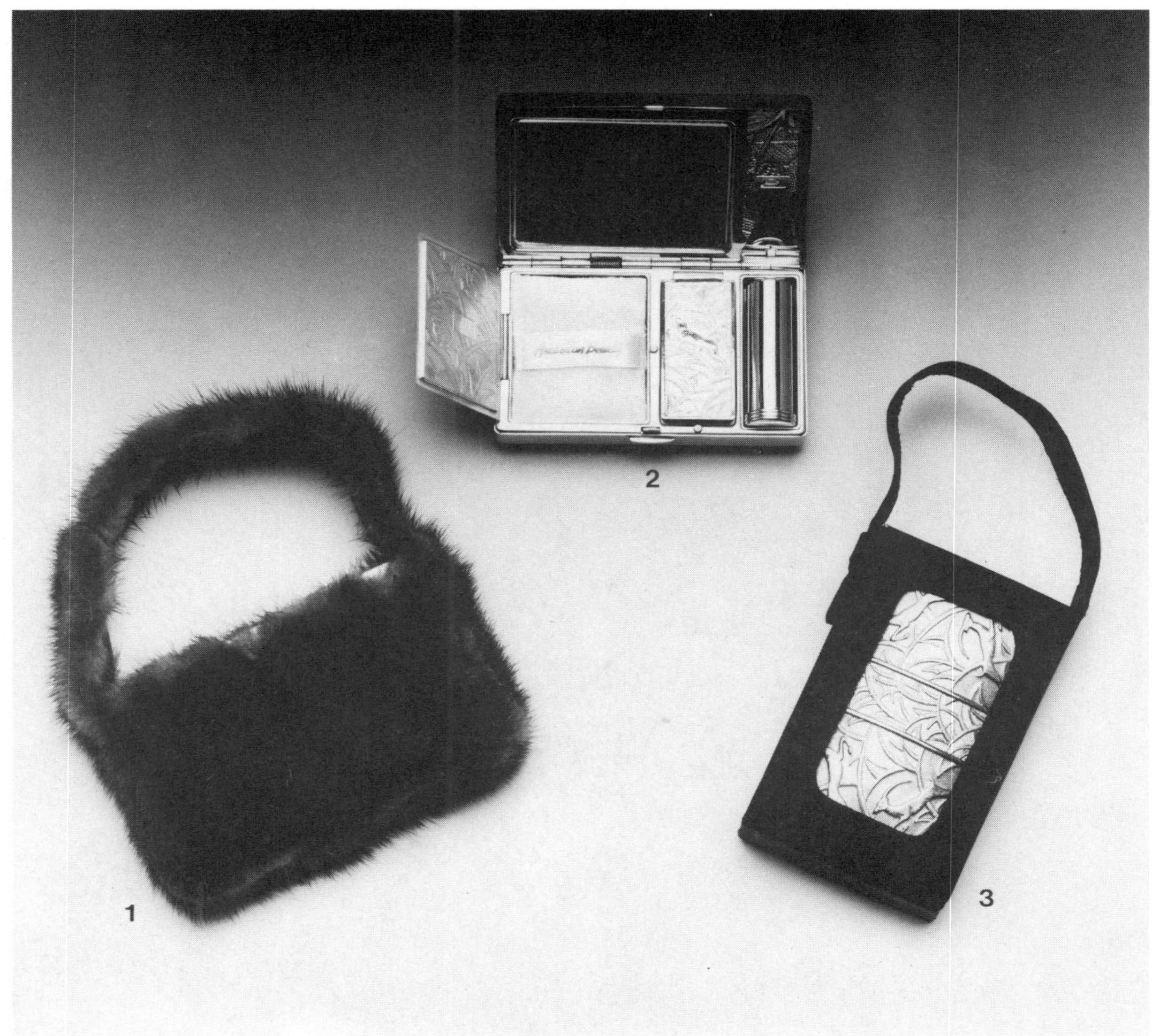

Fig. 85

1, 2, 3 Elgin American "American Beauty" carryall with jeweler's bronze-embossed fawn design; compartments for powder, rouge, lipstick, cigarettes, and bill-clip, c. 1950s (**1** with custom-made mink carrying case, **2** shown open; **3** with original black moiré carrying case).

Fig. 86

1, 2 Volupté "Oval Sophisticase" carryall with silver-embossed gilt lid; center band slides to open compartments for powder and utilities, tassel pulls out to reveal lipstick; black faille carrying case, c. 1950s; (**1** shown open, **2** shown closed).

3, 4 Lin-Bren vanity clutch contains compact, lipstick, and comb (**3**, navy blue faille, shown open; **4**, maroon suede, shown closed).

Fig. 87 Robin Handbags vanity purse with snap closure and drawstring top; compact located at base of purse.
1 navy blue corduroy.
2 silver and gold damask.
3 black faille.
4 black velvet, shown open.

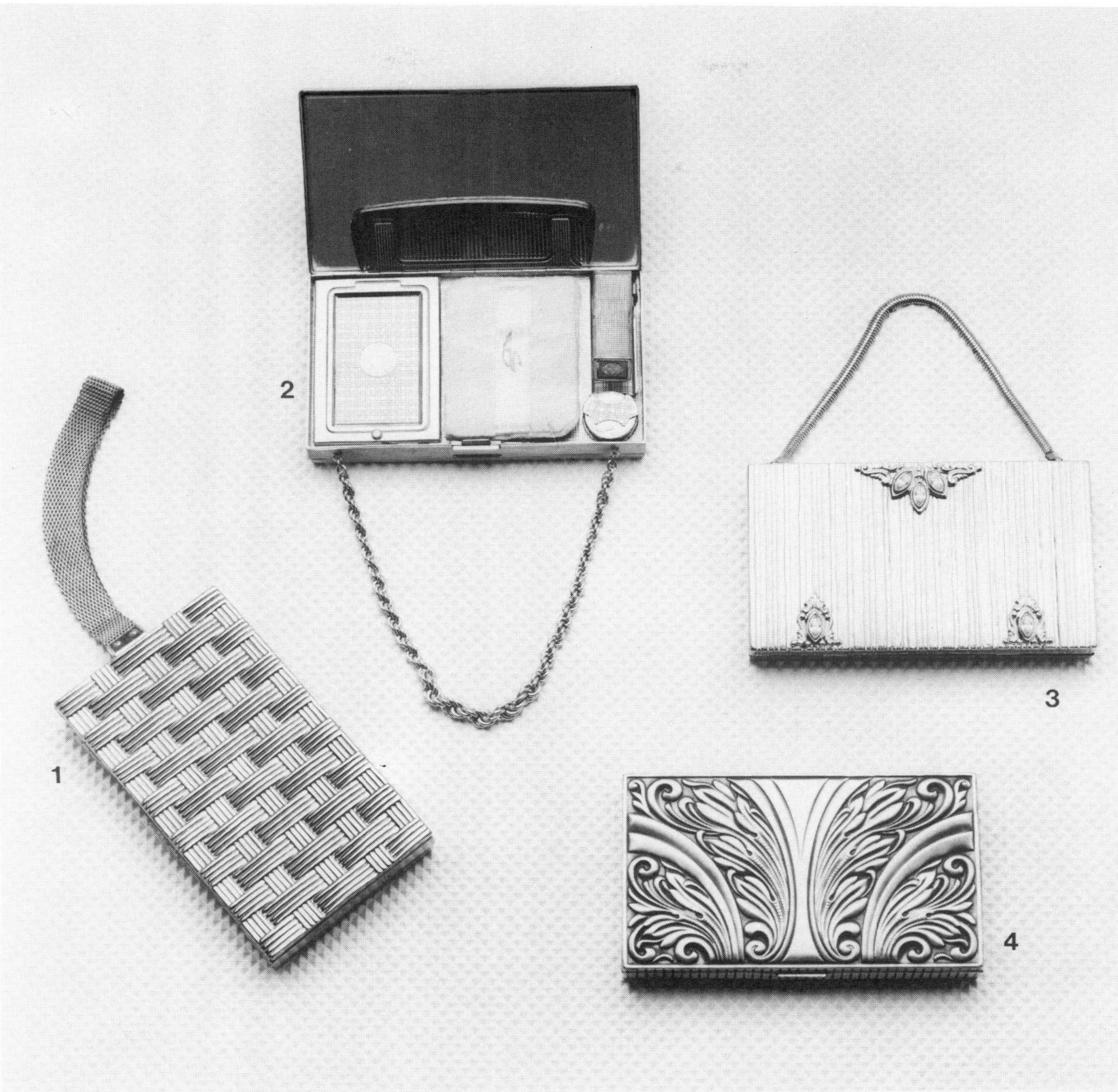

Fig. 88 Evans carryall with carrying chain, compartments for powder, puff, lipstick, comb, and coins, c. 1950s.

1 goldtone basketweave pattern.

2 embossed pink and gilt-colored metal (shown open).

3 goldtone engine-turned with rhinestones.

4 pewter-finish metal clutch with embossed floral design).

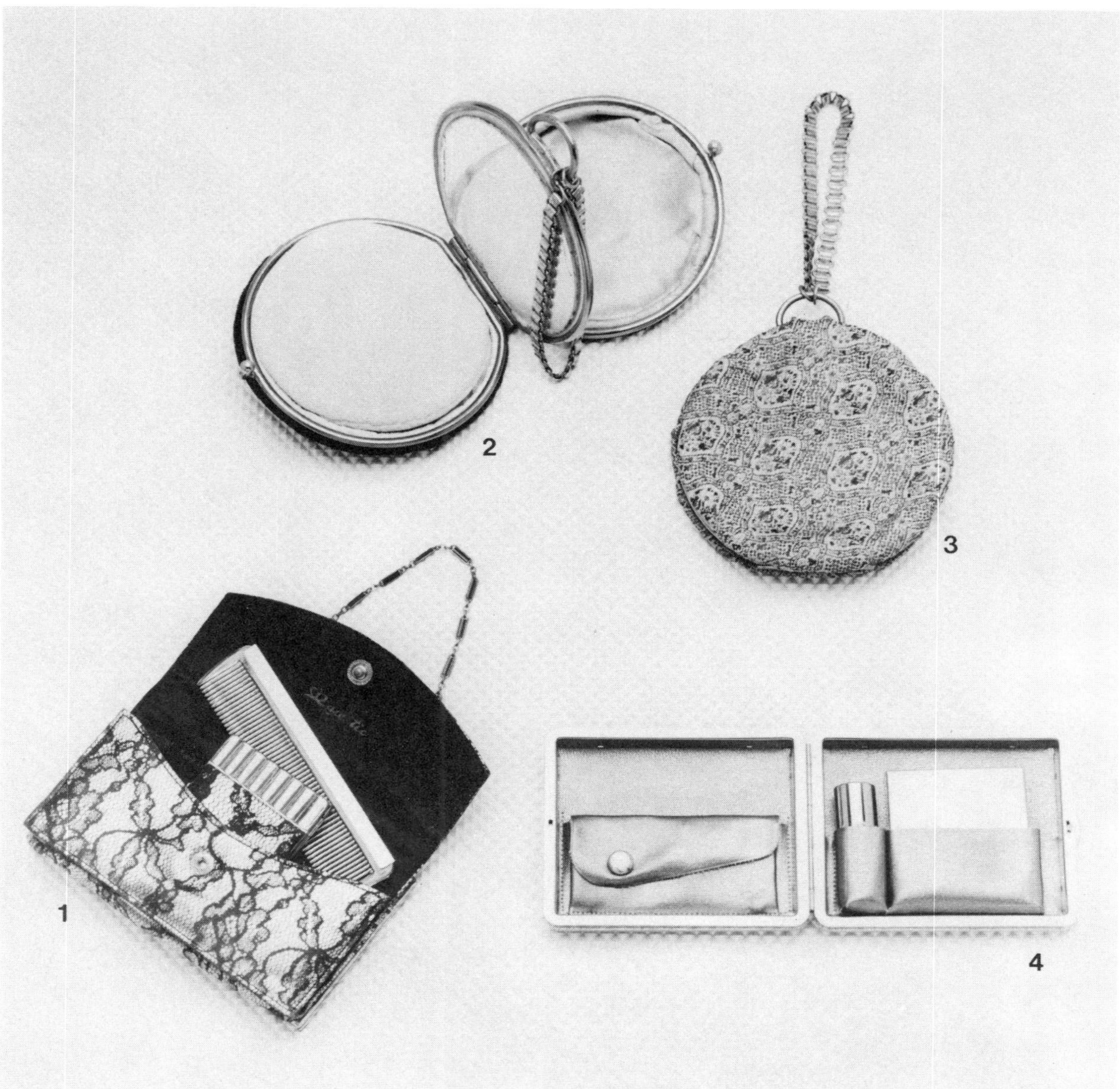

Fig. 89

1 Majestic gold and black lace vanity clutch with black and gold carrying chain and compartments for compact, lipstick, and comb (shown open).

2, 3 Graceline small vanity reticule with wrist chain; compartments for puff, compact, and lipstick, (**2**, maroon velvet, shown open; **3**, multicolor woven fabric, shown closed).

4 Zell gilt-padded vanity clutch with compartments for compact, lipstick, and comb (shown open).

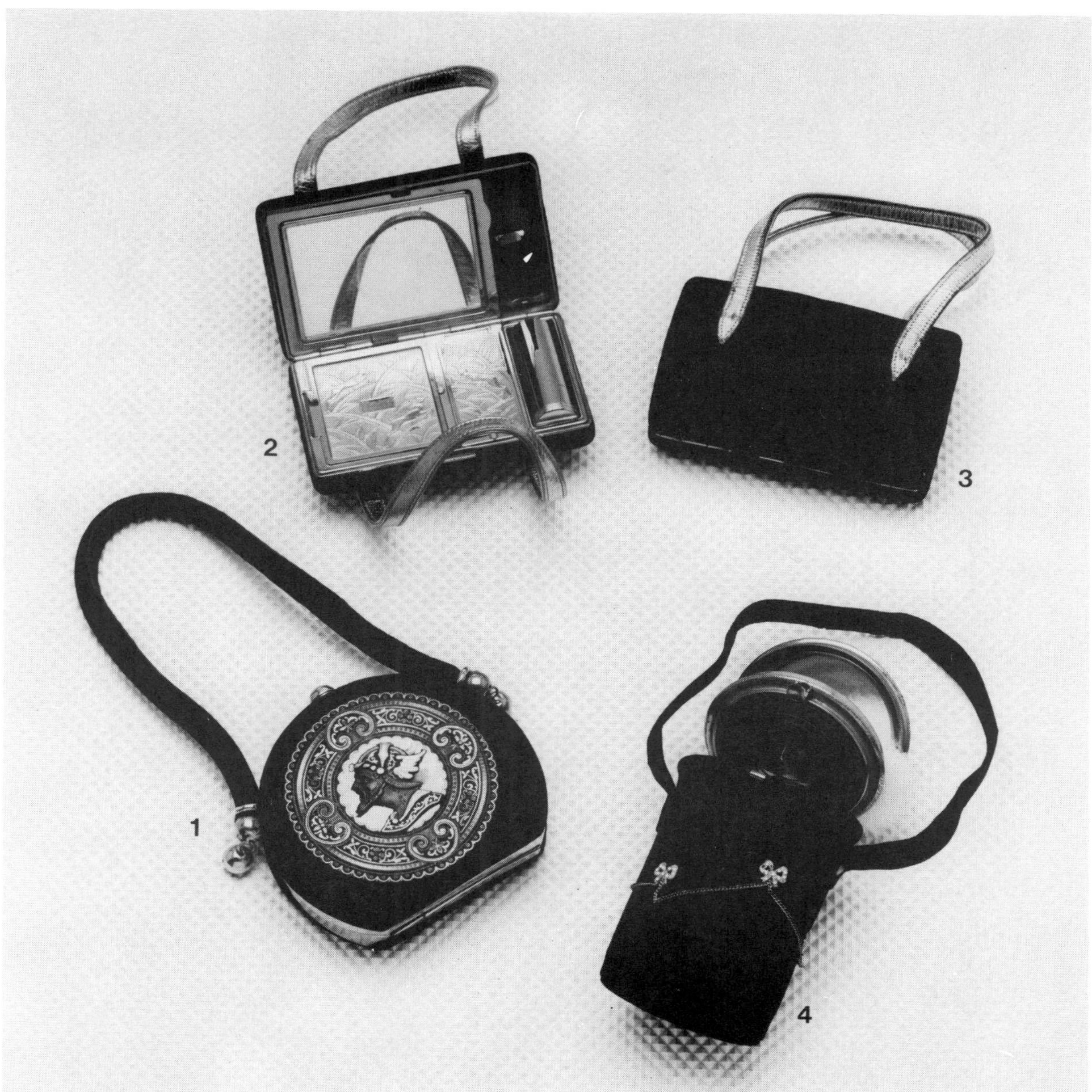

Fig. 90

1 Black suede vanity purse with gilt disk; compartments for powder, lipstick, and rouge, Argentina.

2, 3 Elgin American black suede carryall with gold leather handles; compartments for powder, rouge, lipstick, and bill-clip, c. 1950s (**2** shown open, **3** shown closed).

4 Black suede and brass bolster-shaped vanity purse with rhinestone bows connected by brass chain, France.

Fig. 91

1, 2 Coty "Envelope" goldtone compact, c. 1940s.

3, 4 Vanity case with compartments for powder, rouge, and cigarettes; tassel pulls out to reveal lipstick, probably England (**3**, blue plastic resembling cloisonné top, leather-lined interior, shown open; **4**, black silk, leather-lined interior, shown closed).

5, 6 Le Rage goldtone vanity case with chain-attached lipstick; center lid with enamel painted flowers reveals compartment for rouge, photo, or tablets; interior reveals snap-on comb/whisk-broom combination; second opening reveals powder compartment and perfume container; moiré carrying case contains perfume funnel, England, c. 1950s.

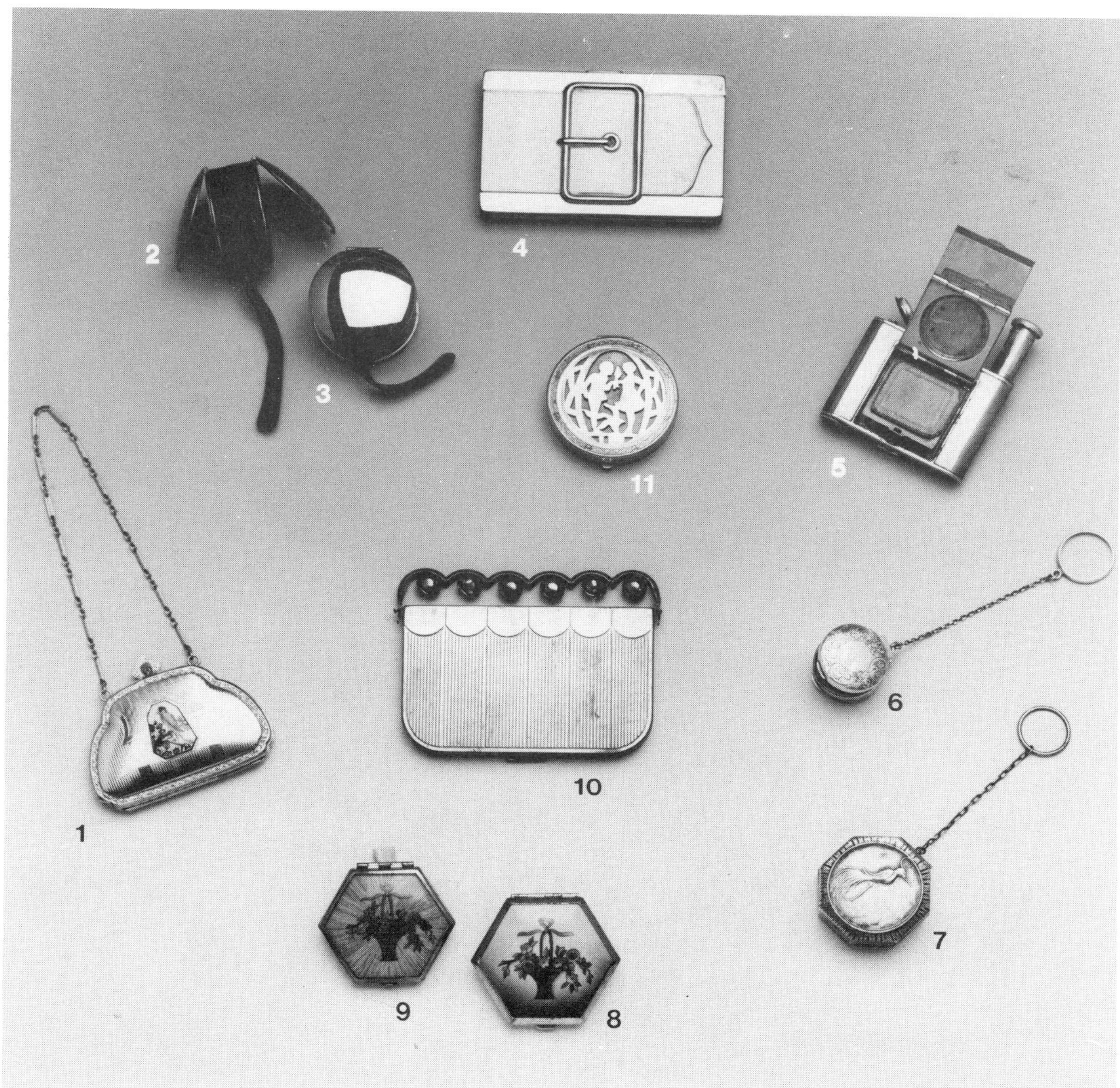

Fig. 92

1 Silvered-metal purse-motif vanity case with enamel bluebird and engine-turned back; contains loose powder sifter, two puffs, rouge, mirror, and carrying chain, c. 1920s.

2, 3 Wadsworth two-sided mini vanity case with powder and rouge compartments and finger loop (**2**, green suede, shown open; **3**, black leather, shown closed).

4 Coty "Buckle" goldtone vanity case with white enamel buckle, c. 1940s.

5 Fillkwik Co. "Van-Mist" silver vanity case designed to resemble camera; compartments for powder, rouge, lipstick, and perfume, c. 1930s.

6 Sterling-silver hallmarked two-sided miniature vanity case with floral-engraved powder and rouge compartments and finger-ring chain, England, c. 1900s.

7 Jonteel repoussé silver-plated compact with finger-ring chain, c. 1920s.

8, 9 Houbigant six-sided vanity case with basket of flowers on lid; compartments for powder and rouge (**8** goldtone small version, **9** silvered-metal larger version).

10 Coty "Jingle Bells" goldtone compact, c. 1940s.

11 Coty silvered-metal compact with cutout design of boy and girl, c. 1920–30s.

Fig. 93

1 Gun-metal clover-shaped purse-motif compact.

2 Sterling-silver hallmarked compact designed to resemble hand mirror; lid decorated with blue faux cloisonné, loop for chain.

3 White enamel compact with "Yes" in green and "No" in red.

4 Six-inch-round pink and goldtone compact with sixteen stars with faux diamonds on lid.

5 Volupté green and yellow triangular checkerboard compact.

6 Gold-filled compact decorated with blackbird; finger-ring chain and tassel, c. 1920s.

7 K & K small oval black enamel compact with rhinestone lipstick tube mounted on lid.

8 Flato goldtone compact with brass key mounted on lid; red leather-like protective case.

9 Majestic goldtone compact with comb and black faille case.

10 Silver compact with blue and white Delft enamel windmill scene.

11 Light and dark blue guilloche enamel 1″ compact, loop for chain.

Fig. 94

1 La Mode gilt and black-striped enamel vanity case with black silhouette on cover; powder, rouge, and lipstick compartments; loop for chain.

2, 3 Slim oval compact designed as a locket with chain; black silhouette on cover (**2**, yellow enamel, shown in presentation box; **3**, red enamel with loop for chain).

4 Divine lavender-striped enamel miniature compact with white silhouette on cover.

5 Ivory-colored enamel vanity case, silver silhouette within black disk; powder and rouge compartments.

6 La Mode ivory and black enamel vanity case with black silhouette on ivory; powder and rouge compartments and through handle.

7 Plastic and goldtone compact with molded silhouette on plastic slip-cover lid.

8 Black enamel and goldtone vanity case with black transfer silhouette; powder and rouge compartments.

9 Rex Fifth Avenue blue plastic and gilt compact with white plastic silhouette on blue lid, c. 1940s.

10 Silver and black-enamel vanity case with white silhouette; finger-ring chain; powder sifter and rouge compartment, c. 1920s.

11 Armand red enamel compact with silhouette on lid, "Pat'd Aug. 14, 1917."

12 Blue and clear plastic compact with white silhouette on screw-top lid.

13 Rigaud "Mary Garden" gilt miniature compact with embossed silhouette on slip-cover lid, c. 1919.

14 Armand silver-plated compact with engraved silhouette on lid and engine-turned back, "Pat. 7–1–24."

15 Rigaud "Mary Garden" brass compact with embossed silhouette on cover, c. 1919.

Fig. 95

1 Black enamel vanity case with lipstick compartment centered on lid; powder and rouge compartments.

2 Kigu blue enamel compact with Limoges-type locket centered on lid, c. 1940–50s.

3 Goldtone vanity case with locket centered on lid; powder, rouge, and lipstick compartments, c. 1930s.

4 Maroon enamel vanity case with lipstick compartment centered on lid; powder and rouge compartments.

5 Lazell goldtone vanity case with powder compartment; rouge compartment centered on lid, "Pat'd. July 18, 1922."

6 Mondaine red enamel vanity case with lipstick compartment centered on lid; compartments for powder and rouge, c. 1920–30s.

7 Silvered-metal compact with goldtone locket centered on lid, c. 1930s.

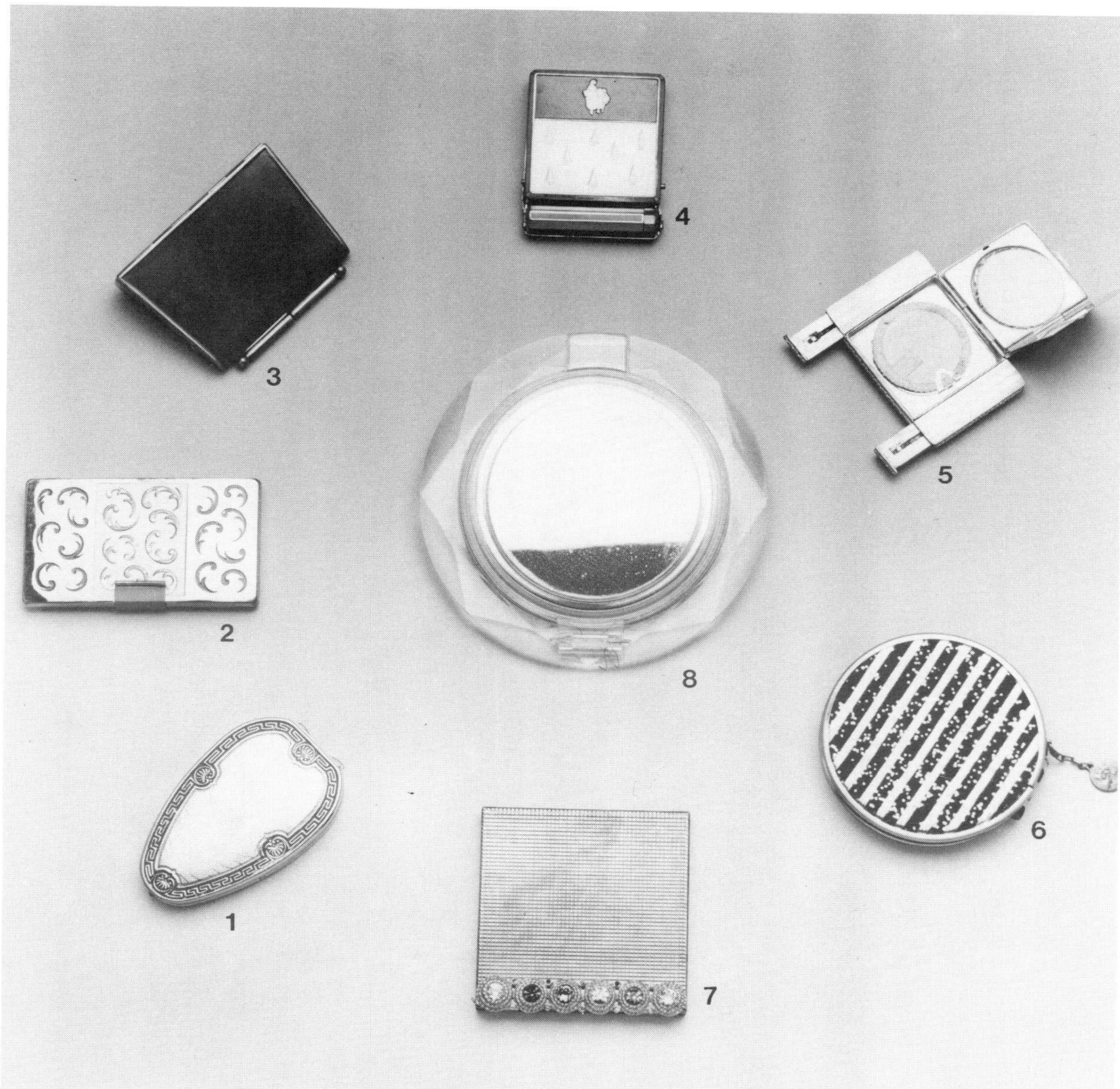

Fig. 96

1 Woodworth "Karess" egg-shaped vanity case of engine-turned silvered metal; edge of lid enameled with blue Greek key design; powder and rouge compartments, c. 1920s.

2 Yardley goldtone vanity case with red, white, and blue embossed design on lid; powder and rouge compartments, c. 1940s.

3 Alwyn blue enamel suitcase-motif compact.

4 Yardley black enamel and goldtone vanity case with powder and rouge compartments and swing-out lipstick, c. 1930s.

5 La Mode goldstone and enameled vanity case with powder and rouge compartments and slide-out lipsticks (shown open).

6 Rosenfeld zippered goldtone compact with multicolor confetti sparkles and thread, Israel.

7 Volupté "Swinglok" stippled goldtone compact with multicolored synthetic gems on swinglok, c. 1940s.

8 Lucite compact mirrored on inner and outer lid, c. 1940s.

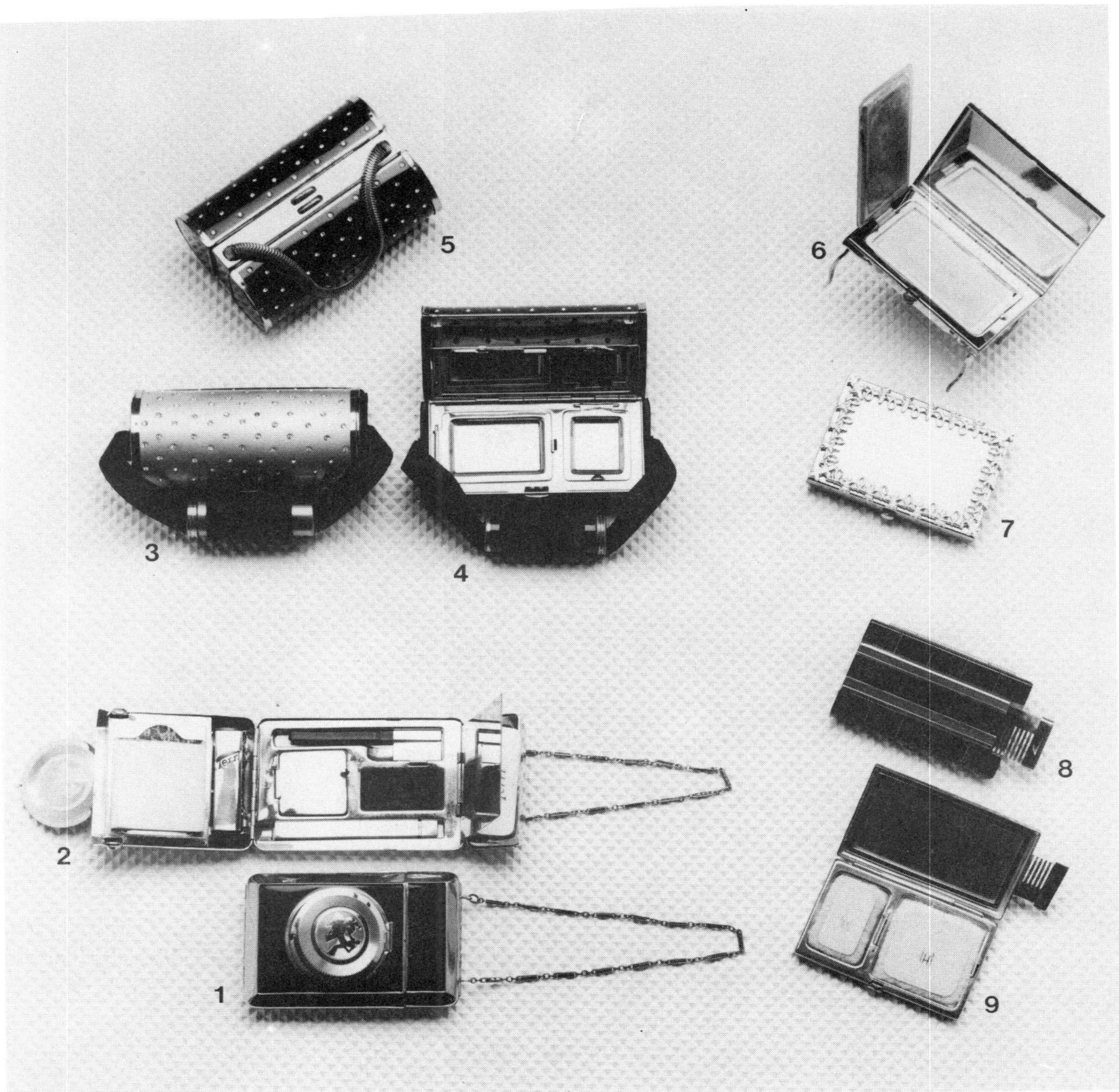

Fig. 97

1, 2 Terri black enamel goldtone vanity case with carrying chain; compartments for powder, rouge, lipstick, and lip-tissues; complete eye makeup kit included, c. 1950s.

3, 4 Rhinestone-studded vanity case; black faille carrying case incorporates sleeves for lipstick and comb; compartments for powder, rouge, and cigarettes (**3**, goldtone, shown closed; **4**, black enamel, shown open).

5 Rhinestone-studded black enamel double vanity case with carrying chain and compartments for powder, rouge, comb, lipstick, and cigarettes.

6, 7 Wadsworth goldtone compact designed to resemble vanity table; collapsible cabriole legs.

8, 9 Houbigant enameled vanity case with powder and rouge compartments and sliding comb on lid (**8**, black enamel, shown closed; **9**, white enamel, shown open).

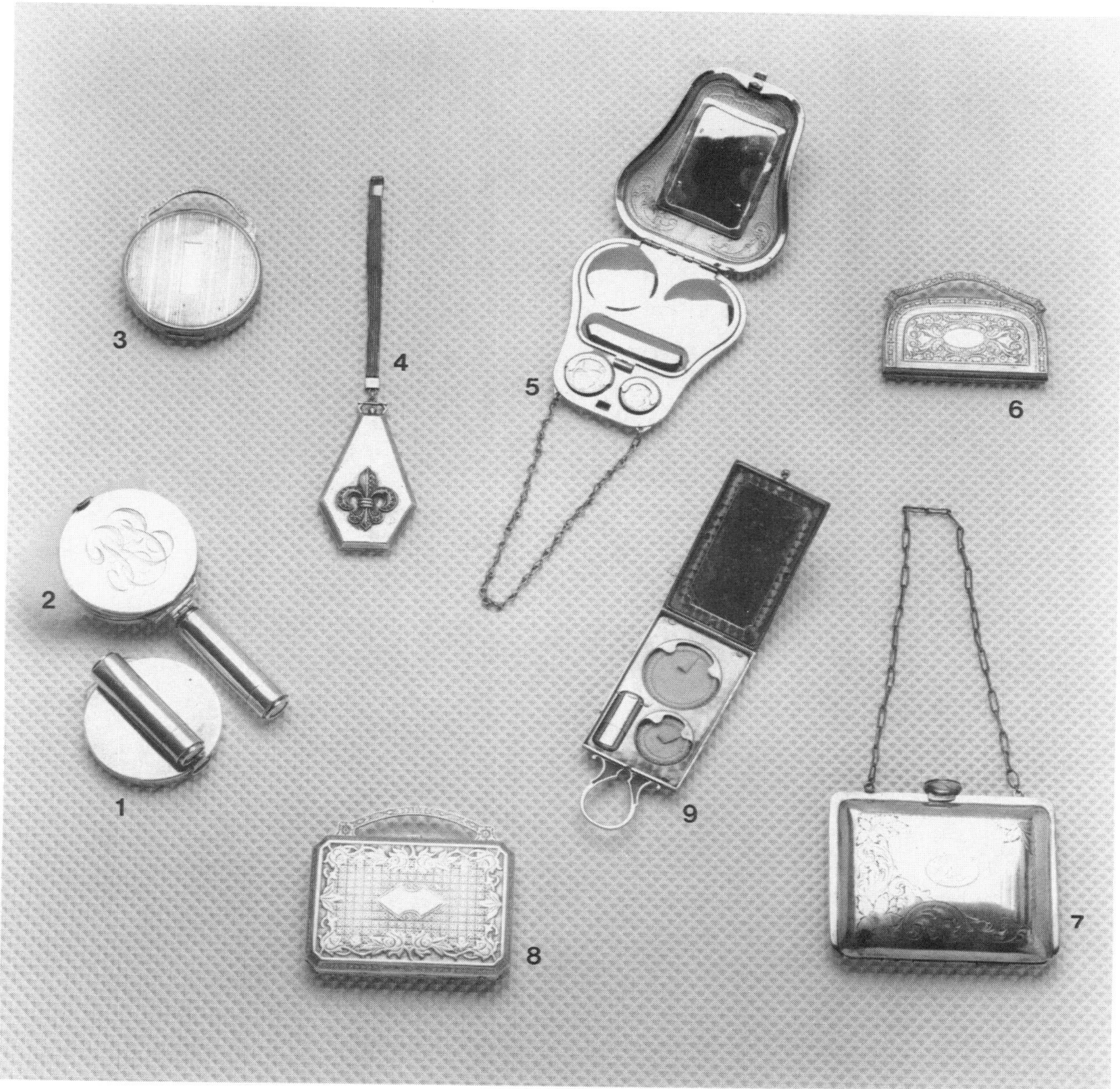

Fig. 98

1, 2 Silver-plated compact with swivel lipstick on lid, c. 1930s.

3 Engine-turned silvered-metal compact with through handle, c. 1920s.

4 Silvered compact with hammered surface and fleur-de-lis mounted on lid; carrying chain, c. 1920s.

5 Silvered vanity case with carrying chain and compartments for powder, rouge, lipstick, and coins, "Pat. Aug. 9, 1921" (shown open).

6 Silver-plated metal miniature vanity case with floral-engraved decoration on all sides; goldtone interior, through handle, and compartments for powder, rouge, and lipstick, c. 1920s.

7 German silver engraved vanity case with carrying chain and compartments for powder, rouge, and coins, c. 1915.

8 Silver-plated metal vanity case with engraved decoration on all sides; goldtone interior, through handle, and compartments for powder, rouge, and lipstick, c. 1920s.

9 Silvered-metal oblong vanity case with through handle and compartments for powder, rouge, and lipstick, c. 1920s (shown open).

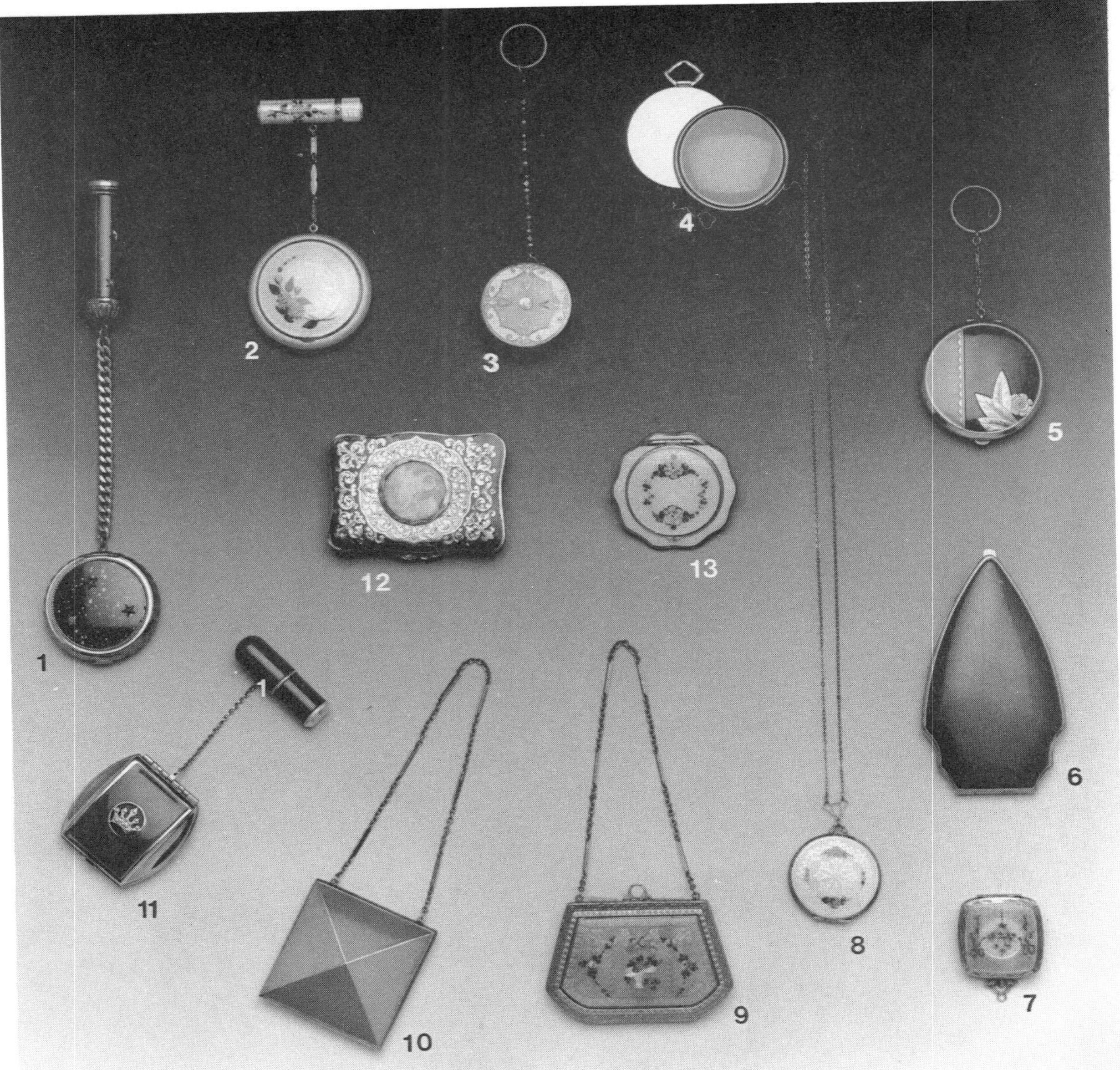

Fig. 99

1 Navy blue enamel on goldtone tango-chain compact and lipstick case with star-shaped studs mounted on a blue celestial scene.

2 B.B.Co. sterling-silver enameled tango-chain with light blue and cream-colored cloisonné flowers on lid, c. 1920s.

3 Blue and white guilloche enamel compact with finger-ring chain, c. 1917.

4 Green enamel round compact with slide-out mirror, Germany.

5 Green and black enamel metal compact with finger-ring chain, c. 1920s.

6 Shaded blue enamel on metal shield-shaped vanity case, c. 1920–30s.

7 R & G Co. green cloisonné and silver miniature compact with painted flowers on lid; loop for chain, c. 1910.

8 Yellow cloisonné locket compact with painted roses on lid; complete with chain, c. 1920s.

9 Blue cloisonné purse-motif vanity case with painted flowers on lid; carrying chain and compartments for powder, rouge, and lipstick, c. 1920–30s.

10 Square blue and ivory-colored enamel vanity case with carrying chain, c. 1920s.

11 Green enamel tango-chain vanity with silvered-metal crown mounted on lid, c. 1920s.

12 Green champlevé vermeil compact with painted ivory disk on lid, Italy, late 19th century.

13 R & G Co. yellow cloisonné vanity case with painted flowers on lid, c. 1920s.

Fig. 100

1 Vermeil sterling-silver oval compact with blue cloisonné decorated lid and finger-ring chain, c. 1920s.

2 R & G Co. sterling-silver yellow cloisonné tango-chain vanity with painted flowers on lid; lipstick and perfume tube suspended from enameled and silver finger-ring chain, c. 1920s.

3 G. L. B. Co. sterling-silver yellow and blue cloisonné vanity case with painted flowers; powder sifter and rouge compartment; enameled finger-ring chain, c. 1920s.

4 Flapjack green cloisonné compact with painted flowers on lid, c. 1930s.

5 Engine-turned silvered-metal compact with enameled disk on lid and finger-ring chain, c. 1920s.

6 May Fair engine-turned goldtone vanity case with enameled disk on lid; powder and rouge compartments; carrying cord and tassel, c. 1920s (shown open).

7 Evans "Tap Sift" black enameled white-nickel triangular vanity case with finger-ring chain, c. 1920s.

8 D. F. B. Co. blue enamel vanity case with painted windmill scene; chain with key; powder sifter and rouge compartment, "Pat'd Feb. 9, 1926."

9 La Mode octagonal green enamel vanity case with etched basket on lid; compartments for powder and rouge and through handle, c. 1920–30s.

10 Lavender and green champlevé vanity case with powder sifter, rouge and coins compartments; carrying chain, c. 1920s.

11 Triangular vanity case with engine-turned decoration and lustrous simulated cloisonné disk on lid; compartments for powder and rouge; carrying chain, c. 1920–30s.

12 Goldtone and silvered-metal vanity case with lavender cloisonné inset on lid; compartments for powder, rouge, and lipstick; carrying chain, c. 1920s.

13 Snakeskin tango-chain compact and lipstick.

Fig. 101

1 Rigid mesh multicolored bolster-shaped vanity bag with faux pearls and blue stones; tassel and carrying chain (shown open).

2 Maroon enamel vanity case with compartments for powder, rouge, lipstick, comb, and eye makeup (shown open).

3 Sterling-silver hallmarked lavender cloisonné compact perfume combination with painted flowers; finger-ring chain suspended from perfume ring.

4 Highly finished white-nickel compact designed as hand mirror.

5 R & G Co. "Nuwite" octagonal green enamel compact with scalework design on lid, c. 1920s.

6 Rigid multicolored mesh purse-motif vanity case; compartments for powder, rouge, and coins; carrying chain (shown open).

7 Daniel black leather compact with plastic dome enclosing portrait of lady, Paris.

8 Black plastic compact with Lucite top enclosing painted picture of lady on sparkling confetti, c. 1920s.

9 Black plastic compact with Lucite top enclosing painted "Pierrot" on sparkling confetti, c. 1920s.

10 Evans goldtone mesh vanity bag decorated with multicolored stones; scene of man and woman on lid; satin lined; wrist chain; metal mirror and powder and rouge compartments, c. 1940–50s.

11 Red damask bolster-shaped vanity bag with tassel and carrying chain with carved plastic ojime bead.

12 Leather-textured blue silvered vanity case with enamel painting on lid; wrist chain, c. 1930s.

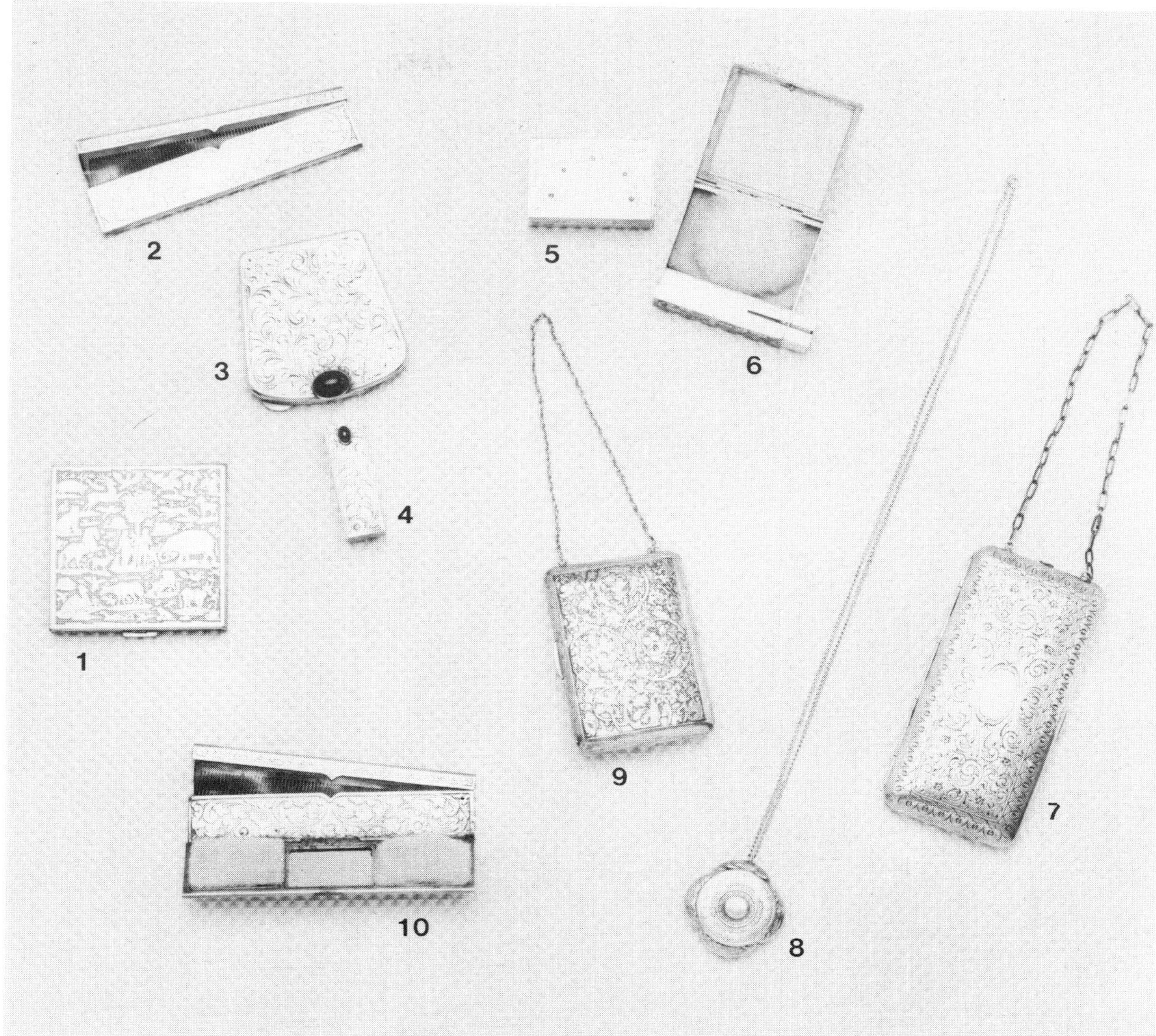

Fig. 102

1 Volupté silvered-metal compact embossed on all sides with "Adam and Eve" as central motif.

2, 3, 4 Sterling-silver engraved compact, lipstick, and comb set with green cabochon on compact and lipstick, Italy.

5 Sterling-silver miniature engraved vanity case with small rubies; sliding lipstick.

6 Sterling-silver engraved vanity case, sliding lipstick (shown open).

7 German silver engraved oblong carryall with carrying chain and compartments for powder, rouge, coins, and bill-clip.

8 Clover-shaped silvered repoussé compact/locket with chain.

9 German silver engraved carryall with carrying chain and compartments for powder, rouge, coins, and bill-clip.

10 Silver engraved compact/comb combination with compartments for powder and rouge in comb case.

Fig. 103

1 Silver filigree compact with two lids mounted with damascene scenes of India; interior lid opens to reveal powder compartment, India.

2 Antique goldtone compact with Oriental scene on lid, Austria.

3 Oriental brass engraved double-tier swivel vanity case (shown open).

4 Octagonal silver compact with repoussé Siamese dancer on lid.

5 Chinese hallmarked handmade silver filigree compact; lid lifts to reveal mirror, drawer pulls out for powder; loop for chain (shown with drawer open).

6 Chinese handmade silver filigree compact; multicolored lid lifts to reveal mirror, drawer pulls out for powder (shown open).

7 Suzuyo sterling-silver compact inlaid with copper bamboo branches, Japan.

8 Silver and black damascene compact with Siamese dancer on lid.

9 Sunc sterling-silver compact with jade cutout mounted on lid, China.

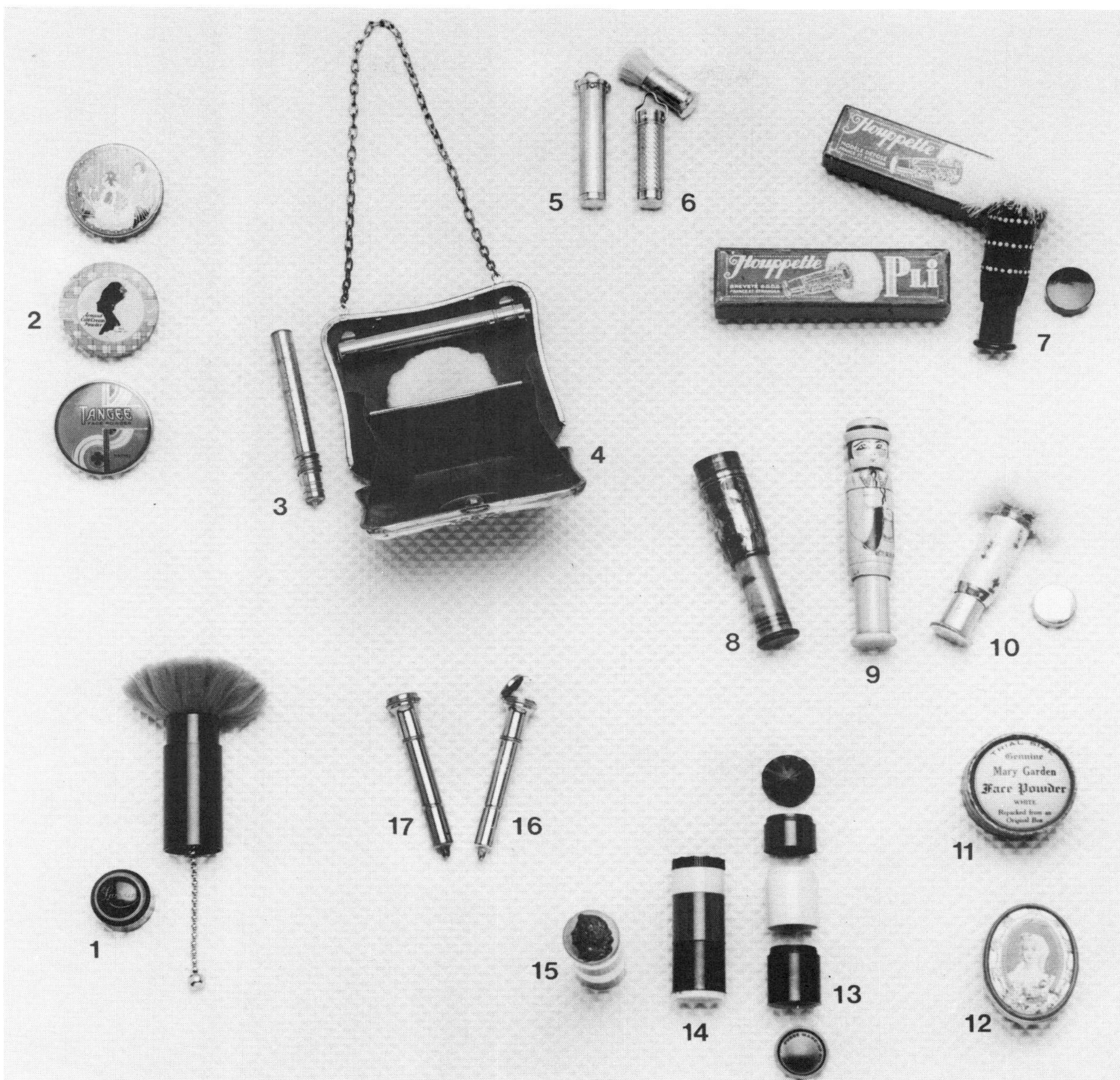

Fig. 104

1 Lamkin pink and black plastic powder-puff container and carrying chain, England.

2 Three miniature powder boxes; Tangee, Armand, and Richard Hudnut, c. 1920s.

3 Paris Fashion Co. silvered powderette, c. 1900s.

4 Silvered repoussé vanity purse with mirror, powder puff, and powderette, "Pat'd Oct. 17, 1914."

5, 6 Gold-filled Puf-Kase, c. 1920s (**5** shown closed; 6, smaller version, shown open).

7, 8 Houppette plastic pli, France, c. 1920s (**7**, turquoise-beaded black, shown open; **8**, goldtone decorated, shown closed).

9 Pink plastic pli painted to resemble doll; hat contains lipstick, France, c. 1920s.

10 Sterling-silver hallmarked pli with vermeil overlay and painted cloisonné, France (shown open).

11 Mary Garden face powder in a puff in original box, c. 1917.

12 Richard Hudnut "Du Barry" face-powder sampler in original box, France, c. 1920s.

13, 14, 15 Colt Purse Make-Up Kit with plastic tubular colored makeup containers, c. 1930s (**13** shown open, **14** shown closed, **15** top view).

16, 17 Princess Pat powderette-lipstick, c. 1920s (**16**, goldtone, shown open, **17**, silvered, shown closed).

Fig. 105

1 Antique embossed goldtone-finish vanity case with multicolored stones; carrying chain and compartments for powder, rouge, and lipstick, turn of the century.

2 Antique goldtone compact with filigree lid set with pearls and turquoise; jeweled tassel and carrying chain, turn of the century.

3 Antique goldtone vanity bag lined with pink satin; multicolored silk back, filigree compact set with pearls and blue stones; jeweled tassel and carrying chain, turn of the century.

4 Antique silvered-metal vanity bag; filigree compact set with multicolored stones; black velvet back, carrying chain, and tassel, turn of the century.

5 Two-sided antique goldtone vanity case; filigree lids set with red stones; powder and rouge compartments; tassel conceals lipstick; carrying chain, turn of the century.

6 Antique silvered-filigree metal vanity bag set with marcasites and blue stones; gray moire lining, jeweled tassel, and carrying chain, turn of the century.

7 Antique goldtone filigree compact set with green stones; lipstick case bonded to top; tassel and carrying chain, turn of the century.

Fig. 106

1 Goldtone vanity case with filigree lid set with colored stones and green cabochon stone; red faille lining, multicolored silk back set with stones; jeweled tassel and carrying chain; compartments for powder, rouge, and lipstick, turn of the century.

2 White cloisonné goldtone vanity reticule with lid mounted with multicolored gemstones and filigree back; silk-lined interior, tassel conceals lipstick; carrying chain, Austria, turn of the century.

3 Embossed brass collapsible compact with edge set with multicolored cabochons, France, turn of the century (shown open).

4 Antique goldtone tango-chain; compact and rouge have filigree lids set with green stones and micro-mosaic disks, c. 1920s.

5 Antique goldtone compact with red stones on embossed lid; tassel and carrying chain, c. 1920s.

6 Goldtone filigree vanity case set with pearls and yellow stones; openings on both sides for powder and rouge, lipstick attached on bottom; tassel and carrying chain.

7 Goldtone compact with honeycomb lid set with multicolored stones; fabric back, turn of the century.

8 E. A. Bliss Co. brass filigree purse-motif vanity case with multicolored stones and carrying chain, turn of the century.

9 Embossed goldtone compact with multicolored stones on lid, Czechoslovakia, late 19th century.

10 Antique goldtone compact; filigree lid incorporates lipstick holder set with blue stones, turn of the century.

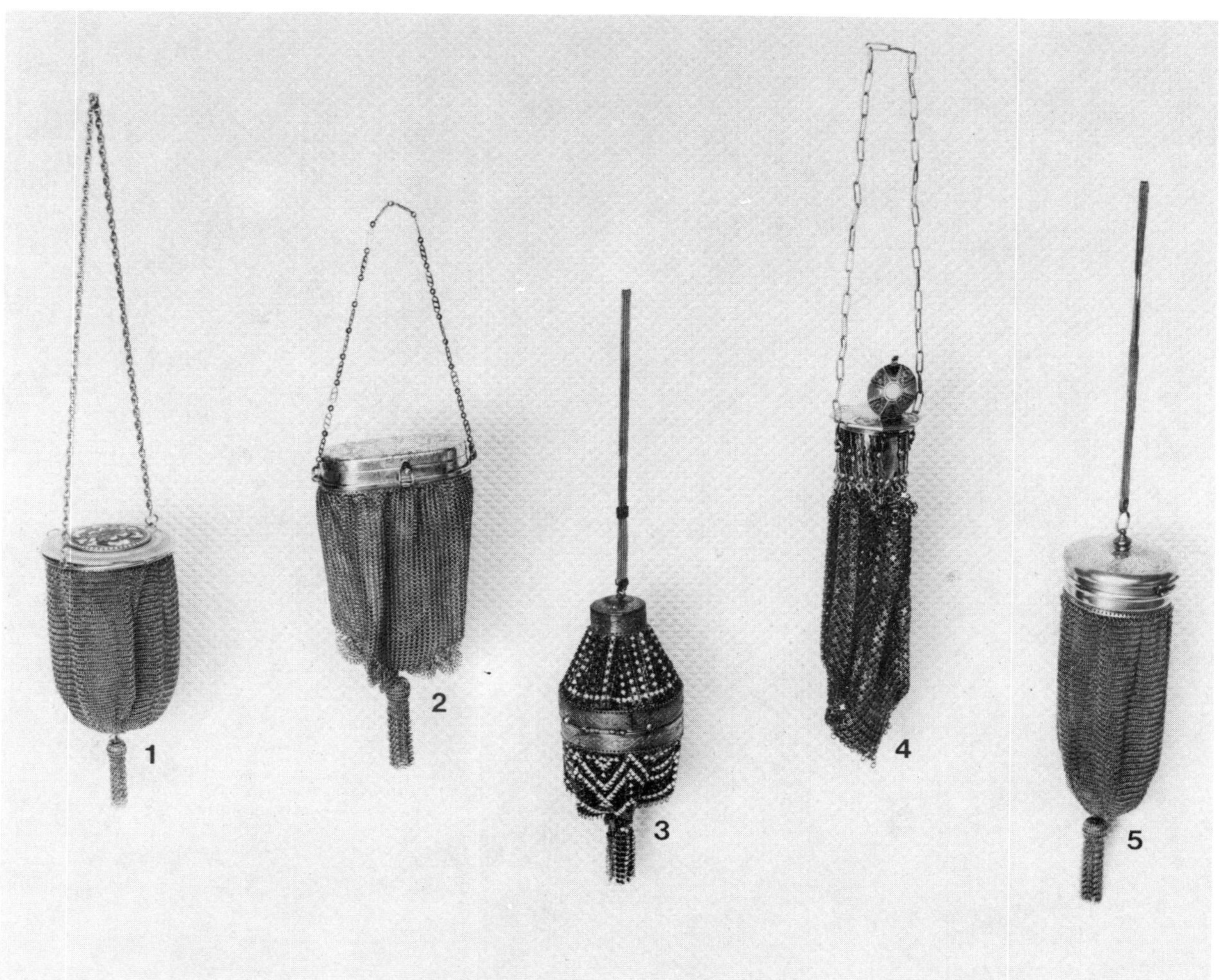

Fig. 107

1 Evans multicolored champlevé mesh vanity bag with carrying chain; metal mirror and compartments for powder and rouge, c. 1940s.

2 Embossed silvered-mesh oval vanity bag with carrying chain and powder and rouge compartments, c. 1920s.

3 Whiting & Davis "Delysia" multicolored mesh vanity bag with sapphire cabochon thumbpiece and carrying chain; powder and rouge compartments, c. 1920s.

4 Silver-plated "extension gate top" mesh vanity bag with carrying chain; compact located on outer cover, c. 1920s (shown open).

5 Goldtone mesh vanity bag with embossed lid; powder and coin compartments; carrying chain and sapphire cabochon thumbpiece, turn of the century.

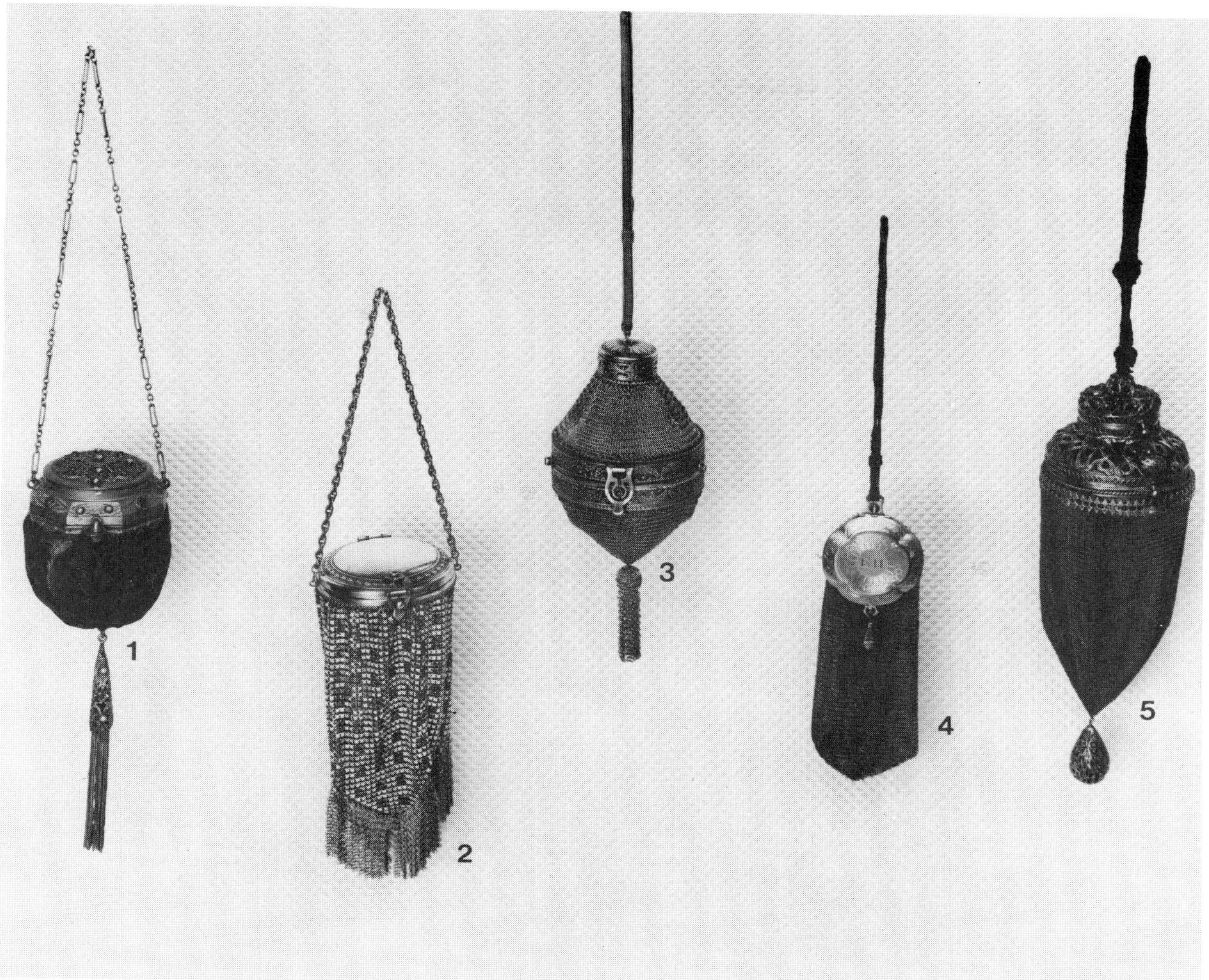

Fig. 108

1 Antique goldtone-colored vanity bag with pearls and red stones on filigree lid; multicolored silk bag; metal jeweled tassel and carrying chain, turn of the century.

2 Whiting & Davis multicolored mesh vanity bag with silvered lid and carrying chain, c. 1920s.

3 Whiting & Davis "Delysia" silvered mesh vanity bag, powder and rouge compartments; sapphire cabochon thumbpiece and carrying chain, c. 1920s.

4 Goldtone mesh vanity bag with sapphire cabochon thumbpiece and carrying chain, turn of the century.

5 Antique goldtone mesh filigree vanity bag with carrying chain and metal tassel; powder and rouge compartments, sliding lipstick, late 19th century.

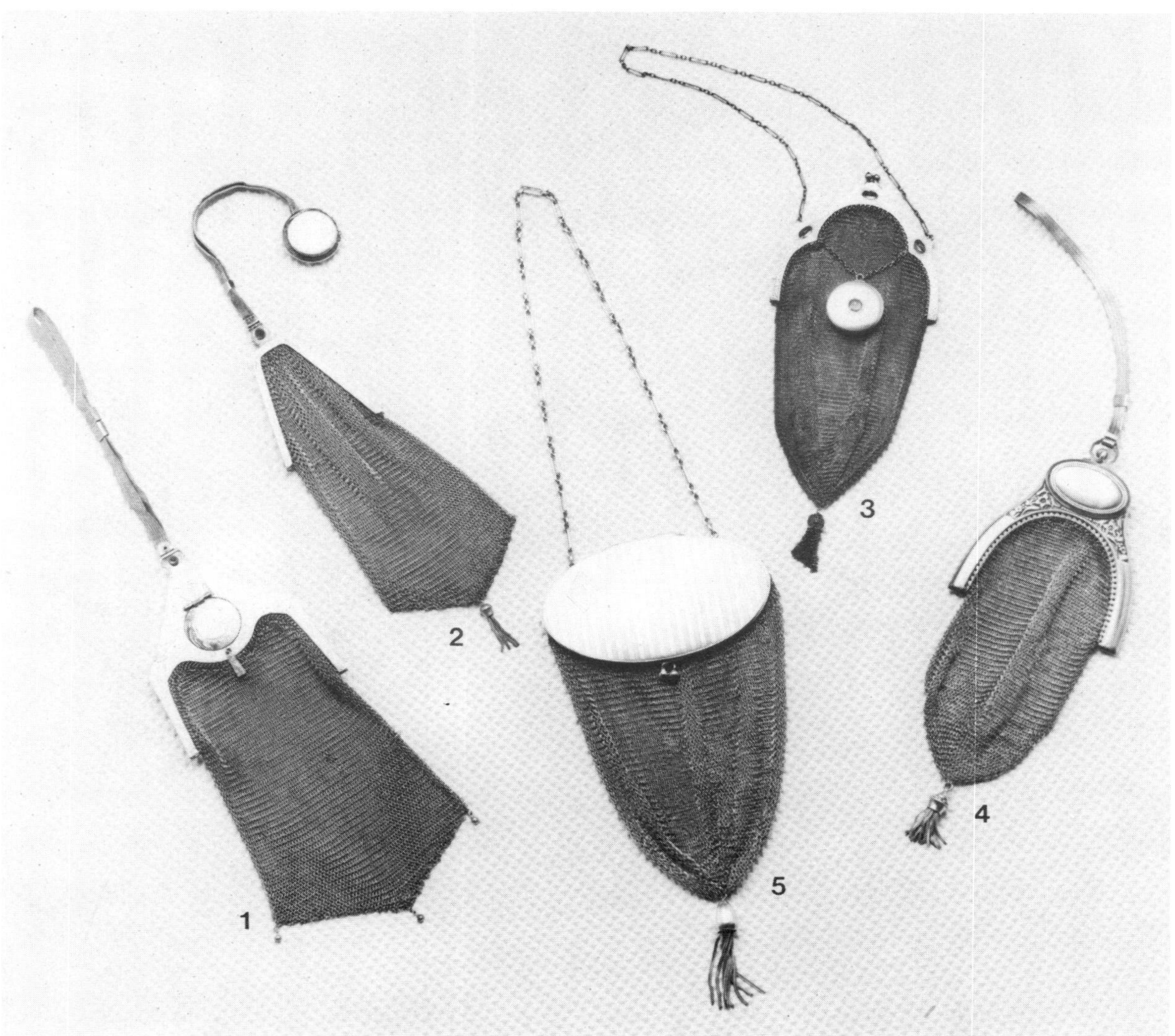

Fig. 109

1 Whiting & Davis "Piccadilly" gilded mesh vanity bag with carrying chain; compact in front lid, c. 1920s.

2 Silver mesh bag with engraved compact attached to mesh carrying chain; sapphire cabochon thumbpiece, Germany, c. 1920s.

3 Sterling-silver compact suspended from sterling frame of soldered-metal mesh bag decorated with sapphire cabochons; carrying chain, c. 1920s.

4 Silver-plated mesh vanity bag with embossed frame and carrying chain, c. 1920s.

5 Sterling-silver mesh vanity bag with monogram engraved on lid; carrying chain, c. 1920s.

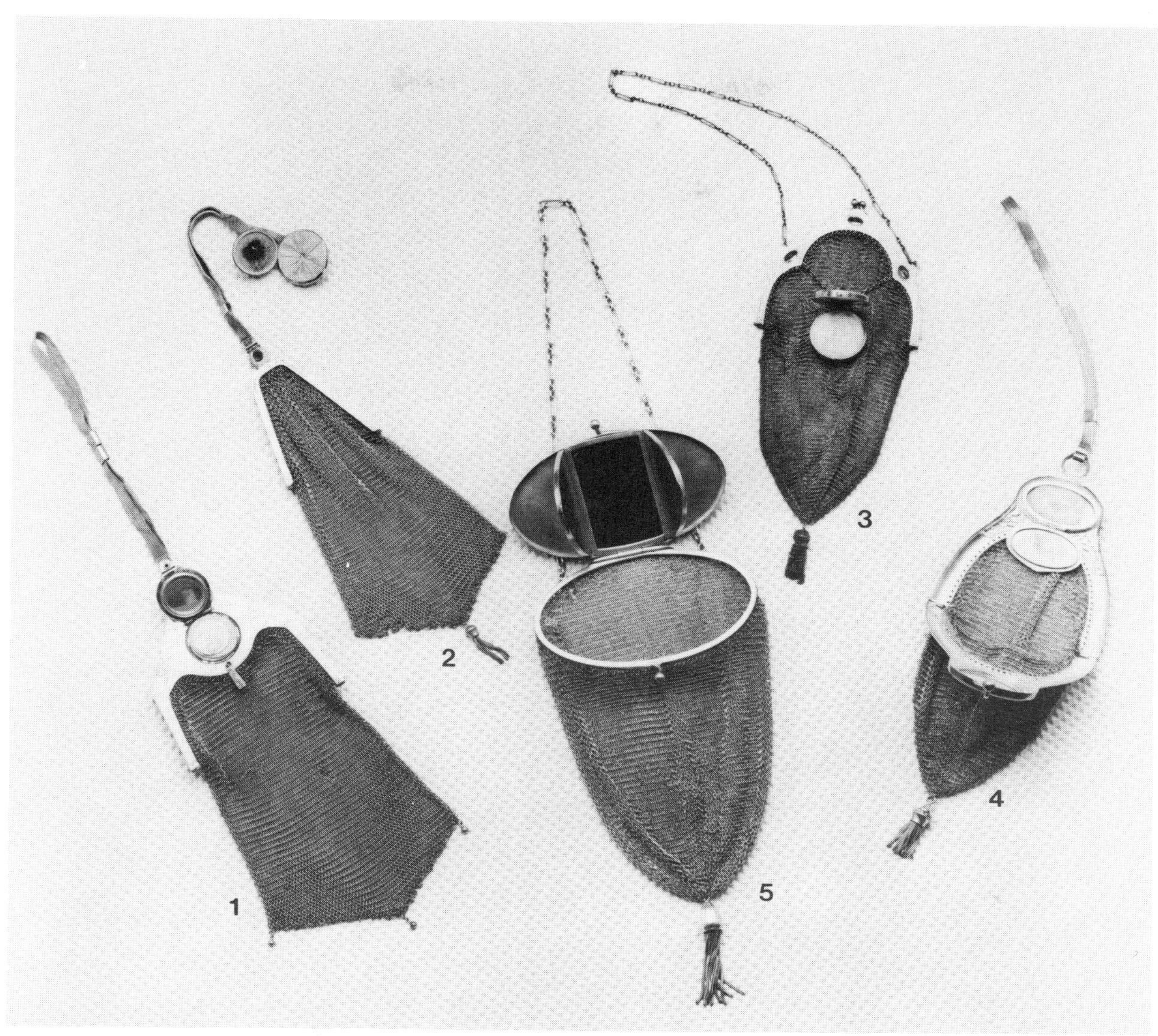

Fig. 110 Vanity bags in Figure 109 shown open.

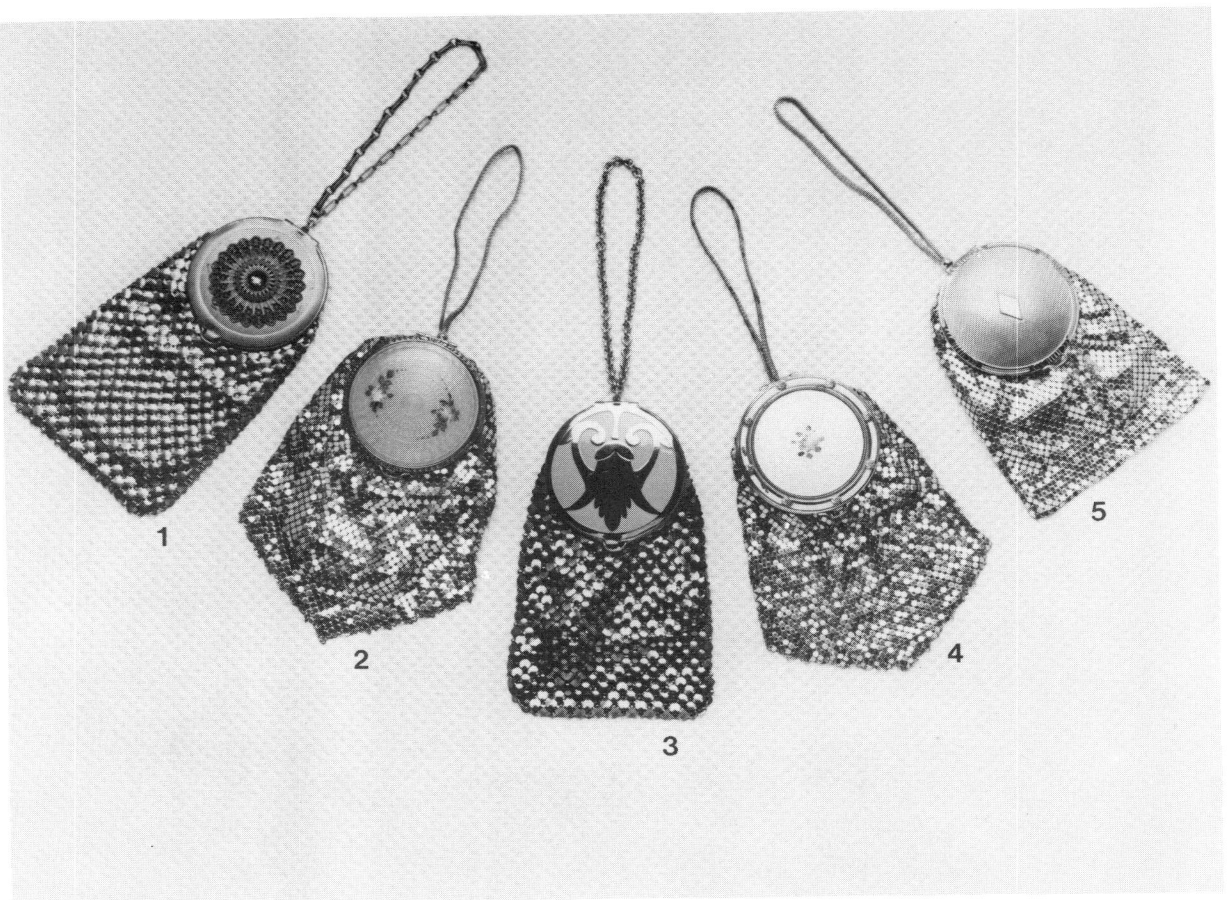

Fig. 111

1 Antique goldtone mesh vanity bag with red stone on lid; lined interior and carrying chain, turn of the century.

2 Evans goldtone mesh vanity bag with blue cloisonné lid decorated with painted flowers; metal mirror and powder and rouge compartments; lined interior, c. 1930s.

3 Antique goldtone mesh vanity bag with blue enamel and goldtone lid; lined interior and carrying chain, turn of the century.

4 Evans goldtone mesh vanity bag with white cloisonné lid with painted flowers; metal mirror and powder and rouge compartments; lined interior, c. 1930s.

5 Evans goldtone mesh vanity bag with embossed lid; metal mirror and powder and rouge compartments; carrying chain, c. 1930s.

Fig. 112

1 Whiting & Davis silvered mesh vanity bag with embossed lid, blue sapphire cabochon thumbpiece, and carrying chain, c. 1920s.

2 Sterling hallmarked mesh vanity bag with deep engraving on lid; diminishing mirror and finger-ring chain, turn of the century.

3 Whiting & Davis multicolored mesh vanity bag with painted fruit on lid; carrying chain, c. 1920.

4 Whiting & Davis black and white mesh vanity bag with carrying chain, c. 1920s.

5 Whiting & Davis silvered mesh vanity bag with heavily embossed frame and carrying chain, c. 1920s.

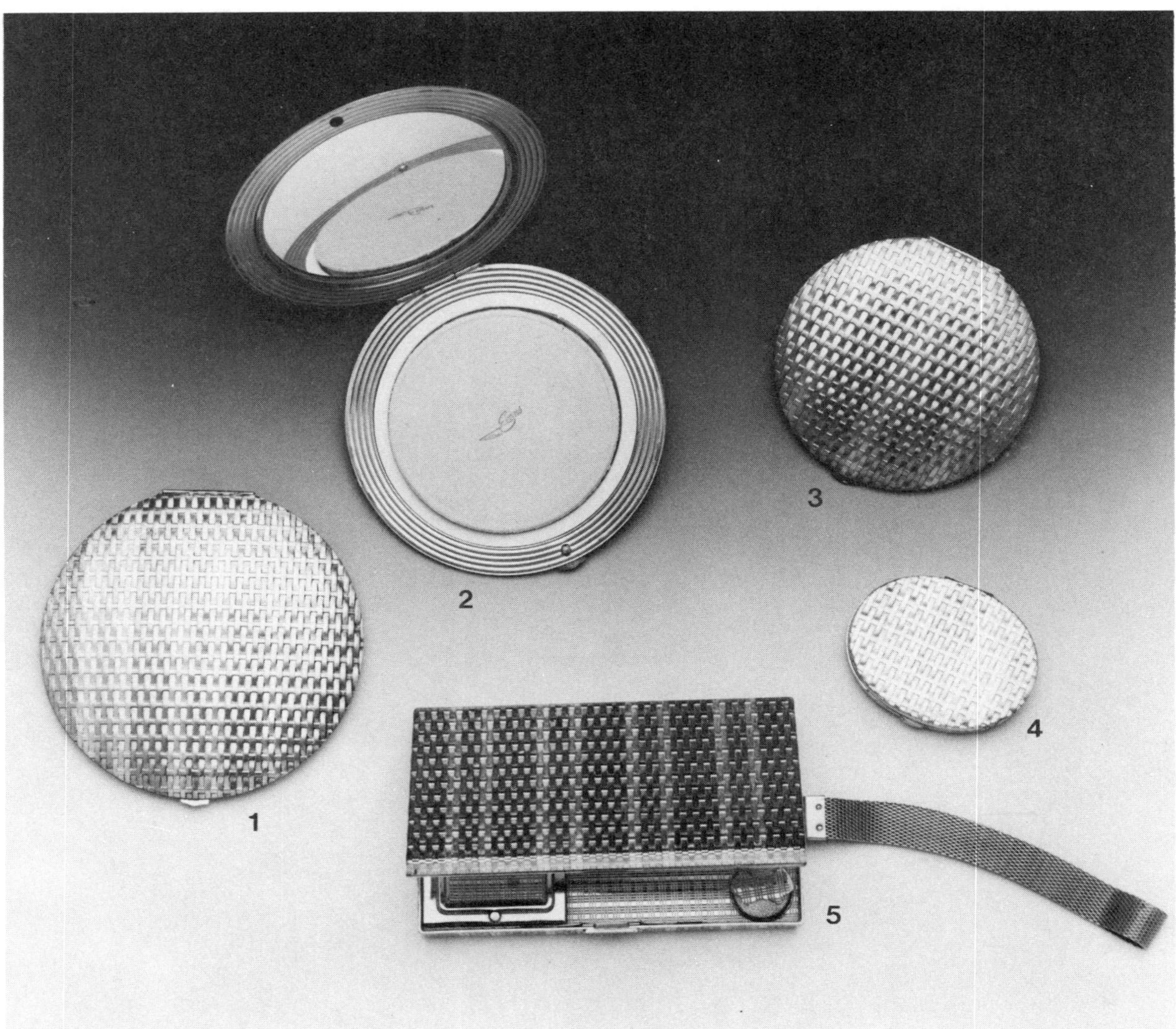

Fig. 113

1 Evans 5″-round sterling gold-wash compact with pink, yellow, and white basketweave.

2 Evans 5″-round sterling compact with pink, yellow, and white basketweave (shown open).

3 Evans 4″-round sterling gold-wash compact with pink, yellow, and white basketweave.

4 Evans oval sterling gold-wash compact with pink, yellow, and white basketweave.

5 Evans pink, yellow, and white basketweave metal carryall c. 1940–50s (shown open).

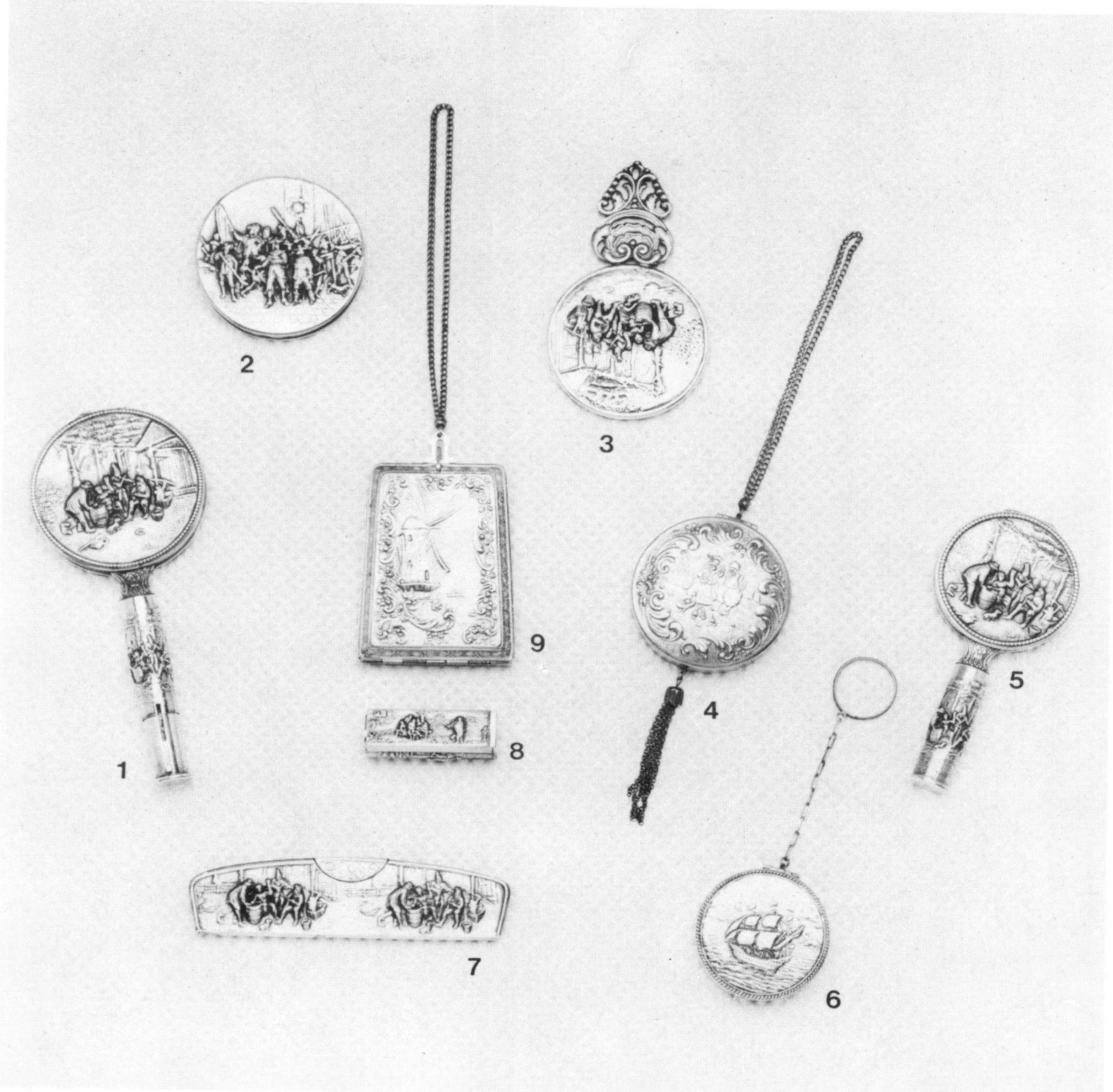

Fig. 114

1 S & F silver-plated compact designed to resemble hand mirror; lipstick in handle; repoussé cracker-barrel scene on lid, Denmark.

2 Silver-plated compact with Danish scene on lid, Denmark.

3 Silver-plated mirror with repoussé cracker-barrel scene, Denmark.

4 Silver-plated compact with Dutch scene on lid; tassel and carrying chain, c. 1920s.

5 S & F silver-plated compact designed to resemble hand mirror; lipstick in handle; repoussé cracker-barrel scene on lid, Denmark.

6 Silver-plated vanity case with sailing ship on lid; powder and rouge compartments and finger-ring chain, c. 1920s.

7 Silver-plated comb with repoussé cracker-barrel scene, Denmark.

8 Silver-plated lipstick with repoussé cracker-barrel scene, Denmark.

9 Silver-plated vanity case with Dutch scene on lid; compartments for powder, rouge, and lipstick, and carrying chain, c. 1920s.

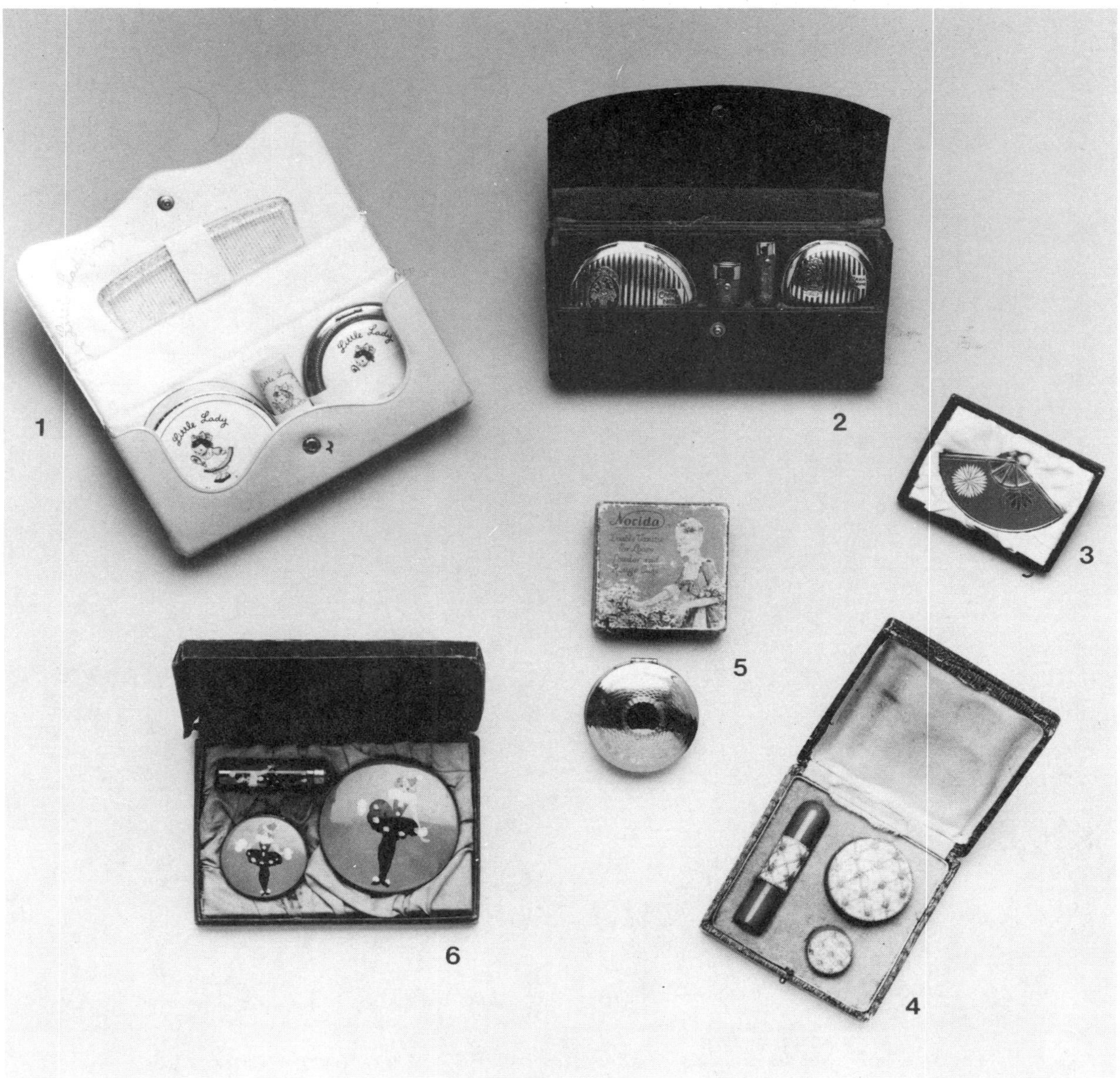

Fig. 115

1 Little Lady child's vanity box containing compact, lipstick, powder, and comb in blue carrying case.

2 Langlois "Cara Noma" blue vanity clutch containing silver-plated powder compact, rouge, lipstick, and eye makeup containers, "Pat. 7-1-24."

3 Goldtone miniature red enamel fan-motif compact in original fitted presentation box, c. 1950s.

4 Edouardo "Bag-Dabs" green and white plastic compact; lipstick and sachet container decorated with red flowers; original fitted presentation box, France.

5 Norida nickel-silver vanity case with powder and rouge compartments in original box, "Pat. Aug. 5, 1924."

6 Goldtone compact with painted clown, rouge and lipstick set in original fitted presentation box.

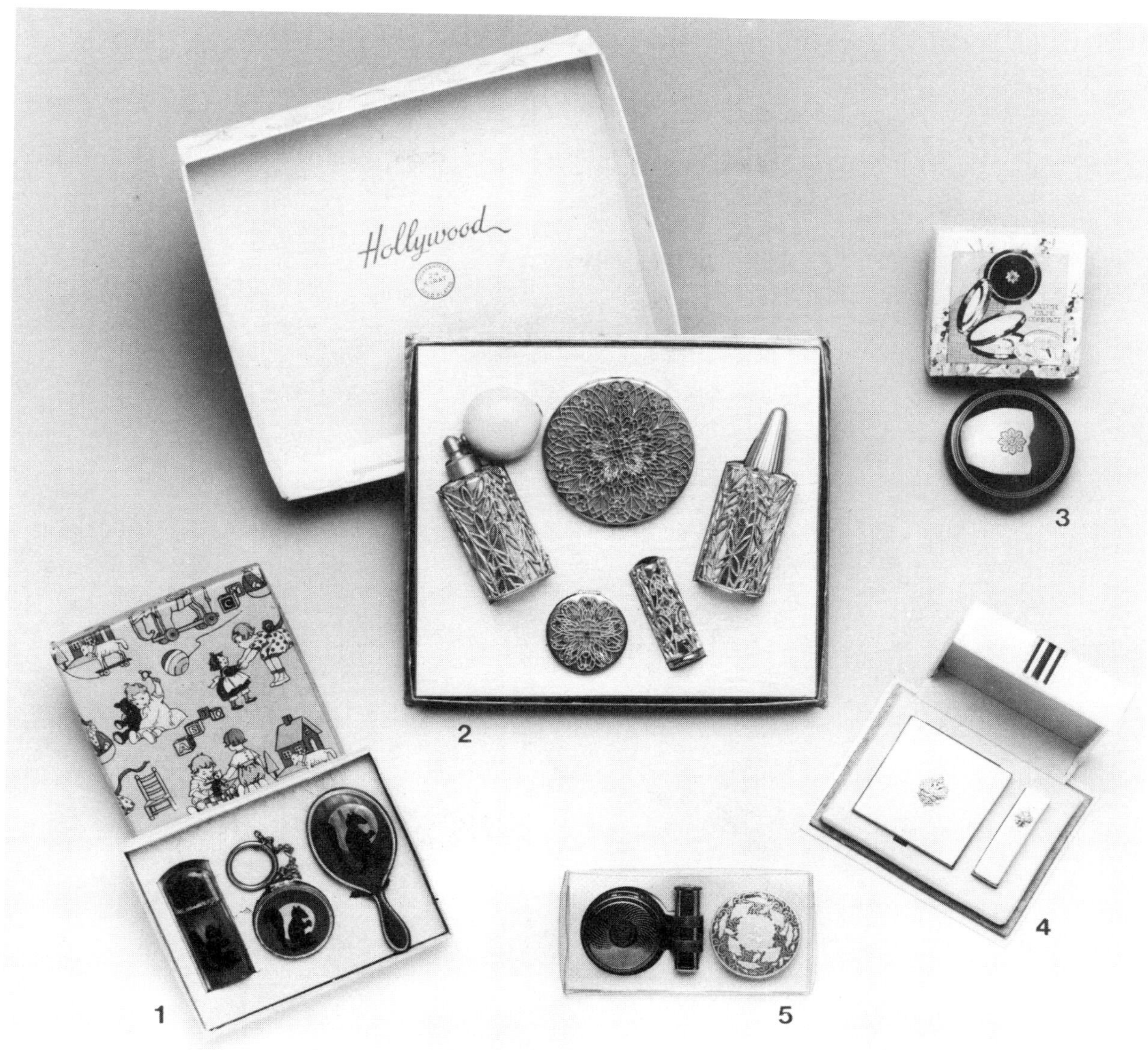

Fig. 116

1 Annette "Chypre" child's green cosmetic set; compact with finger chain; hand mirror and perfume bottle; original fitted presentation box.

2 Hollywood 24-karat gold-plated multicolored stone-studded filigree cosmetic set with compact, rouge case, lipstick, perfume bottle with atmomizer, and lotion bottle in original fitted presentation box.

3 Colgate & Co. "Watch Case" brown metal vanity case with powder and rouge compartments in original presentation box.

4 Anna Pavlova white and gold enamel goldtone compact and lipstick-case set with goldtone coat-of-arms in original fitted presentation box, c. 1930s.

5 Coty "Trio" goldtone metal rouge and lipstick case; tandem set in red plastic "invitation"-size face powder, c. 1930s.

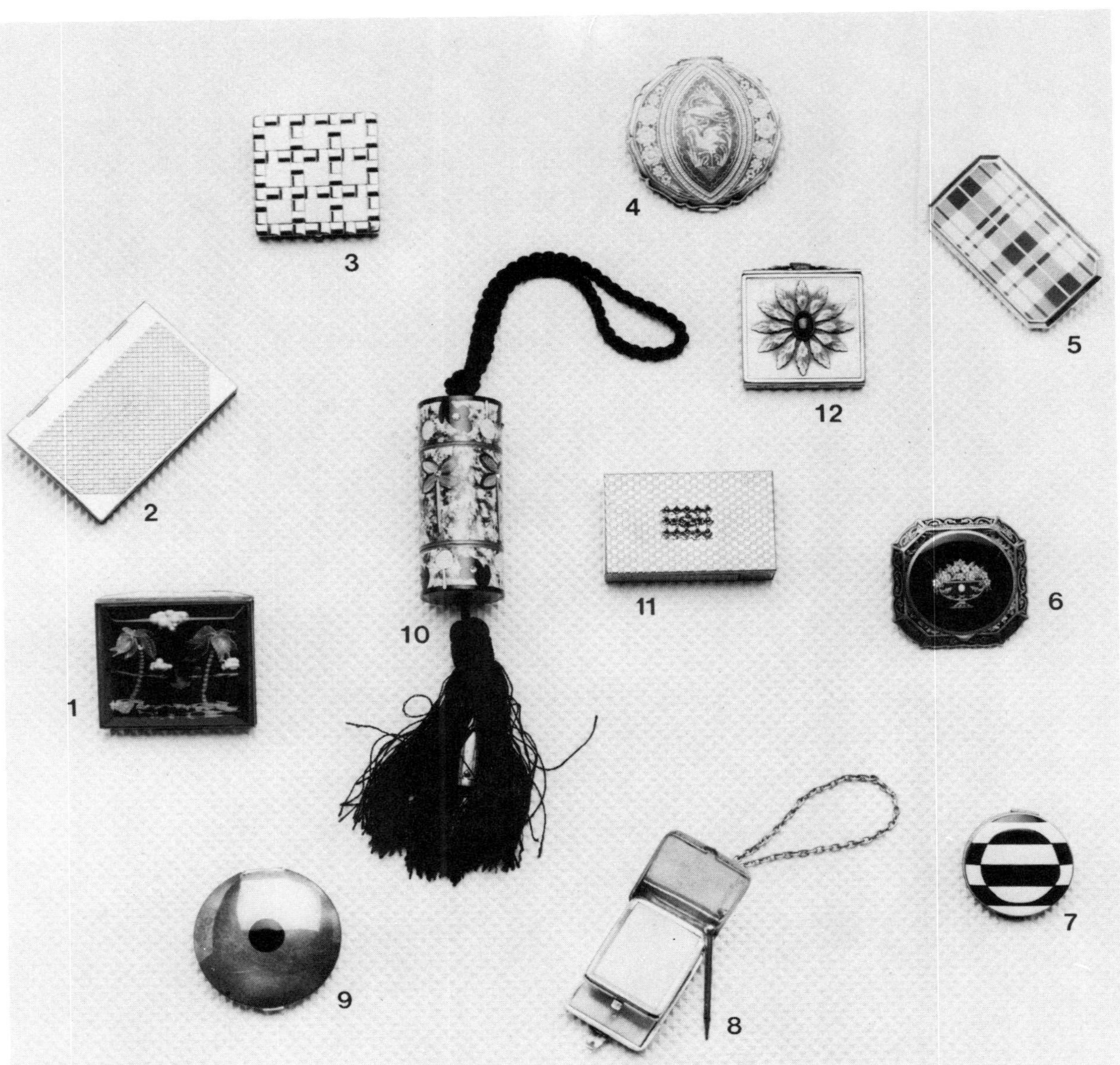

Fig. 117

1 Goldtone compact with colorful South Seas scene encased in Lucite lid.

2 Coty goldtone embossed book-motif compact, c. 1940s.

3 Majestic copper-colored basketweave compact.

4 Damascene goldtone and black metal compact, c. 1930s.

5 Blue and white enamel plaid vanity case with powder and rouge compartments.

6 Octagonal silvered and black enamel compact with powder sifter, c. 1920s.

7 Black and white plastic compact.

8 B C brass engine-turned vanity case with powder and rouge compartments, mirror and writing slate, and brass writing pencil enclosed on side lid, Germany, c. 1920s.

9 Copper compact with black enamel bull's-eye center.

10 Black plastic bolster-shaped vanity bag with painted blue and white flowers set with rhinestones; black carrying cord; lipstick concealed in tassel, c. 1920s.

11 Volupté goldtone basketweave compact with red stones on lid; sliding lipstick, c. 1940s.

12 Antique goldtone compact with goldtone leaves mounted on lid and red cabochon stone in center, c. 1930s.

Fig. 118

1 B.Co. green crackle plastic vanity case with enamel decoration on lid, carrying chain and compartments for powder, rouge, and lipstick.

2 Volupté blue enamel "Watchcase Compact," set with faux pearls with painted disk on lid and black tassel, c. 1940s.

3 Red and black enamel tango-chain vanity with red and black enamel chain; powder sifter, rouge compartment, and metal mirror, c. 1920s.

4 Silvered-metal compact with enameled medallion on lid and through handle, c. 1920s.

5 Zell simulated lavender cloisonné vanity case (shown open).

6 Marbleized brown Bakelite tango-chain vanity with red enamel disk on lid.

7 Chrome cookie-shaped compact with loop for chain, c. 1910.

8 Richard Hudnut black and goldtone enamel vanity case; metal mirror and powder and rouge compartments, c. 1920s.

9 Schildkraut rhinestone compact with black faille and rhinestone carrying case.

10 Square champlevé compact with blue, gold, and green enamel flowers and yellow cabochon stone on lid; engraved sides, Czechoslovakia.

11 Goldtone compact with Lucite dome enclosing heather on a plaid background.

12 Orange enamel metal vanity case with metal mirror and powder and rouge compartments; lipstick compartment centered on back lid, c. 1920s.

Fig. 119

1 Horseshoe-shaped zippered compact with painted dancing girl on lid, signed Annette Honeywell.

2 Avon oval compact with blue and green checkerboard lid.

3 Royal blue ribbed-silk compact; catch set with blue stones, England.

4 Dorset Fifth Avenue bolster-shaped goldtone compact.

5 Terri silvered-metal vanity case with black carrying cord, c. 1950s.

6 Majestic brass compact with spinning roulette wheel set on lid.

7 Volupté brass and black enamel oblong vanity case with compartments for powder, rouge, lipstick and comb.

8 Wooden painted compact, c. 1940s.

9 E.A.M. sterling pentagonal vanity case with goldtone engraved interior; powder and rouge compartments and carrying chain, c. 1920s (shown open).

Fig. 120 Kigu brown marbleized enameled compact/camera combination; working camera incorporates compact, lipstick holder, and 16 mm film-cartridge holder, England, c. 1940–50s.

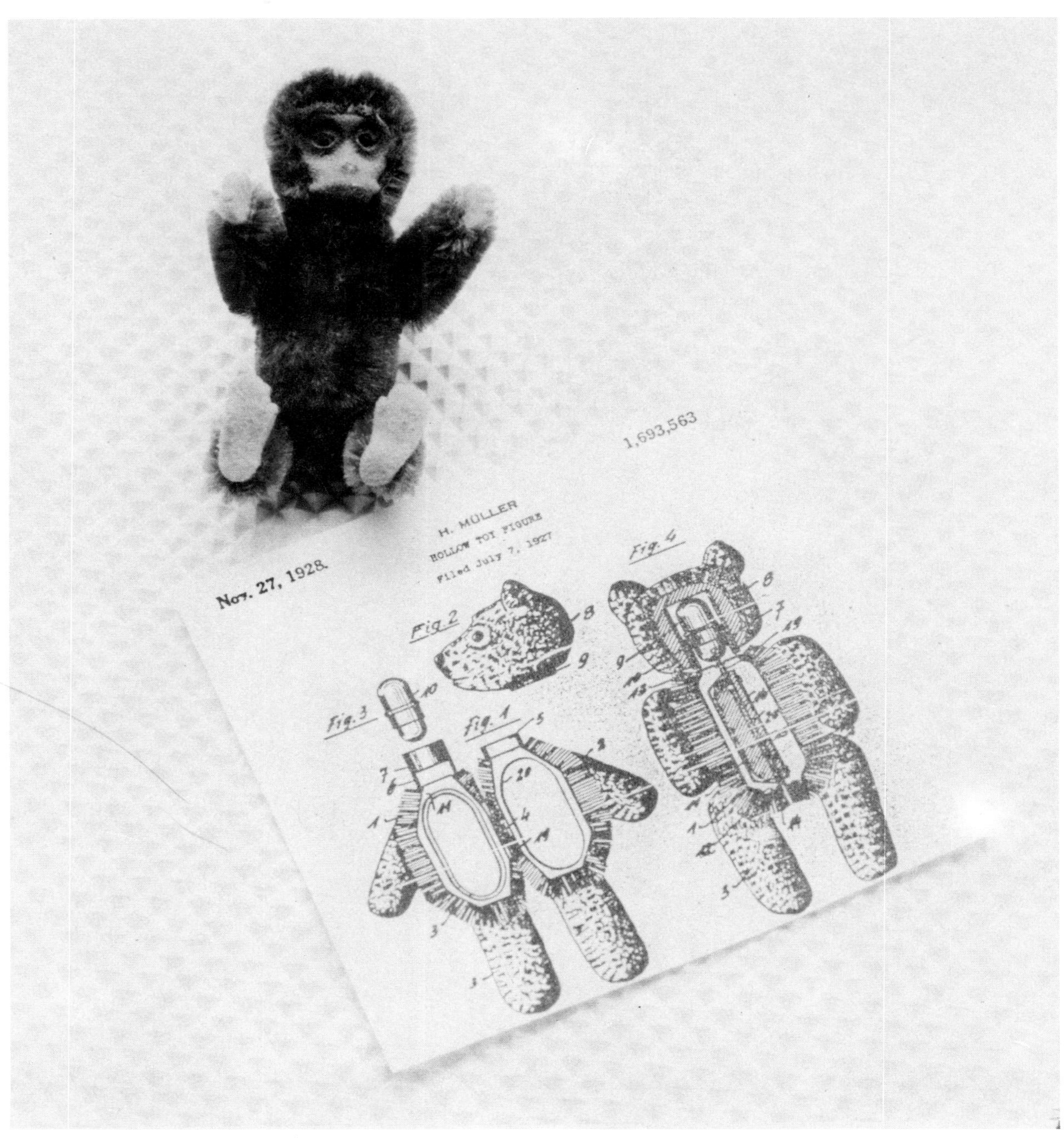

Fig. 121 Schuco miniature monkey that opens to reveal compact and lipstick; patent shown is for hollow toy teddy-bear compact/lipstick combination, c. 1920s.

Fig. 122 Schuco miniature monkey in Figure 121 shown open.

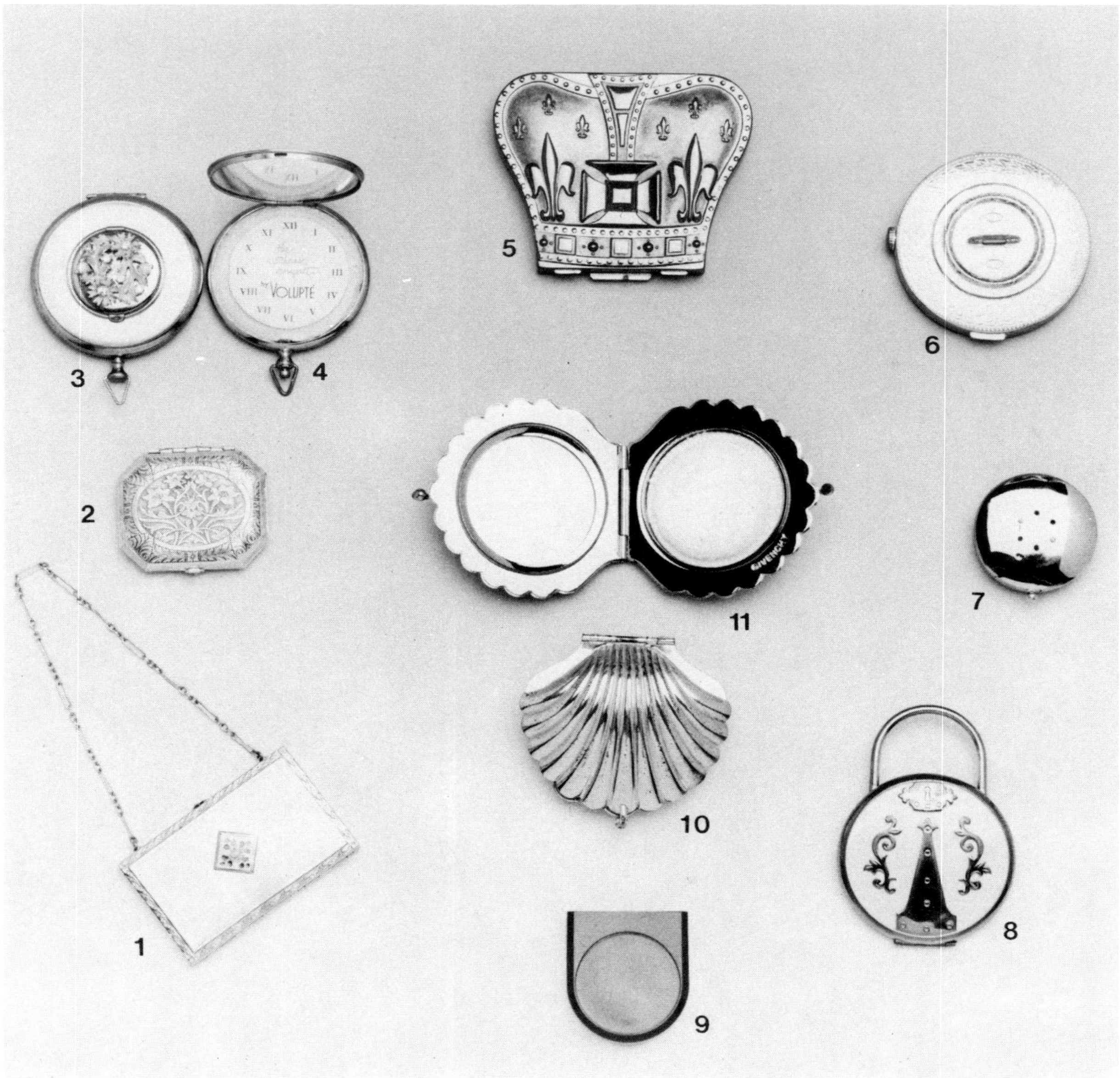

Fig. 123

1 Nickel-silver engine-turned vanity case with painted enamel flowers on lid, carrying chain and compartments for powder, lipstick, and rouge, c. 1920s.

2 Woodworth "Karess" embossed silvered-metal miniature vanity with compartments for powder, rouge, and lipstick, c. 1920s.

3, 4 Volupté "Watchcase Compact" with picture locket on flower-decorated lid, c. 1940s (**3** shown closed, **4** shown open).

5 Stratton goldtone compact with crown motif, c. 1940–50s.

6 Elizabeth Arden engraved goldtone powder-sifter compact, Switzerland.

7 Richard Hudnut nickel-silver complimentary powder sifter, c. 1920s.

8 White enamel goldtone compact with lock motif.

9 Coty "Sub-Deb" red and white plastic compact, c. 1940s.

10 Napier sterling-silver clamshell compact, c. 1940s.

11 Givenchy goldtone clamshell compact with blue stone thumbpieces, c. 1940s (shown open).

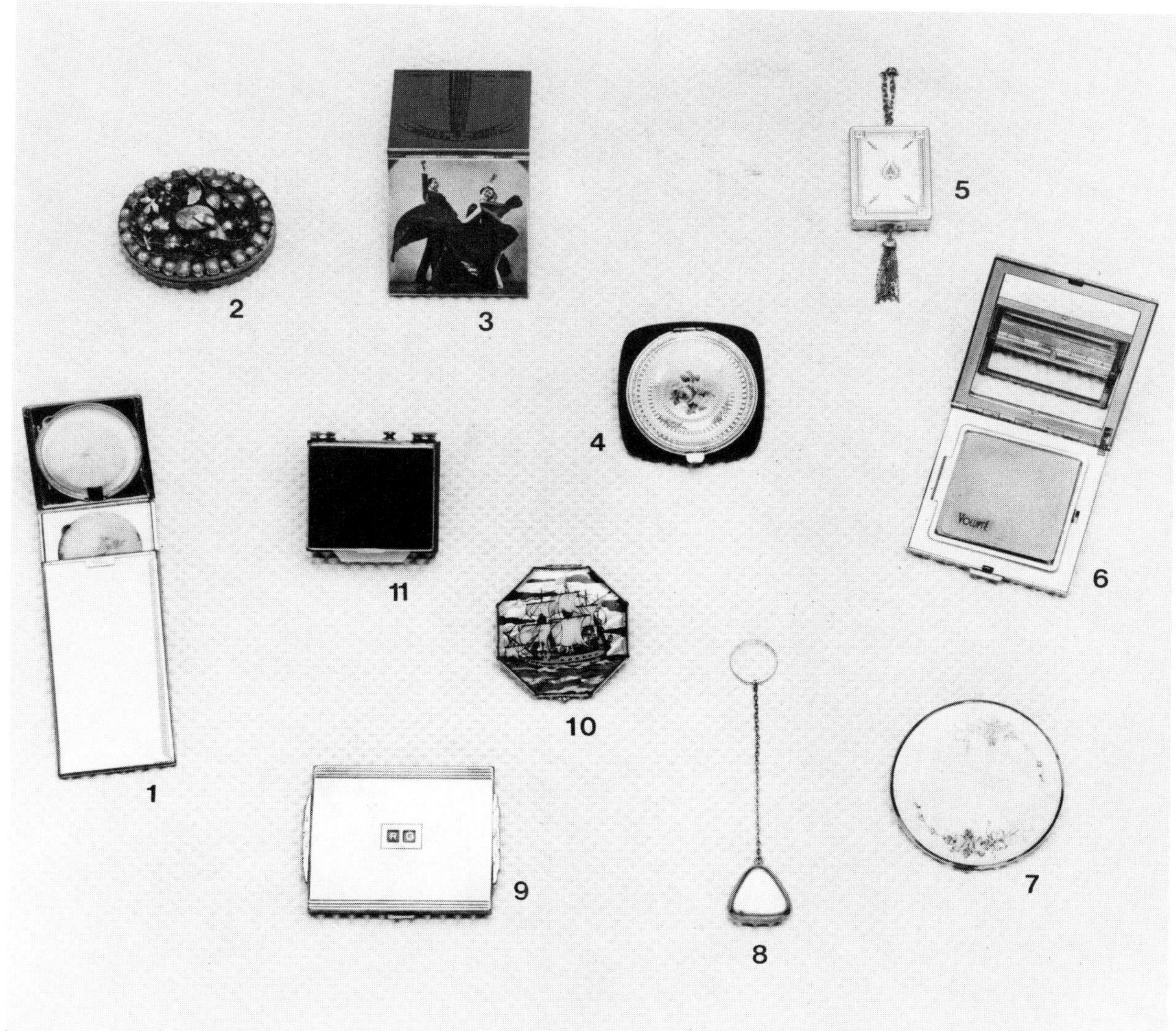

Fig. 124

1 Yardley goldtone embossed vanity case; sliding mirror reveals powder and rouge compartments, England, c. 1930–40s.

2 Evans oval antique goldtone compact encrusted with faux cabochon jade and pearls.

3 The Rainbow Room and Grill "First Prize for Dancing" compact with picture of dancers.

4 Brown plastic and goldtone compact with painted flowers on lid.

5 Melba goldtone engraved vanity case with powder and lipstick compartments, tassel, and finger-ring chain.

6 Volupté engraved goldtone compact with swivel mirror lid.

7 La Mode cloisonné flapjack vanity case.

8 Goldtone and silvered miniature triangular compact with finger-ring chain.

9 Agme goldtone compact with adjustable initials on lid, Switzerland.

10 Gwenda octagonal painted foil compact.

11 Cambi illuminated, enameled goldtone and plastic vanity case with powder compartment, sliding lipstick, and eye makeup in lid, France.

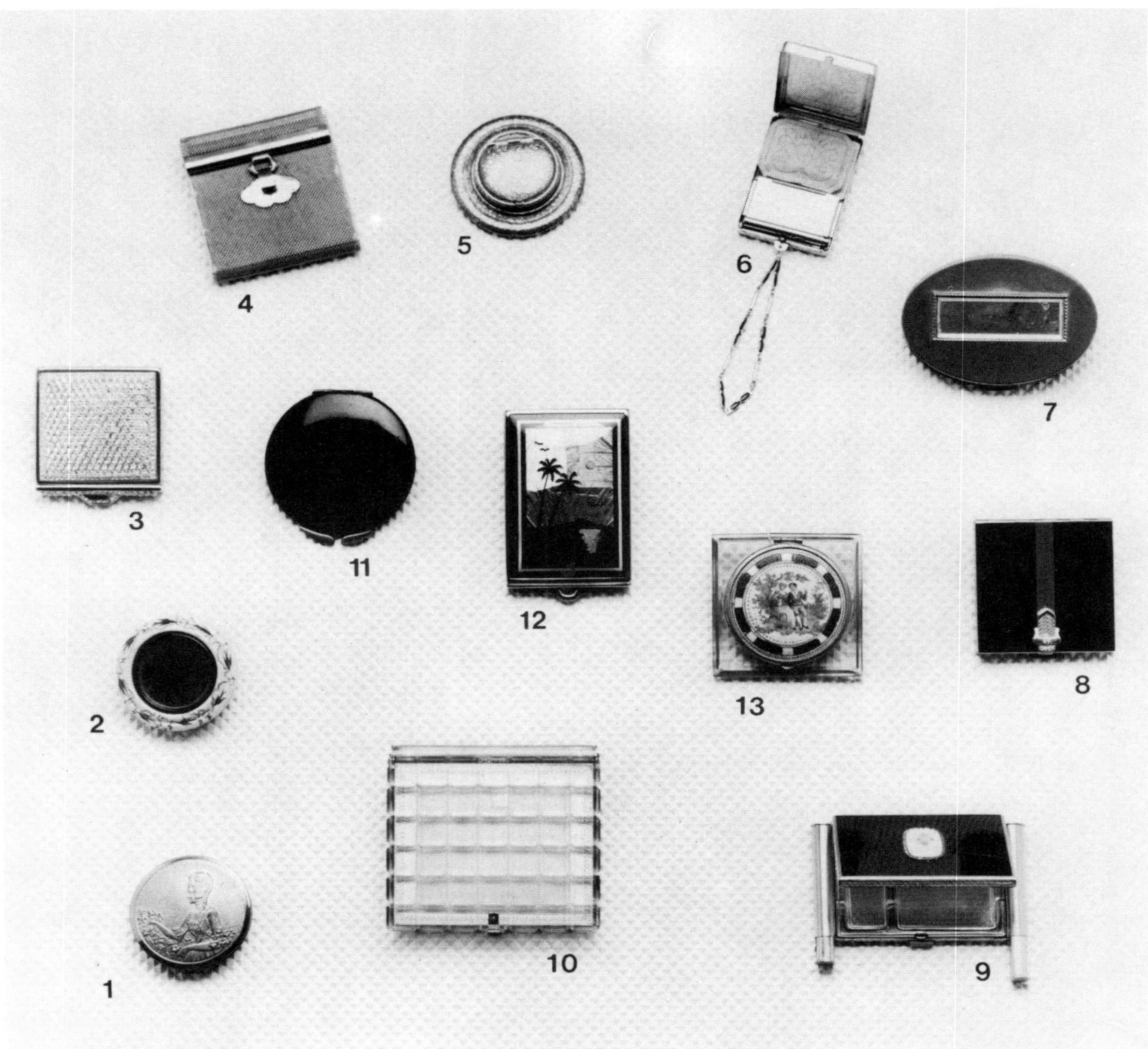

Fig. 125

1 Norida hammered goldtone-metal compact with powder sifter, c. 1920s.

2 French ivory compact with mirror encircled with bluebirds on lid; "Compliments of Van Raalte" on inner lid.

3 Rhinestone silvered-metal compact, c. 1930s.

4 Volupté rigid goldtone mesh compact with buckle closure.

5 Embossed goldtone cookie-shaped compact, c. 1910.

6 Woodworth "Karess" blue enamel goldtone vanity case with carrying chain and compartments for powder, rouge, and lipstick, c. 1920s.

7 Rex Fifth Avenue oval red enamel goldtone compact; lid inset with mirror.

8 Volupté black enamel and goldtone buckle-motif compact.

9 La Mode black enamel vanity case with painted enamel disk on lid; powder and rouge compartments and sliding lipstick on either side.

10 Wadsworth crystal deep-cut cross-bar plastic compact with polished goldtone back, c. 1930s.

11 Gucci black enamel goldtone compact.

12 Oblong black enamel polished goldtone compact with colorful butterfly-wing scene under clear plastic on lid, c. 1930s.

13 Compact set into square yellow plastic frame with transfer scene on lid.

Fig. 126

1 Engine-turned brass-tone metal vanity case with multicolored stones encrusted on lid; powder and rouge compartments and carrying chain.

2 Enameled silvered-metal miniature vanity case with powder sifter and rouge compartment; finger-ring chain, c. 1920s.

3 Silvered-metal compact decorated with red stones.

4 Black silk compact decorated with beaded pink fan, France.

5 Silvered-metal compact designed in shape of a hat with repoussé cherub on lid.

6 Imperial-plate goldtone-metal vanity case with flower design on lid; finger-ring chain, c. 1920s.

7 Daniel satin-finish goldtone compact with three-dimensional white plastic courting scene under plastic dome.

8 Engraved silvered-metal powder-vial container with puff, metal mirror, and finger-ring chain.

9 Damascene scalloped goldtone compact with windmill scene on lid.

10 Engraved, embossed goldtone compact with harlequin-shaped lid decorated with two large yellow stones, France.

11 Oval goldtone compact with blue plastic lid set with faux gems.

Fig. 127

1 R & G Co. sterling-top mesh vanity bag with painted flowers on white cloisonné lid; powder and rouge compartments and double-faced mirror; carrying chain and sapphire cabochon thumbpiece.

2 Silver mesh vanity bag with Japanese lettering and painted black bamboo shoots on blue enamel lid, tassel and black braided carrying cord; mirror and powder and rouge compartments.

3 Whiting & Davis blue, white, and yellow mesh vanity bag with blue sapphire cabochon thumbpiece, c. 1915.

4 R & G Co. sterling-top mesh vanity bag with painted flowers on white cloisonné lid; powder and rouge compartments, double-faced mirror, carrying chain, and sapphire cabochon thumbpiece.

5 Alpacca silvered mesh vanity bag with blue enamel lid and carrying chain, Germany.

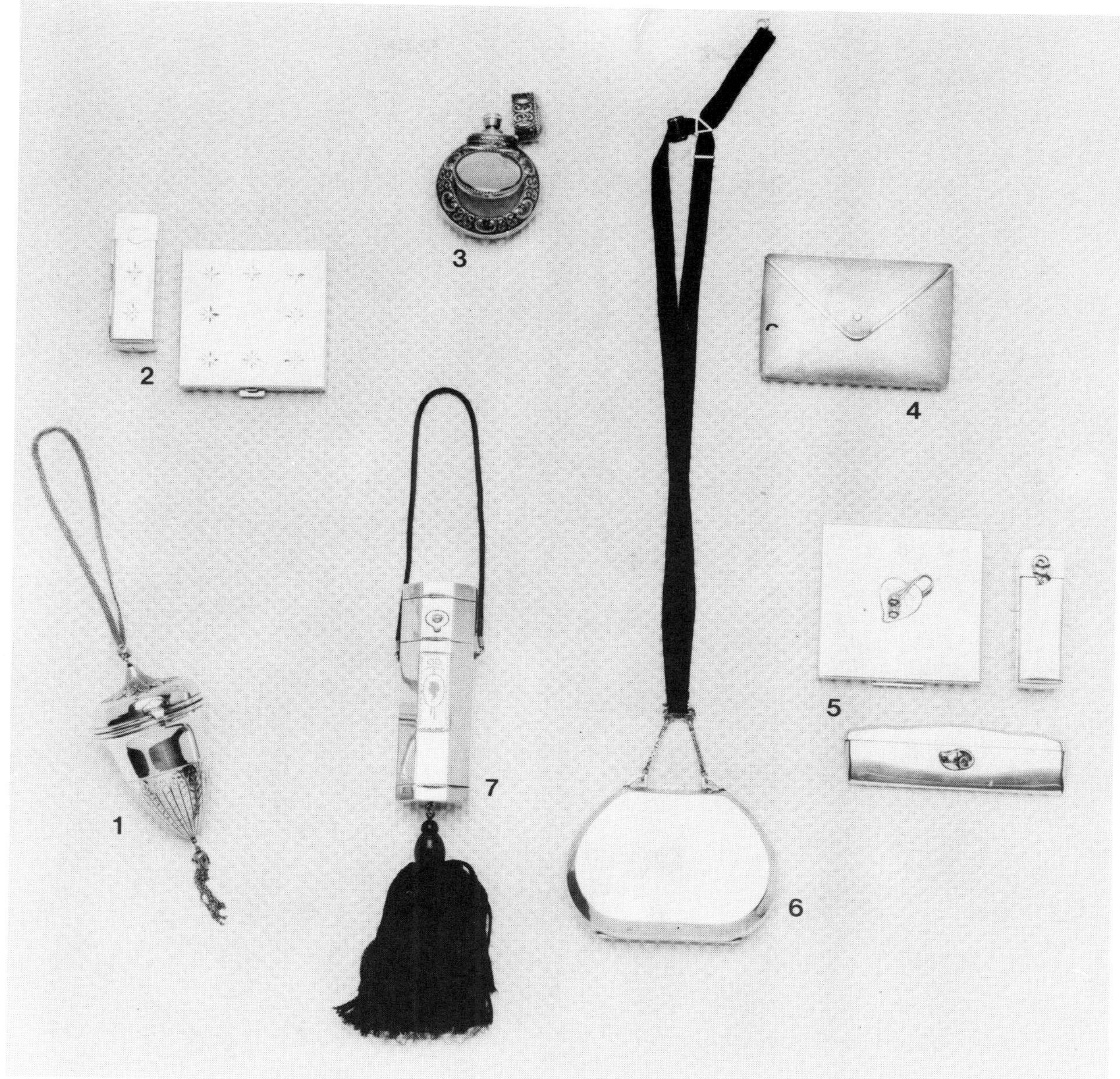

Fig. 128

1 Silver embossed acorn-shaped vanity case with tassel and mesh chain; powder and rouge compartments, turn of the century.

2 Tiffany & Co. sterling-silver compact and lipstick-case set with etched snowflakes.

3 Sterling-silver compact/perfume combination with repoussé leaf design around edges, Germany, turn of the century.

4 Tiffany & Co. sterling-silver antique-finish compact designed to resemble envelope, Italy.

5 Sterling-silver compact, lipstick, and comb set with grape leaf, possibly Georg Jensen.

6 Sterling hallmarked purse-motif vanity case with carrying cord; powder and rouge compartments, lipstick tube, and mirror, England, turn of the century.

7 Sterling-silver hallmarked necessaire, silhouettes on lid and front; cord and tassel; sliding lipstick and compartments for powder, rouge, and cigarettes.

Fig. 129

1 Yardley "Quadruple" goldtone carryall with black enamel (flying horse) intaglio decoration; interior contains powder, rouge, lipstick, perfume, and bill-clip; coral cabochon thumbpiece, c. 1940s.

2 Three-sided brown sponge-effect enameled minaudière with mesh carrying handle; first sectioned compartment for powder and rouge; second for cigarettes, coin holder, and billfold; third for comb, necessities, writing slate, retrievable brass pencil, mirror, and comb.

3 Fifth Avenue "Cosmetist" aquamarine enamel vanity case containing powder, rouge, lipstick, cleansing cream, and mascara, England.

4 Engraved goldtone carryall with carrying chain; compartments for powder, rouge, lipstick, coins, and billfold.

5 Silver-plated floral repoussé screw-lid compact and puff compartment; "H. Reade, Nov. 19, '92" inscribed on lids, probably England.

6 M.M.R's black plastic triangular vanity case with red-stone design on lid; red and black carrying ribbon; compartments for powder, rouge, and lipstick, c. 1920s.

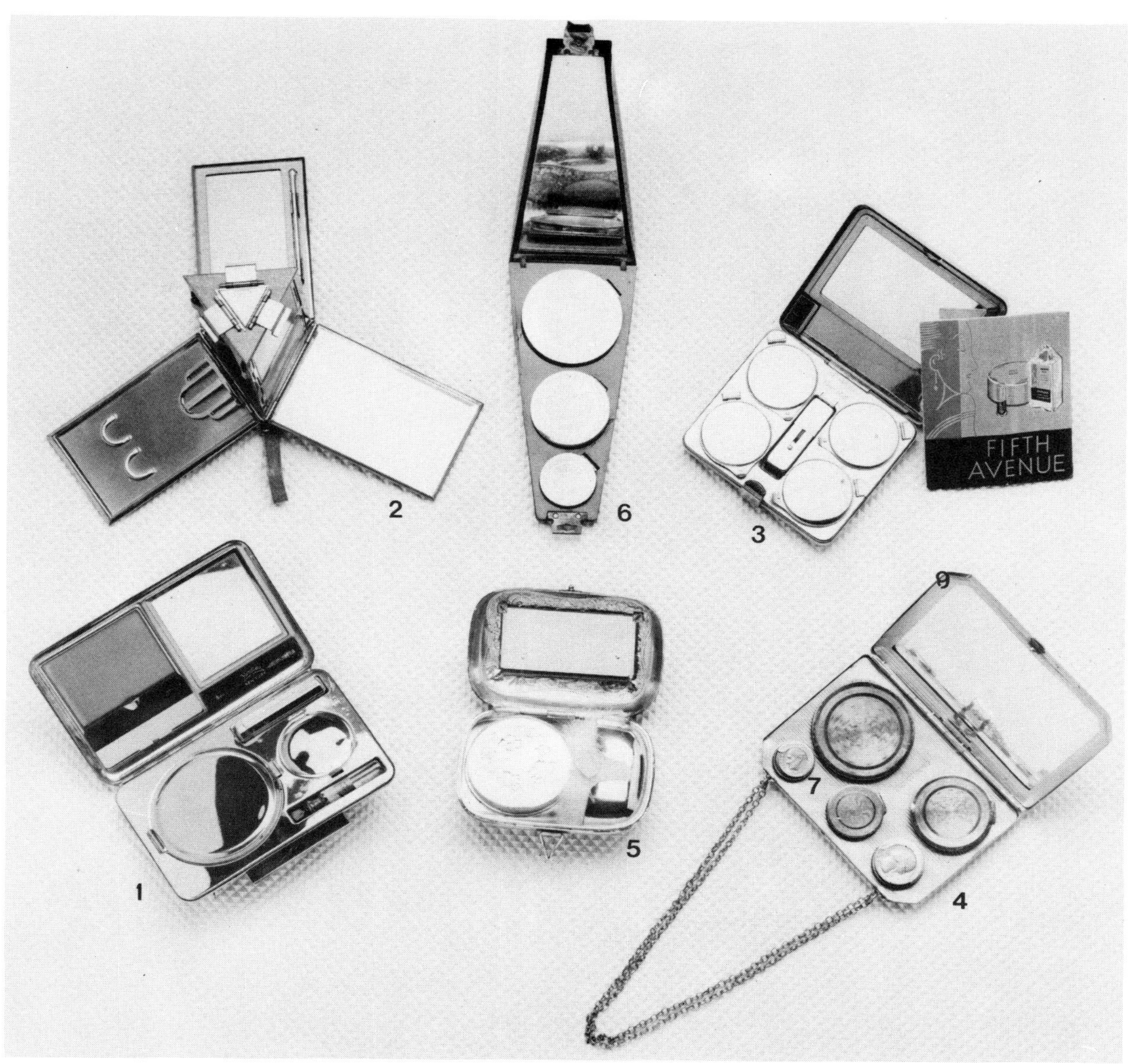

Fig. 130 Compacts shown in Figure 129 shown open.

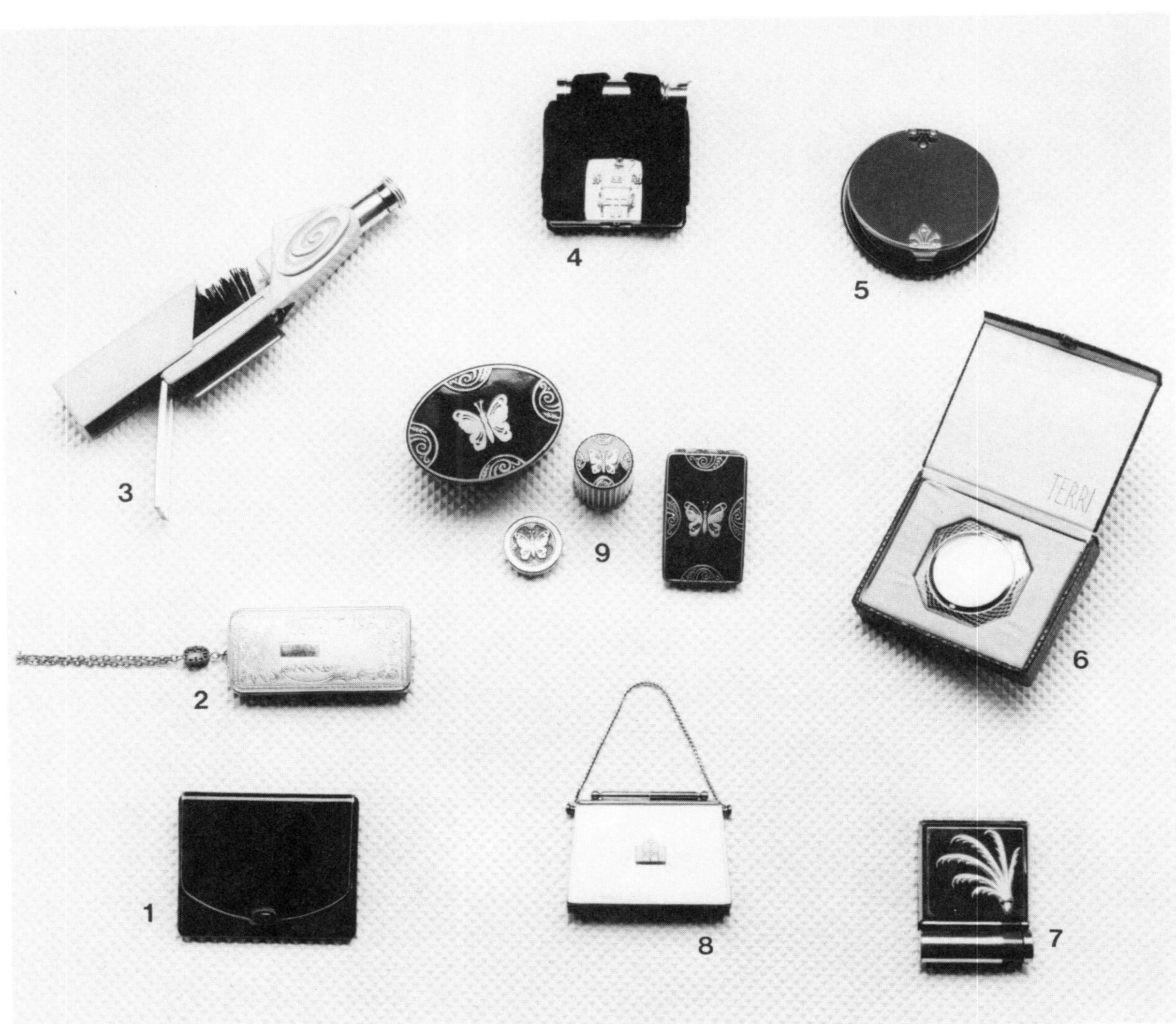

Fig. 131

1 Brown marbleized enamel compact designed to resemble envelope, with cabochon blue stone on lid, Germany.

2 Richard Hudnut "Du Barry Beauty Box" engraved goldtone vanity box with carrying chain; compartments for powder, rouge, and lipstick.

3 Light blue plastic novelty carryall with concealed compact, lipstick, hairbrush, and comb.

4 Flato goldtone compact with jeweled horse and carriage mounted on lid in blue velvet protective case with lipstick sleeve.

5 Kreisler red and black enamel goldtone compact with ornate hinge and closure.

6 Terri octagonal goldtone compact with scalework engraved edges and dancers on lid; original fitted presentation box.

7 Yardley goldtone vanity case with white enamel feather on lid; powder and rouge compartments and tandem lipstick, c. 1940s.

8 Satin goldtone compact designed to resemble purse, with blue enamel disk on lid, carrying chain.

9 Lucretia Vanderbilt blue enamel silvered-metal set decorated with silver butterflies: miniature round compact, oblong vanity case, boudoir-size face powder container, and sample-size extract container.

Fig. 132

1 Silvered and goldtone vanity case with blue enamel profile of woman on lid; faded blue tassel and carrying cord; compartments for powder, rouge, and lipstick, turn of the century.

2 Art Deco blue enamel and goldtone vanity case with compartments for powder and rouge.

3 Sterling-silver hallmarked Art Nouveau compact with silhouette of dancing woman; carrying cord and tassel.

4 D. F. Briggs Co. engine-turned silvered carryall with oval disk of woman applying makeup centered and black enamel border; carrying chain and compartments for powder, rouge, lipstick, coins, and necessities.

5 Chantrey bronze-colored metal vanity case and lipstick set with red and black silhouettes of man and woman.

6 Black and white enamel vanity case with compartments for powder and lipstick.

7 Richard Hudnut "Le Debut" octagonal vanity case with black-enamel celestial scene; powder and rouge compartments and finger-ring chain.

8 E.A.M. Art Deco blue enamel tango-chain with red and yellow abstract design; powder sifter and attached lipstick; finger-ring chain, c. 1920s.

9 E.A.M. Art Deco enameled compact with blue, yellow, and gray abstract design; powder sifter and carrying chain, c. 1920.

10 Octagonal Art Deco compact with pink, yellow, and blue abstract design; powder sifter and carrying chain, c. 1920.

11 Horseshoe-shaped pewter and leather zippered compact with repoussé woman on lid.

Fig. 133

1, 2 Goldtone and black lip-blotter tissue case with mirrored lid (**1** shown closed, **2** shown open).

3 Dorothy Gray engine-turned goldtone compact designed to resemble a hat, c. 1940s.

4 Lederer "Sacs" goldtone compact with red pompom black suede beret; original presentation box, France.

5 Miniature red enamel goldtone bolster-shaped compact (shown open).

6 Multicolored micro-mosaic goldtone compact, Italy.

7 Wadsworth polished and satin-finish engraved compact designed to resemble a fan.

8 Octagonal wood-marquetry compact inlaid with light and dark wood veneers.

9 Brass cookie-shaped basketweave compact, c. 1920s.

10 Langlois "Shari" green enamel and goldtone vanity case with compartments for powder, rouge, and lipstick (shown open).

11, 12 Two goldtone and red cloisonné compacts in original silk-lined leather fitted presentation box (**11** shown open, **12** shown closed).

13 Goldtone tango-chain vanity case with black painted strapwork.

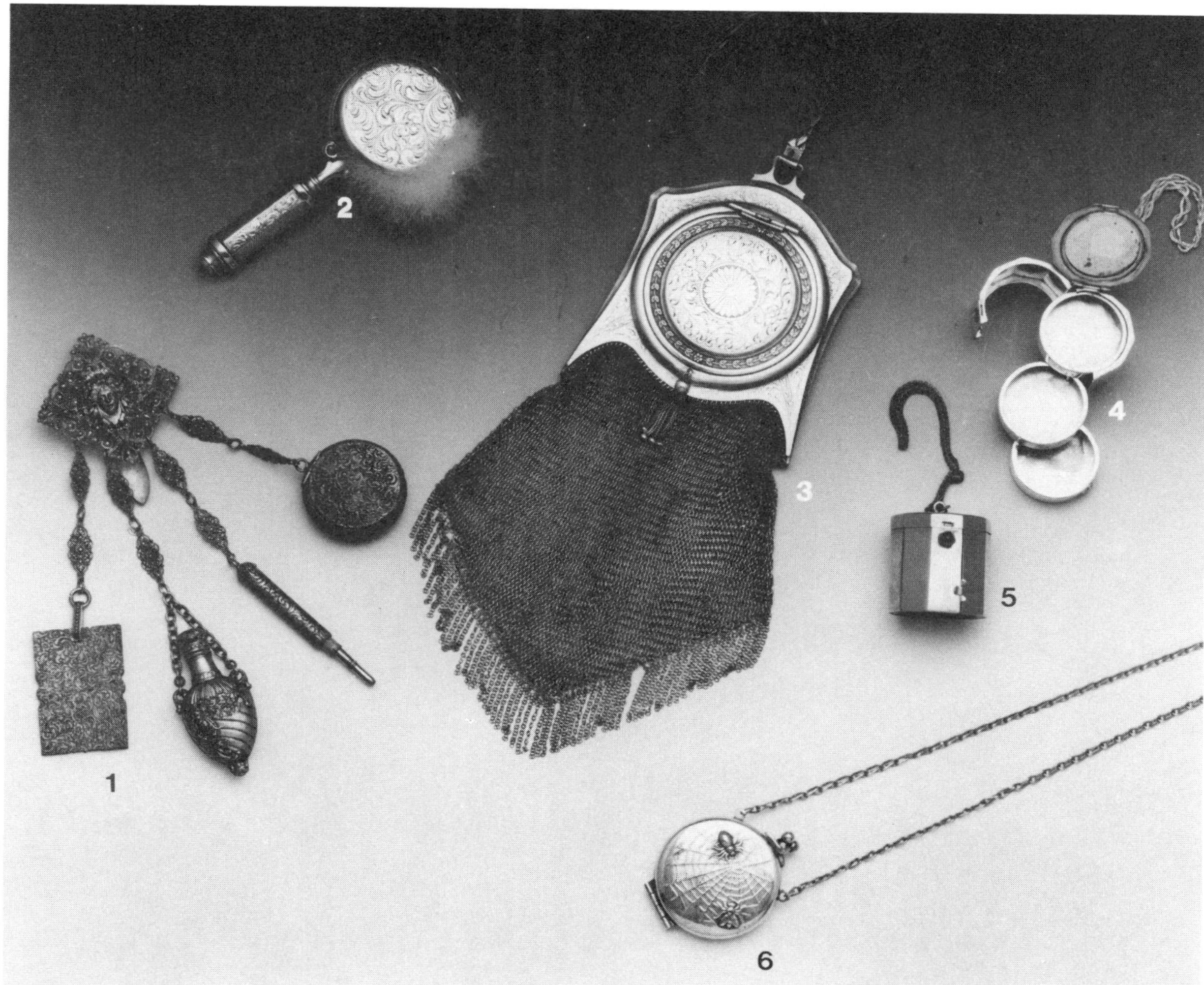

Fig. 134

1 Antiqued silver-filigree and engraved belt chatelette with compact, pencil, perfume holder, and writing slate, Continental, 19th century.

2 Engraved silver compact shaped as a hand mirror with lipstick in handle, Italy, turn of the century.

3 Whiting & Davis silvered mesh vanity bag with etched and engraved lid and braided carrying chain, c. 1920s.

4, 5 Powder-Tier triple-tier vanity case with swivel compartments for powder, rouge, and lipstick, c. 1920s (**4**, sterling silver, shown open; **5**, silvered metal, shown closed).

6 Silvered compact with spider and fly repoussé on both sides; neck chain.

Fig. 135

1 Simulated, painted enamel goldtone compact/cigarette-case combination with tandem lipstick and carrying chain.

2 Kigu silvered and goldtone compact/cigarette-case combination with tandem lipstick and carrying chain, England, c. 1940–50s.

3 Dorothy Gray textured goldtone compact with buckle design on lid; tandem lipstick.

4 Evans goldtone and mother-of-pearl compact/lipstick combination, c. 1940–50s.

5 Yardley engine-turned goldtone vanity case with picture centered on lid; lipstick, swivel tandem metal mirror, and powder and rouge compartments, c. 1930s.

6 Flato goldtone compact with open umbrella mounted on lid; lipstick sleeve in black faille case.

7 Yardley enamel and goldtone vanity case with enameled flowers on lid; lipstick, swivel tandem metal mirror, and powder and rouge compartments, c. 1930s.

8 Black mother-of-pearl goldtone compact with small crown on lid; lipstick and perfume container on either side.

9 Black silk compact with multicolored embroidered flowers; lipstick in lid.

10 Satin-finish metal compact with rhinestone lid and tandem lipstick, c. 1930s (shown open).

11 Evans goldtone and red leather compact/lipstick combination, c. 1940–50s.

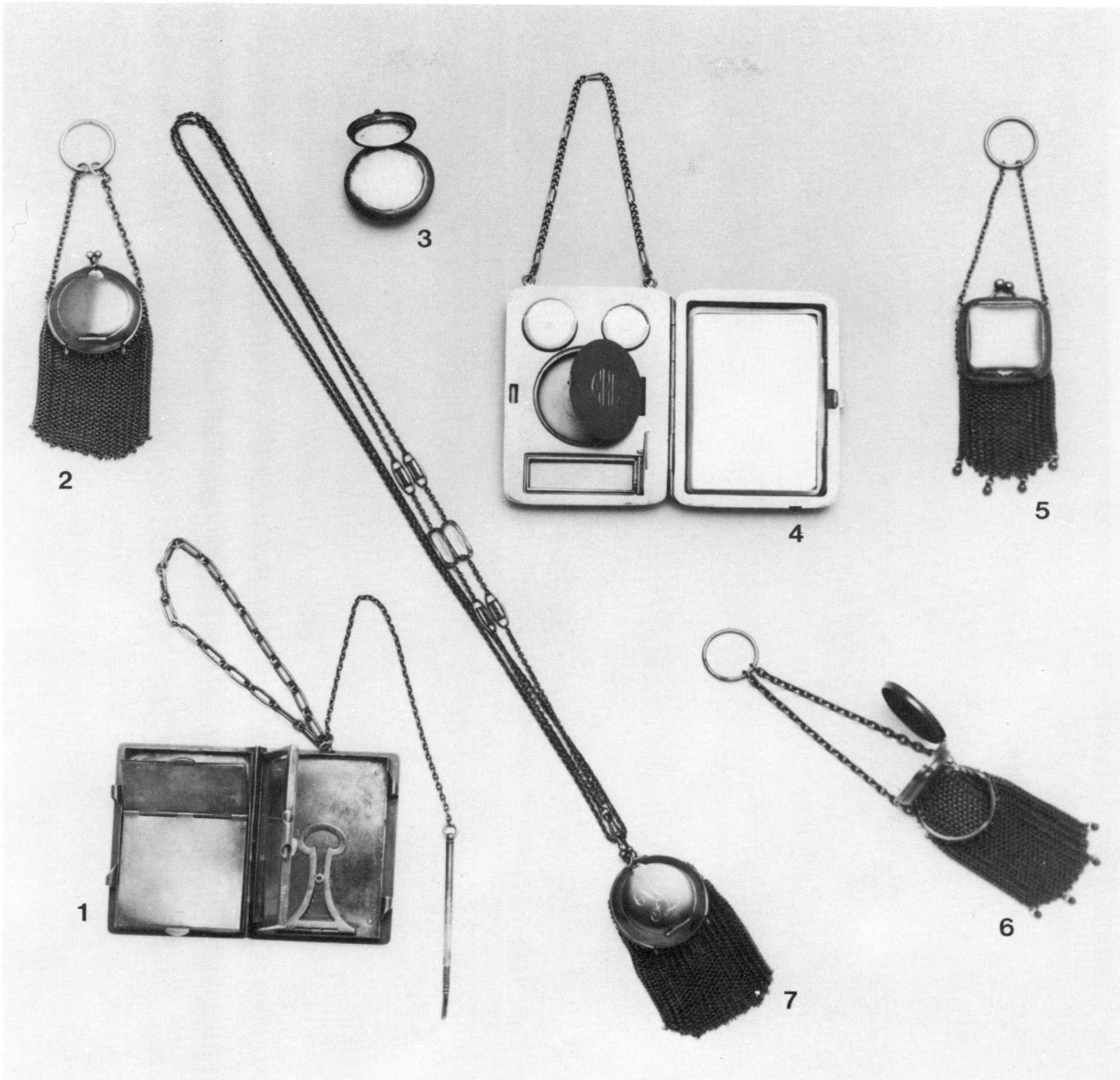

Fig. 136

1 Gun-metal mini carryall designed to resemble book, with four faux amethysts on lid; carrying chain and compartments for powder, rouge, bills, writing slate, and slim metal pencil (shown open).

2 Gun-metal mini mesh vanity bag with diminishing mirror and finger-ring chain, France.

3 Gun-metal mini compact with loop for chain, Germany.

4 Gun-metal black beaded mini carryall monogrammed ERC; carrying chain and compartments for powder, lipstick, and coins (shown open).

5 Gun-metal mini-mesh vanity bag with finger-ring chain.

6 Gun-metal mini-mesh vanity bag with finger-ring chain, France.

7 Gun-metal mini-mesh vanity bag with monogrammed lid; diminishing mirror and neck chain, France.

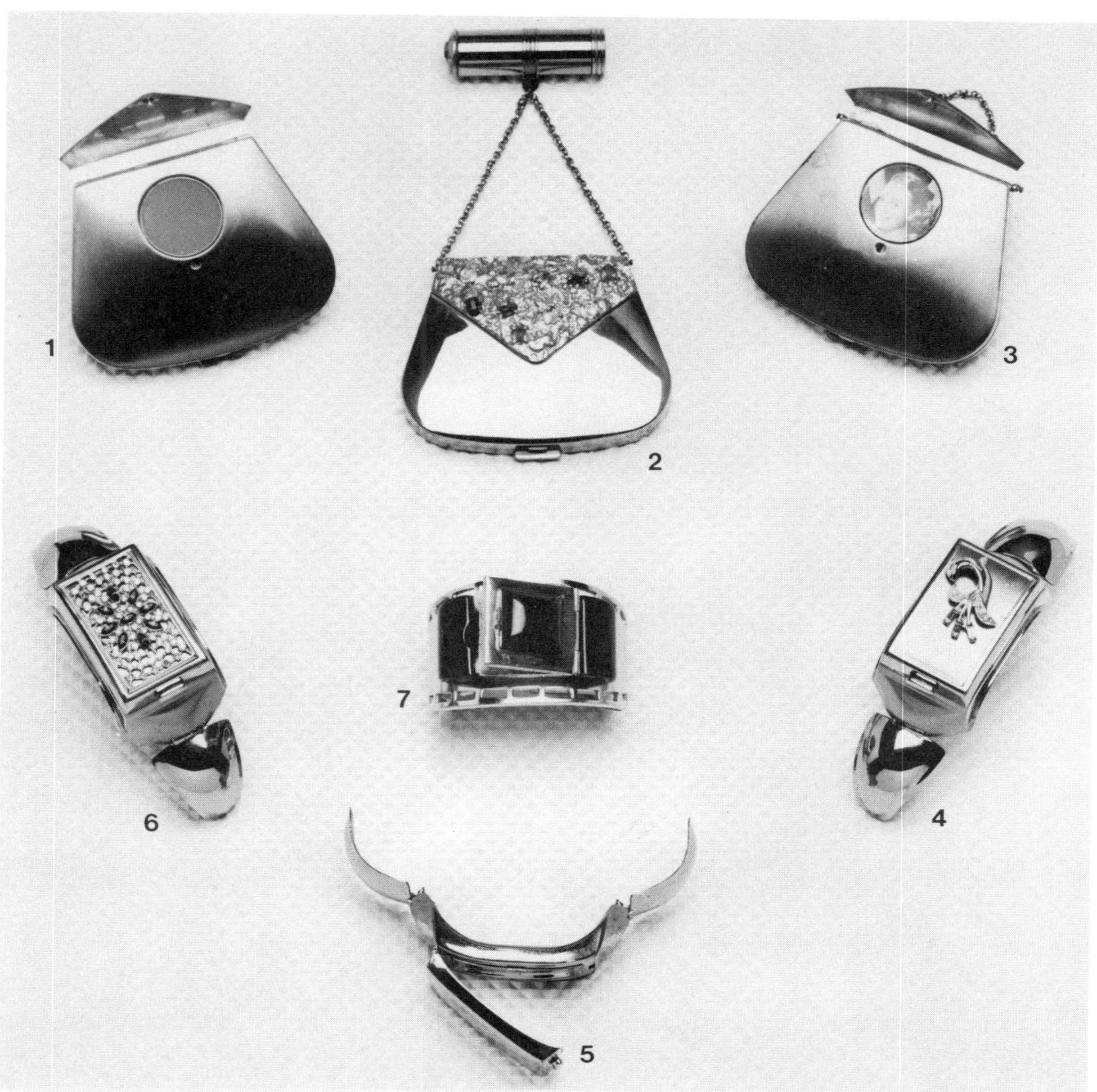

Fig. 137

1 Volupté "Lucky Purse" satin-finish metal compact; outer lid reveals rouge, c. 1940s (shown open).

2 Volupté "Lucky Purse" polished-metal tango-chain compact with multicolored stones; lipstick, c. 1940s.

3 Volupté "Lucky Purse" satin-finish metal compact; outer lid reveals picture locket, c. 1940s (shown open).

4 K & K polished satin-finish compact/bracelet set with pearls and blue stones; hinged bracelet.

5 K & K polished satin-finish compact/bracelet; hinged bracelet (shown open).

6 K & K polished satin-finish compact/bracelet set with rhinestones and red stones; hinged bracelet.

7 Deva-Dassy polished goldtone compact/bracelet set with large green stones, France.

Fig. 138

1 Hexagonal engine-turned brass tango-chain compact.

2 Sterling-silver engraved miniature compact with locket mounted on top.

3 Brass ball compact with pair of dice under plastic dome lid.

4 Champlevé goldtone compact with painted ivory disk on lid, Italy.

5 Goldtone miniature compact with Limoges painting set in pearl disk on filigree lid.

6 Green champlevé and vermeil compact, Italy.

7 Green cloisonné and silver four-leaf-clover vanity case with painted flowers on lid; goldtone interior; metal mirror and powder sifter and rouge compartment, c. 1920s.

8 Evans engine-turned nickel-silver triangular vanity case with yellow cloisonné lid with painted flowers; powder and rouge compartments and through handle.

9 Terri blue plastic compact with silver dancers on metal lid.

10 Goldtone compact with micro-mosaic flowers on lid and four stones set around base.

11 Divine miniature orange enamel compact with white silhouette on lid.

12 Divine miniature pink enamel compact with white picture on lid (shown open).

13 Divine miniature yellow compact with painted picture of woman on lid.

14 White enamel compact with molded pink and green plastic floral design on lid, c. 1930s.

15 Flato goldtone compact with etched cat with green cabochon stone eyes on lid; lipstick sleeve in maroon velvet case, c. 1950s.

16 Blue enamel goldtone compact with multicolored painted flowers on lid, France.

17 Cheramy "Cappi" goldtone vanity case with powder and rouge compartments and sliding mirror, c. 1920s (shown open).

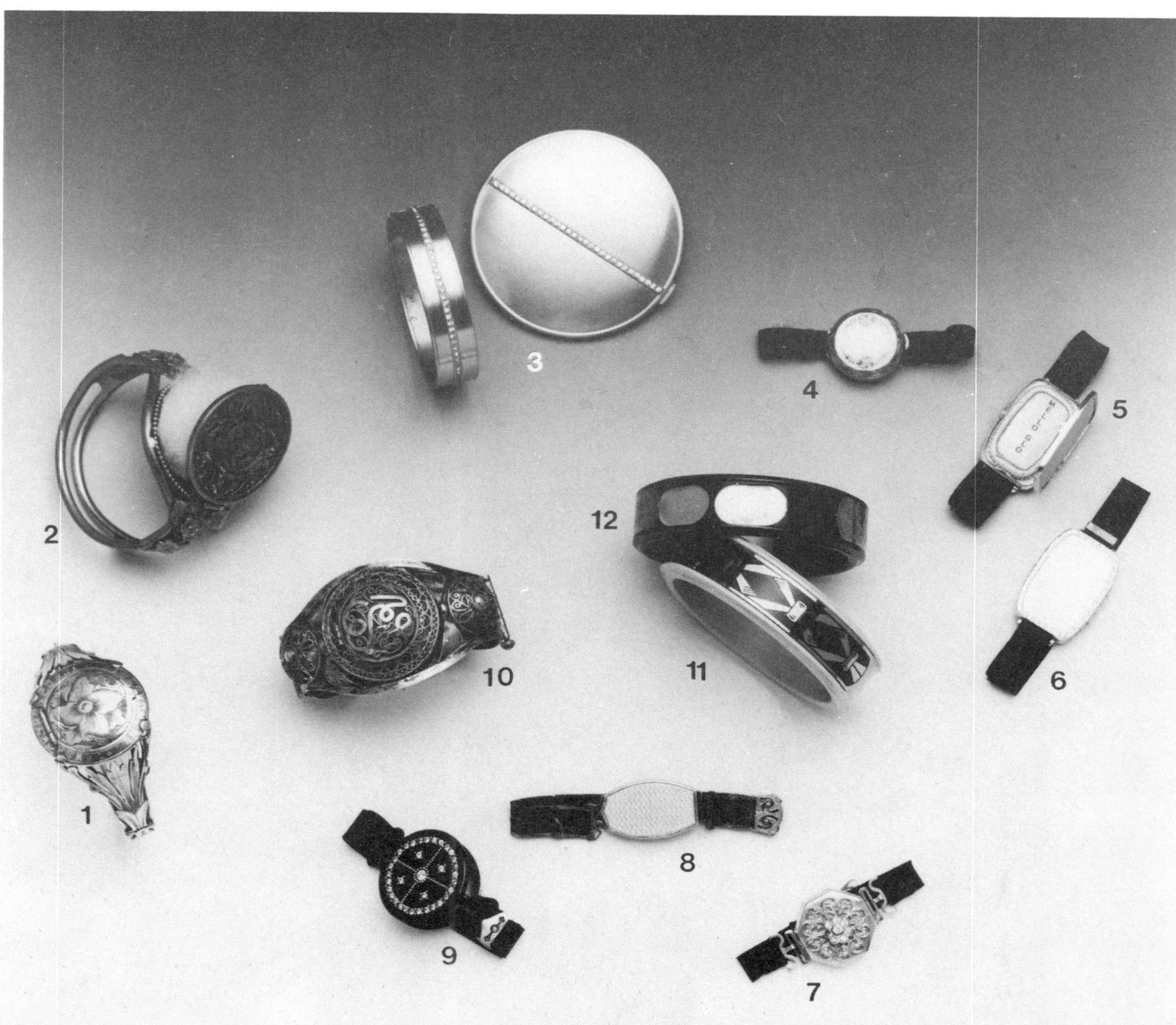

Fig. 139

1 E. A. Bliss Co. vermeil nickel-silver compact/bracelet with etched floral decoration on lid; applied cutout leaf-shape metal band, turn of the century.

2 F. J. Co. antique goldtone compact/bracelet with filigree lid and flowers on band, c. 1930s.

3 La Mode satin-finish flapjack vanity case and bracelet set with rhinestone trim.

4 Sterling-silver hallmarked vermeil cloisonné compact/bracelet with painted flowers on lid and grosgrain band, Continental.

5, 6 Mello-Glo nickel-silver "Wrist Compact" with grosgrain band, c. 1920s.

7 Octagonal goldtone compact/bracelet with rhinestone and filigree overlay on lid and grosgrain band.

8 Sterling-silver hallmarked blue cloisonné compact/bracelet with black grosgrain band, Continental, turn of the century.

9 Black plastic compact/bracelet set with rhinestones; grosgrain band, c. 1920s.

10 Silvered compact/bracelet with filigree and engraved decoration; removable pin-hinge closure, Continental, 19th century.

11, 12 Marlowe Co. "Parisienne" plastic cosmetic bracelet with decorative metal band that slides to reveal two mirrors and five cosmetic compartments (**11**, ivory, shown closed, **12**, black, shown open).

Fig. 140

1 French ivory plastic bolster-shaped vanity case with rhinestones and blue stones; faded blue carrying cord with lipstick concealed in tassel, c. 1920s.

2 Crystal plastic compact with blue Wedgwood disk on lid.

3 Vani-Pak black plastic compact/cigarette-case combination with sliding mirror (shown open).

4 Black plastic vanity case with rhinestone geometric design on lid; front opens to reveal mirror and powder and rouge compartments; back contains coin pocket; black carrying cord with lipstick concealed in tassel, c. 1920s.

5 Richelieu yellow plastic egg-shaped vanity case with monogrammed lid; powder and rouge compartments.

6 Goldtone and orange plastic compact with filigree overlay on lid set with stones; neck chain.

7 Oval simulated-tortoise shell plastic compact with raised grape and leaf design on lid; sterling-silver catches, c. 1940s.

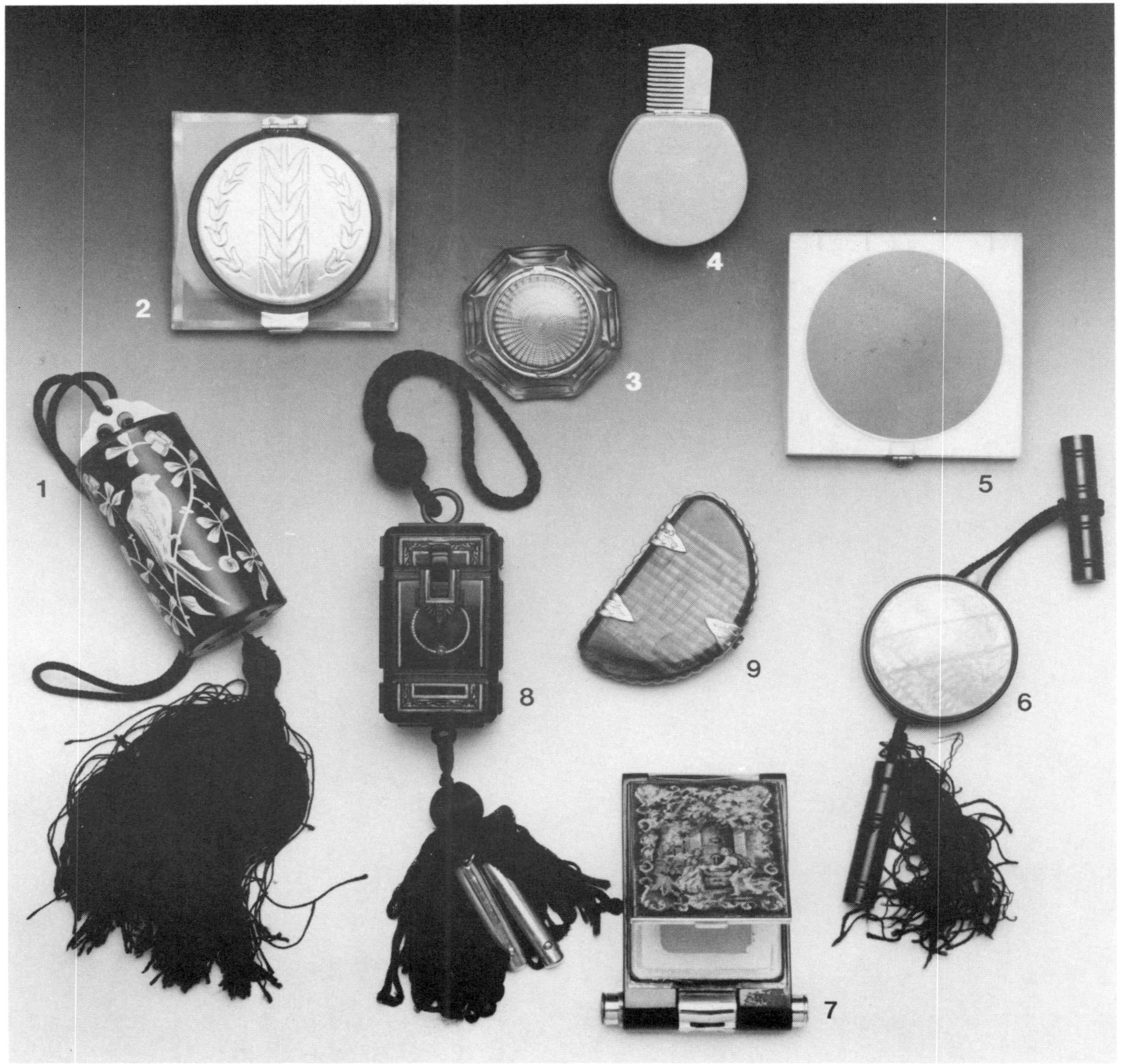

Fig. 141

1 Black plastic bolster-shaped vanity case with French ivory bird and trees, c. 1920s.

2 Crafters crystal Lucite compact with embossed chrome lid, c. 1940s.

3 Clear yellow plastic octagonal compact with green cloisonné lid and mirror on back, c. 1930s.

4 Fuller horseshoe-shaped marbleized-plastic mini compact with comb in lid, c. 1920s.

5 Lenthéric square Lucite and black compact, c. 1940s.

6 Yellow marbleized and black compact; perfume container on carrying cord; lipstick concealed in tassel.

7 Evans "Air-Flo" black plastic vanity case with tapestry lid; rouge and lipstick contained at base, c. 1930s.

8 Rectangular ebony plastic vanity case with engraved goldtone decoration and hinged clasp; carrying cord with lipstick and rouge concealed in tassel.

9 Shields Inc. amber plastic halfmoon-shaped compact with metal mirror and silvered and goldtone hinges.

Fig. 142

1 K & K brass-colored, engine-tooled, basket-shaped compact with dice enclosed in plastic domed lid; embossed swinging handle.

2 Kigu engraved brass-colored, basket-shaped compact with filigree flowers centered with faux pearl on lid; embossed swinging handle, England, c. 1940–50s.

3 K & K brass-colored, engine-tooled, basket-shaped compact with embossed swinging handle (shown open).

4 K & K brass-colored, engine-tooled, basket-shaped compact with satin-finish lid and embossed swinging handle.

5 K & K brass-colored, engine-tooled, basket-shaped compact with multicolored silk flowers enclosed in plastic domed lid; embossed swinging handle.

6, 7 Brass walnut-motif compact; inner partition incorporates writing slate and diminishing mirror; compartments for powder and combination hinged scent bottle and pin holder; loop for chain, 19th century (**6** shown open, **7** shown closed).

8 Silvered-metal walnut-motif compact; inner partition has picture locket and diminishing mirror; compartments for powder and hinged scent bottle; loop for chain (shown open).

9 Zell goldtone engraved basket-motif compact with engraved pink and green flowers and embossed rigid handle.

10 Polished goldtone basket compact with red, white, and green painted flowers on lid and engraved swinging handle.

Fig. 143

1 Blue plastic sphere-shaped compact with multicolored plastic flowers; carrying cord and tassel.

2 Polished goldtone ball-shaped compact with roulette wheel enclosed in plastic domed lid.

3 Green lizard oval compact with brass decoration and closure and lizard wrist strap.

4 Ebony enamel "eight ball" compact.

5 Kigu brass musical globe compact, England, c. 1940–50s.

6 Henriette brass compact, c. 1930s (shown open).

7 Vogue Vanities "PomPom" ivory enamel ball compact decorated with painted flowers; powder sifter and multicolored tassel, England.

8 Enameled red, white, and blue air-balloon-motif compact; balloon basket contains rouge.

9 Asprey sterling-silver hallmarked miniature ball compact with vermeil blue enamel; loop for chain.

10 Henriette polished brass-ball compact with multicolored flowers enclosed in plastic domed lid, c. 1930s.

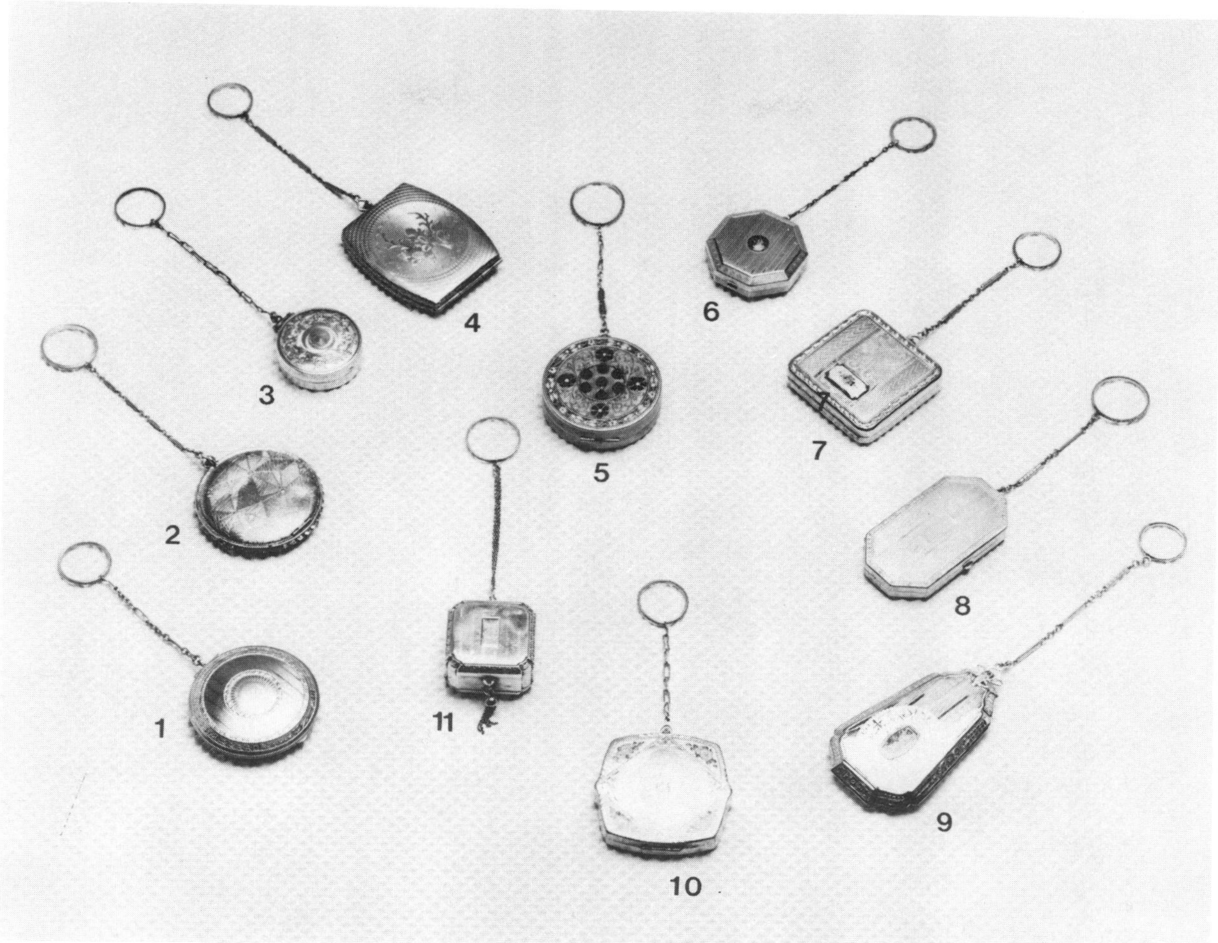

Fig. 144

1 Engine-turned silvered-metal vanity case with powder sifter, rouge compartment, and finger-ring chain, c. 1920–30s.

2 Etched silvered-metal compact with rhinestone decoration around rim and finger-ring chain, c. 1920–30s.

3 Silver-plated compact with finger-ring chain, c. 1920–30s.

4 Rounded-oblong silvered and goldtone vanity case with powder sifter, rouge compartment, and finger-ring chain, c. 1920–30s.

5 Engine-turned goldtone vanity case with blue and white enamel flowers set with cabochon blue stones; powder sifter, rouge compartments, and finger-ring chain, c. 1920–30s.

6 Engine-turned nickel-finish octagonal compact with green enamel disk on lid and finger-ring chain, c. 1920–30s.

7 May Fair goldtone vanity case with yellow cloisonné disk on lid; compartments for powder and rouge and finger-ring chain, c. 1920–30s.

8 Silvered goldtone oblong octagonal vanity case with powder and rouge compartments and finger-ring chain, c. 1920–30s.

9 Silver-plated engine-turned vanity case with green enamel disk on lid; powder sifter, rouge compartment and lipstick, and finger-ring chain, c. 1920–30s.

10 Engine-turned silvered-metal vanity case with yellow cloisonné on lid; powder and rouge compartments and finger-ring chain, c. 1920–30s.

11 Sterling-silver hallmarked double-sided vanity case with powder and rouge compartments and finger-ring chain, Continental.

Fig. 145

1 Stratton scalloped oblong multicolor enamel goldtone compact with lipstick in lid.

2 Volupté goldtone carryall with multicolored enameled animals on lid; compartments for powder, rouge, cigarettes, and comb.

3 K & K satin and polished goldtone diamond-shaped compact.

4 Coro halfmoon-shaped goldtone compact with enameled Persian design on lid.

5 Coro halfmoon-shaped satin and polished goldtone compact (shown open).

6 Miref engine-turned goldtone compact designed to resemble pocketwatch; carrying ring, France.

7 Rex Fifth Avenue red, white, and blue enamel oval compact with military emblem on lid.

8 Volupté scalloped goldtone compact with black enamel border and finger-ring cord.

9 Black silk vanity case with embroidered birds on lid; blue beaded tassel with green ojime bead and carrying ring; compartments for powder, rouge, and lipstick, c. 1920s.

10 Shaded yellow enamel horseshoe-shaped vanity case with coat-of-arms on lid; powder and rouge compartments.

11 Zell Fifth Avenue goldtone compact with picture locket in lid.

Fig. 146

1 Goldtone compact with painted peacock on plastic disk set with red stones.

2 Melba miniature oblong compact with enameled scene on lid.

3 Woodworth "Karess" polished goldtone vanity case with powder and rouge compartments, c. 1920s.

4 Navy blue enamel silvered-metal vanity case with marcasite flower on lid; lid opens to reveal pop-up-mirror and compartments for powder, rouge, and lipstick.

5 Pale yellow vanity case with raised mountain scenes; tassel and carrying cord; compartments for powder, rouge, and lipstick, c. 1920s.

6 Evans goldtone tap-sift powder compact with red enamel goldtone lid.

7 Multicolored damask compact with wallet-type closure and plastic ring on lid, France.

8 Estée Lauder Lucite compact with monogrammed metal lid.

9 Silvered-metal vanity case with abalone disk; "Chicago, Ill" printed on cover, c. 1920s.

10 Oblong engine-turned silvered-metal vanity case with raised basket on lid; sliding mirror reveals powder and rouge compartments.

Fig. 147

1 Mary Dunhill satin goldtone compact with hinges and thumbpiece set with rhinestones and green stones.

2, 3 Jet set, compact and matching pillbox.

4 Volupté brown oblong vanity case with compartments for powder, rouge, pills, and comb (shown open).

5 Silvered compact with purple enamel lid set with rhinestones.

6 Dorothy Gray blue enamel and silvered compact with mirror on outside lid.

7 Engine-turned nickel-finish compact/cigarette-case/lighter combination with raised giraffe and palm trees on lid.

8 Sterling-silver mini compact with yellow enameled lid decorated with flowers and finger-ring chain.

9 Harriet Hubbard Ayer engine-turned goldtone vanity case with center-opening compartments for powder, rouge, and lipstick (shown open).

10 Double-sided painted filigree metal vanity case set with colored stones; powder and rouge compartment and hanging bead chain.

11 Brown plastic compact with lid inset with embroidery under plastic; interior and exterior mirrors.

Fig. 148

1 Triangular goldtone compact with raised elephants.

2 Wadsworth bolster-shaped black enamel goldtone vanity case with compartments for powder, lipstick, and cigarettes (shown open).

3 Volupté satin and polished goldtone strapwork-design compact with raised flowers and small orange stones on lid.

4 Richard Hudnut marbleized blue plastic vanity case with silver-plated engraved lid; powder and rouge compartments; original fitted presentation box.

5 Painted plastic compact with ballet scene on lid.

6, 7 Stratton blue enamel scalloped compact and matching lipstick holder.

8 Beaded compact with multicolored beaded flowers on white beaded background, France.

9 Polished goldtone oblong vanity case with leaves on lid; powder and rouge compartments.

10 Vitoge polished goldtone compact and lipstick case with four-leaf clovers; protective carrying case.

11 Elgin American silvered compact with engraved lid.

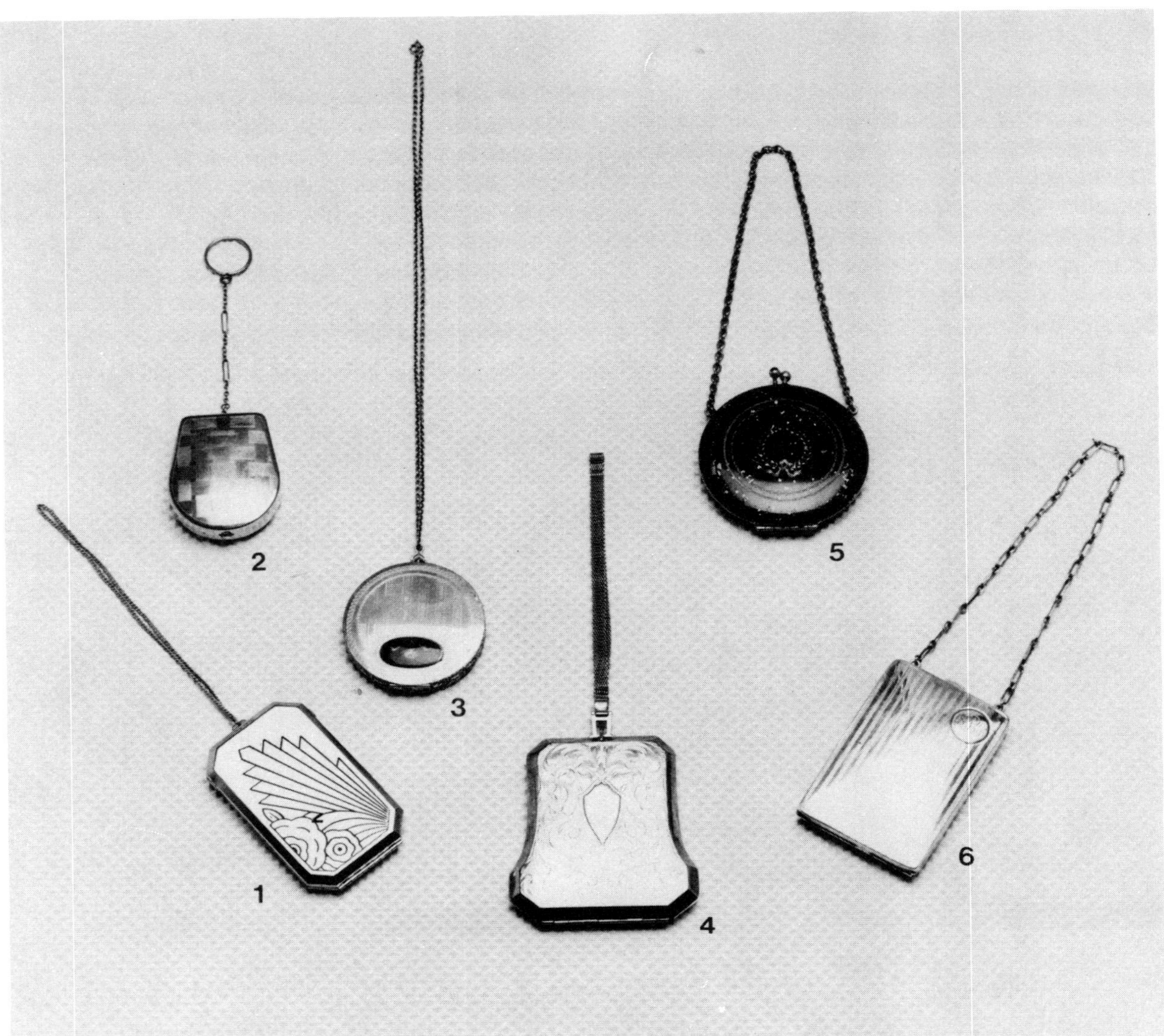

Fig. 149

1 Melba goldtone vanity case with blue enameled flower design on lid; carrying chain and compartments for powder, rouge, and lipstick.

2 Silvered-metal horseshoe-shaped vanity case with basketweave design on lid; powder and rouge compartments, swivel mirror, and finger-ring chain, c. 1920s.

3 D. F. Briggs Co. gold-filled engine-turned vanity case with enamel disk on lid; carrying chain and compartments for powder, rouge, lipstick, and eye makeup.

4 Goldtone engraved vanity case with mesh carrying chain and compartments for powder, rouge, lipstick, and coins.

5 Goldtone and green enamel vanity case with goldtone interior and green cabochon thumbpieces; carrying chain and compartments for powder and coins.

6 Sterling-silver hallmarked engine-turned vanity case with monogrammed lid; carrying chain and compartments for powder, coins, and bills, Continental.

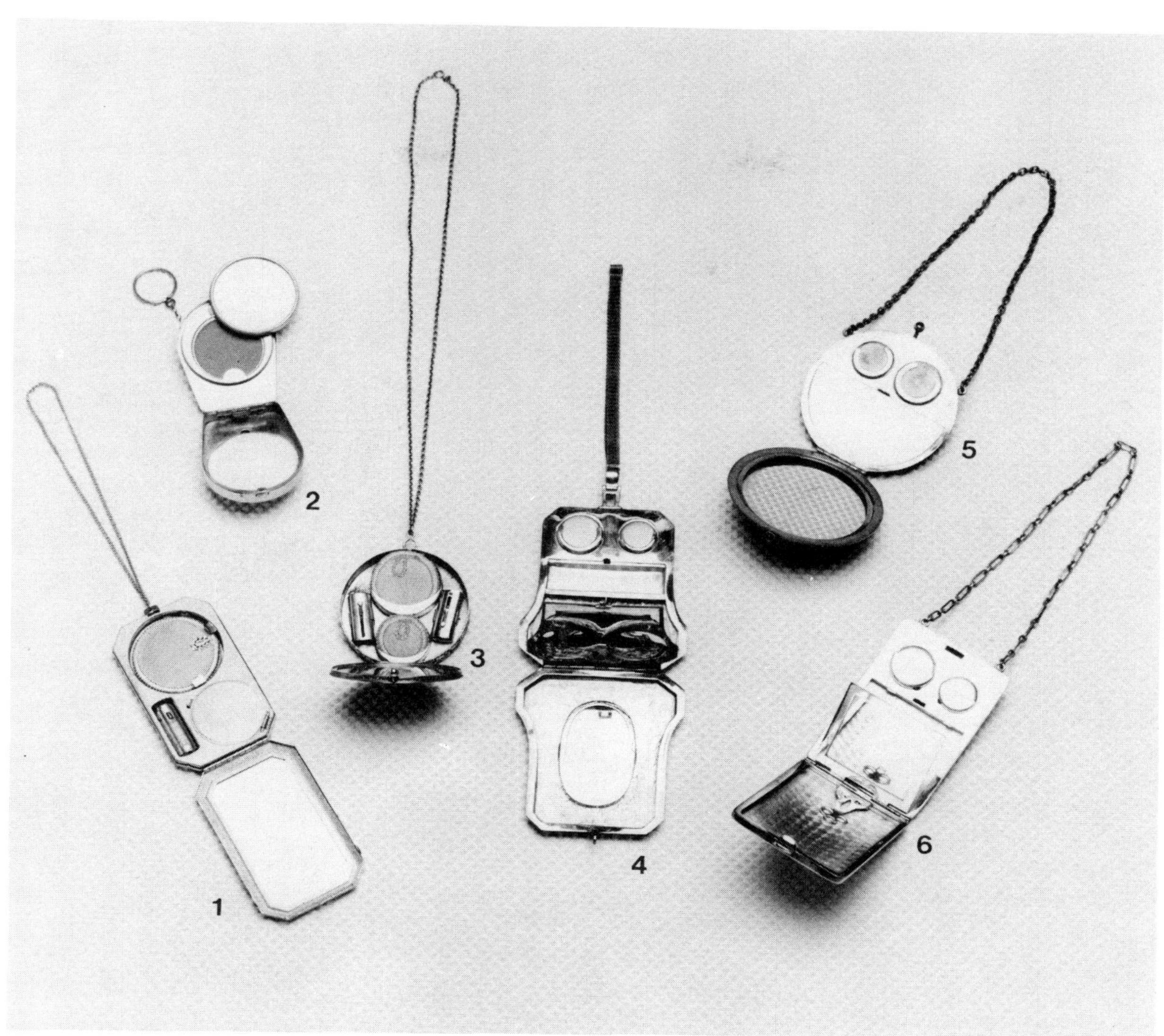

Fig. 150 Vanity cases in Figure 149 shown open.

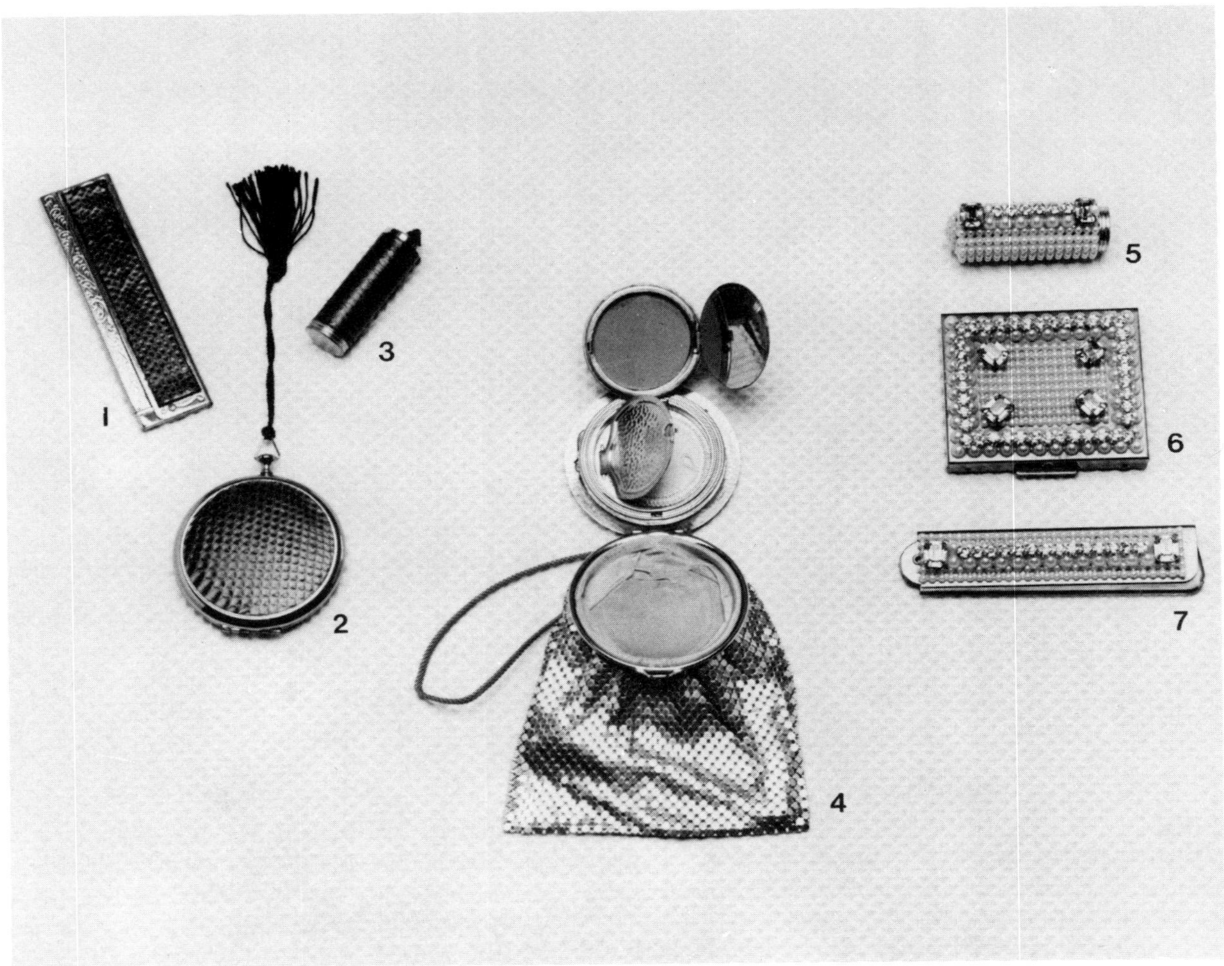

Fig. 151

1, 2, 3 Zell Fifth Avenue brown lizard compact, lipstick, and comb set; compact designed to resemble pocketwatch.

4 Silvered-mesh vanity bag with powder and rouge compartments and carrying chain (shown open).

5, 6, 7 Compact, lipstick, and comb set decorated with pearls, rhinestones, and blue stones.

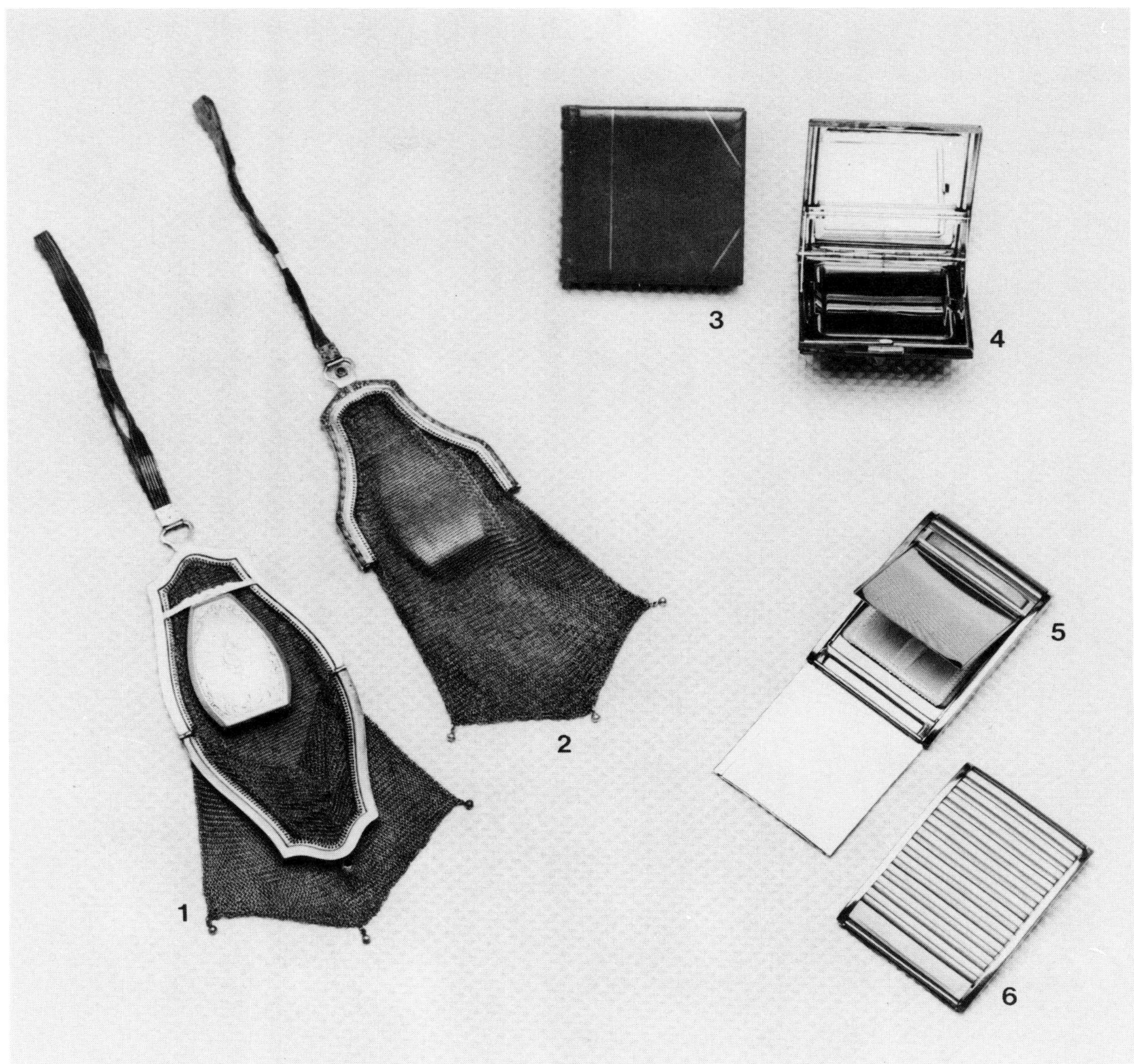

Fig. 152

1, 2 W B silvered-metal mesh vanity bag with compact suspended on bar inside bag, c. 1920s (**1** shown open, **2** shown closed).

3, 4 Dunhill "Clearview" brown leather windshield-wiper compact designed to resemble book, c. 1930s (**3** shown closed, **4** shown open).

5, 6 Blue enamel and goldtone roll-top compact, Germany, c. 1940s (**5** shown open, **6** shown closed).

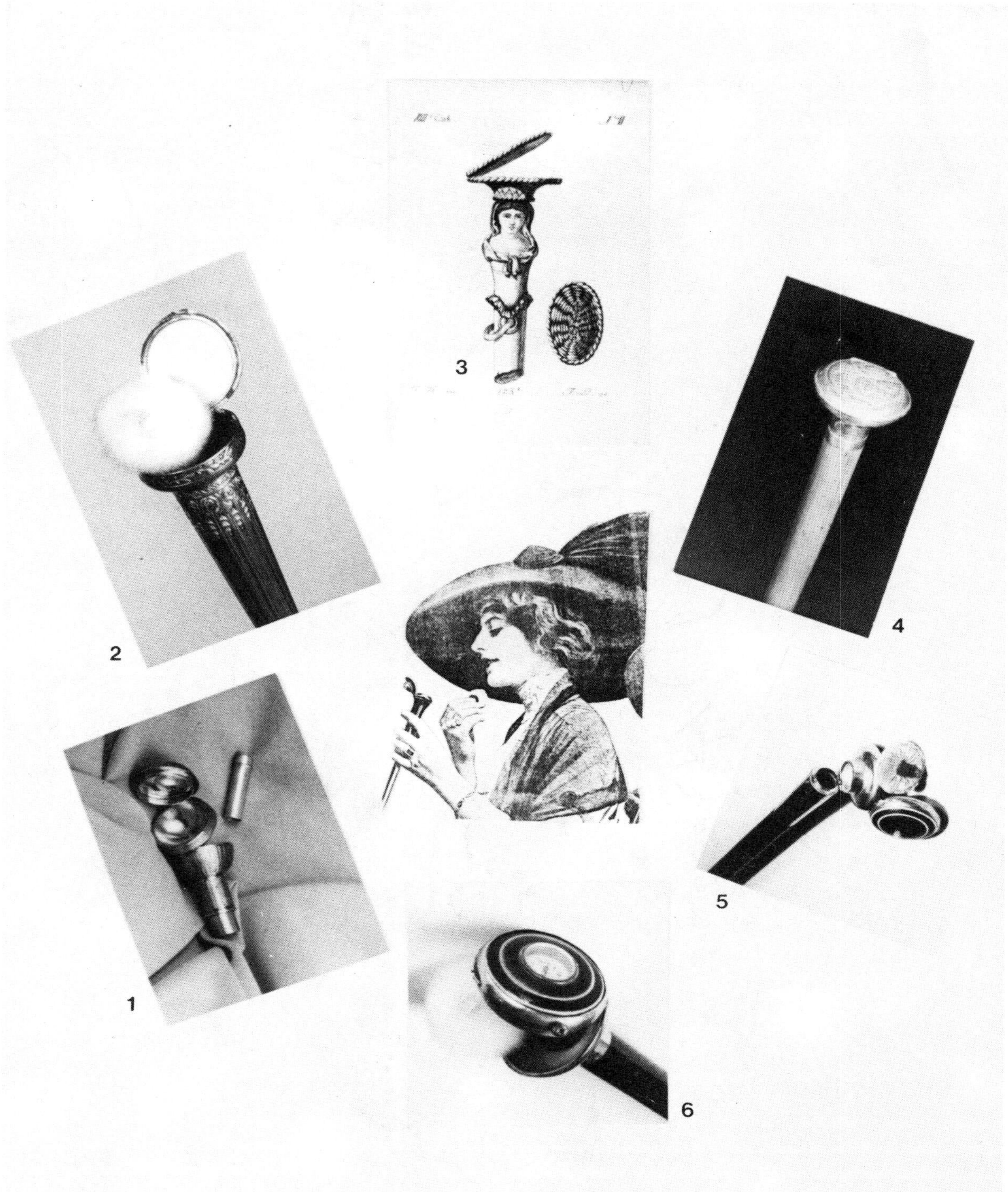

Fig. 153

1 Powder/lipstick/cane made to order for Hermès, Paris; lipstick slides into bottom part of handle, c. 1900s.

2 Silver compact/cane.

3 Compact/cane powder box, France, early 19th century.

4 Compact/cane (shown closed).

5 Compact/cane, hinged to allow access to lipstick or perfume bottle, c. 1912.

6 Compact/watch/cane with gold and green enamel case; white enamel watch dial with Swiss movement hidden under mirror, c. 1912.

Reproduced with permission from Catherine Dike, "Cane Curiosa."

Value Guide

IT is impossible to give absolute prices for articles as varied as compacts. Dealers' retail prices are determined by a number of factors:

Condition. Mint? Scratched, dented, cracked, or chipped? Mirror intact? Original puff, mirror, chain, and powder sifter? Original pouch and presentation box?

Production. Handmade? Mass-produced? Hand painted? Commissioned? Personalized? Limited edition?

Decoration. Precious metals, gold, silver? Silver plate, base metals? Precious stones—diamonds, rubies, emeralds, sapphires? Gemstones? Synthetic stones? Enameled? Manmade materials?

Maker or manufacturer?

Date of manufacture?

Place of purchase. Demand and selection varies from one part of the country to another.

This is merely an "average price range" Value Guide and not a price list. Prices may be higher or lower than listed depending on the above conditions. Values given are for items in mint condition and with original parts.

Value Listing

Fig. 1

	Amount ($)
	N/A

Fig. 2

	Amount ($)
	N/A

Fig. 3

	Amount ($)
1	300–350
2	125–150
3	250–350

Fig. 4

	Amount ($)
	200–250

Fig. 5

	Amount ($)
	VR

Fig. 6

	Amount ($)
	40–60

Fig. 7

	Amount ($)
	250–300

Fig. 8

	Amount ($)
	400–500R

Fig. 9

	Amount ($)
	60–80

Fig. 10

	Amount ($)
1	N/A
2	N/A

Fig. 11

	Amount ($)
	VR

Fig. 12

	Amount ($)
	R

Fig. 13

	Amount ($)
	VR

Fig. 14

	Amount ($)
	300–400

Fig. 15

	Amount ($)
1	VR
2	400–500
3	350–400

Figs. 16–18

	Amount ($)
	VR

Figs. 19–20

	Amount ($)
1	150–200
2	350–450
3	1,000–1,500

Fig. 21

	Amount ($)
1	40–60
2	75–100
3	30–50
4	150–200
5	60–80
6	100–120
7	50–70
8	60–100
9	80–100

Fig. 22

	Amount ($)
1	75–95
2	120–140
3	100–120
4	150–200

Fig. 23

	Amount ($)
1	50–75
2	80–100
3	50–75
4	60–75
5	150–200

Fig. 24

	Amount ($)
1	30–50
2	30–50
3	50–60
4	75–100
5	75–100
6	20–30
7	50–60
8	200–300

Fig. 25

	Amount ($)
1	100–150
2	225–275
3	150–200
4	75–100
5	150–200
6	250–300
7	100–150
8	40–60

Fig. 26

	Amount ($)
1	150–200
2	150–200
3	50–75
4	30–50
5	100–125
6	200–250R
7	150–200
8	40–60
9	50–75
10	80–110
11	VR

Fig. 27

	Amount ($)
1	50–75
2	150–200
3	150–200
4	150–200
5	150–200
6	200–250
7	200–250
8	100–150
9	50–75
10	50–75
11	100–150
12	75–100
13	100–150

Fig. 28

	Amount ($)
1	50–75
2	40–60
3	30–40
4	150–200
5	75–100
6	75–100
7	75–100
8	50–75
9	90–100
10	35–50
11	50–75
12	75–100
13	60–75
14	60–75
15	150–200
16	175–200

Fig. 29

	Amount ($)
1	100–125
2	150–200
3	80–100
4	40–60
5	40–60
6	75–100
7	60–80
8	150–200

Fig. 30

	Amount ($)
1	75–100
2	75–100
3	50–75
4	50–75
5	30–50
6	60–80
7	75–100
8	60–80
9	50–75

Fig. 31

	Amount ($)
1	200–250
2	150–200
3	80–100
4	80–100
5	75–100
6	75–95
7	65–80
8	60–80
9	70–90
10	80–100
11	80–100
12	75–95
13	60–80

Fig. 32

	Amount ($)
1	40–60
2	70–90
3	60–80
4	75–100
5	30–50
6	80–100
7	30–50
8	60–80
9	40–60
10	70–90

Fig. 33

	Amount ($)
1	70–90
2	40–60
3	150–175
4	150–175
5	150–175
6	60–75
7	200–250

R = rare; VR = very rare; N/A = not applicable.

	Amount ($)
8	40–60
9	60–80
Fig. 34	
1	150–200
2	50–70
3	30–50
4	100–125
5	150–200
6	100–125
7	60–80
8	50–70
9	80–100
10	50–70
Fig. 35	
1	40–60
2	60–80
3	100–125
4	50–70
5	50–70
6	60–80
7	40–60
8	75–85
9	40–60
10	100–125
11	40–60
12	120–150
Fig. 36	
1	200–250
2	200–250
Fig. 37	
1	200–250
2	125–150
3	125–150
4	125–150
5	150–175
6	125–150
Fig. 38	
1	60–80
2	125–150
3	80–100
4	125–150
5	125–150
6	125–150
7	125–150
8	100–150

	Amount ($)
Fig. 39	
1	100–150R
2	100–150R
3	100–125
4	100–125
5	80–100
6	80–100
7	150–200R
8	80–100
9	125–150
10	150–200
Fig. 40	
1	100–125
2	100–125
3	125–150
4	125–150
5	125–150
6	100–125
7	125–150
8	150–175
9	150–175
Fig. 41	
1	125–150
2	125–150
3	125–150
4	125–150
5	100–125
6	125–150
Fig. 42	
1	80–100
2	40–60
3	200–250R
4	80–100
5	75–100
6	VR
7	125–150
8	100–125
9	125–150R
Fig. 43	
	150–175
Fig. 44	
	175–225
Fig. 45	
1	60–80
2	50–70

	Amount ($)
3	50–70
4	60–80
5	50–70
6	50–70
7	100–125
8	80–100
9	60–80
Fig. 46	
1	150–175
2	60–80
3	175–225
4	125–150
5	125–150
6	125–150
7	125–150
8	150–175
Fig. 47	
1	60–80
2	60–80
3	75–100
4	200–225
5	100–125
6	40–60
7	30–50
8	40–60
Fig. 48	
1	100–125
2	150–200
3	60–80
4	125–150
5	100–125
6	30–50
7	40–60
8	80–100
Fig. 49	
1	20–40
2	60–80
3	30–50
4	30–50
5	30–50
6	80–100
7	30–50
Fig. 50	
1	75–100
2	60–80
3	60–80

	Amount ($)
4	60–80
5	60–80
6	60–80
7	75–100
8	60–80
9	60–80
Fig. 51	
1	60–80
2	80–100
3	70–90
4	80–100
5	100–125
6	80–100
7	70–90
Fig. 52	
1	60–100
2	80–100
3	150–200R
4	80–100
5	60–80
6	60–80
7	VR
Fig. 53	
	R
Fig. 54	
1	80–100
2	100–125
3	125–150
4	200–250
5	200–250
6	250–300
7	60–80
8	40–60
9	100–125
10	125–150
11	125–150
12	125–150
Fig. 55	
1	100–125
2	60–75
3	30–50
4	50–75
5	80–100
6	80–100
7	50–75
8	40–60

R = rare; VR = very rare; N/A = not applicable.

	Amount ($)
9	40–60
10	30–50
11	30–50

Fig. 56

	Amount ($)
1	125–150
2	125–150
3	100–125
4	150–200
5	100–125

Fig. 57

	Amount ($)
1	R
2	R

Fig. 58

	Amount ($)
1	80–100
2	80–100
3	40–60
4	100–150
5	60–80
6	40–60
7	100–125
8	60–80
9	60–80
10	80–100
11	80–100
12	40–60
13	50–60
14	50–60

Figs. 59–60

	Amount ($)
1	60–80
2	40–60
3	40–60
4	60–80
5	60–80
6	75–100
7	40–60
8	60–80

Fig. 61

	Amount ($)
1	300–400
2	250–350
3	150–200
4	150–200
5	200–300

Fig. 62

	Amount ($)
1	100–125
2	150–175
3	150–175

Figs. 63–64

	Amount ($)
1	200–250
2	250–350
3	125–150
4	200–250

Figs. 65–66

	Amount ($)
1	150–200
2	200–225
3	80–100
4	40–60
5	50–70
6	150–200
7	150–200
8	60–80

Figs. 67–68

	Amount ($)
1	200–300
2	200–300
3	300–350
4	VR

Figs. 69–70

	Amount ($)
	VR

Fig. 71

	Amount ($)
1	200–250
2	250–300
3	300–350

Fig. 72

	Amount ($)
1	150–200
2	200–250R
3	200–250R
4	200–250
5	200–250
6	175–200

Figs. 73–74

	Amount ($)
1	250–300R
2	175–200R
3	250–300R

Fig. 75

	Amount ($)
1	100–150
2	100–150
3	100–150
4	100–125
5	100–150
6	150–200
7	150–175

Fig. 76

	Amount ($)
1	100–125
2	125–150
3	—
4	125–150
5	125–150
6	150–200

Fig. 77

	Amount ($)
1	125–175
2	150–175
3	200–250
4	200–225
5	300–350R
6	100–125
7	250–300

Fig. 78

	Amount ($)
1	175–200
2	250–300
3	250–300
4	150–175
5	175–200

Figs. 79–80

	Amount ($)
1	100–125
2	100–150
3	125–150
4	VR
5	200–250
6	125–150

Fig. 81

	Amount ($)
1	150–200
2	150–200
3	100–125
4	125–150
5	150–200

Fig. 82

	Amount ($)
1	80–100
2	80–100
3	100–125
4	100–125

Figs. 83–84

	Amount ($)
1	VR
2	VR
3	VR

Fig. 85

	Amount ($)
1	VR
2	100–125
3	125–150

Fig. 86

	Amount ($)
1	125–150
2	125–150
3	60–80
4	60–80

Fig. 87

	Amount ($)
	80–100

Fig. 88

	Amount ($)
	125–150

Fig. 89

	Amount ($)
1	60–80
2	50–70
3	50–70
4	40–60

Fig. 90

	Amount ($)
1	100–125
2	125–150
3	125–150
4	175–225

Fig. 91

	Amount ($)
1	60–80
2	60–80
3	100–125
4	100–125
5	VR
6	VR

Fig. 92

	Amount ($)
1	60–80
2	40–60
3	40–60
4	60–80
5	60–80
6	125–150
7	60–80
8	40–60
9	40–60
10	60–80
11	40–60

R = rare; VR = very rare; N/A = not applicable.

	Amount ($)
Fig. 93	
1	60–80
2	75–100
3	80–100
4	125–150
5	50–70
6	75–100
7	100–125
8	50–60
9	40–60
10	50–60
11	60–80
Fig. 94	
1	100–125
2	80–100
3	80–100
4	30–50
5	30–50
6	80–100
7	40–50
8	60–80
9	40–60
10	80–100
11	40–60
12	20–30
13	40–60
14	60–80
15	60–80
Fig. 95	
1	50–60
2	50–60
3	50–60
4	50–60
5	60–70
6	60–70
7	60–75
Fig. 96	
1	30–40
2	40–60
3	40–60
4	40–60
5	100–150
6	30–50
7	40–60
8	60–80
Fig. 97	
1	150–175

	Amount ($)
2	150–175
3	80–100
4	80–100
5	100–125
6	R
7	R
8	80–100
9	80–100
Fig. 98	
1	125–150
2	125–150
3	100–125
4	100–125
5	125–150
6	100–125
7	100–125
8	125–150
9	125–150
Fig. 99	
1	100–150
2	250–300
3	75–100
4	60–80
5	100–125
6	40–60
7	125–150
8	100–125
9	150–200
10	100–125
11	100–125
12	125–150
13	135–150
Fig. 100	
1	100–125
2	250–300
3	225–250
4	60–80
5	100–125
6	100–125
7	80–100
8	150–200
9	70–90
10	175–200
11	80–100
12	150–200
13	125–150

	Amount ($)
Fig. 101	
1	100–125
2	60–80
3	300–350R
4	60–80
5	100–125
6	125–150
7	80–100
8	150–175
9	125–150
10	300–400
11	100–125
12	80–100
Fig. 102	
1	60–80
2	250–300
3	250–300
4	250–300
5	150–175
6	175–200
7	175–200
8	80–100
9	125–150
10	75–100R
Fig. 103	
1	200–250R
2	60–80
3	250–300R
4	100–150
5	VR
6	VR
7	175–200
8	100–150
9	R
Fig. 104	
1	50–75
2	25 each
3	50–100R
4	VR
5	125–150R
6	100–125R
7	60–80
8	60–80
9	100–130
10	150–200
11	VR
12	40–60
13	40–60

	Amount ($)
14	40–60
15	60–90
16	50–75
17	50–75
Fig. 105	
1	100–150
2	175–225
3	350–400R
4	350–400R
5	200–250
6	350–400R
7	200–250R
Fig. 106	
1	300–325
2	400–450R
3	250–300R
4	75–100
5	200–250
6	350–400
7	200–250
8	150–200
9	125–175
10	250–300
Fig. 107	
1	350–450
2	350–450R
3	450–550R
4	250–350
5	350–450R
Fig. 108	
1	350–450R
2	250–350
3	450–550
4	350–450
5	VR
Figs. 109–10	
1	150–250
2	400–500R
3	400–500R
4	350–450R
5	500–700R
Fig. 111	
1	250–300
2	250–300
3	250–300

R = rare; VR = very rare; N/A = not applicable.

	Amount ($)
4	250–300
5	250–300
Fig. 112	
1	350–450
2	400–500
3	300–400
4	300–400
5	350–450
Fig. 113	
1	200–250
2	200–250
3	175–200
4	125–150
5	125–150
Fig. 114	
1	125–150
2	50–75
3	30–50
4	125–150
5	100–125
6	100–125
7	20–30
8	40–60
9	125–150
Fig. 115	
1	50–75
2	125–150R
3	50–60
4	VR
5	60–80
6	80–100
Fig. 116	
1	R
2	R
3	40–60
4	80–100
5	60–80
Fig. 117	
1	40–60
2	40–60
3	30–50
4	30–40
5	40–60
6	75–90
7	20–30

	Amount ($)
8	125–150
9	60–80
10	250–300
11	50–60
12	40–60
Fig. 118	
1	80–100
2	60–80
3	125–150
4	100–125
5	40–60
6	80–100
7	30–50
8	40–60
9	80–100
10	100–125
11	40–60
12	75–100
Fig. 119	
1	50–75
2	20–30
3	100–125
4	50–60
5	60–80
6	60–80
7	30–50
8	40–60
9	150–175
Fig. 120	
	VR
Fig. 121	
	VR
Fig. 122	
	VR
Fig. 123	
1	80–100
2	60–80
3	50–70
4	50–70
5	80–100
6	60–100
7	R
8	60–80
9	25–40
10	200–250

	Amount ($)
11	100–125
Fig. 124	
1	60–80
2	40–60
3	80–100
4	40–60
5	40–60
6	60–80
7	50–70
8	40–60
9	80–100
10	40–60
11	60–80
Fig. 125	
1	40–60
2	30–50
3	80–100
4	80–100
5	40–60
6	60–80
7	60–80
8	60–80
9	100–125
10	100–125
11	60–80
12	75–90
13	50–75
Fig. 126	
1	80–100
2	40–60
3	40–60
4	60–80
5	100–125
6	80–100
7	60–80
8	VR
9	30–40
10	80–100
11	40–60
Fig. 127	
1	450–550
2	450–550R
3	250–350
4	400–500
5	350–450

	Amount ($)
Fig. 128	
1	750–1,000VR
2	400–500
3	R
4	250–300
5	500–600
6	500–600R
7	1,000–1,500VR
Fig. 129–30	
1	125–150
2	250–300R
3	150–175
4	125–150
5	VR
6	250–300
Fig. 131	
1	60–80
2	60–80
3	R
4	80–100
5	40–60
6	80–100
7	40–60
8	100–125
9	R
Fig. 132	
1	100–125
2	60–80
3	150–175
4	150–200
5	100–125
6	60–80
7	100–150
8	150–200
9	150–200
10	150–200
11	R
Fig. 133	
1	20–40
2	20–40
3	60–80
4	100–125
5	25–30
6	80–100
7	60–80
8	75–100
9	60–80

R = rare; VR = very rare; N/A = not applicable.

	Amount ($)
10	80–100
11	100–125
12	100–125
13	100–125

Fig. 134

1	VR
2	150–200
3	400–500
4	300–350
5	100–150
6	100–125

Fig. 135

1	40–60
2	60–80
3	60–80
4	30–40
5	40–60
6	100–125
7	40–60
8	40–60
9	80–100
10	80–100
11	40–60

Fig. 136

1	200–225R
2	150–200
3	50–75
4	200–250
5	150–200
6	150–200
7	200–250

Fig. 137

1	80–100
2	100–125
3	80–100
4	150–200
5	125–150
6	150–200
7	150–200

Fig. 138

	Amount ($)
1	100–125
2	100–125
3	80–100
4	40–60
5	60–80
6	80–100
7	100–125
8	100–125
9	30–40
10	60–80
11	40–60
12	40–60
13	40–60
14	60–80
15	80–100
16	100–125
17	80–100

Fig. 139

1	150–200VR
2	200–250VR
3	150–200
4	200–250
5	75–125
6	75–125
7	40–60
8	200–250
9	200–250R
10	VR
11	200–250
12	200–250

Fig. 140

1	250–300
2	60–80
3	60–80
4	250–300
5	40–60
6	80–100
7	60–80

Fig. 141

1	250–300
2	60–80
3	40–60
4	40–60
5	60–80
6	200–250
7	100–125
8	VR
9	60–80

Fig. 142

	Amount ($)
1	80–100
2	80–100
3	60–80
4	60–80
5	80–100
6	200–250
7	200–250
8	200–250
9	80–100
10	60–80

Fig. 143

1	125–150
2	80–100
3	150–175
4	80–100
5	300–350R
6	60–80
7	100–125
8	VR
9	150–200
10	80–100

Fig. 144

1	80–100
2	80–100
3	40–60
4	80–100
5	100–125
6	80–100
7	80–100
8	60–80
9	80–100
10	90–100
11	200–250

Fig. 145

1	60–80
2	125–150
3	40–60
4	40–60
5	40–60
6	80–100
7	40–60
8	40–60
9	150–200
10	40–60
11	40–60

Fig. 146

	Amount ($)
1	40–60
2	40–60
3	20–30
4	60–80
5	150–175
6	40–60
7	30–40
8	40–60
9	60–80
10	100–125

Fig. 147

1	60–80
2	40–60 set
3	40–60 set
4	40–45
5	50–60
6	40–60
7	80–100
8	40–60
9	60–80
10	150–175
11	60–80

Fig. 148

1	30–40
2	80–100
3	40–60
4	80–100
5	60–80
6	60–80 set
7	60–80 set
8	75–100
9	40–60
10	60–80
11	40–60

Figs. 149–50

1	80–100
2	60–80
3	80–100
4	125–150
5	100–125
6	150–200

Fig. 151

1	200–250 set
2	200–250 set
3	200–250 set
4	250–300
5	125–150 set
6	125–150 set
7	125–150 set

Fig. 152

1	350–450

R = rare; VR = very rare; N/A = not applicable.

	Amount ($)
2	350–450
3	80–100
4	80–100
5	100–125
6	100–125

Fig. 153

1–6	N/A

Plate 1

1	150–200R
2	VR
3	200–250
4	80–100
5	150–200
6	R
7	R
8	R
9	150–200
10	150–200
11	40–60
12	200–250
13	250–300
14	150–200R
15	200–250R
16	100–150
17	300–350R

Plate 2

1	175–200
2	300–350R
3	150–200
4	250–300
5	250–300R
6	50–75
7	250–300
8	250–300
9	300–350R
10	VR
11	80–120

Plate 3

	Amount ($)
1	200–250
2	200–250
3	100–125
4	100–125
5	150–200
6	200–250
7	150–200
8	150–200
9	125–150
10	200–250
11	150–175
12	300–350
13	150–200
14	150–200
15	200–250

Plate 4

1	200–250R
2	250–300
3	80–100
4	60–80
5	60–80
6	R
7	250–300
8	150–200
9	60–80
10	300–350

Plate 5

1	125–150
2	250–350
3	250–300
4	125–150
5	200–250
6	150–200
7	150–200
8	100–125
9	125–150
10	150–200
11	100–125
12	125–150
13	300–350
14	200–250

Plate 6

1	150–200
2	100–150
3	200–250
4	200–250
5	250–300
6	250–300
7	150–200
8	R
9	200–250
10	125–150
11	250–300
12	150–200
13	200–250
14	150–200

	Amount ($)

Plate 7

1	100–125
2	80–100
3	100–125
4	30–50
5	30–50
6	R
7	75–100
8	75–100
9	75–100
10	150–200
11	80–120
12	R
13	125–150

Plate 8

1,000–1,200R

Plate 9

VR

Plate 10

VR

Plate 11

1	400–500R
2	350–450R
3	400–500R
4	300–400
5	400–500R
6	300–350
7	VR

Plate 12

1	550–700
2	250–350
3	VR
4	750–1,000
5	500–700
6	500–700
7	VR
8	300–400
9	200–300
10	VR

Plate 13

	Amount ($)
1	60–80
2	60–80
3	VR
4	60–100
5	125–150
6	100–150
7	100–125
8	100–125
9	150–200
10	100–150
11	80–100
12	100–150R

Plate 14

1	300–400
2	125–150
3	250–350
4	200–225
5	300–350
6	300–350
7	100–125
8	200–250
9	100–125
10	100–125
11	100–125
12	175–275
13	125–150

Plate 15

1	250–350
2	250–350
3	200–300
4	125–150
5	150–250
6	150–250
7	200–300
8	80–100
9	100–125
10	150–250

Plate 16

1	R
2	800–1,000
3	500–600
4	300–400
5	VR
6	R

Plate 17

VR

Plate 18

400–500

Plate 19

1	150–200

R = rare; VR = very rare; N/A = not applicable.

	Amount ($)		Amount ($)		Amount ($)		Amount ($)
2	200–250 set	**10**	300–350R	**18**	100–125	**4**	R
3	200–250 set	**11**	60–80	**19**	50–75	**5**	R
4	300–350	**12**	250–300	**20**	150–175	**6**	R
5	300–350	**13**	350–400			**7**	R
6	200–250	**14**	350–450R	**Plate 20**		**8**	R
7	300–350	**15**	R	**1**	R	**9**	R
8	300–350	**16**	200–250	**2**	R		
9	175–225	**17**	200–250	**3**	R		

R = rare; VR = very rare; N/A = not applicable.

Patents

Patent Numbers Issued by Year

Date	Patent Numbers	Date	Patent Numbers	Date	Patent Numbers
1859	22,477– 26,641	1893	488,976– 511,743	1927	1,612,790–1,654,520
1860	26,642– 31,004	1894	511,744– 531,618	1928	1,654,521–1,696,896
1861	31,005– 34,044	1895	531,619– 552,501	1929	1,696,897–1,742,180
1862	34,045– 37,265	1896	552,502– 574,368	1930	1,742,181–1,787,423
1863	37,266– 41,046	1897	574,369– 596,466	1931	1,787,424–1,839,189
1864	41,047– 45,684	1898	596,467– 616,870	1932	1,839,190–1,892,662
1865	45,685– 51,783	1899	616,871– 640,166	1933	1,892,663–1,941,448
1866	51,784– 60,684	1900	640,167– 664,826	1934	1,941,449–1,985,877
1867	60,685– 72,958	1901	664,827– 690,384	1935	1,985,878–2,026,515
1868	72,959– 85,502	1902	690,385– 717,520	1936	2,026,516–2,066,308
1869	85,503– 98,459	1903	717,521– 748,566	1937	2,066,309–2,104,003
1870	98,460–110,616	1904	748,567– 778,833	1938	2,104,004–2,142,079
1871	110,617–122,303	1905	778,834– 808,617	1939	2,142,080–2,185,169
1872	122,304–134,503	1906	808,618– 839,798	1940	2,185,170–2,227,417
1873	134,504–146,119	1907	839,799– 875,678	1941	2,227,418–2,268,539
1874	146,120–158,349	1908	875,679– 908,435	1942	2,268,540–2,307,006
1875	158,350–171,640	1909	908,436– 945,009	1943	2,307,007–2,338,080
1876	171,641–185,812	1910	945,010– 980,177	1944	2,338,081–2,366,153
1877	185,813–198,732	1911	980,178–1,013,094	1945	2,366,154–2,391,855
1878	198,733–211,077	1912	1,013,095–1,049,325	1946	2,391,856–2,413,674
1879	211,078–223,209	1913	1,049,326–1,083,266	1947	2,413,675–2,433,823
1880	223,210–240,372	1914	1,083,267–1,123,211	1948	2,433,824–2,457,796
1881	240,373–254,835	1915	1,123,212–1,166,418	1949	2,457,797–2,492,943
1882	254,836–269,819	1916	1,166,419–1,210,388	1950	2,492,944–2,536,015
1883	269,820–291,015	1917	1,210,389–1,251,457	1951	2,536,016–2,580,378
1884	291,016–310,167	1918	1,251,458–1,290,026	1952	2,580,379–2,624,045
1885	310,168–353,493	1919	1,290,027–1,329,351	1953	2,624,046–2,664,561
1886	353,494–355,290	1920	1,329,352–1,364,062	1954	2,664,562–2,698,433
1887	355,291–375,719	1921	1,364,063–1,401,947	1955	2,698,434–2,728,912
1888	375,720–395,304	1922	1,401,948–1,440,361	1956	2,728,913–2,775,761
1889	395,305–418,664	1923	1,440,362–1,478,895	1957	2,775,762–2,818,566
1890	418,665–443,986	1924	1,478,896–1,521,589	1958	2,818,567–2,866,972
1891	443,987–466,314	1925	1,521,590–1,568,039	1959	2,866,973–2,919,442
1892	466,315–488,975	1926	1,568,040–1,612,789	1960	2,919,443– —

Note: This guide does not apply to design patents in which the letters *D* or *DES* precede the numbers.

A Sampling of Important Patents

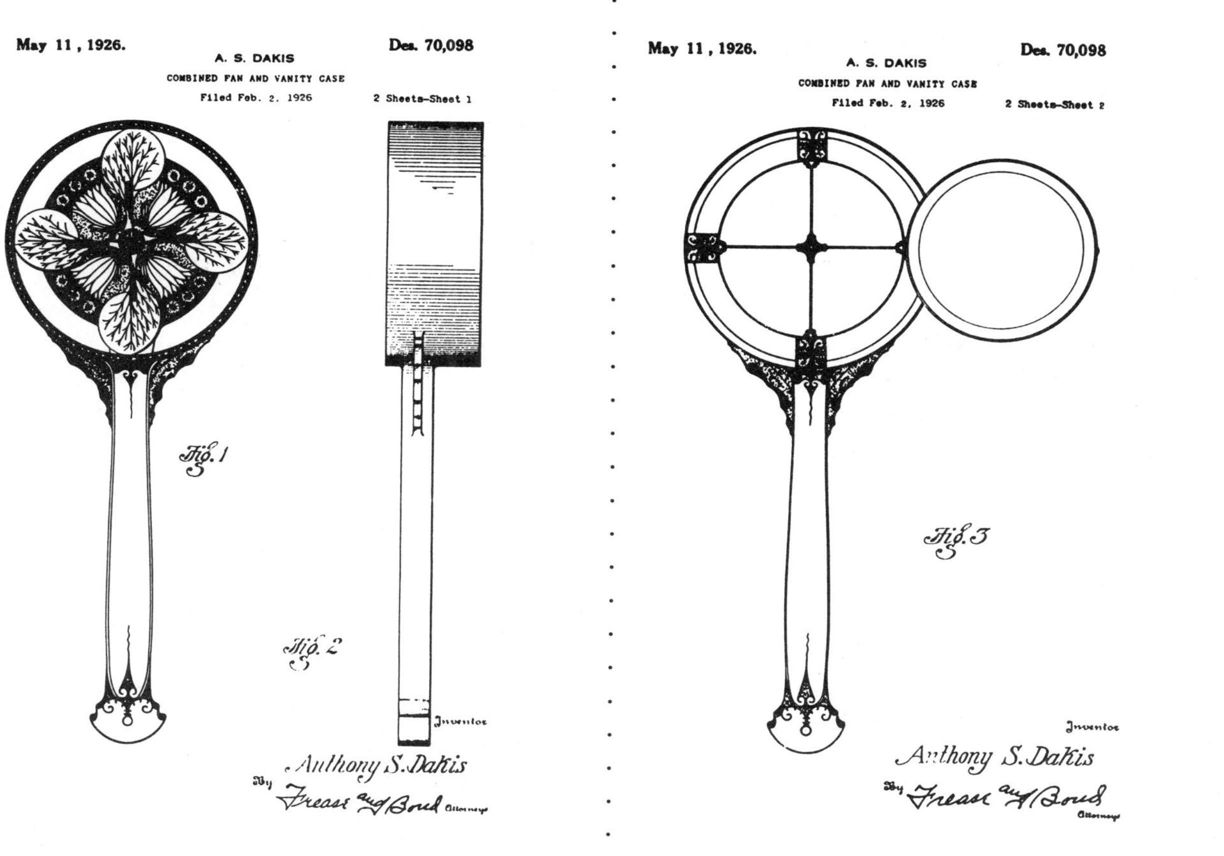

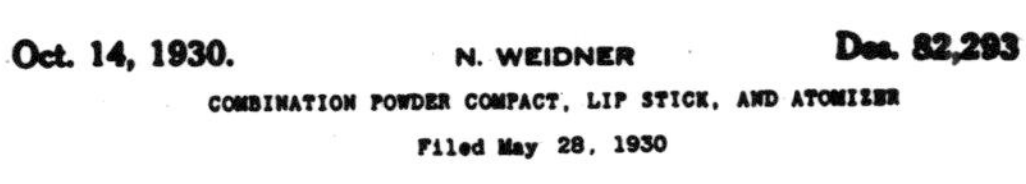

Oct. 14, 1930. N. WEIDNER Des. 82,293

COMBINATION POWDER COMPACT, LIP STICK, AND ATOMIZER

Filed May 28, 1930

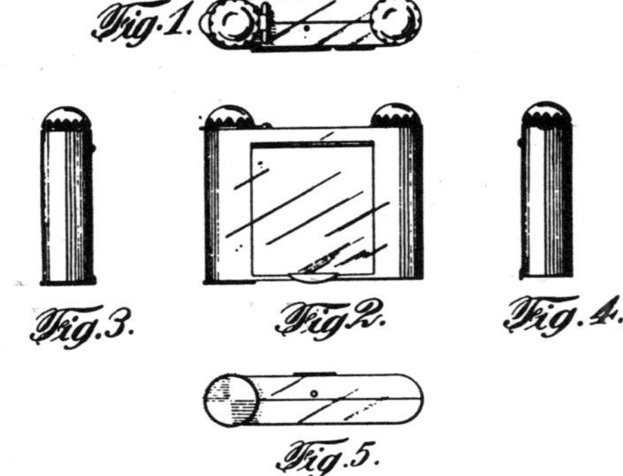

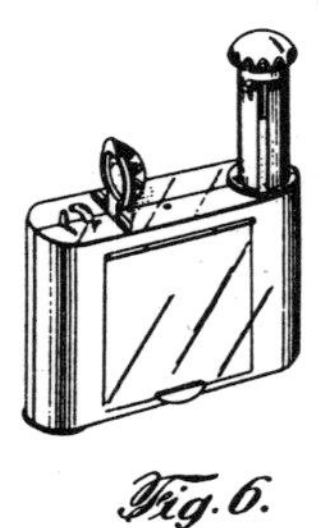

INVENTOR
Nathan Weidner
BY
ATTORNEY

Oct. 10, 1939. M. V. EASTLEY Des. 117,092

COMBINED COSMETIC CONTAINER AND APPLICATOR

Filed Nov. 26, 1938

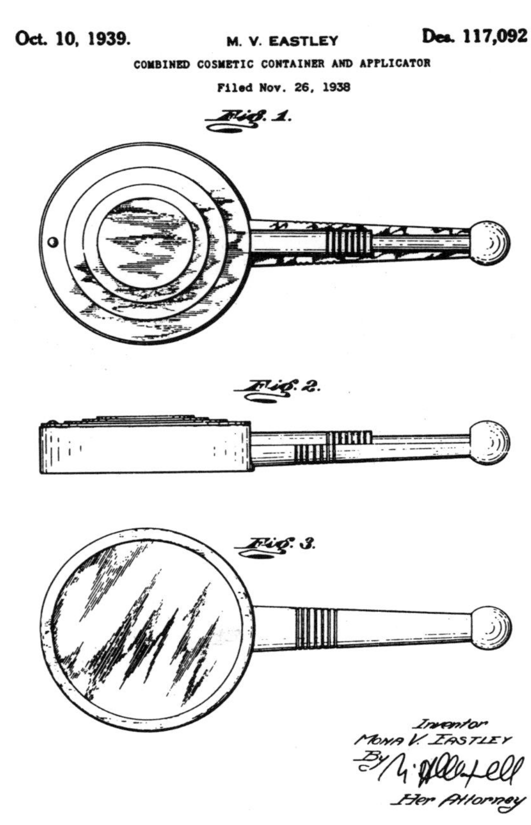

March 5, 1940. A. A. ROSENBERG Des. 119,284

COMBINED COMPACT, MEMO PAD, AND PENCIL

Filed Jan. 17, 1940

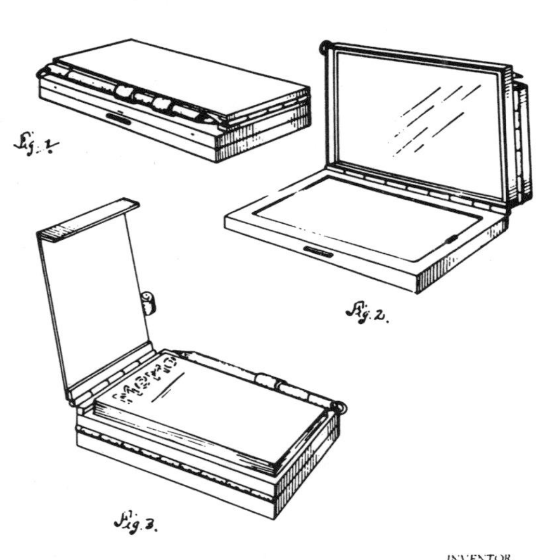

INVENTOR
ARTHUR A. ROSENBERG
BY S Bernard Gahm
ATTORNEY

May 7, 1940. R. W. MASON Des. 120,347

VANITY CASE

Filed Feb. 10, 1940

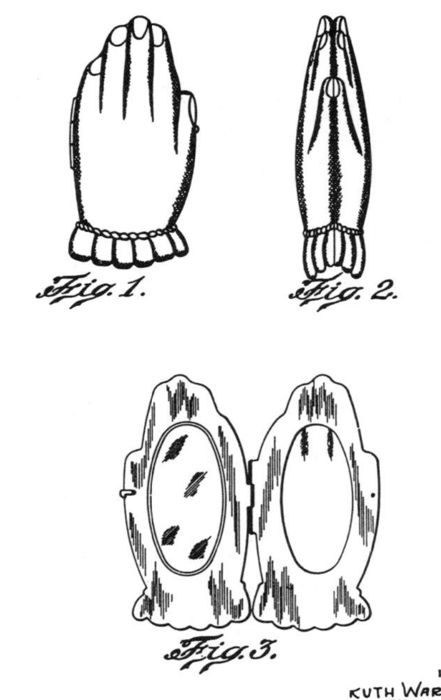

INVENTOR
RUTH WARNER MASON
BY
ATTORNEY

Feb. 4, 1941. A. R. BOTHAM Des. 124,949

VANITY CASE

Filed Nov. 29, 1940

FIG. 1

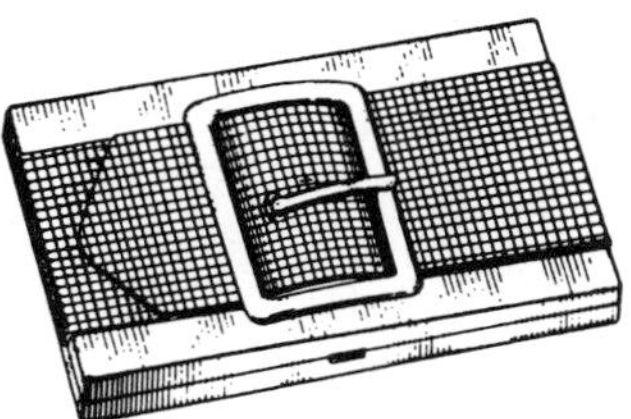

FIG. 2

INVENTOR.

Feb. 4, 1941. A. R. BOTHAM Des. 124,950

COMBINED LIPSTICK AND VANITY CASE

Filed Nov. 29, 1940

FIG. 1

FIG. 2

INVENTOR.

Feb. 4, 1941. A. R. BOTHAM Des. 124,952

COMBINED LIPSTICK AND VANITY CASE

Filed Nov. 29, 1940

FIG. 1

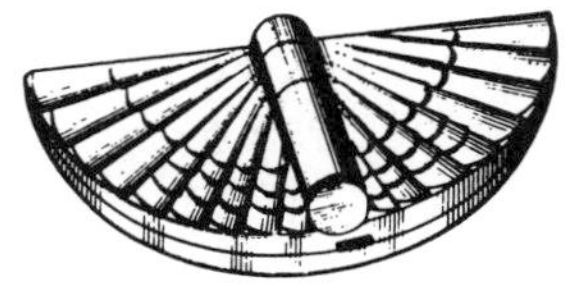

FIG. 2

FIG. 3

INVENTOR.

Feb. 4, 1941. A. R. BOTHAM Des. 124,954

VANITY CASE

Filed Nov. 29, 1940

FIG. 1

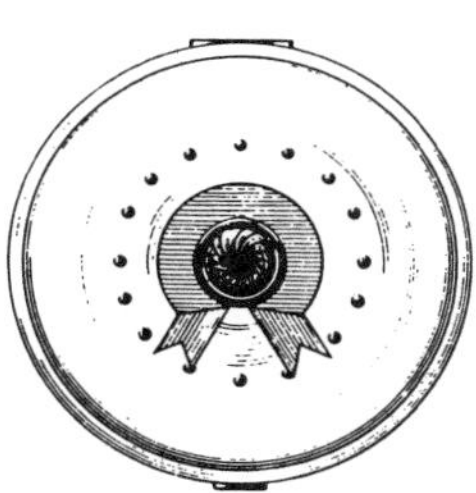

FIG. 2

INVENTOR.

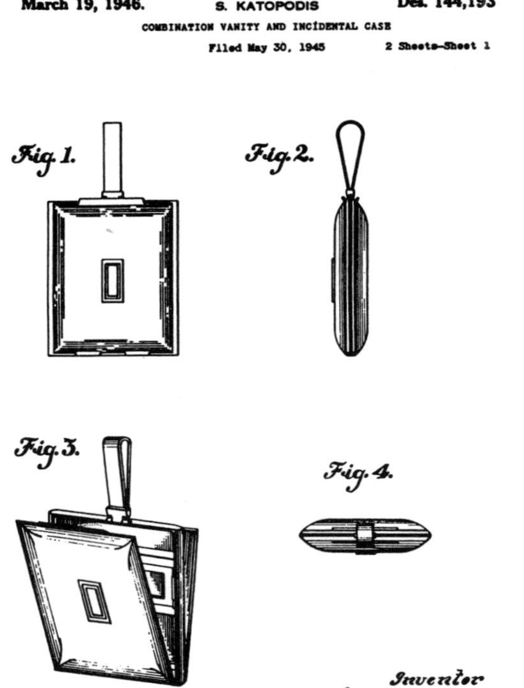
March 19, 1946.
S. KATOPODIS
Des. 144,193
COMBINATION VANITY AND INCIDENTAL CASE
Filed May 30, 1945
2 Sheets-Sheet 1
Fig. 1.
Fig. 2.
Fig. 3.
Fig. 4.
Inventor
Spiros Katopodis
by Harold E. Cole
Attorney.

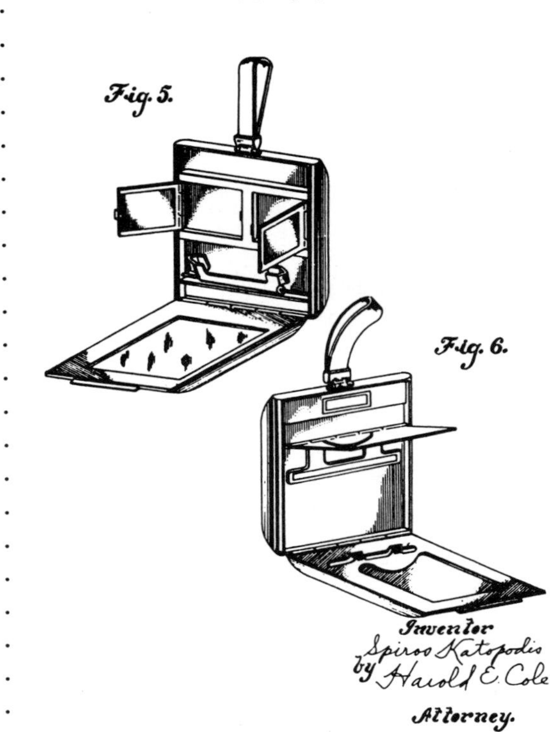
March 19, 1946.
S. KATOPODIS
Des. 144,193
COMBINATION VANITY AND INCIDENTAL CASE
Filed May 30, 1945
2 Sheets-Sheet 2
Fig. 5.
Fig. 6.
Inventor
Spiros Katopodis
by Harold E. Cole
Attorney.

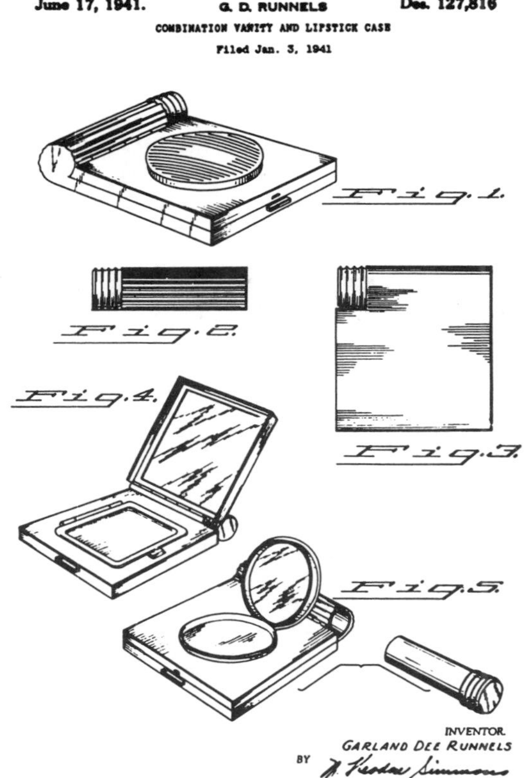
June 17, 1941.
G. D. RUNNELS
Des. 127,816
COMBINATION VANITY AND LIPSTICK CASE
Filed Jan. 3, 1941
Fig. 1.
Fig. 2.
Fig. 3.
Fig. 4.
Fig. 5.
INVENTOR
GARLAND DEE RUNNELS
BY
ATTORNEY.

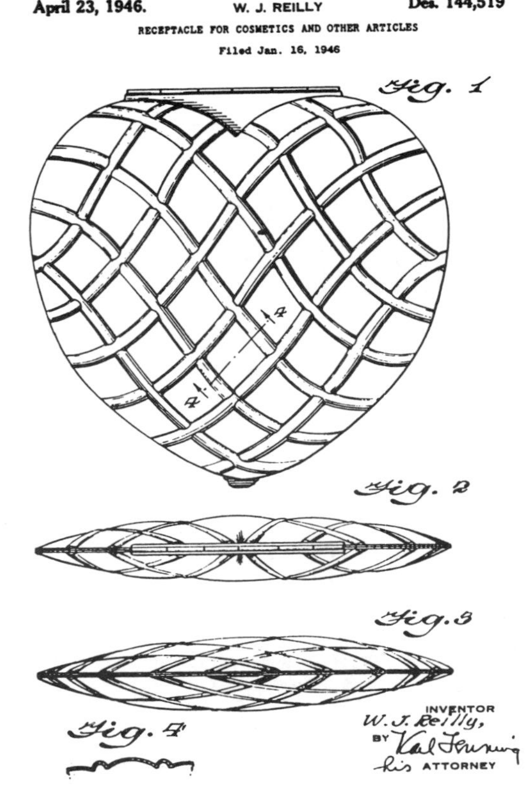
April 23, 1946.
W. J. REILLY
Des. 144,519
RECEPTACLE FOR COSMETICS AND OTHER ARTICLES
Filed Jan. 16, 1946
Fig. 1
Fig. 2
Fig. 3
Fig. 4
INVENTOR
W. J. Reilly,
BY
his ATTORNEY

Jan. 27, 1948. L. MEDGYES Des. 148,478

COMBINED VANITY CASE AND LIPSTICK HOLDER

Filed July 11, 1946

Fig. 1.

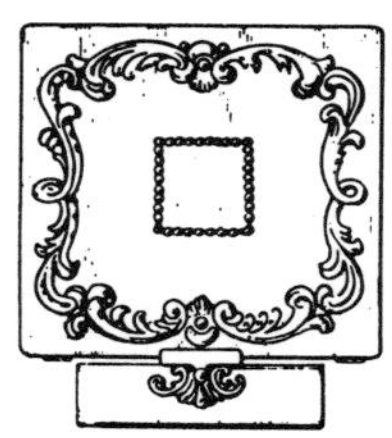

Fig. 2.

Fig. 3.

LADISLAS MEDGYES
INVENTOR
BY
ATTORNEY

Aug. 2, 1949. H. L. LAMBERT Des. 154,687

COMBINED WATCH AND COSMETIC CASE

Filed June 26, 1948

Fig. 1.

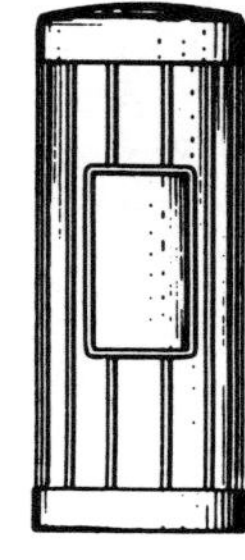

Fig. 3.

Fig. 2.

INVENTOR.
BY
ATTORNEY.

Feb. 14, 1950 S. KAUFMAN Des. 157,265

COMBINED VANITY CASE AND LIPSTICK HOLDER

Filed March 22, 1948

Fig. 2. Fig. 3. Fig. 4.

Fig. 1.

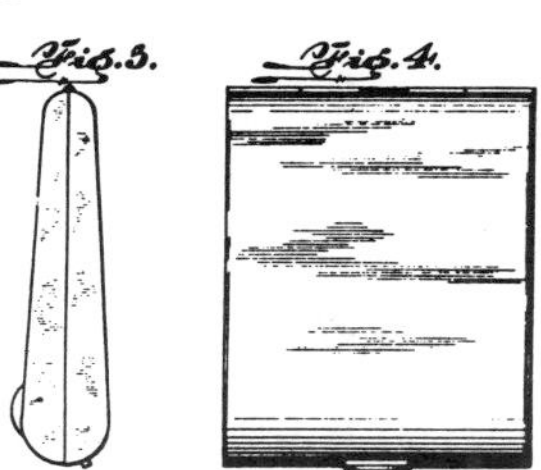

Fig. 5.

Fig. 6.

INVENTOR.
SOL KAUFMAN.
BY
ATTORNEY.

Nov. 28, 1950 P. E. FLATO Des. 161,011

COMPACT OR SIMILAR ARTICLE

Filed June 5, 1950

Fig. 1.

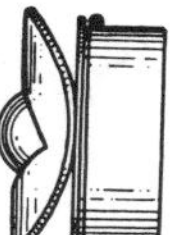

Fig. 2.

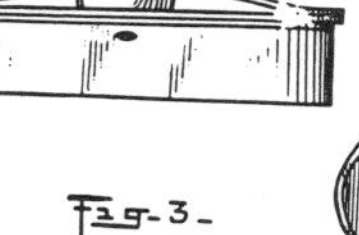

Fig. 3.

Fig. 4.

PAUL E. FLATO,
INVENTOR
ATTORNEY

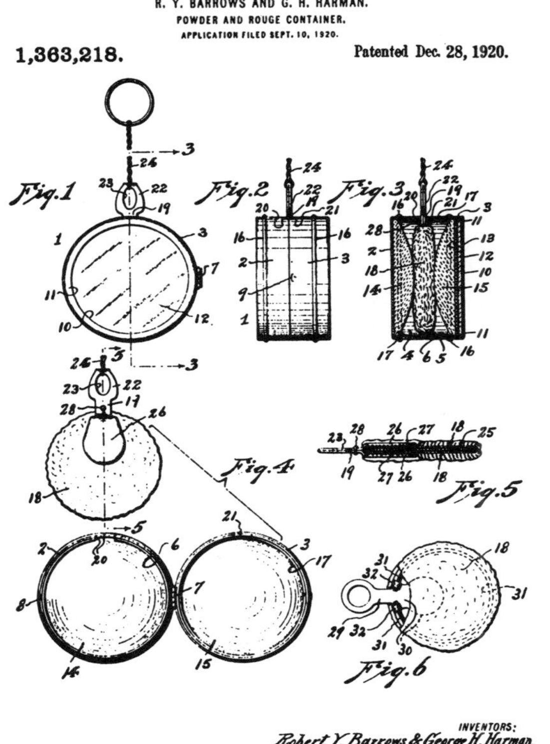
R. Y. BARROWS AND G. H. HARMAN.
POWDER AND ROUGE CONTAINER.
APPLICATION FILED SEPT. 10, 1920.
1,363,218.
Patented Dec. 28, 1920.
Fig. 1
Fig. 2
Fig. 3
Fig. 4
Fig. 5
Fig. 6
INVENTORS:
Robert Y. Barrows & George H. Harman,
BY
Frauntzel & Richards
ATTORNEYS

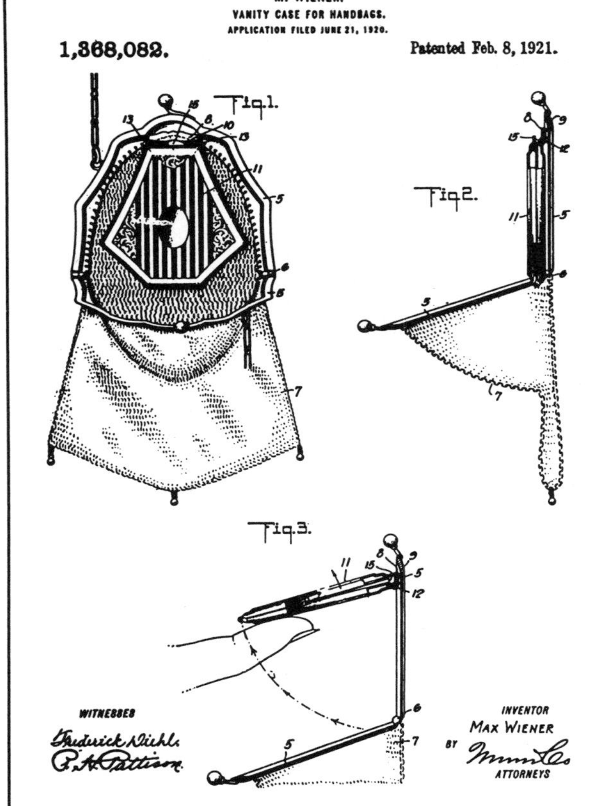
M. WIENER.
VANITY CASE FOR HANDBAGS.
APPLICATION FILED JUNE 21, 1920.
1,368,082.
Patented Feb. 8, 1921.
Fig. 1.
Fig. 2.
Fig. 3.
WITNESSES
INVENTOR
MAX WIENER
BY
Munn & Co
ATTORNEYS

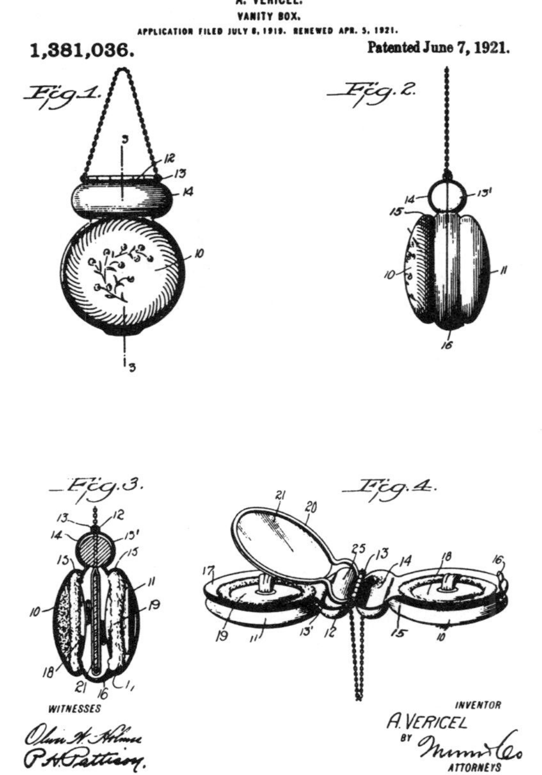
A. VERICEL.
VANITY BOX.
APPLICATION FILED JULY 8, 1919. RENEWED APR. 5, 1921.
1,381,036.
Patented June 7, 1921.
Fig. 1.
Fig. 2.
Fig. 3.
Fig. 4.
WITNESSES
INVENTOR
A. VERICEL
BY
Munn & Co
ATTORNEYS

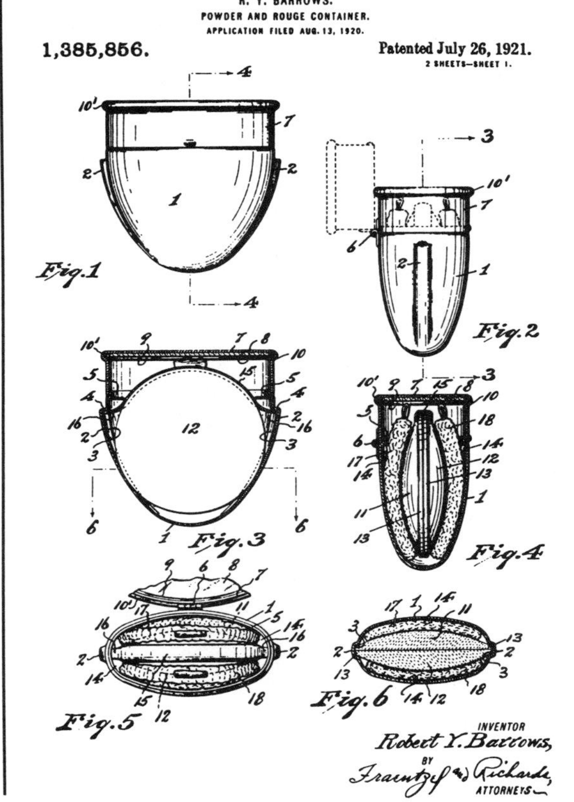
R. Y. BARROWS.
POWDER AND ROUGE CONTAINER.
APPLICATION FILED AUG. 13, 1920.
1,385,856.
Patented July 26, 1921.
2 SHEETS—SHEET 1.
Fig. 1
Fig. 2
Fig. 3
Fig. 4
Fig. 5
Fig. 6
INVENTOR
Robert Y. Barrows,
BY
Frauntzel & Richards
ATTORNEYS

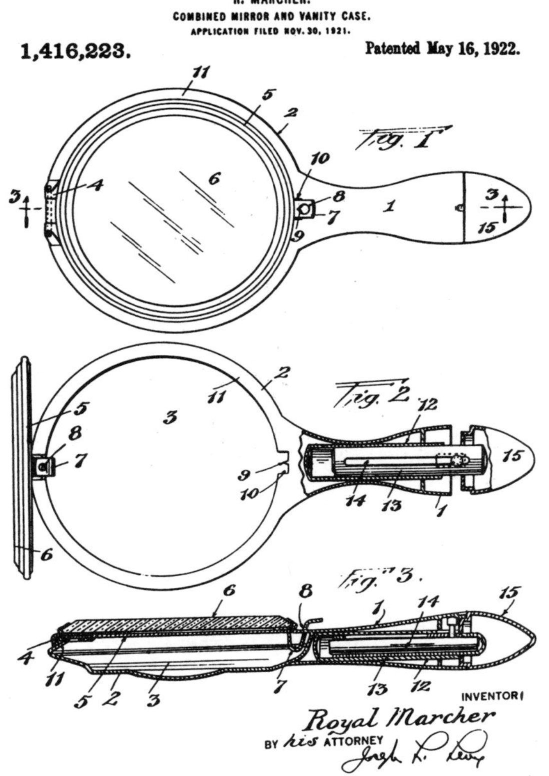
R. MARCHER.
COMBINED MIRROR AND VANITY CASE.
APPLICATION FILED NOV. 30, 1921.
1,416,223.
Patented May 16, 1922.
INVENTOR
Royal Marcher
BY his ATTORNEY

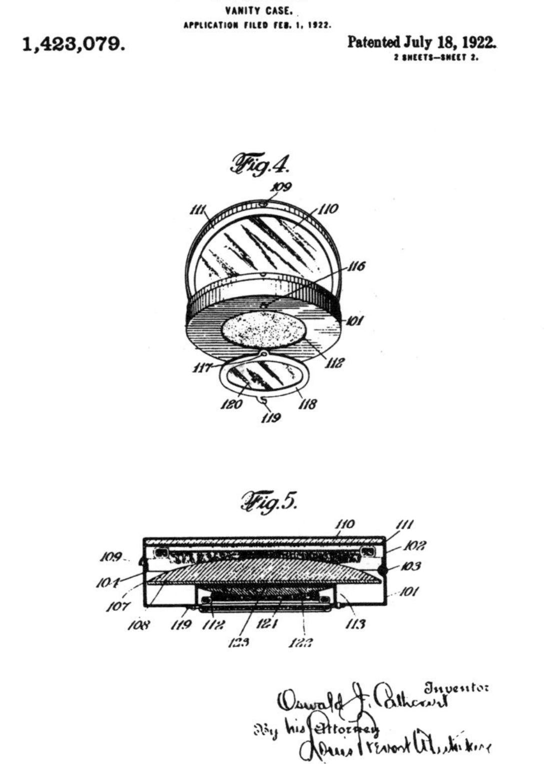
O. J. CATHCART.
VANITY CASE.
APPLICATION FILED FEB. 1, 1922.
1,423,079.
Patented July 18, 1922.
2 SHEETS—SHEET 2.
Fig. 4.
Fig. 5.
Inventor
By his Attorney

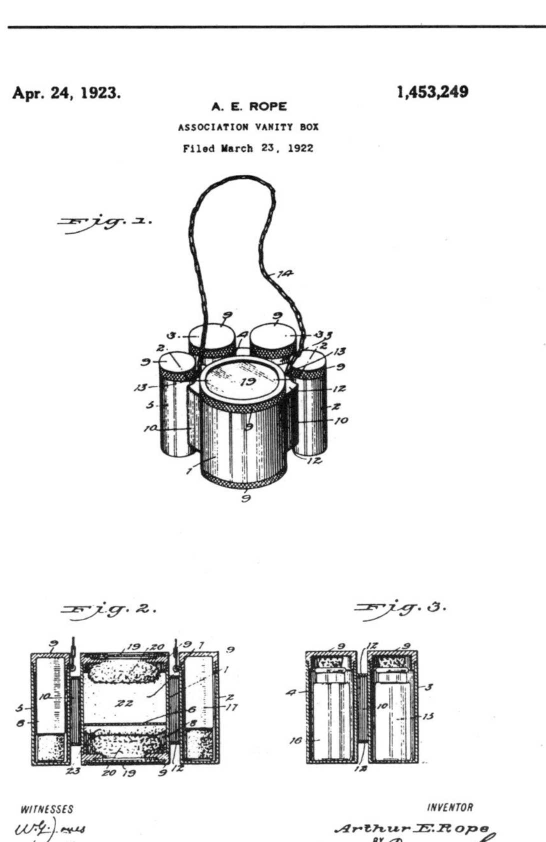
Apr. 24, 1923.
A. E. ROPE
1,453,249
ASSOCIATION VANITY BOX
Filed March 23, 1922
Fig. 1.
Fig. 2.
Fig. 3.
WITNESSES
INVENTOR
Arthur E. Rope
BY
ATTORNEYS

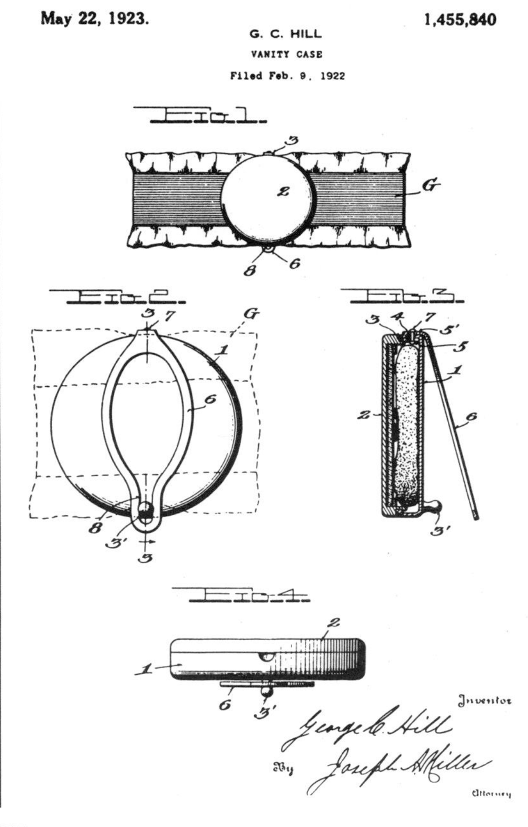
May 22, 1923.
G. C. HILL
1,455,840
VANITY CASE
Filed Feb. 9, 1922
Inventor
George C. Hill
By

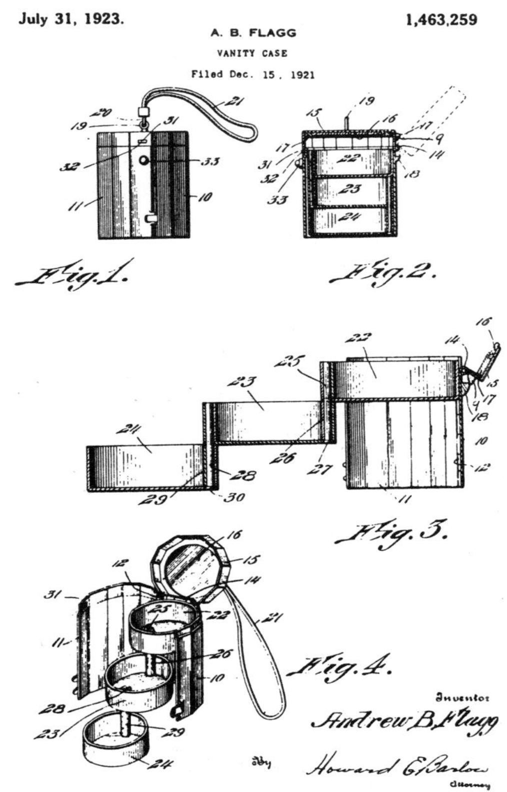
July 31, 1923.
A. B. FLAGG
1,463,259
VANITY CASE
Filed Dec. 15, 1921
Fig. 1.
Fig. 2.
Fig. 3.
Fig. 4.
Inventor
Andrew B. Flagg
By Howard E. Barlow
Attorney

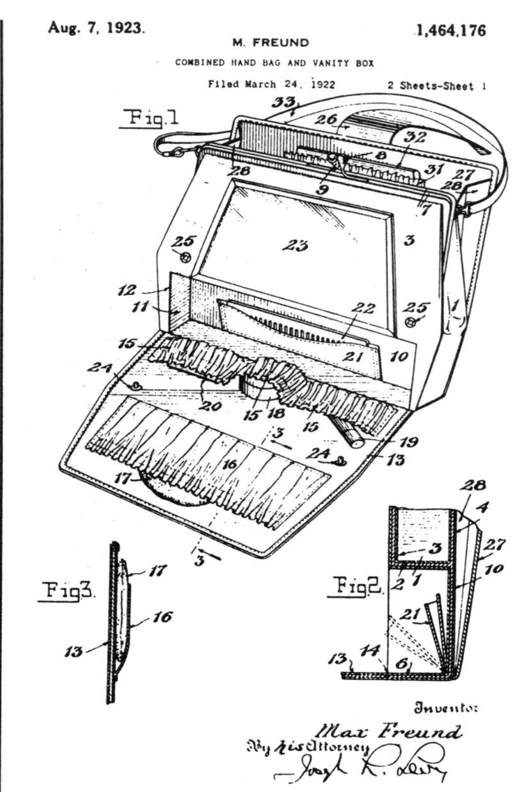
Aug. 7, 1923.
M. FREUND
1,464,176
COMBINED HAND BAG AND VANITY BOX
Filed March 24, 1922
2 Sheets-Sheet 1
Fig. 1
Fig. 2
Fig. 3.
Inventor
Max Freund
By his Attorney
Joseph R. Levy

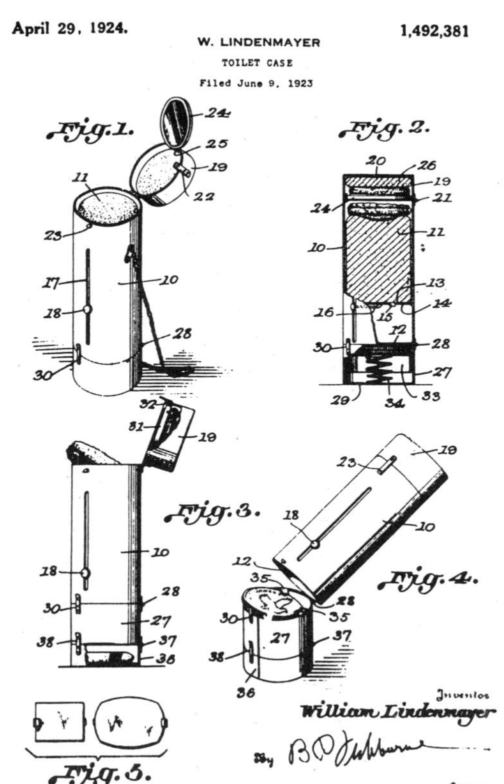
April 29, 1924.
W. LINDENMAYER
1,492,381
TOILET CASE
Filed June 9, 1923
Fig. 1.
Fig. 2.
Fig. 3.
Fig. 4.
Fig. 5.
Inventor
William Lindenmayer
By
Attorney

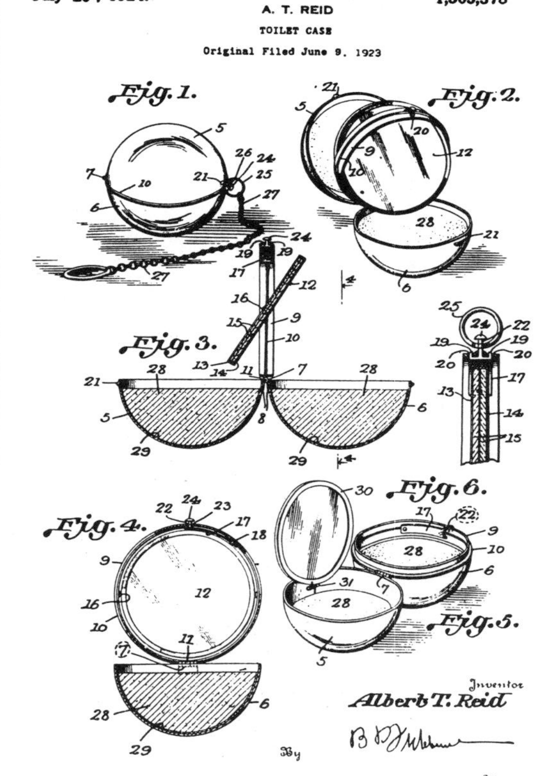
July 29, 1924.
A. T. REID
1,503,378
TOILET CASE
Original Filed June 9, 1923
Fig. 1.
Fig. 2.
Fig. 3.
Fig. 4.
Fig. 5.
Fig. 6.
Inventor
Albert T. Reid
By
Attorney

Aug. 5, 1924. A. CALLAHAN 1,503,979

COMBINATION VANITY CASE AND PURSE

Filed July 24, 1923

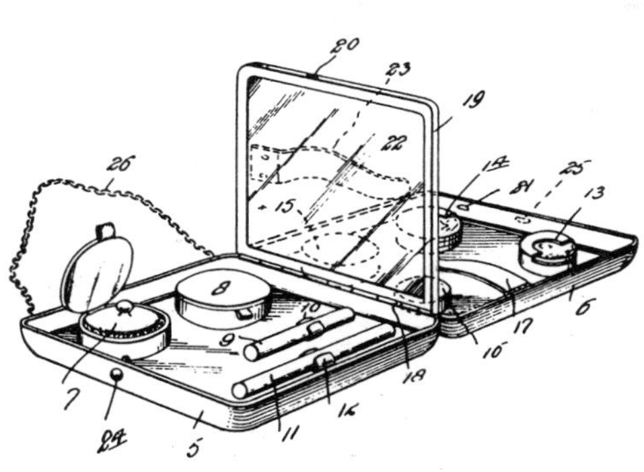

Witnesses:

Annie Callahan, Inventor

Attorney

Sept. 9, 1924. M. GOLDSMITH 1,507,915

COMBINED VANITY AND CAMERA CASE

Filed April 7, 1924

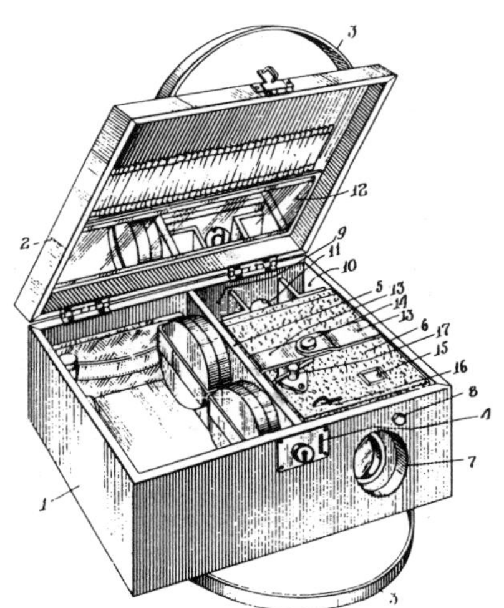

Maurice Goldsmith

INVENTOR

BY

ATTORNEY

March 17, 1925. L. F. FOREMAN 1,530,162

AUTOMOBILE VANITY CASE

Filed Nov. 27, 1923

Fig. 1.

Fig. 2.

Fig. 3.

WITNESSES

Howard D. Orr

Lillian F. Foreman, INVENTOR,

BY

ATTORNEY

July 7, 1925. S. E. MILLER 1,544,852

TOILET CASE

Filed Nov. 5, 1923 2 Sheets-Sheet 1

Fig. 1

Fig. 2

Witnesses:

B. J. Richards

Inventor:

Sommerfield E. Miller

His Attorney.

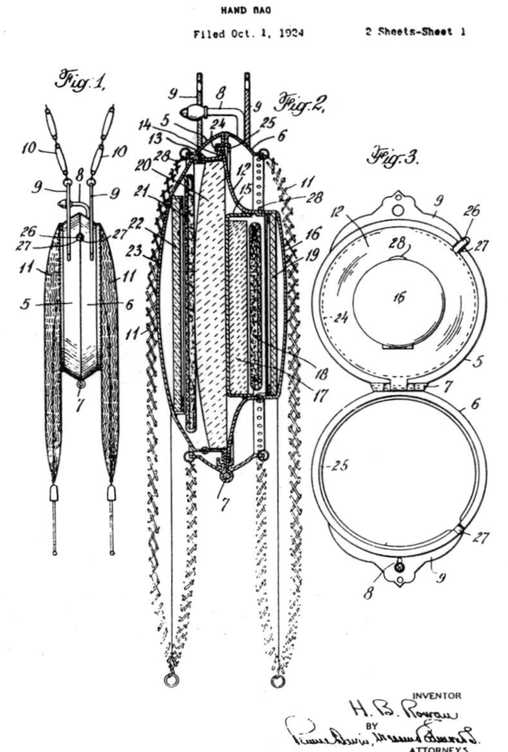
Dec. 22 1925.
H. B. ROWAN
HAND BAG
Filed Oct. 1, 1924
1,566,773
2 Sheets-Sheet 1
Fig. 1.
Fig. 2.
Fig. 3.
INVENTOR
H. B. Rowan
BY
ATTORNEYS.

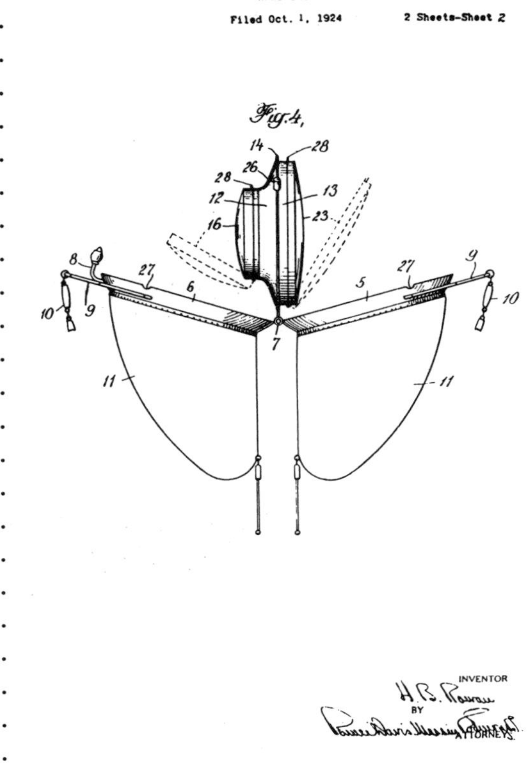
Dec. 22, 1925.
H. B. ROWAN
HAND BAG
Filed Oct. 1, 1924
1,566,773
2 Sheets-Sheet 2
Fig. 4.
INVENTOR
H. B. Rowan
BY
ATTORNEYS

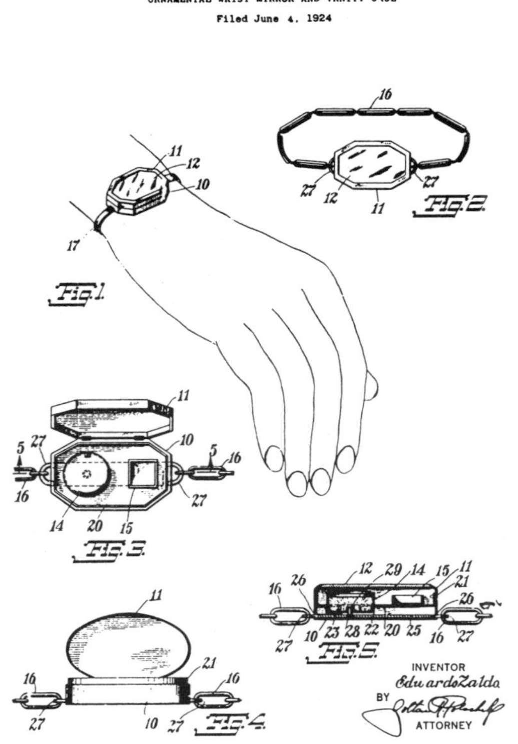
May 11, 1926.
E. ZALDO
ORNAMENTAL WRIST MIRROR AND VANITY CASE
Filed June 4, 1924
1,584,205
Fig. 1
Fig. 2
Fig. 3
Fig. 4
Fig. 5
INVENTOR
Eduardo Zaldo
BY
ATTORNEY

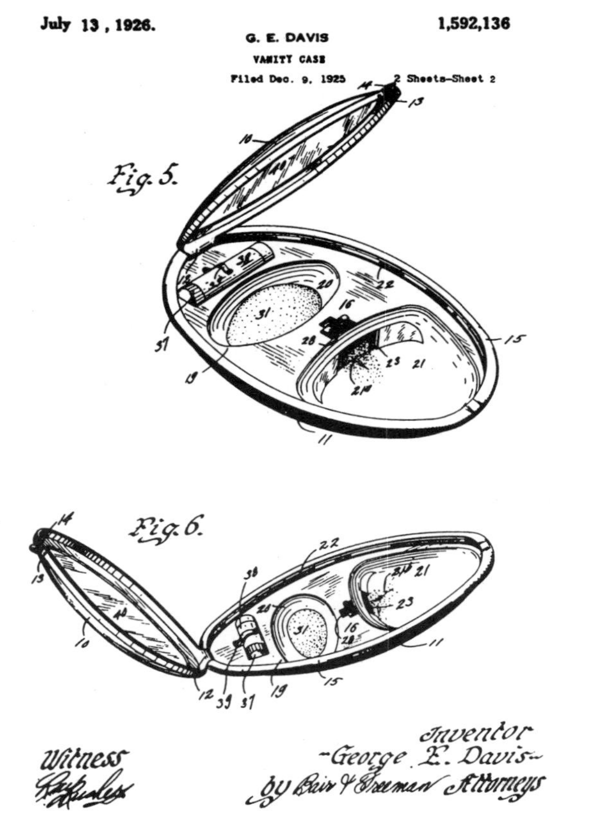
July 13, 1926.
G. E. DAVIS
VANITY CASE
Filed Dec. 9, 1925
1,592,136
2 Sheets-Sheet 2
Fig. 5.
Fig. 6.
Witness
Inventor
George E. Davis
by Bair & Freeman Attorneys

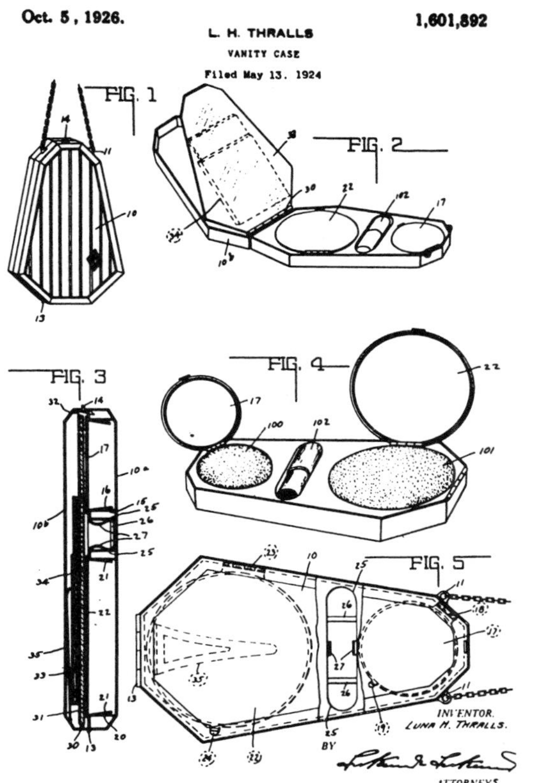
Oct. 5, 1926.
L. H. THRALLS
VANITY CASE
Filed May 13, 1924
1,601,892
FIG. 1
FIG. 2
FIG. 3
FIG. 4
FIG. 5
INVENTOR.
LUNA H. THRALLS.
BY
ATTORNEYS.

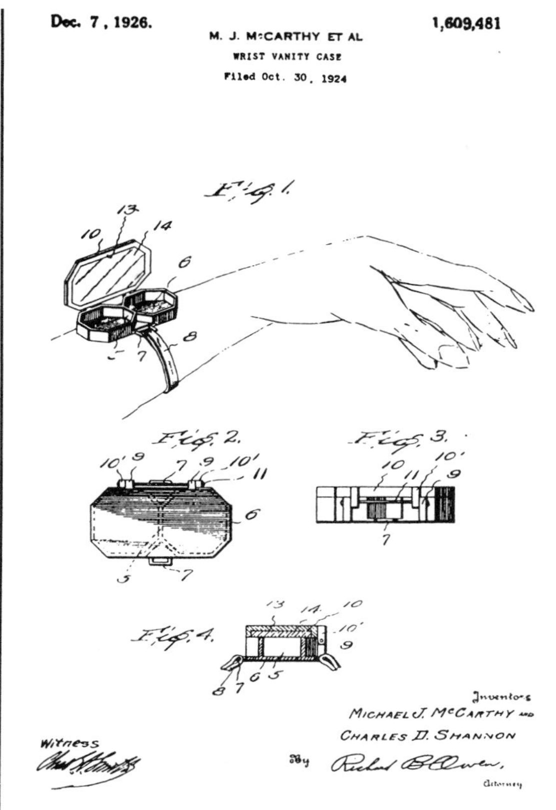
Dec. 7, 1926.
M. J. McCARTHY ET AL
WRIST VANITY CASE
Filed Oct. 30, 1924
1,609,481
Fig. 1.
Fig. 2.
Fig. 3.
Fig. 4.
Inventors
MICHAEL J. McCARTHY and
CHARLES D. SHANNON
Witness
By
Attorney

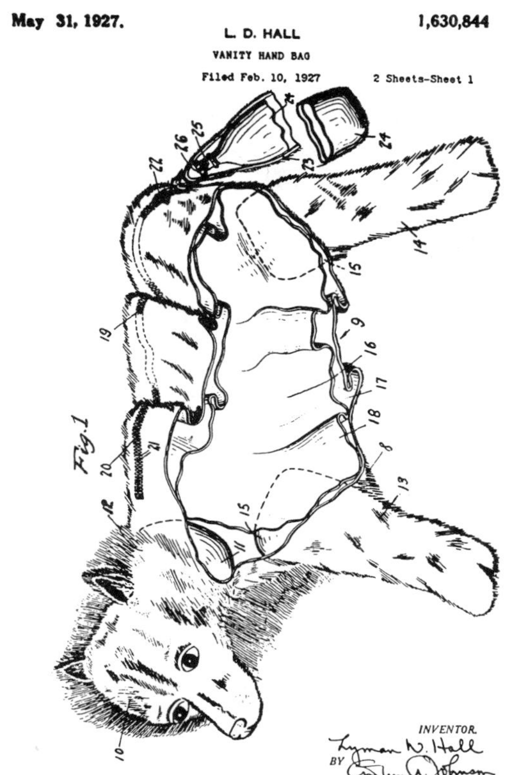
May 31, 1927.
L. D. HALL
VANITY HAND BAG
Filed Feb. 10, 1927
2 Sheets-Sheet 1
1,630,844
Fig. 1
INVENTOR.
Lyman N. Hall
BY
ATTORNEYS.

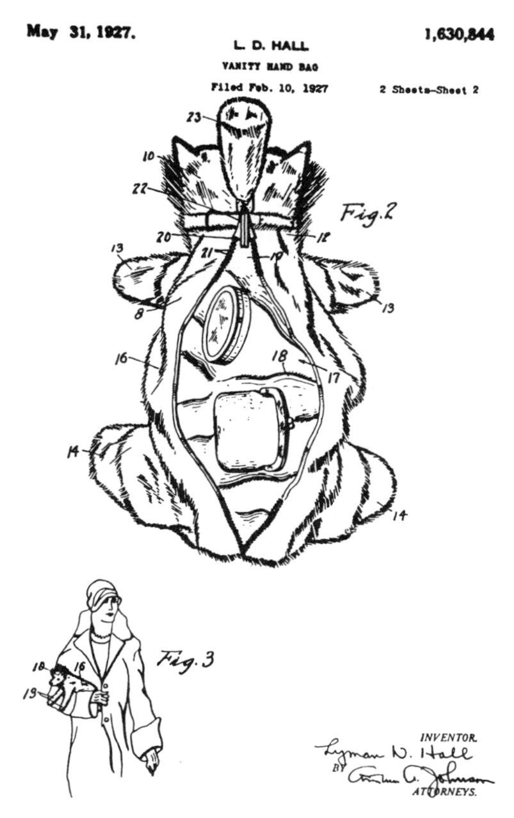
May 31, 1927.
L. D. HALL
VANITY HAND BAG
Filed Feb. 10, 1927
2 Sheets-Sheet 2
1,630,844
Fig. 2
Fig. 3
INVENTOR.
Lyman N. Hall
BY
ATTORNEYS.

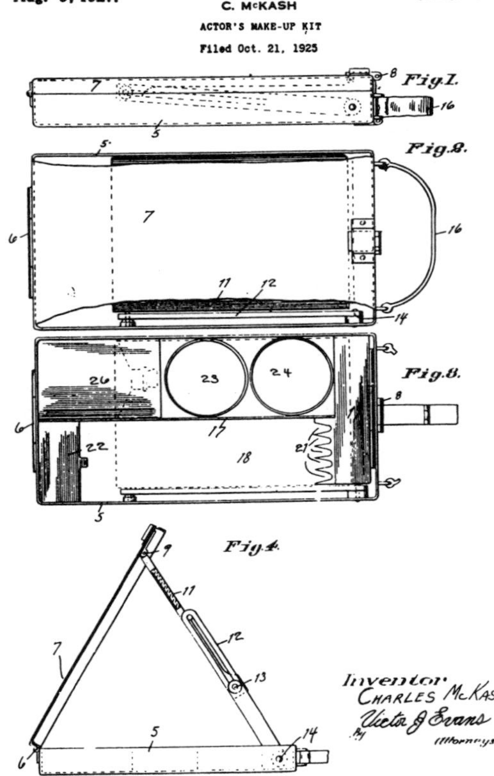
Aug. 9, 1927.
C. McKASH
1,638,356
ACTOR'S MAKE-UP KIT
Filed Oct. 21, 1925
Fig.1.
Fig.2.
Fig.3.
Fig.4.
Inventor
CHARLES McKASH
Victor J. Evans
Attorneys.

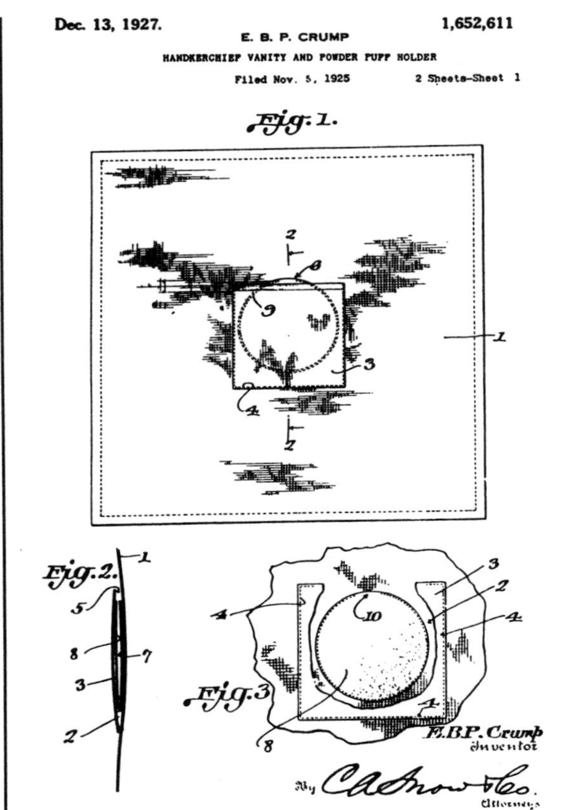
Dec. 13, 1927.
E. B. P. CRUMP
1,652,611
HANDKERCHIEF VANITY AND POWDER PUFF HOLDER
Filed Nov. 5, 1925
2 Sheets-Sheet 1
Fig.1.
Fig.2.
Fig.3
E.B.P. Crump
Inventor
By C.A. Snow & Co.
Attorneys

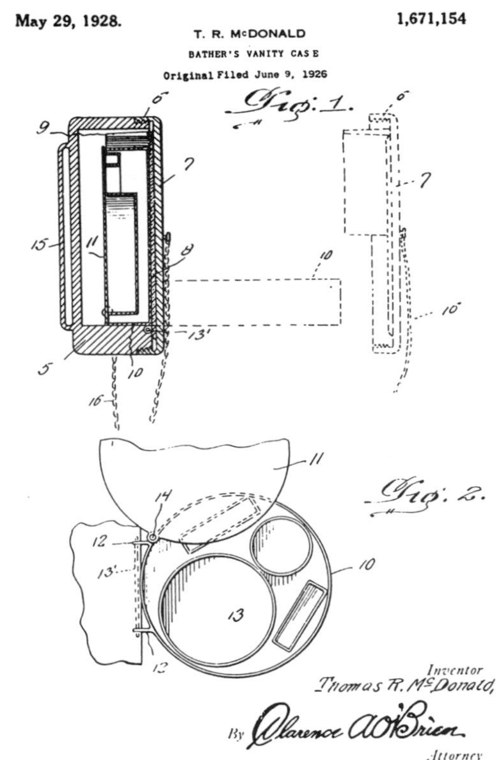
May 29, 1928.
T. R. McDONALD
1,671,154
BATHER'S VANITY CASE
Original Filed June 9, 1926
Fig. 1.
Fig. 2.
Inventor
Thomas R. McDonald,
By Clarence A. O'Brien
Attorney

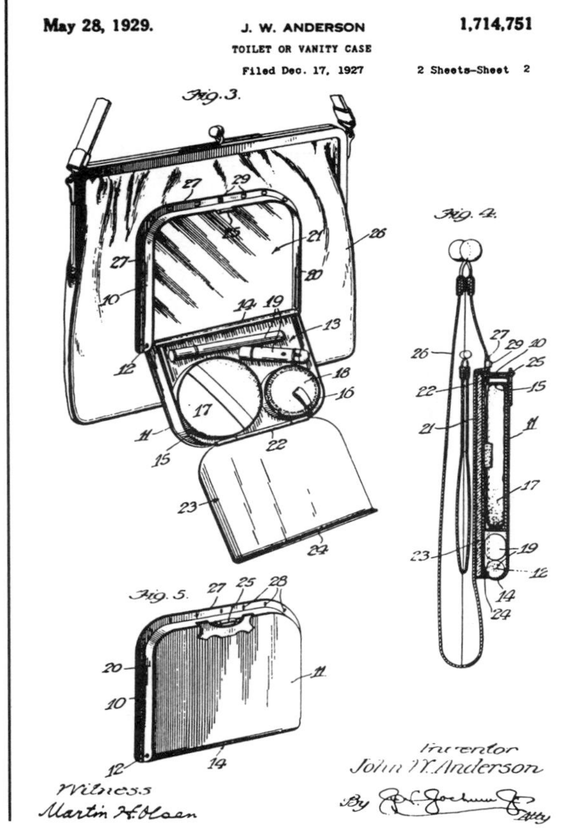
May 28, 1929.
J. W. ANDERSON
1,714,751
TOILET OR VANITY CASE
Filed Dec. 17, 1927
2 Sheets-Sheet 2
Fig. 3.
Fig. 4.
Fig. 5.
Inventor
John W. Anderson
Witness
Martin H. Olsen

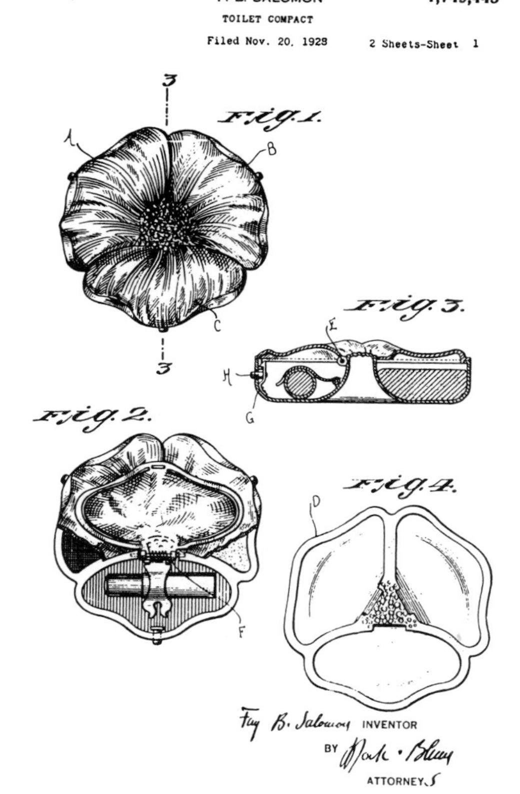
March 4, 1930.
F. B. SALOMON
1,749,445
TOILET COMPACT
Filed Nov. 20, 1928
2 Sheets-Sheet 1
Fig. 1.
Fig. 2.
Fig. 3.
Fig. 4.
INVENTOR
BY
ATTORNEYS

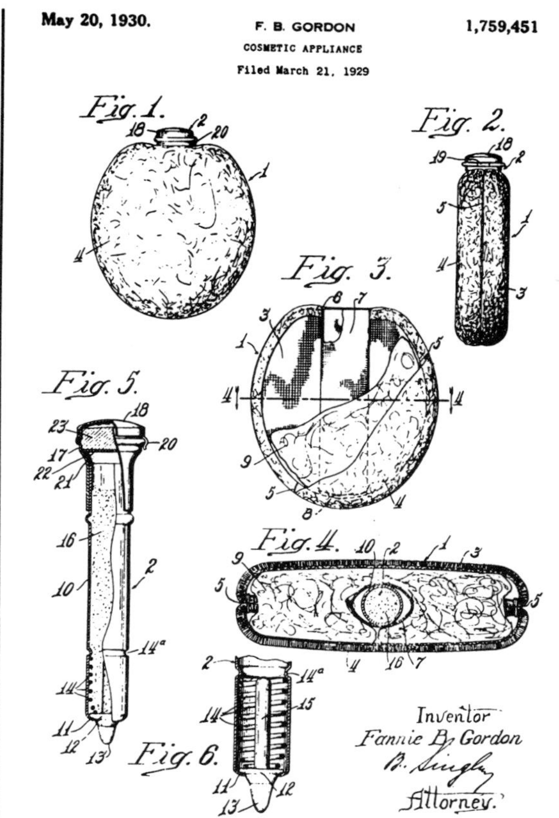
May 20, 1930.
F. B. GORDON
1,759,451
COSMETIC APPLIANCE
Filed March 21, 1929
Fig. 1.
Fig. 2.
Fig. 3.
Fig. 4.
Fig. 5.
Fig. 6.
Inventor
Fannie B. Gordon
Attorney.

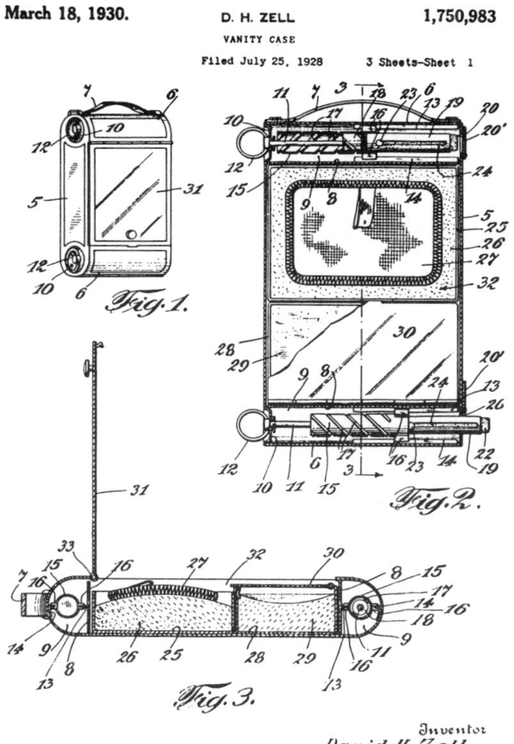
March 18, 1930.
D. H. ZELL
1,750,983
VANITY CASE
Filed July 25, 1928
3 Sheets-Sheet 1
Fig. 1.
Fig. 2.
Fig. 3.
Inventor
David H. Zell
By his Attorney

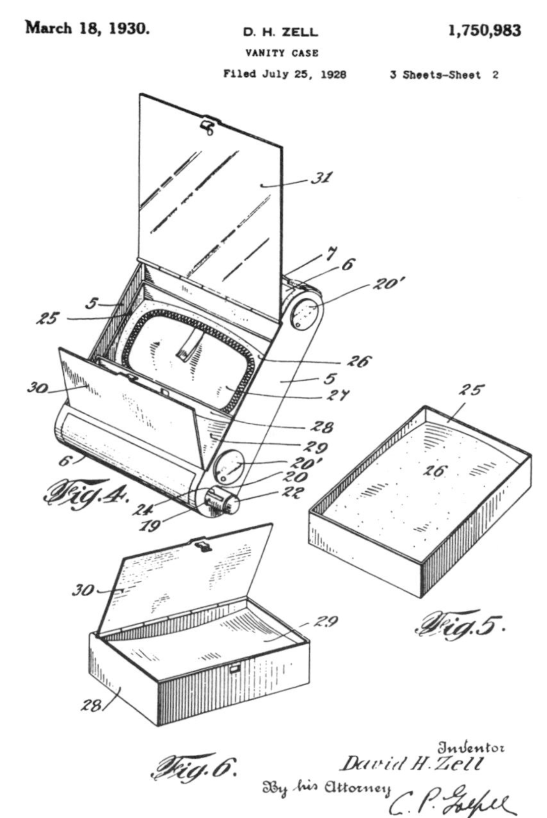
March 18, 1930.
D. H. ZELL
1,750,983
VANITY CASE
Filed July 25, 1928
3 Sheets-Sheet 2
Fig. 4.
Fig. 5.
Fig. 6.
Inventor
David H. Zell
By his Attorney

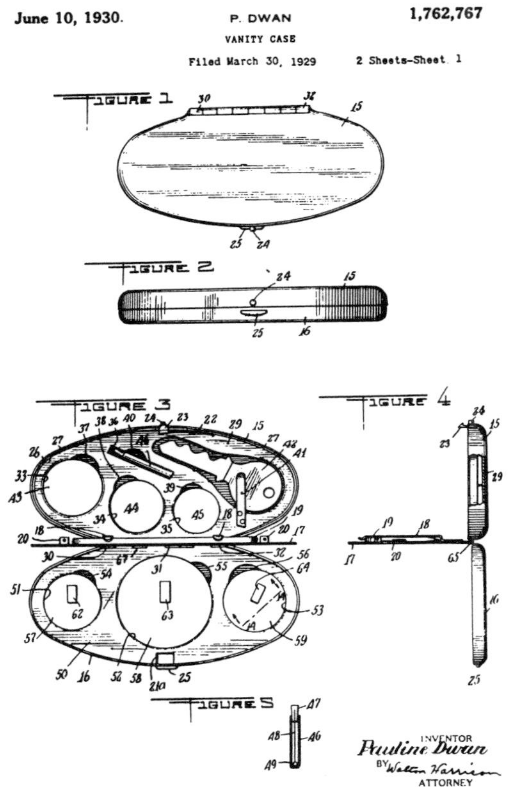

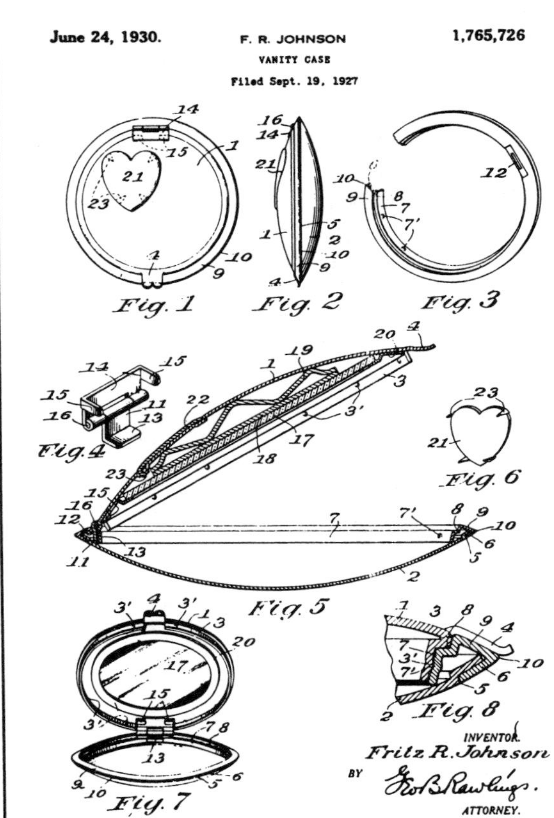

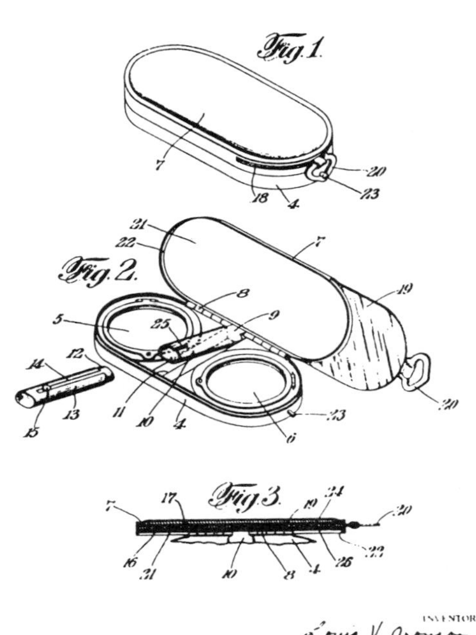

June 7, 1932. G. M. ROBERTS 1,861,644

COMBINED WATCH AND VANITY CASE

Filed Jan. 10, 1929 2 Sheets-Sheet 1

Fig. 1

Fig. 2

Fig. 3

Fig. 4

Fig. 5

INVENTOR.
GEORGE M ROBERTS
BY
ATTORNEY.

June 7, 1932. G. M. ROBERTS 1,861,644

COMBINED WATCH AND VANITY CASE.

Filed Jan. 10, 1929 2 Sheets-Sheet 2

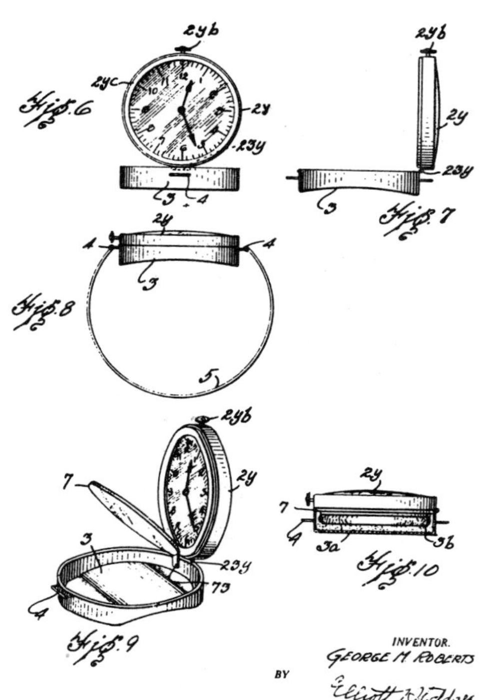

July 19, 1932. A. ERMITAÑO 1,867,815

FAN AND COMPACT

Filed Aug. 10, 1931

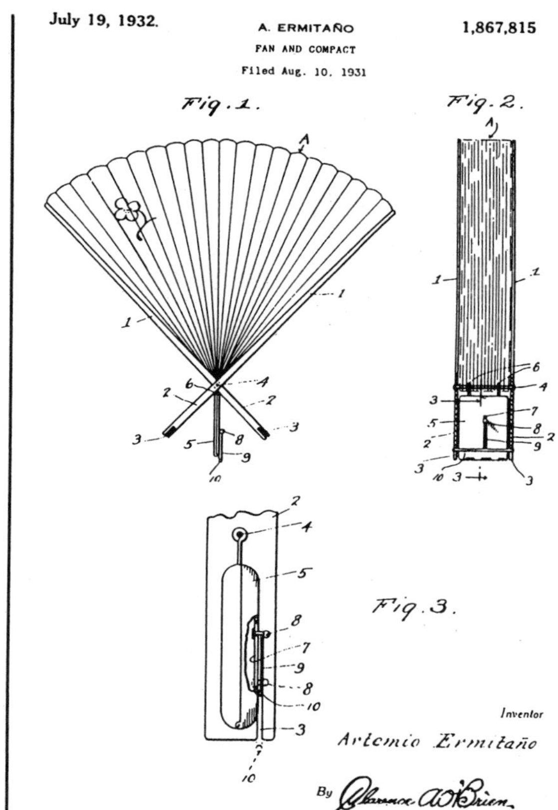

Nov. 27, 1934. E. GEBHARDT 1,982,248

HANDKERCHIEF CARRYING VANITY ACCESSORY

Filed July 27, 1932

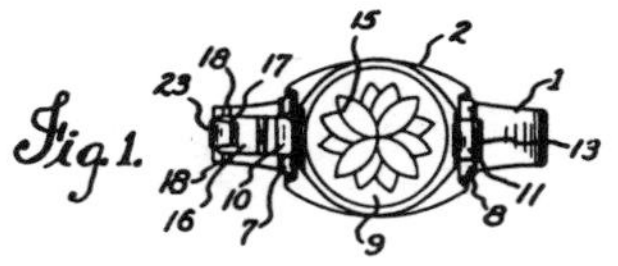

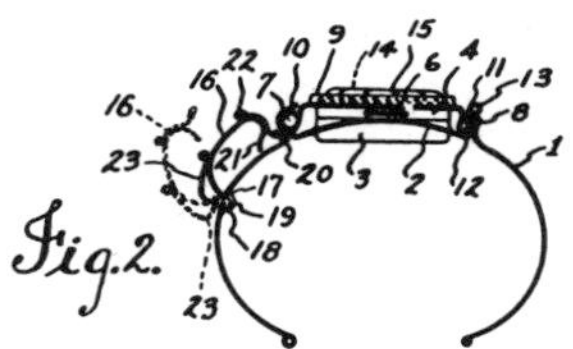

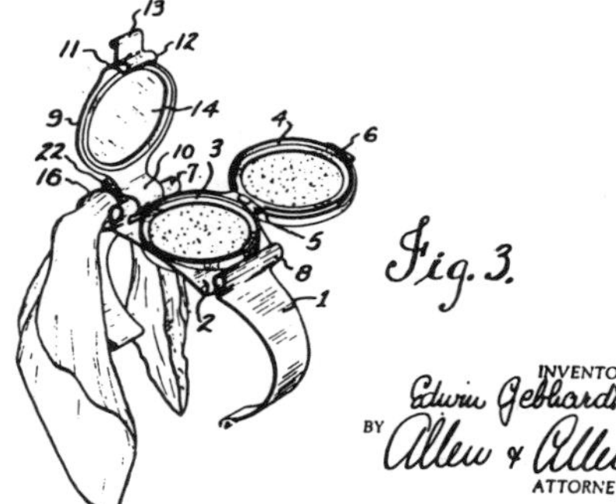

March 12, 1935. G. G. McDONALD 1,993,938

VANITY GEAR SHIFT KNOB

Filed June 28, 1933

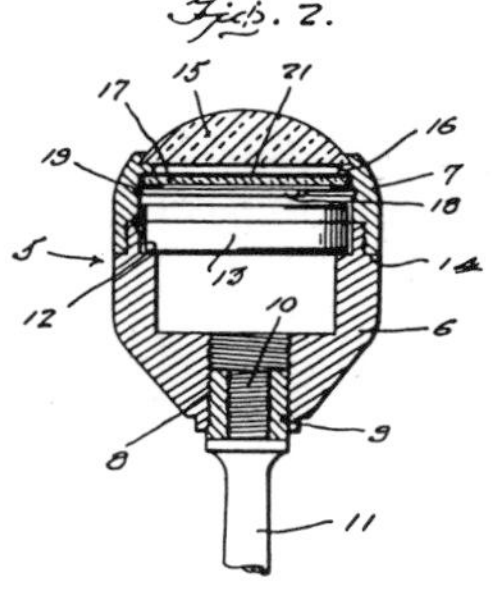

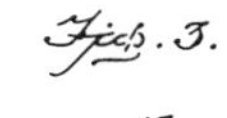

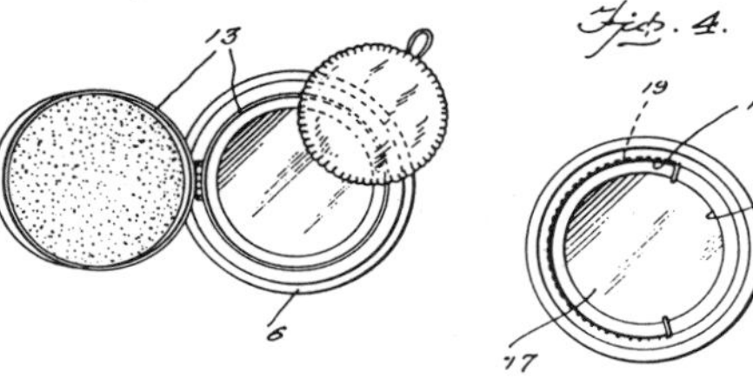

Inventor

G. G. McDonald

By Clarence A. O'Brien

Attorney

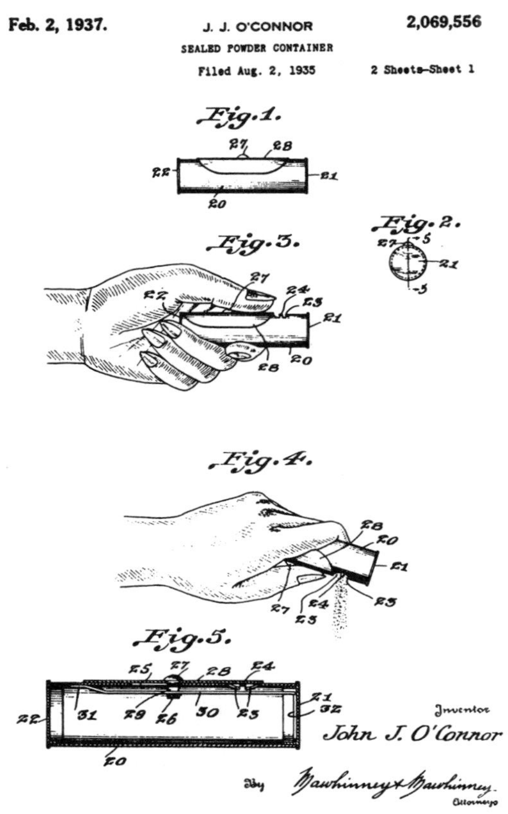
Feb. 2, 1937.
J. J. O'CONNOR
2,069,556
SEALED POWDER CONTAINER
Filed Aug. 2, 1935
2 Sheets-Sheet 1
Fig. 1.
Fig. 2.
Fig. 3.
Fig. 4.
Fig. 5.
Inventor
John J. O'Connor
By Mawhinney & Mawhinney
Attorneys

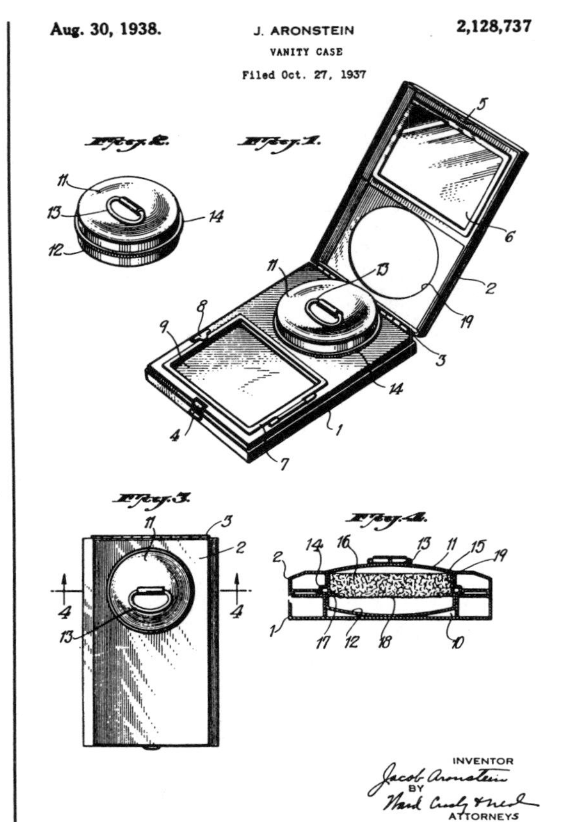
Aug. 30, 1938.
J. ARONSTEIN
2,128,737
VANITY CASE
Filed Oct. 27, 1937
INVENTOR
Jacob Aronstein
BY
ATTORNEYS

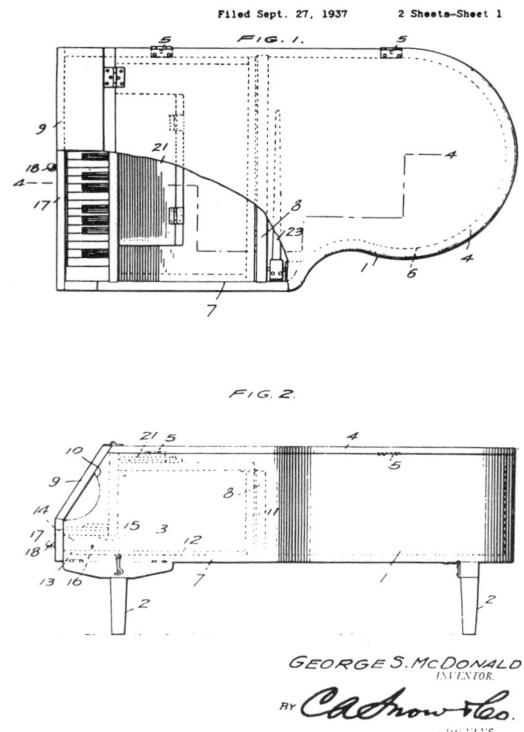
Oct. 11, 1938.
G. S. McDONALD
2,132,989
VANITY BOX
Filed Sept. 27, 1937
2 Sheets-Sheet 1
FIG. 1.
FIG. 2.
GEORGE S. McDONALD
INVENTOR.
BY C.A. Snow & Co.
ATTORNEYS.

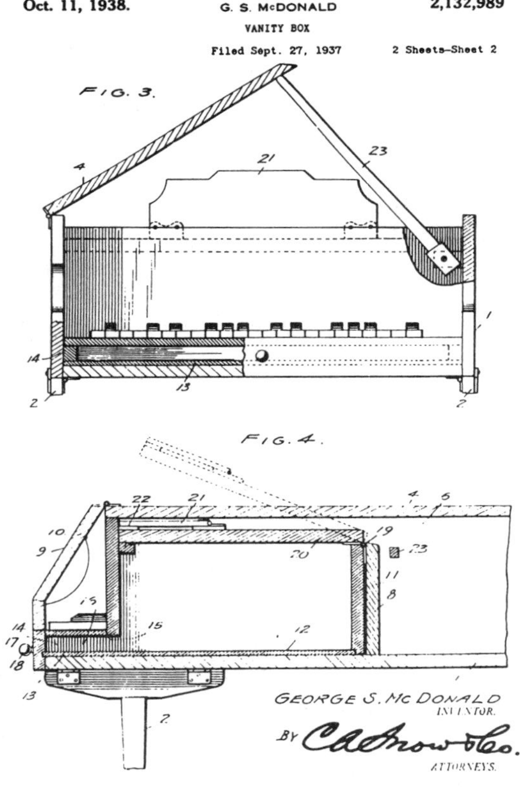
Oct. 11, 1938.
G. S. McDONALD
2,132,989
VANITY BOX
Filed Sept. 27, 1937
2 Sheets-Sheet 2
FIG. 3.
FIG. 4.
GEORGE S. McDONALD
INVENTOR.
BY C.A. Snow & Co.
ATTORNEYS.

Jan. 24, 1939. F. M. WILLIAMSON 2,145,035

WIPER FOR VANITY CASES

Filed Aug. 16, 1937

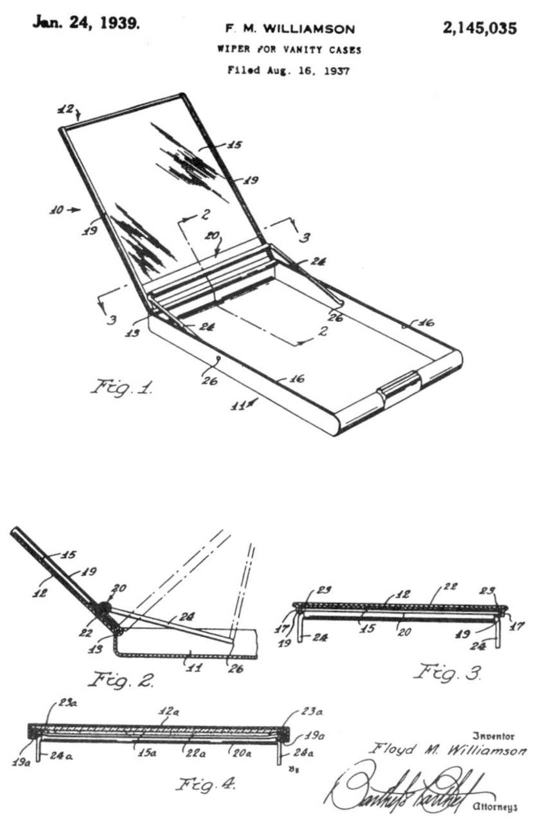

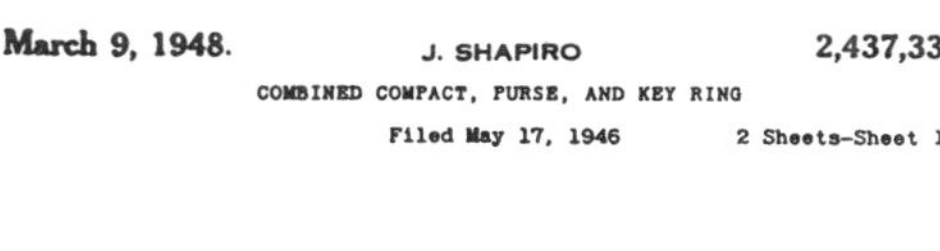

Jan. 14, 1941. C. PICINICH 2,228,845

VANITY CASE

Filed Aug. 22, 1938

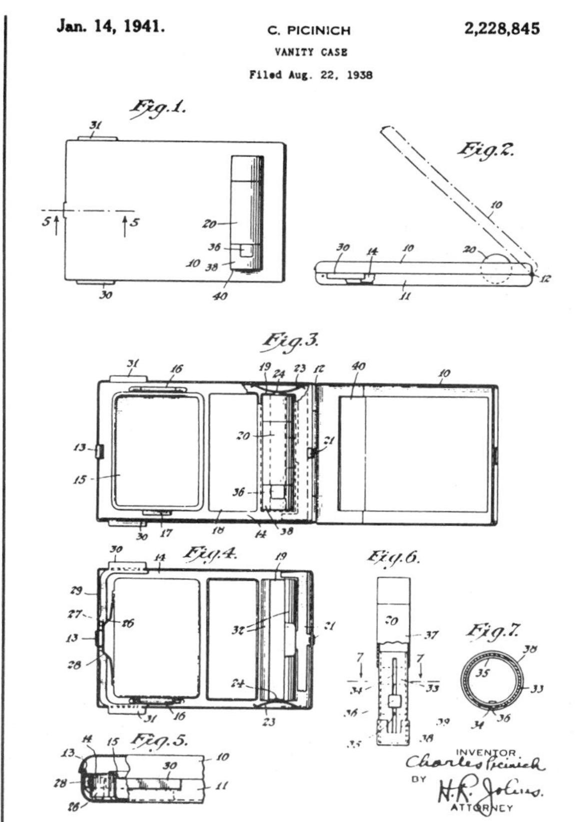

March 9, 1948. J. SHAPIRO 2,437,335

COMBINED COMPACT, PURSE, AND KEY RING

Filed May 17, 1946 2 Sheets-Sheet 1

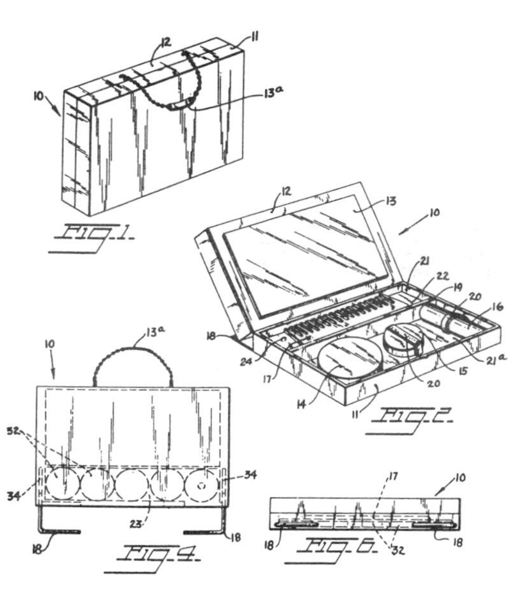

May 11, 1948. B. WESSON ET AL 2,441,303

VANITY CASE

Filed March 4, 1946 3 Sheets-Sheet 3

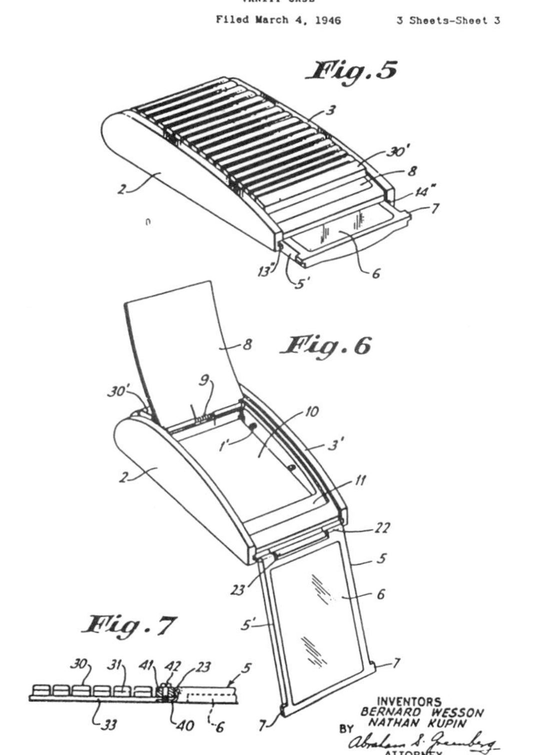

April 12, 1949. R. Z. SARFF 2,466,783

HOLDER FOR COSMETICS

Filed Feb. 11, 1947

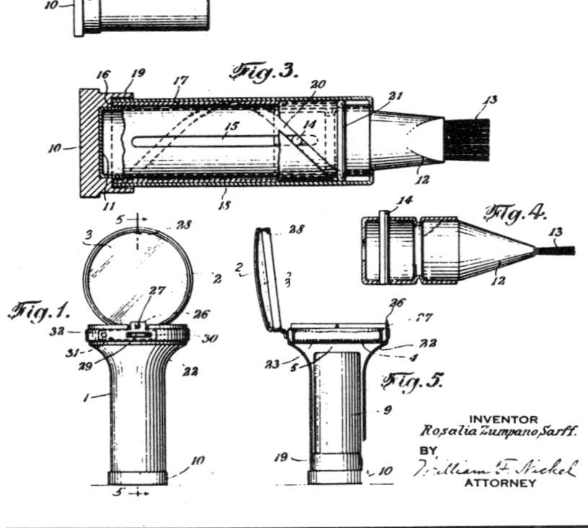

Oct. 25, 1949. A. M. COHAN 2,485,814

OUTSIDE LOCKET VANITY CASE

Filed Oct. 11, 1945

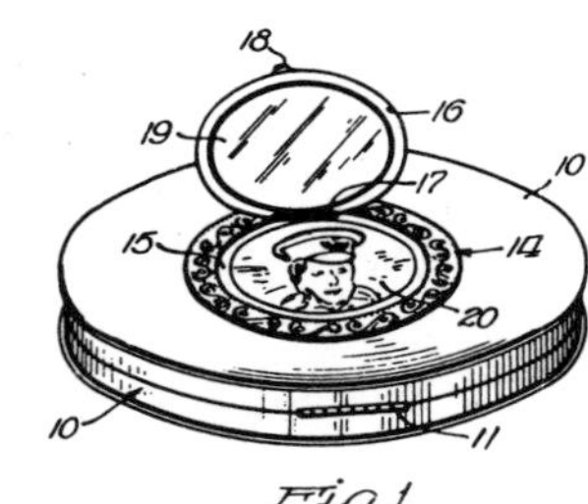

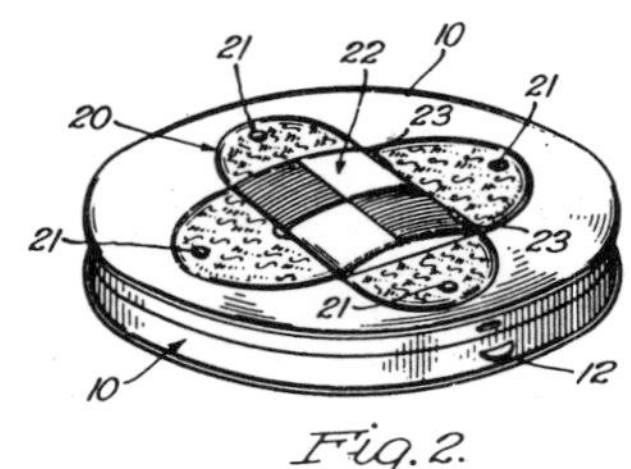

INVENTOR.
Albert M. Cohan
BY
Charles M. Woodin
Agent.

Nov. 22, 1949 J. B. HELMS 2,488,910

COSMETIC COMPACT AND APPLICATOR

Filed Aug. 2, 1946

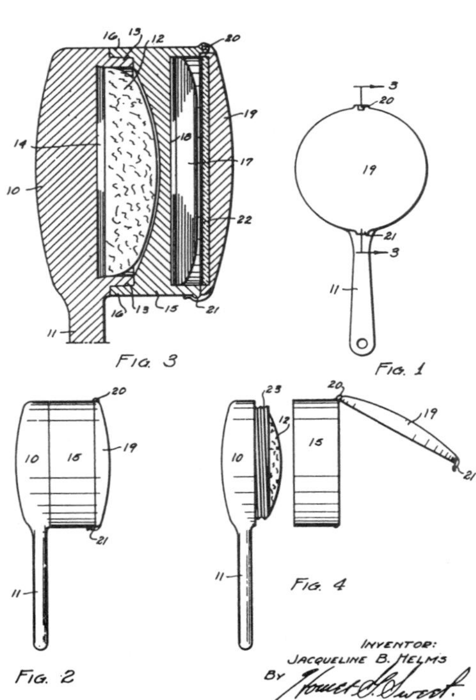

Jan. 3, 1950 A. KORODY 2,493,074

COMPACT HOLDER AND BRUSH

Filed Nov. 8, 1948

Fig. 1. Fig. 2. Fig. 3. Fig. 4. Fig. 5. Fig. 6. Fig. 7.

INVENTOR.
ALEXANDER KORODY.
BY Ralph W. Bumstead
ATTORNEY.

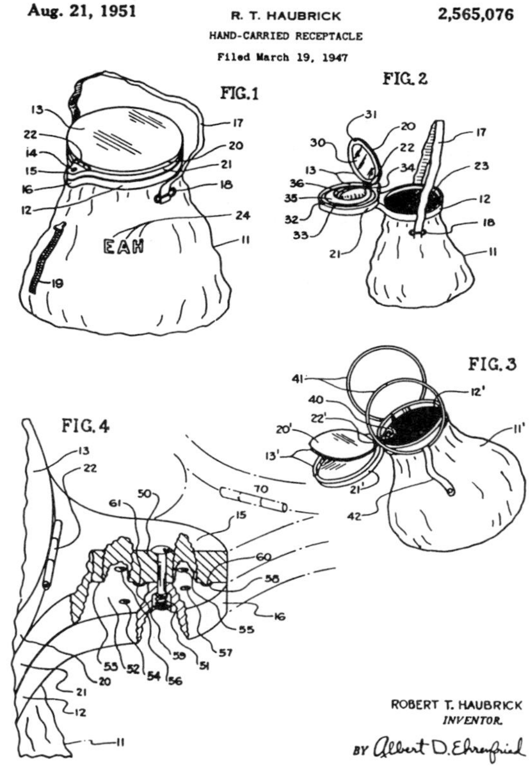

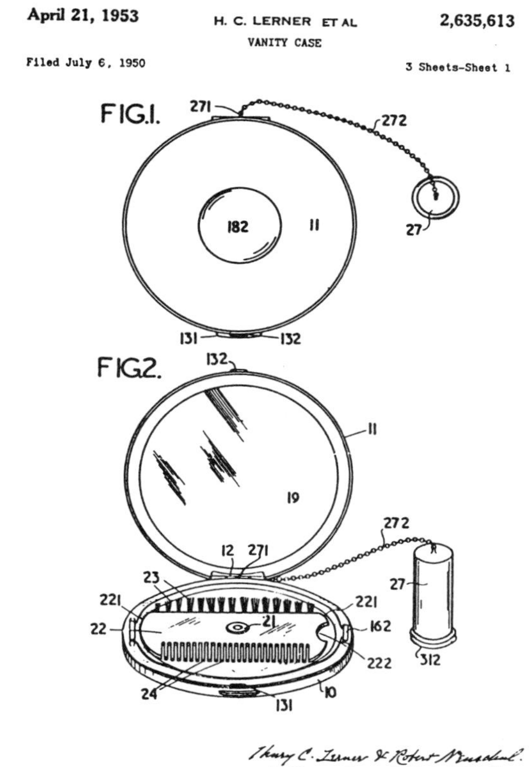

Aug. 21, 1951 R. T. HAUBRICK 2,565,076

HAND-CARRIED RECEPTACLE

Filed March 19, 1947

FIG.1
FIG.2
FIG.3
FIG.4
EAH

ROBERT T. HAUBRICK
INVENTOR
BY Albert D. Ehrenfried

April 21, 1953 H. C. LERNER ET AL 2,635,613

VANITY CASE

Filed July 6, 1950 3 Sheets-Sheet 1

FIG.1.
FIG.2.

Henry C. Lerner & Robert Neuschel
by Hanway, Jenney, Witter & Hildreth Attys.

April 21, 1953 H. C. LERNER ET AL 2,635,613

VANITY CASE

Filed July 6, 1950 3 Sheets-Sheet 2

FIG.3.
FIG.4A.
FIG.4.

Henry C. Lerner & Robert Neuschel
by Hanway, Jenney, Witter & Hildreth Attys.

April 21, 1953 H. C. LERNER ET AL 2,635,613

VANITY CASE

Filed July 6, 1950 3 Sheets-Sheet 3

FIG.5.

Henry C. Lerner & Robert Neuschel
by Hanway, Jenney, Witter & Hildreth Attys.

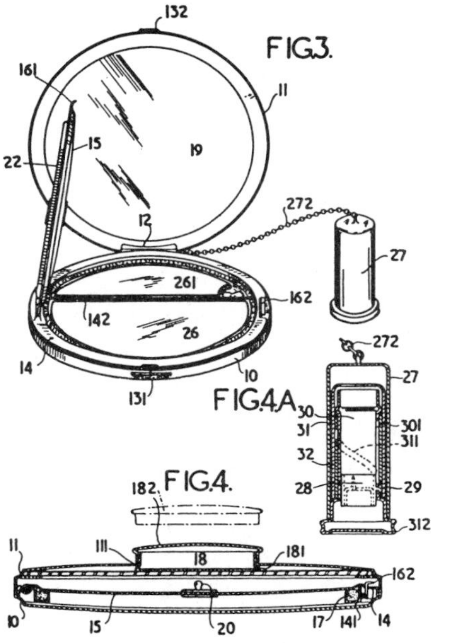

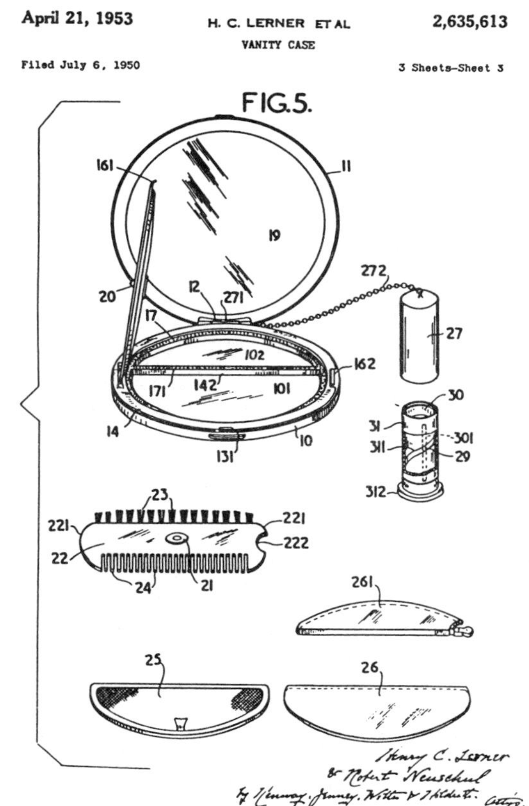

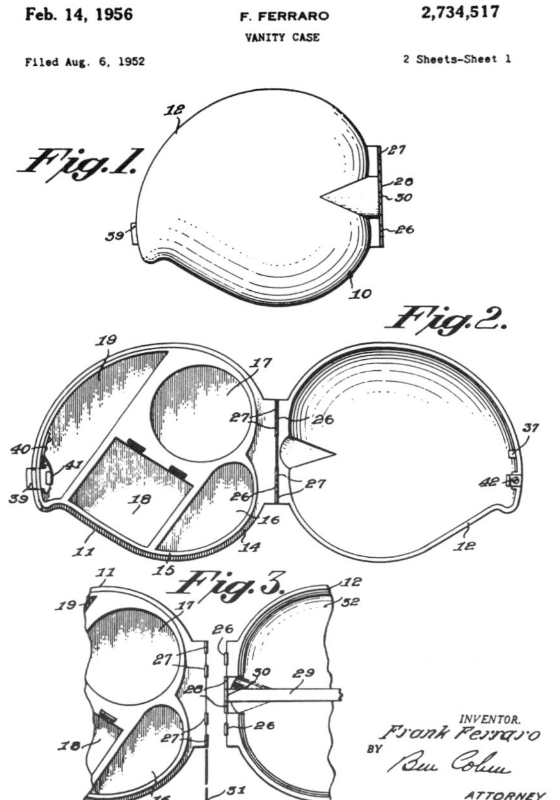
Feb. 14, 1956
F. FERRARO
2,734,517
VANITY CASE
Filed Aug. 6, 1952
2 Sheets-Sheet 1
Fig.1.
Fig.2.
Fig.3.
INVENTOR.
Frank Ferraro
BY
Ben Cohen
ATTORNEY

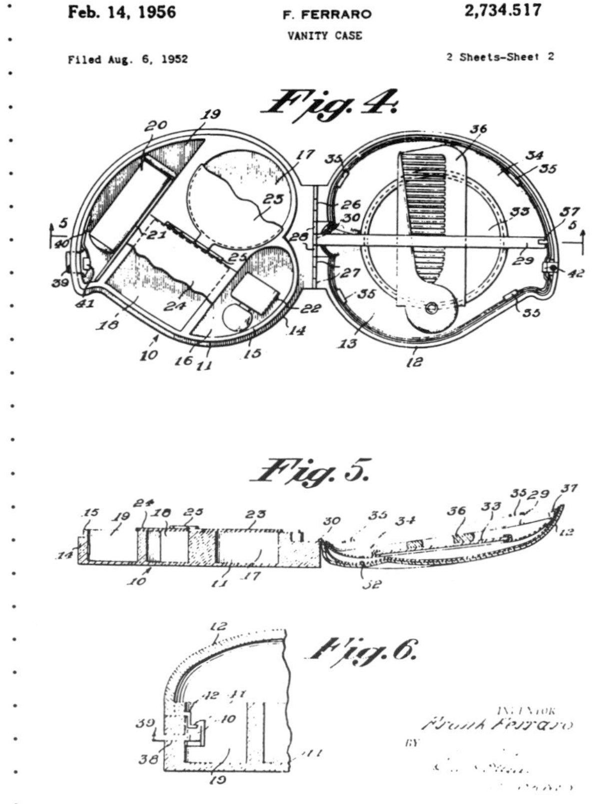
Feb. 14, 1956
F. FERRARO
2,734.517
VANITY CASE
Filed Aug. 6, 1952
2 Sheets-Sheet 2
Fig.4.
Fig.5.
Fig.6.
Frank Ferraro

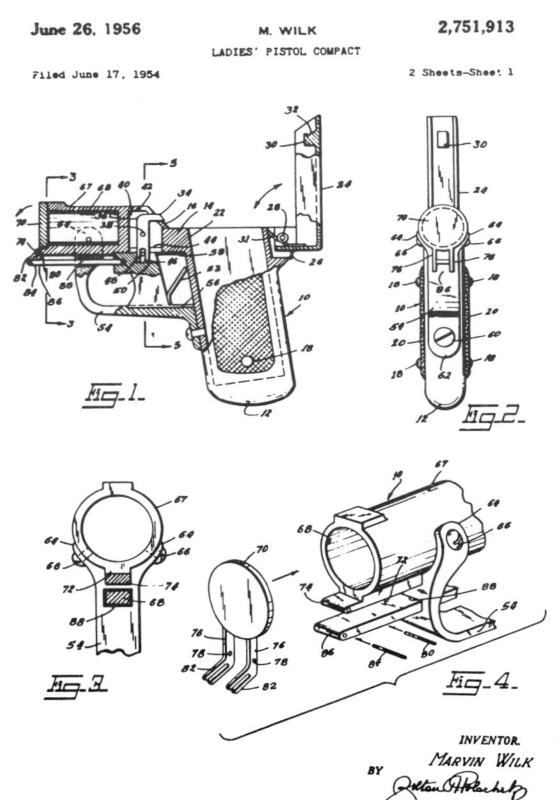
June 26, 1956
M. WILK
2,751,913
LADIES' PISTOL COMPACT
Filed June 17, 1954
2 Sheets-Sheet 1
Fig-1-
Fig-2-
Fig-3
Fig-4-
INVENTOR.
MARVIN WILK
BY
ATTORNEY

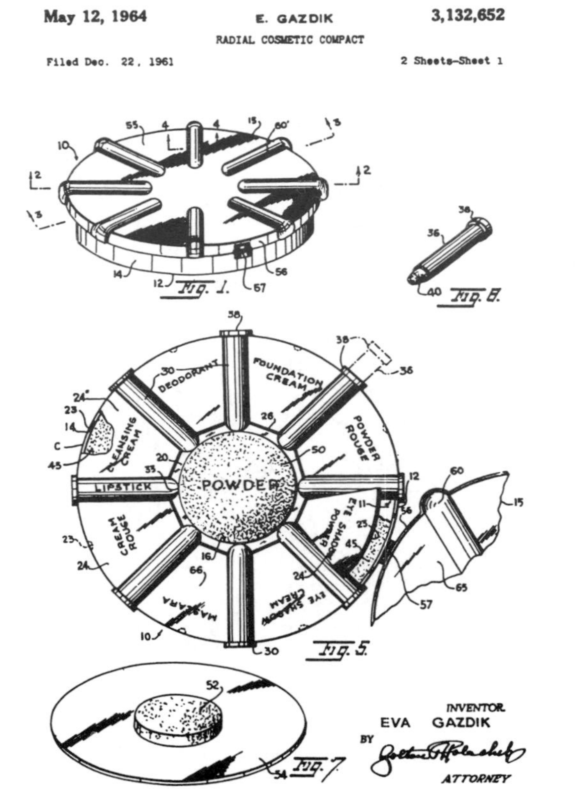
May 12, 1964
E. GAZDIK
3,132,652
RADIAL COSMETIC COMPACT
Filed Dec. 22, 1961
2 Sheets-Sheet 1
Fig. 1.
Fig. 8.
DEODORANT
FOUNDATION CREAM
POWDER ROUGE
CLEANSING CREAM
POWDER
LIPSTICK
CREAM ROUGE
EYE SHADOW POWDER
MASCARA
EYE SHADOW CREAM
Fig. 5.
Fig. 7
INVENTOR
EVA GAZDIK
BY
ATTORNEY

Manufacturing Information

List of Materials

Alligator
Aluminum
Bakelite
Beads
Bird feathers
Brass
Brocade
Bronze
Butterfly wings
Celluloid
Chrome
Delft
Fur
Gemstones
German silver
Glass
Gold
Grosgrain
Gun-metal
Ivory
Jade
Lace
Lacquer
Leather
Lizard
Lucite
Marcasite
Mesh
Moiré
Mosaic
Mother-of-pearl
Paper
Pearl
Pewter
Plastic
Porcelain
Precious gems
Rhinestone
Satin
Sequins
Shagreen
Shell
Silk
Silver
Snakeskin
Steel
Suede
Synthetic stones
Taffeta
Tortoiseshell
Velvet
Wedgwood
Wood
Wool

Compact Manufacturers and Trade Names

A. Bourjois & Co., Inc.
A. L. Siegel Co. (Handysift)
A. S. Brown (England)
AC Belkin Company
Adrienne
AGME (Switzerland)
Aklar
Alpacca (Germany)
Alpaccahoka
Alwyn
Ameré (Switzerland)
American Beauty
American Maid
Amita
Anna Pavlova
Annette
Ansico
Antoine
Arden, Elizabeth
Armand
Armond Co.
Arpels
Artcraft
Asprey
Aveon, N.Y.
Avon

B.B.Co
B & B Co.
B.Co.
BC
Bag-Dabs
Bagirette
Baird North
Barbara Gould
Beauty-Full
Belais
Bertie (Paris)
BG
Bigney
Blanchette DeCorday
Black, Starr and Frost
Bliss Brothers
E. A. Bliss Co.
Blumpak
Bond Street, Laaco
Bonnjolie
Botony Lanolin
Boucheron
Bourdier (Paris)
Bree
D. F. Briggs
Britemode
Broderie Main (France)
Buccellati
Buchner
C & N
C. Fauré
Cambi (France)
Campus Make Up
Cappi (Cheramy)
Cara Mia
Cara Noma
Cartier (Paris, London, New York)
Chament
Chanel
Chantrey
Charbert
Charlton
Charles of the Ritz
Chaumet
Cheramy
Chez ReLew
Cigogne, Inc.
Ciner
Clarece Jane
Cleopatra Vanity, Rex Co.
Clercygne-Pierrette (Paris)
Clover
Colgate & Co.
Colleen Moore Cosmetics
Colt Purse Make-Up Kit
Columbia Creation
Columbia Fifth Ave.
Compant
Concord
Coro
Coty
Crafters (Chicago)
Creme-Puff
Croco (Israel)
Crysta
D. B. H. Sterling (England)
D. F. B. CO.
Daniel (Paris)
Darnee (New York)
Dassy (France)
De Mendor-Lazell
De Meridor
Deerie
Deletron
Delettrez
Dermay
Deva (France)
Deva-Dassy
Divine
Djer-Kiss
Donmark Creations
Dorette
Dorine
Dorothy Gray
Dorset, 5th Ave. (New York)
Dorset, Rex 5th Ave. (New York)
Doucette
Dovell Co.
Dover Briars
Dreisen & Co.
DuBarry
Dunhill Vanity
Dunhill, N.Y.
Duro Gloss
E.A.M. (*see* Elgin American)
E.P.M.S.
Edna Wallace Hopper
Edouardo
Edward's Bag, Ltd.
Egme (England)

Eisenberg
Elgin American Co., Inc.
(also owned Clarece Jane)
E.A.M.
Elgin Vanity
Elgina
Elginite
Elizabeth Arden
Elmo
Enco
Entièrement
Estée Lauder
Evans
Evanshire
Evening In Paris
Eversmart Manicure Compact
F & Co.
F & J
F M Co.
F & B
F. H. Sadler
F. J. Co.
Fabergé (Russian)
Fiancee
Fifth Avenue
Fillkwik Co.
Fitch
Fladium (France)
Flamond (France)
FM Co.
Foreum
Foster
Foster & Bailey
Framies
Framus
Fuller
G. L. B. Co.
Gaess & Hollander
Gainsborough
Garden Court
Gayanne
Georg Jensen (Denmark and New York)
Gibbs
Girey (U.S.A.)
Givenchy
Graceline
Gucci (Italy)
Gwenda (England)
H.F.B.
Hammacher Schlemmer
Hampton
Harmony of Boston
Harriet Hubbard Ayer
Hattie Carnegie
Helane Roma Firenze
Helena Rubinstein
Helene Curtis
Henriette (U.S.A.)
Hingeco (Rhode Island)
Hoechst
Hollywood
Houbigant
Houppette
Illinois Watch Case Co. (Welwood Watch)
Ingram Co.
International Silver
Ivan Britzin (Moscow)
J. F. Creations J.F.B. Co.
J. M. Fisher Co.
J. M. F. Co.
Janesich
Jaquet
Jason Wherler & Sons Mfg.
Jean Panand
Jean Pesprès
Jonteel
JRS (Denmark)
Jules Richard
K & K (Kotler & Kopet, Inc.)
Karess
Karnee
Kaycroft
Kigu of London
Kissproof
Komai/Amita (Japan)
Komdi (Kyota, Japan)
Krank
Kreisler
Kyrill
L. T. Piver (Paris)
La Bohême
La Faveur de Paris
La Jaynees
La Mode
La Mode (R & G Co. Sterling)
La Ray, Inc.
La Santo
La Vedelte
La-May Vanity

Labco
Lablache
Lacherche (Paris)
Lady Esther (Chicago)
Lady Lee
Lady Vanity
Lamkin
Lampl
Lanado
Lanchère
Langlois (New York)
Larue
Larvé
Lazell
Le Debut
Le Rage (England)
Le Tresor
Lee Fran
Lederer (Paris)
Lenthéric
Leon
Léon Farchery (Paris)
Lesco (Bond Street)
Liberty of London
Lilly Daché
LIN-BREN
Linc Vautrin
Little Lady
LOOS PACT
Lubin
Lucien Lelong
Lucky Purse
Lucretia Vanderbilt (New York)
Luschous
Lushus
Luxor Limited (Chicago)
Lyric
M.M.R's
Ma Poudre
Marenello Co.
Majestic (New York)
Man Five
Manna (Naples)
Mara
Marathon
Marcee
Marhill
Marie Earle
Marion Bialac (New York)
Mark Cross
Marlene
Marlowe Co.
Marly (Les Parfums)
Mary Dunhill
Mary Dunhill Co.
Mary Garden
Mary Garden, Rigaud (Paris)
Mary Lewis (England)
Mascot A.S.B.
Maubousson, Park and 55th (N.Y.)
Mavco
Mavis
Max Factor
Maxim
Maxley K.K.
May Co. (Calif)
May-Fair
Medana (West Germany)
Melba Compacte
Melissa (England)
Mello-Glo
Metalfield
Milrone
Mignon
Mingeco (U.S.A.)
Minois
Miref
Mireve
Misof of Paris
MMR Company (1920)
MMR Red Seal
Molinard (France)
Mondaine
Montré à Poudre (France)
Morss
Movado
Murat
Nan Co-Ed
Napier
New Light-Nissei Co., Ltd. (Toyko)
Norida
Novex
Nylotis (Nyal Co.)
Nymfaun
Old Spice
Opaline
Osaka (Japan)
Ostertag (Paris)
Paris Fashion Co.
Parklane LSM

Patrys (Paris)
Pattie Duette Vivaudou
Paul Flato
Personal Beauty Ware
Pilcher Mfg. Co., Inc.
Platé
PN Co. (Chicago)
Pomone
Pompeian
Poster
Powder-Tier
Primrose House
Prince Matchabelli
Princess Marcella Borghese
Princess Pat
Profile Et Modile (France)
Puf-Kase
Pygmalion (England)
Quinlon
Quinto
R & G Co.
RAC
Raymond Templier
Regent
Regent of London
Remé (Switzerland)
Renard (New York)
Revels Glamour Kit
Revlon
Rex Products Corp.
RH Co.
RHO-JAN
Richard Hudnut
Ricard Limoges (France)
Richelieu
Rigaud
RION (Brazil)
RITZ
Robin Handbag
Roger & Gallet
ROGER EDET
Ronson
Rosenfeld (Israel)
Rowenta
Rumpp
S and F
S.G.D.G (France)
Sabor (France)
Sam Fink
Samaral (Madrid)
Schildkraut 5th Ave.
Schleps & Hausemann
Schlumberger
Schuco
Segal
Seventeen Toiletries
Shari
Shields MFG Inc.
Shields Inc.
Silroy
Silvaray
Stadium Girl
Starlet Compact
Stearns of Detroit and Paris
Stratnoid (England)
Stratton (England)
Sue et Mave
Sunc (China)
Suncer Flanjack (Austria)
Superb (U.S.A.)
Suzuyo (Sterling-Oriental)
Swinglok
Tangee
Tattoo
Tre-Jur
Terri Vanities
The D. L. Avld Co. (Columbus, Ohio)
The Marhill Co. Inc.
Tien
Tiffany & Co. (New York and Paris)
Timepact
Tokalon (Paris)
Ton Ton 5th Ave.
Trabert & Hoeffec, Inc.
Tradition
Trio-Ette
Tu Adore
Tussy
Tyrolean
Vade Mecum
Van Cleef & Arpels (Fifth Avenue, New York, Paris, Palm Beach, London)
Van-Mist
Vanace Fifth Ave.
Vanderbilt
Vani-Pac
Vanstyle (U.S.A.)
Vantine
Vashé
Venine

Venus
Venus-Ray Spotlight
Verdura (New York)
Viegay
Vitoge
Vivaudou, Inc.
Vogue Vanities
Volante-Dure
Volupté Inc.
W & H Co.
W. B. Mfg. Co.
W. M. Co.
Wadsworth
Wadsworth Watch Case Co.
Wand Art
Warner of California
Webster Co.
Weltzunder
Whiting
Whiting & Davis Co.
Wiesner of Miami
Wilardy
Woodbury
Woodworth
Yardley
Yurat
Yves Saint Laurent
Zell 5th Ave.
Ziegfeld Girl
ZP Okasa

Landmark Ads from the Heyday of Compacts

Fabric vanity-case advertisement from the 1922 Montgomery Ward catalog.

Face-rouge compact advertisement from the 1922 Montgomery Ward catalog.

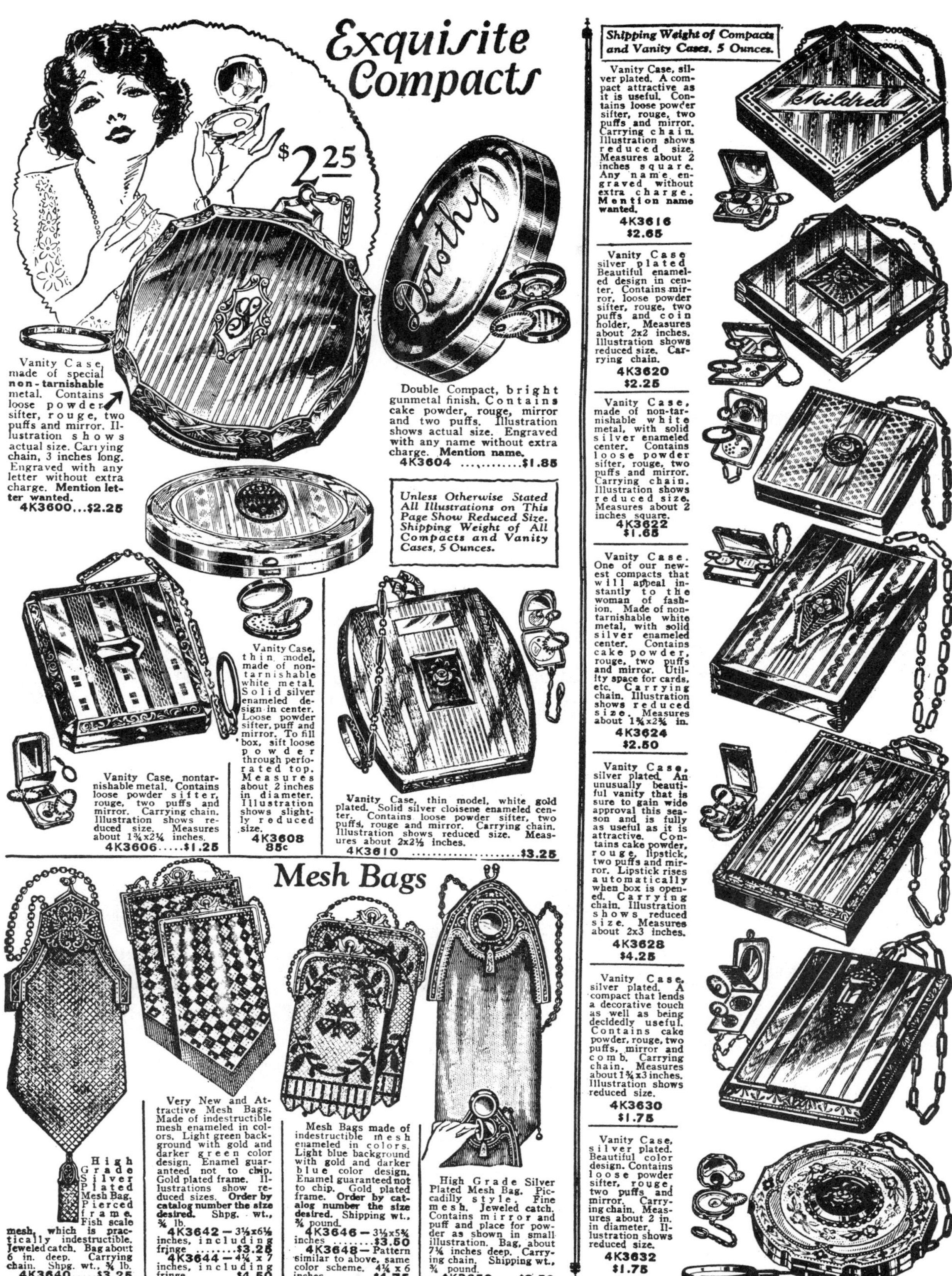

Compact advertisement from the 1927 Sears, Roebuck catalog.

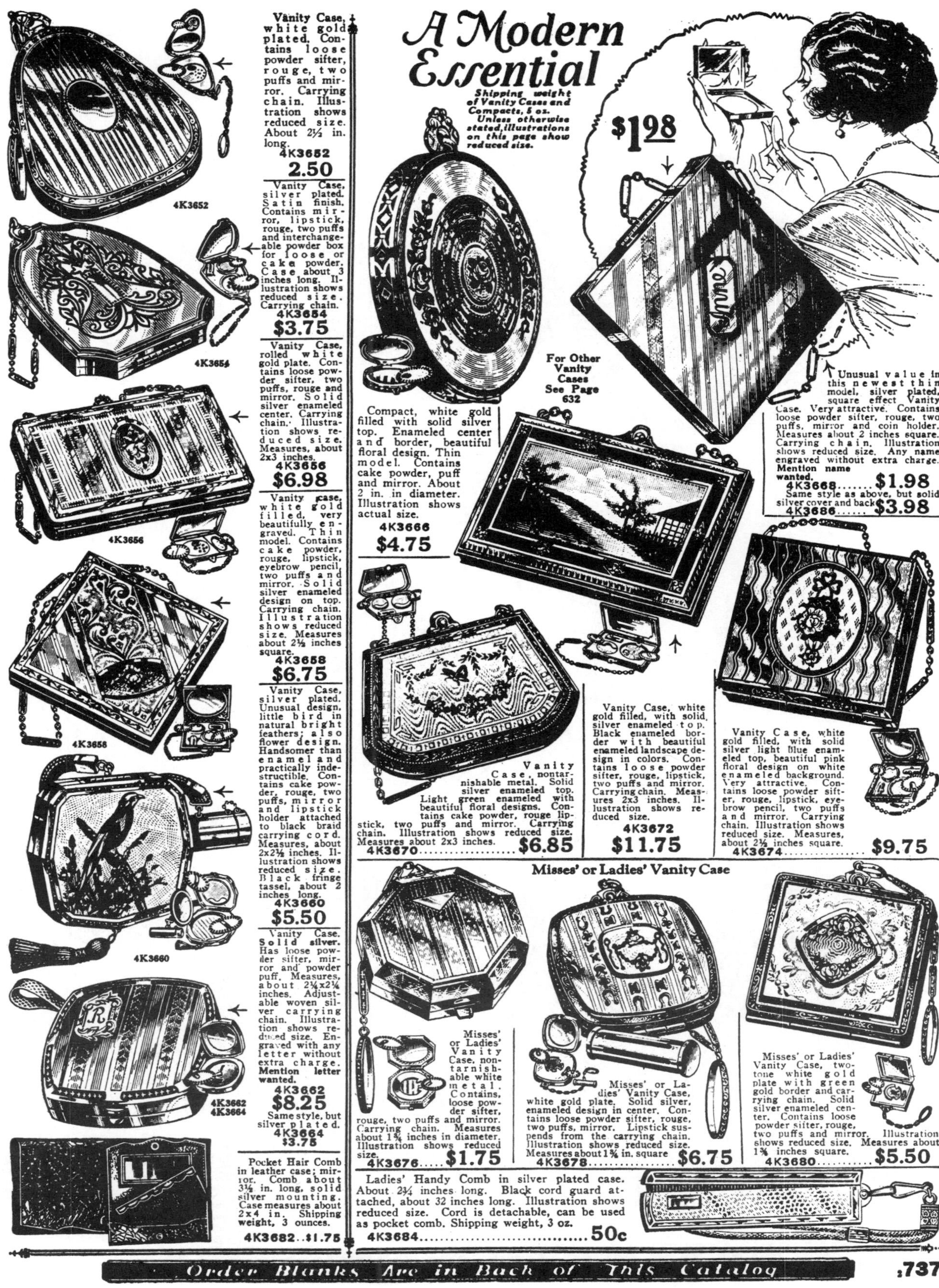

Compact advertisement from the 1927 Sears, Roebuck catalog.

La Dorine compact advertisement from a 1919 issue of *Theatre Magazine*.

Norida nonspilling loose powder vanitie advertisement from the August 1925 *People's Home Journal.*

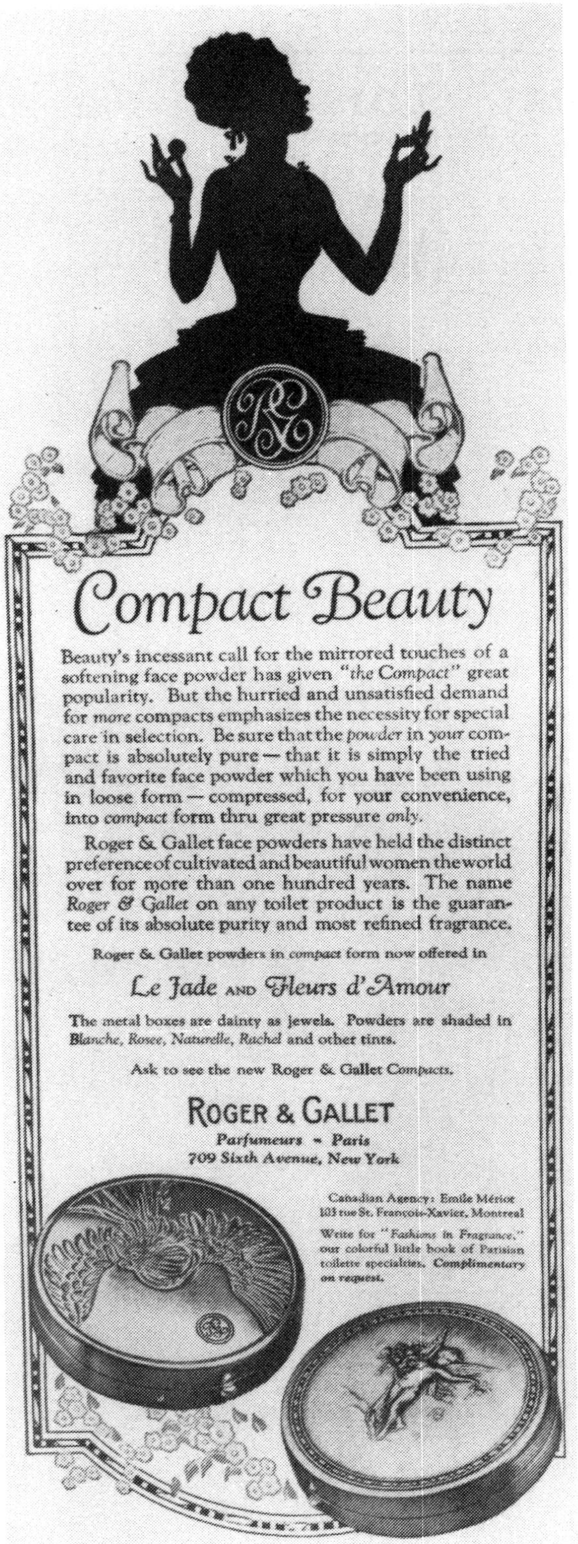

Roger & Gallet compact advertisement from a 1926 issue of *Theatre Magazine.*

The Hagn Merchandiser, Chicago

INVENTORY SALE—EVANS COMPACTS

REAL CLOISONNE and PETIT POINT NEWEST SHAPES—Golden Bronze Finish

AT ATTRACTIVE PRICE REDUCTIONS FOR QUICK CLEARANCE — ACT NOW!

•

No. 723J211—Thin Cookie Vanity. Genuine Dresden hand-painted cloisonne center in either white or canary color. Golden Bronze finish with large clear glass mirror, large puff and loose powder container. Popular because of its spaciousness. Each............ **$1.20**

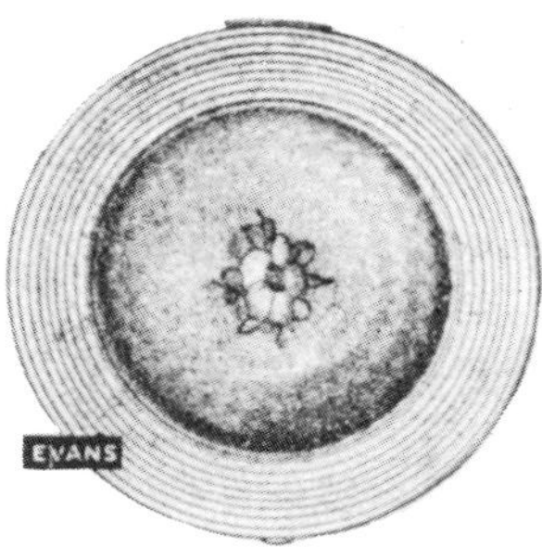

No. 723J211

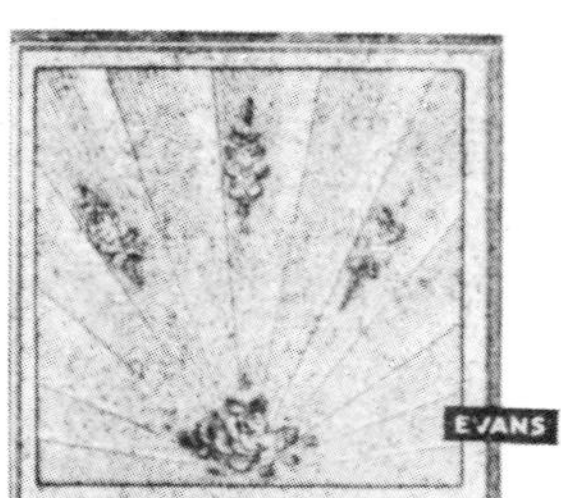

No. 723J165—Wafer Thin Genuine Dresden Hand-Painted Cloisonne Single Compact. Beautiful sunburst design in your choice of popular colors; Blue, White, Green and Canary. Golden Bronze finish with English grosgrain engine-turned back. Fitted with large clear glass mirror, large puff and loose powder container. Has style and beauty. Each......... **$1.20**

No. 723J210—Wafer Thin Single Compact. Genuine Imported Petite Point top. Golden Bronze finish with English grosgrain engine-turned back. The beauty and depth of coloring and design is unexcelled. In black or beige background. Fitted with large clear glass mirror, large puff and loose powder container. Each **$1.20**

ASSORTMENT
No. 723J212—Any six of the above compacts at a special price of
$6.95 PER ASSMT.

No. 723J160—Knife-Edge Double Vanity. The fine workmanship and graceful lines combine to make this a compact of outstanding beauty. Golden Bronze finish English grosgrain design with genuine hand-painted cloisonne decoration and French enamel ends in matching color. Your choice of colors include Blue, White, Canary and Green. Fitted with large clear glass mirror, 2 puffs, rouge and loose powder container. Each **$1.20**

•

REGULAR $3.00 LIST VALUES YOUR CHOICE

LIMITED STOCK AVAILABLE AT . . . $1.20 EACH

LESS 2% CASH DISCOUNT

ILLUSTRATIONS ABOUT ⅔ ACTUAL SIZE.

EVANS COMBINATION COMPACT CIGARETTE CASE

CLOISONNE PANEL FRONT

NATURAL GOLD COLOR

No. 727J54—Combination Double Vanity and Cigarette Case. Golden Bronze finish with English grosgrain engine-turned design. Front panel is genuine hand-painted white cloisonne. Fitted with large mirror, 2 puffs, rouge and loose powder container. Holds 6 cigarettes. Size 2⅞"x2⅛"x⅝". Specially priced. Each.

• **$2.00** •

PRICES LESS 2% CASH DISCOUNT

BLACK ENAMEL FRONT ON GOLD BRONZE

No. 727J55—Combination Double Vanity and Cigarette Case. Golden Bronze finish with English grosgrain engine-turned design. Black enameled front panel with yellow polished signet. Fitted with large mirror, 2 puffs, rouge and loose powder container. Holds 6 cigarettes. Size, 2⅞"x 2⅛"x⅝". Always a popular gift with the ladies. Each.

• **$1.50** •

CLAMSHELL WATCH VANITY

. . . MADE BY ELGIN AMERICAN MFG. COMPANY

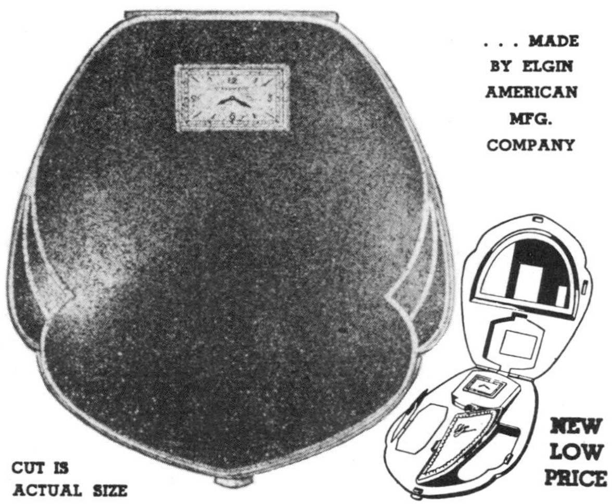

NEW LOW PRICE

CUT IS ACTUAL SIZE

No. 723J152—Clamshell Thin Edge Watch Vanity. A combination of two indispensable articles in one. Yellow gold-plated interior contains large powder compartment, paste rouge, puff and large half circle mirror. Choice of all bronze finish or gloss enamel front and back in black or white with bronze trim. Makes a popular salesboard and premium item in addition to being an ideal and unusual gift and promotional item.

GUARANTEED TIMEPIECE

The American-made Weldwood movement used in this watch is fully guaranteed and is made by a well known reputable manufacturer. Price, each, $4.00, less 2% cash discount or............................ **$3.92 NET**

PRICES SUBJECT TO CHANGE WITHOUT NOTICE 35

Evans compact inventory-sale advertisement from the 1938 Hagn Merchandiser, Chicago, catalog.

The Hagn Merchandiser, Chicago

COMPACTS AND CIGARETTE CASES

EVERY NUMBER IS AN OUTSTANDING VALUE

No. 723J89—"Marie Antoinette" Compact. Genuine tapestry covered top in an attractive floral pattern with black enamel border. Full size non-glare magnifying mirror on back. Yellow embossed edge. Contains full size regular mirror, powder container and large puff. Diameter, 3 9/16 ins. Each .... **75c** | Price, per dozen...... **$8.40**

No. 723J155—Lightweight Double Compact. The catalin border comes in assorted colors—red, green, crystal and shell—and shapes, and is a very effective contrast to the genuine tapestry covered top. Has a large size non-glare magnifying mirror on back. Contains cake rouge, powder sifter, 2 puffs and double unbreakable mirror. Diameter, 3 ins. Try an assortment today. Each.. **60c**

No. 723J154—Velvet Topped Compact. Assorted beautiful colored scenes done in a special Viennese process which cannot rub off. To appreciate the beauty and coloring of these compacts, they must be seen. Full size non-glare magnifying mirror on back, yellow embossed edge. Contains full size regular mirror, powder sifter and large puff. Diameter, 3 9/16 ins. Each........ **$1.00**

No. 723J153—Always Popular, Double Pouch Powder Compact. Yellow lightweight armour mesh combined with genuine tapestry top makes it one of our most outstanding numbers. The effect is both beautiful and rich. Contains cake rouge, 2 puffs, double unbreakable mirror and loose powder sifter. Each .... **85c** | Price, per dozen...... **$9.00**

No. 727J35—Extremely Smart Ladies' Cigarette Case. Your choice of either crystal or shell, cross bar deep cut pattern. The polished yellow band, hinges and lock make a very effective contrast. Holds 10 cigarettes. Size, 3¾x3 ins. Each.......................... **$1.00**

No. 723J156—Stylish Loose Powder Compact with Genuine Tapestry covered top in a beautiful floral pattern. The yellow polished sides and shell back give it the appearance of a much higher priced piece of merchandise. Contains full size mirror, powder container and large puff. Size, 2⅞x2⅞x½ ins. Each............ **85c**

No. 823J157—As above, with simulated cloisonne top in assorted colors. Each.................... **85c**

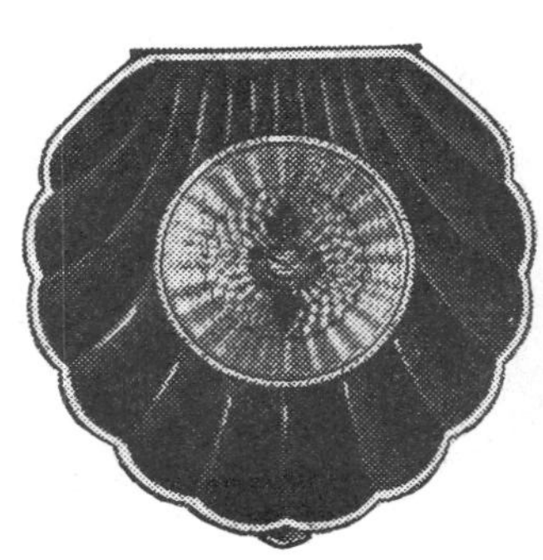

No. 723J204—Clamshell Compact. Highly polished yellow interior and trim. Genuine hand-painted cloisonne center in assorted colors. Black or white glossy enamel cover and back. Contains loose powder compartment, paste rouge, puff and unbreakable mirror. Elgin-American quality. Size, 2¾"x2¾". Each............ **88c**

No. 727J37—New and Fashionable Combination Cigarette Case and Compact. The cigarette case is made of lightweight catalin in your choice of the most popular colors—green, lapis, red and shell. The Genuine Tapestry covered double compact is set in the cover of the case, giving it a unique and attractive appearance. The hinges, frame and lock are polished yellow finish. Compact contains loose powder sifter, double unbreakable mirror, cake rouge and 2 puffs. Size, 3¾x3 ins. A remarkable value for this type of merchandise. Each...... **$1.25**

No. 727J36—Same as above in crystal with simulated cloisonne compact. Each............ **$1.25**

No. 823J209—Clarice Jane Compact and Lipstick Set. Thin knife edge compact, beautifully enameled front and back in lively, glossy colors, making a very modern contrast to the El-Bronze trim and wings. Contains glass mirror, cream rouge, powder compartment and puff. Sleek square shape lipstick in matching case with glass mirror on top. Put up in attractive display box. Compact, size, 2½x2½ ins. Lipstick, 2x⅝x¼ ins. Colors: Black, Wine and Green. An attractive set at a very special price. Per set.................. **$1.20**

Made by Elgin-American

KEEP EVERY NUMBER IN STOCK, THEY ARE PROVEN SELLERS 33

Compact and cigarette case-advertisement from the 1938 Hagn Merchandiser, Chicago, catalog.

COMPACTS THAT ARE DEFINITELY NEW

ILLUSTRATIONS ARE ABOUT 2/3 ACTUAL SIZE

CHARLEY McCARTHY

No. 823J228—Charlie McCarthy Compact by Evans. This clever compact is an immediate hit when shown. Golden bronze finish, hard-baked, glossy, white enamel cover with raised Charlie McCarthy head. English grosgrain engine-turned back. Contains large glass mirror, large puff and loose powder compartment.
Each **85c**

TOPAZ AND AMETHYST STONES

No. 823J220—Glamourous Jeweled Compact, set with simulated full-cut, sparkling stones. 5 topaz, 8 amethysts and 2 simulated emeralds. Deep golden bronze finish with attractive raised filigree border. Contains large, beveled-edge mirror, loose powder compartment, lip paste, cake rouge and 2 puffs.
Each **$3.00**

LUSTROUS SIMULATED CLOISONNE

No. 823J223—Book-Shape Compact. Sparkling simulated cloisonne top in popular colors of pink, gold and turquoise with enameled border to match. Yellow gold-plated engine-turned back and trim, floral decoration in center. Contains unbreakable mirror, large-size cake rouge, loose powder compartment and 2 puffs. Each **65c**

YELLOW FINISH THIN MODEL

No. 823J221—Wafer Thin Compact. Beautifully etched top in assorted attractive patterns with black enamel inlay. Polished yellow finish. Contains large, beveled-glass mirror, large powder compartment and puff. Engine-turned back. Each **80c**

"LOUVRE" COMPACTS

Hand-Painted Reproductions of priceless paintings by famous artists grace the top of these convenient slender compacts. The artists name and the name of the original are on the back. A border of deep ivory sets the exquisite paintings off to advantage. Some of the subjects are Romeo and Juliet, Wood by the Winds, A Gallant Gentleman, April Showers, etc. All have real mirrors and generous puffs. Loose powder styles only.

A Gallant Gentleman

No. 823J227—Cookie Style. Yellow-plated, embossed sides and trim. A very popular size.
Each .... **85c** Per dozen....... **$9.00**

WOOD BY THE WINDS

No. 823J226—Square Style. Yellow-plated, polished sides and trim.
No. 823J226S—As above with hand-painted garden and cottage scenes taken from original oil paintings.
Each .... **85c** | Per dozen....... **$9.00**

RHINESTONE BASKET ORNAMENT

•

YELLOW GOLD PLATED

No. 823J214—Double Compact. Fine quality, hard-baked, glossy enamel front and back. Raised rhinestone basket ornament with pastel enameled flowers. Yellow gold-plated, embossed edge and interior. Contains unbreakable mirror, loose powder compartment, cake rouge and 2 puffs. Colors are black, white and pastel blue.
Each **$1.00**

FULL SIZE LIPSTICK

No. 823J229—Triple-Style Compact by Evans. Golden bronze finish with English grosgrain and engine-turned design. Polished signet for engraving. Contains loose powder compartment, cake rouge, full-size swivel lipstick, unbreakable mirror and 2 puffs.
Each **$1.40**

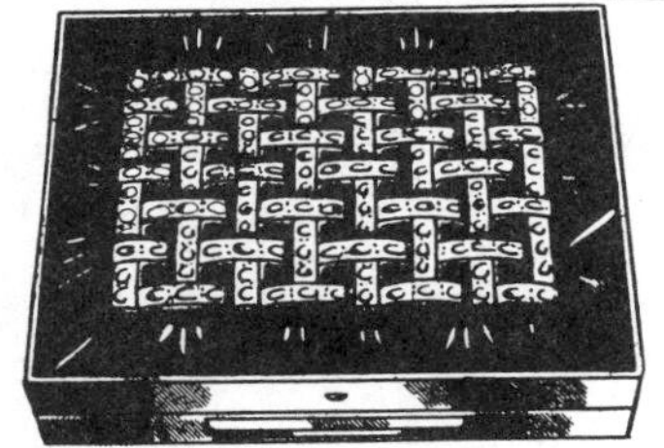

GORGEOUSLY RHINESTONE SET

No. 823J216—Thin Model Compact. Extremely smart design. Fine quality, hard-baked, glossy enamel front and back, elaborate rhinestone decoration on cover. Contains loose powder compartment, lip paste, cake rouge, 2 puffs and large unbreakable mirror. Black or white enamel. Gold-plated interior and edges.
Each **$2.50**

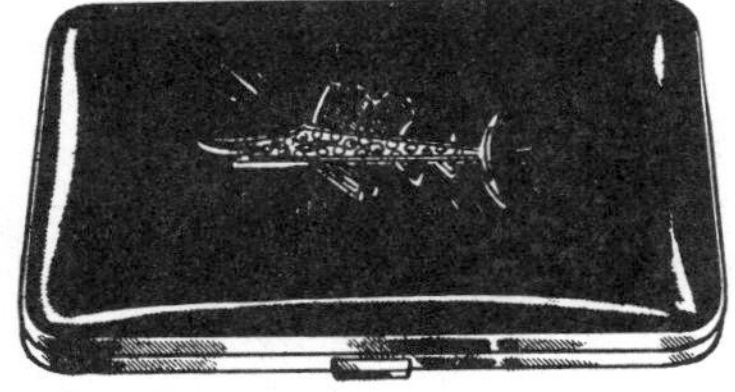

RHINESTONE SWORDFISH MOTIF

No. 823J218—Thin Model Book Compact. Fine quality, hard-baked, glossy enamel front and back. Raised rhinestone swordfish with pastel enamel trim. Yellow gold-plated interior and edge. Contains unbreakable mirror, loose powder compartment, cake rouge and 2 puffs. In black, pastel blue and white.
Each **$1.00**

YELLOW FINISH MESH STYLE

No. 823J223—Large-Size Powder Pouch. Beautifully etched top with black enamel inlay in assorted designs. Yellow gold finish, lightweight armour mesh. Fitted with large-size velour puff, unbreakable mirror and loose powder sifter.
Each **85c**

34 A GIFT THAT IS ALWAYS APPRECIATED

New compacts advertisement from the 1938 Hagn Merchandiser, Chicago, catalog.

Lablache advertisement from the December 1924 issue of *The Ladies' Home Journal.*

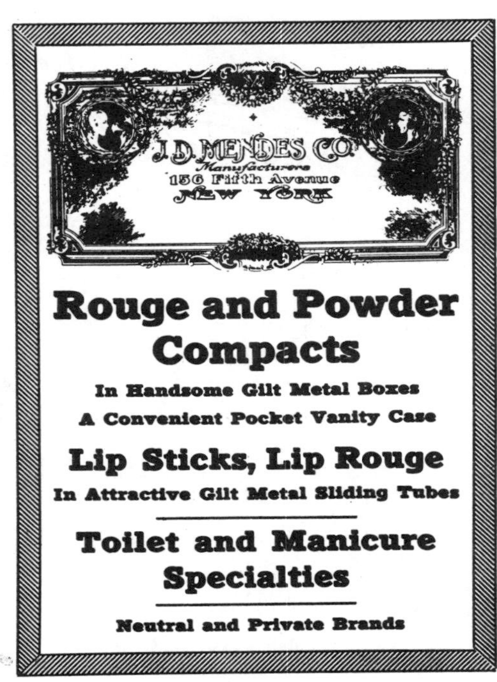

The J. D. Mendes Co. rouge and powder compact advertisement from the December 1920 issue of *The American Perfumer.*

Powder compact advertisements from the 1922 Montgomery Ward catalog.

Here's the perfect way to mark a special occasion in any woman's life—an *Elgin American* compact! It's a gift of jewelry she'll display with pride... a gift of beauty she'll use with pleasure. And because it's made by *Elgin American*, she'll love it for its quality and value ... and because the giver thought enough to choose the finest.

Craftsmanship in Every Fine Detail

If *Elgin American* specializes in any one thing... it's attention to every exacting detail. Not just what you see on the surface, but everything that goes into an *Elgin American* is selected and worked with the utmost care and precision.

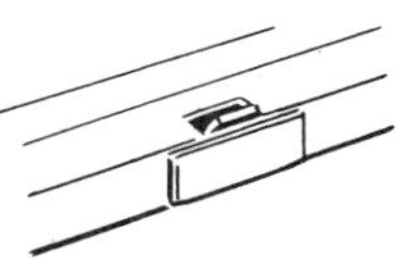

CLASP

Elgin American's clasp holds its own...safely! Keeps your compact closed, keeps powder in place, protects everything in your purse!

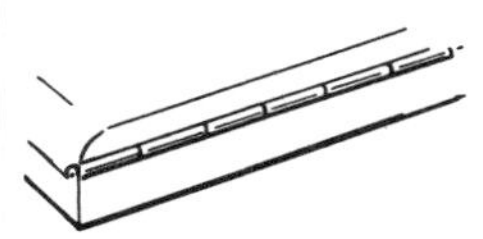

HINGE

Reinforced hinges are part of the case itself. Thus, shifting and slipping are eliminated...wear and tear reduced...limitless service assured.

SMOOTH EDGES

The fine finish of *Elgin American* compacts extends to the very edges! Satin-smooth, they meet perfectly and feel glorious to the touch!

INTERIORS

Elgin American craftsmen pay as much attention to the interior of their compact as the outside design. Every detail is worked out perfectly to preserve its beauty.

LEAKPROOF POWDER DOORS

Powder enjoys privacy in an *Elgin American* compact. Leakproof doors keep it in a world of its own... apart from other objects in her purse.

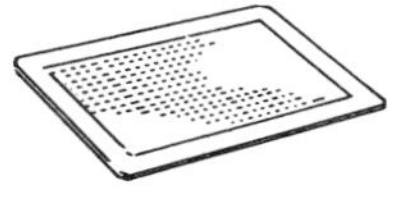

SNUG SIFTERS

In *Elgin American* compacts, sifters sit super-snugly. Unexpected spills are avoided, saving powder (and temper!)...adding proof of superior value.

MIRROR

Perfectly backed and finished, *Elgin American* mirrors are made for each compact. No distortion... you see yourself as others see you!

2

Elgin American compact craftsmanship from the 1952–53 Elgin American catalog.

The Elgin American Carryall from the 1952–53 Elgin American catalog.

THE EXCITING NEW Carryalls IN JEWELER'S BRONZE

1461/035

1461/035 — Engraved bronze bird and leaf design on satin silver finish. Size 4¼" x 2½". Black moire carrying case. Matches lighter 1414/035, page 18.

1461/036—Cover ornamented with multi-color stones in overall design. Satin finish jeweler's bronze trim. Size 4¼" x 2½". With black moire carrying case.

1461/036

1461/025

1461/025—Jeweler's bronze carryall with overall brown alligator covering. Size 4¼" x 2½". With black moire carrying case.

1461/027 — Inlaid mother-of-pearl with aqua blue stones on jeweler's bronze background. Size 4¼" x 2½". With black moire carrying case.

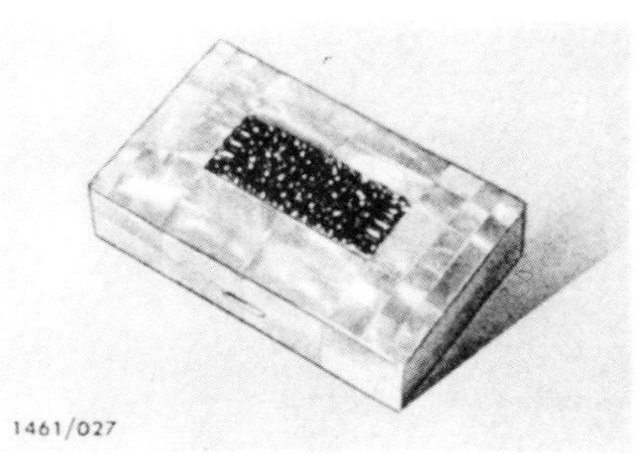
1461/027

1461/026

1461/026—Jeweler's bronze carryall with overall inlaid mother-of-pearl. Size 4¼" x 2½". With black moire carrying case.

1461/034 — Inlaid mother-of-pearl. Cover ornamented with rhinestone design on bronze background. Size 4¼" x 2½". With black moire carrying case.

1461/034

ACCESSORIES

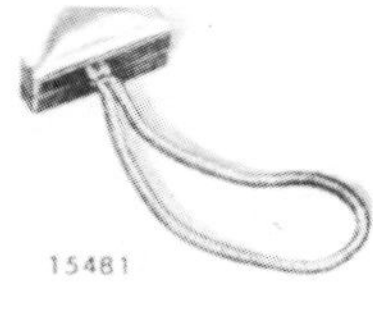
15481

15480

15481—Gold finish tubular link chain handles.

15480—Gold finish close curb chain handles.

15482—Gold finish mesh chain handles.

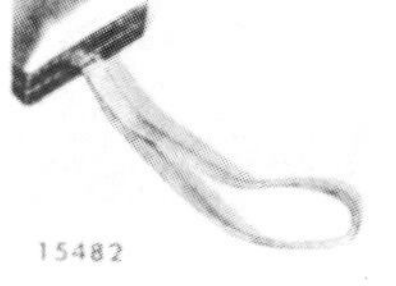
15482

5880—Navy blue leather with gold tooled design, without handles. Accommodates carryalls 1461/008, 021, 022, 031, 035 and 010.

5880

5881

5882—Black and gold brocade, with handles. Will accommodate carryalls 1461/026, 1461/036, 1461/027 and 1461/034.

5881—Black and gold brocade, without handles.

5883 — Dark "gold moonmist" crushed goatskin, without handles. Will accommodate carryalls 1461/008, 1461/010, 1461/021, 1461/022, 1461/031, and 1461/035.

5882

5883

All *Elgin American* Masterpieces Beautifully Cased for Gift Presentation.

25

The Elgin American Carryall and Carryall accessories from the 1952–53 Elgin American catalog.

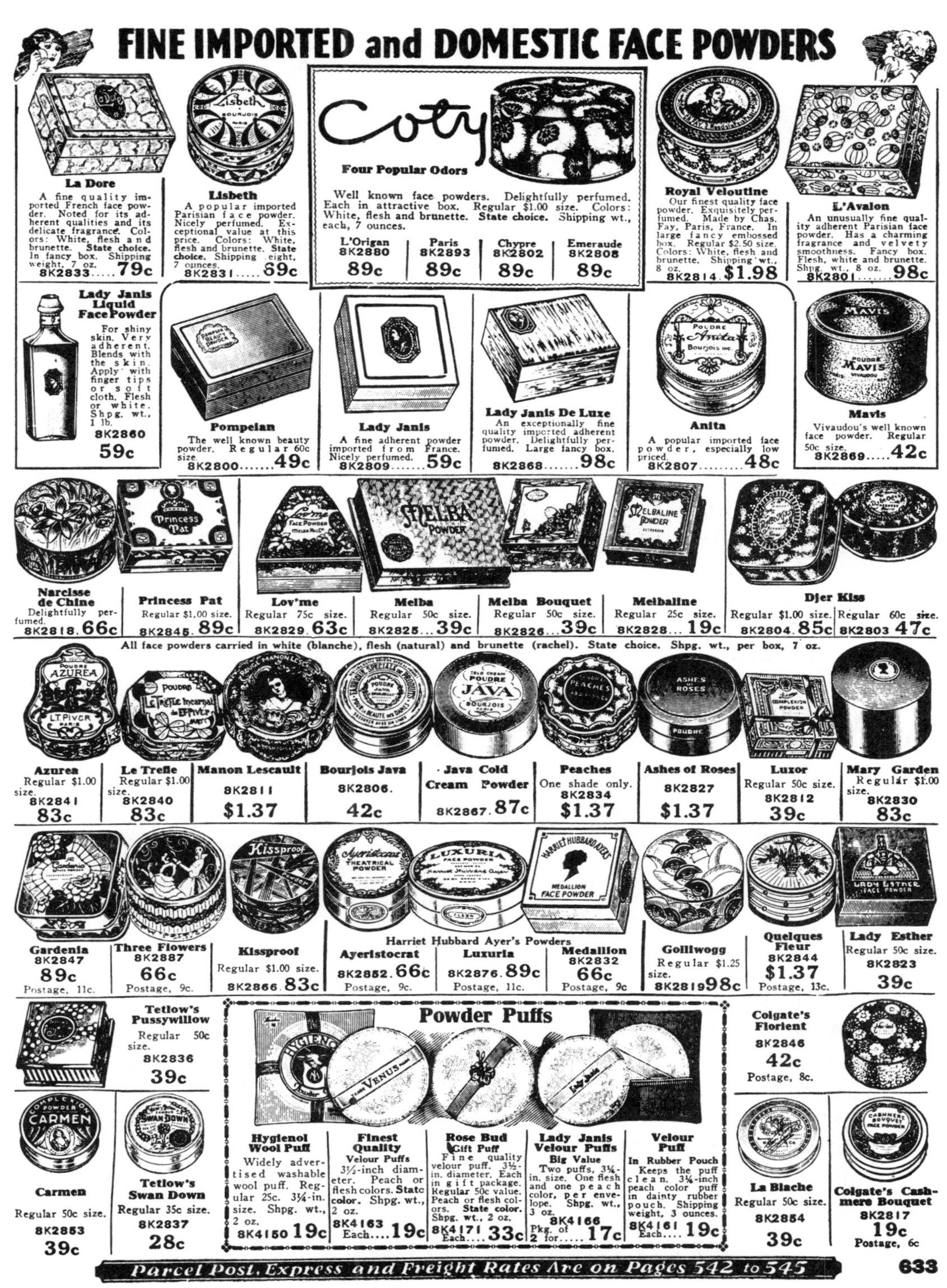

Face powder advertisement from the 1927 Sears, Roebuck catalog.

Glossary

alloy. Base metal fused with a precious ore to change its color or to harden it.

Art Deco (1920–30). An angular style of geometric patterns and abstract designs that originated in France.

Art Nouveau (1890–1910). A free-flowing style introduced in England, with emphasis on curved lines, natural motifs, and women with long flowing hair.

Bakelite. Trademark for an opaque synthetic plastic developed in 1909.

bar brooche. A narrow, horizontal decorated pin.

baroque pearl. Pearls with an irregular shape.

base metal. All metals other than the three primary precious metals: silver, gold, and platinum.

basse-taille. A decorative enameling technique in which the metal is etched, engraved, or cut and then filled with transparent enamels. Also known as translucent enameling.

brass. An alloy composed of two-thirds copper and one-third zinc.

brocade. Silk fabric with a woven raised design.

bronze. A reddish-brown alloy of copper and tin.

cabochon. A highly polished dome-shaped stone with no facets.

cabriole. An elongated S-shaped support.

cameo. A gem, shell, or stone with a design or figure carved in relief against a background of a darker or lighter color.

carryall. Mass-produced version of a minaudière.

celluloid. Trademark for a type of plastic developed in 1868.

champlevé. An enameling technique in which cut-out or depressed areas in the metal are filled with enamel.

chatelaine. An ornamental clasp from which five to nine chains are suspended to accommodate various small objects.

chatelette. A chatelaine with shorter and fewer chains.

chinoiserie. European decoration with a Chinese motif.

chrome. A hard, brittle gray metal used to plate other metal with a bright mirror-like finish.

circa. Approximate date an item was manufactured.

clip. A hinged support on the back of a pin or brooch that clips onto an article of clothing.

cloisonné. An enameling technique in which narrow strips of gold or silver wires are soldered to a metal base to form compartments (cloisons), which are then filled with enamel.

compact. A small portable makeup container consisting of a mirror, powder, and puff.

damascene. Decorative inlaid pattern of gold or silver on metal.

déposé. French word for patent or copyright.

enamel. A form of powdered colored glass that is fused onto metal surfaces for decoration.

engraving. A pattern or design cut into the surface of a hard material with a sharp instrument.

fede. A decorative form consisting of a pair of clasped right hands symbolizing faith and trust.

flapjack. A slim, thin compact resembling a "flap-jack" pancake.

French ivory. Trademark for plastic imitation ivory.

German silver. A white alloy of nickle, zinc, and copper. Also called nickle silver, although it contains no silver.

gilt or gild. To cover a base metal with a thin layer of gold or gold color.

gold. A soft precious metal usually combined with copper or nickle, depending on the color and hardness desired.

gold filled. A base metal (usually copper) plated with gold, usually by electroplating.

grosgrain. A stiffly corded silk fabric.

guilloché enamel. An engraved decoration on metal, usually geometric or floral, covered with a translucent enamel.

hallmark. A mark stamped on some objects of gold and silver to denote the quality, purity, origin, and manufacturer. First used in Great Britain.

inlay. A decorative technique in which a design in metal is etched or cut out and another hard material inserted in the recessed pattern to make a flat or even shape.

intaglio. A form of engraving or carving that gives the object a hollow, three-dimensional effect. The reverse of the cameo.

jet. A glossy black variety of hard coal. A name commonly used for imitation or genuine black stones.

karat. A term denoting the amount of pure gold in an article. 24 karats equals pure gold; 18 karats equals 18 parts pure gold and 6 parts of another metal.

Limoges. A translucent enamel of colorful portraits or scenes on copper that originated in Limoges, France.

lusterware. A glaze used on pottery to give a metallic or iridescent appearance.

marcasite. Natural marcasite is crystallized white iron pyrites. Imitation marcasite is made of cut steel that is formed and faceted.

marquetry. A decorated wooden inlaid veneer.

minaudière. A rigid metal, usually box-shaped evening bag with compartments for powder, lipstick, rouge, mirror, coins, and cigarettes.

mosaic. A picture or design composed of small varicolored stones or glass. A micro-mosaic is created with tiny pieces of glass or stones.

mother-of-pearl. The hard, smooth iridescent lining of pearl oyster shells.

motif. In the style of or resembling.

necessaire. Bolster-shaped version of the minaudière with fewer compartments.

obelisk. A four-sided tapering shaft with a pyramidal top.

ojime. A sliding bead or button on a cord used to tighten or loosen an inro.

parure. A set of matching pieces of jewelry.

petit-point. One-half the cross of a cross-stitch done in fine thread on a fine canvas.

pewter. A silver-white alloy of tin and lead.

plastic. Synthetic material, such as Bakelite, celluloid, or Lucite, that is molded by heat into a variety of shapes and colors. Natural, organic plastics (amber, Ivory, tortoiseshell, and horn) can be softened and molded or pressed into shape.

pli. A makeup tube containing powder and a puff-brush.

plique-à-jour. An enameling technique in which transparent enamel is placed across soldered bands of metal to produce a stained-glass effect.

reticule. A small handbag that is held in the hand or carried over the arm.

rhinestone. A form of rock crystal faceted to resemble diamonds.

seed pearl. A tiny pearl.

shagreen. Green-dyed leather made from the skin of a shark.

silver. A precious metal usually combined with copper for hardness.

sterling silver. The purest alloy of silver, containing 0.925 parts of silver and 0.075 parts of copper.

strapwork. A pattern of crossed and interwoven bands that resemble straps.

synthetic stone. Man-made imitations of precious or semiprecious stones.

taffeta. A bright, shiny thin silk fabric.

tango chain. A short chain that attaches a compact and lipstick case.

thumbpiece. A small knob that releases a catch when pressed.

tooling. A design in leather produced by a heated tool.

tortoiseshell. The transluscent shell of a tortoise, which can be molded by heat.

transfer. A commercial pattern or design applied to another surface.

vanity bag. A dainty mesh evening bag incorporating a compact as an integral part of the bag.

vanity box. Fitted traveling cosmetic box.

vanity case. A compact that contains rouge and/or a lipstick.

vanity clutch. A fitted cosmetic bag with sleeves attached to the inside lining to accommodate compact, lipstick, and rouge.

vanity pouch. Drawstring powder pouch with a mirror at the base.

vanity purse. Leather, fabric, metal or beaded purse incorporating a vanity case an an integral part of the purse.

velvet. A fabric made of silk with a smooth pile surface.

vermeil. A layer of gold over silver, copper, or bronze.

vinaigrette. A small ornamental receptacle that contains scented vinegar or ammonia.

Bibliography

Books

Andacht, Sandra.
Oriental Antiques and Art: An Identification and Value Guide.
Wallace-Homestead
Greensboro, NC: 1987.

Baker, Lillian.
100 Years of Collectible Jewelry.
Collector Books
Paducah, KY: 1978.

———.
Fifty Years of Collectible Fashion Jewelry, 1925–1975.
Collector Books
Paducah, KY: 1986.

Battersby, Martin.
The Decorative Twenties.
Walker and Company
NY: 1971.

———.
The Decorative Thirties.
Collier Books
New York: 1971.

Carter, Rosalynn.
The First Lady from Plains.
Houghton Mifflin
Boston: 1984.

Chandro, Moti.
Journal of the Indian Society of Oriental Art, vol. 8.
Abanindranath Tagore and Stella Kramrisch, eds. 1940.

Coty.
The History of Coty
(235 East 42nd Street, New York, N.Y. 10017).

de Fontenoy, The Marquise.
Eve's Glossary.
Herbert Stone & Co.
Chicago and New York: 1897.

Haertig, Evelyn.
Antique Combs & Purses
Gallery of Graphics Press
Carmel, CA: 1983.

Hainworth, Henry.
A Collector's Dictionary.
Routledge & Kegan Paul
Boston and London: 1981.

Heide, Robert, and John Gilman.
Dime-Store Dream Parade.
E. P. Dutton
New York: 1979.

Hillier, Bevis.
The Style of the Century, 1900–1980.
E. P. Dutton
New York: 1983.

———.
The World of Art Deco.
Studio-Vista, Dutton
New York: 1971.

———.
Art Deco of the 20's & 30's.
Studio-Vista, Dutton
New York: 1968.

Holiner, Richard.
Antique Purses.
Collector Books
Paducah, KY: 1982.

Kaplan, Arthur Guy.
Official Price Guide to Antique Jewelry, fifth edition.
The House of Collectibles
Westminster, MD: 1985.

Kelley, Lyngerda, and Nancy Schiffer.
Plastic Jewelry.
Schiffer Publishing Ltd.
Exton, PA: 1987.

Klein, Dan; Nancy A. McClelland; Malcolm Haslam.
In the Deco Style.
Rizzoli
New York: 1986.

Lester, Katharine Morris, and Bess Viola Oerke.
Accessories of Dress.
Charles A. Bennett Co.
Peoria, IL: 1940.

Loring, John.
Tiffany's 150 Years.
Doubleday
New York: 1987.

McClinton, Katherine Morrison.
Art Deco: A Guide for Collectors.
Clarkson N. Potter
New York: 1972.

Mebane, John.
Collecting Nostalgia: The First Guide to the Antiques of the 30's and 40's.
Castle Books
New York: 1972.

Patterson, Jerry E.
Matchsafes.
Smithsonian Institution
Washington, D.C.: 1981.

Sloan, Jean.
Perfume and Scent Bottle Collecting.
Wallace-Homestead
Lombard, IL: 1986.

Sotheby's (ed.).
The Andy Warhol Collection.
Abrams
New York: 1988.

Whiting & Davis Co.
Tercentenary Booklet, 1876–1930.
Plainville, MA.

Articles

Baker, Stanley L.
"Collecting Compacts."
The Antique Trader Weekly
(Dubuque, IA), July 27, 1977.

Bayer, Patricia.
"Collecting Compacts."
Antiques World
(April 1979).

Gelatt, Dorothy S.
"$25 Million for Andy Warhol's 10,000 Favorite Things."
Maine Antique Digest
(June 1988).

Hillier, Bevis.
"Open-and-Shut Cases."
Los Angeles Times Magazine
December 29, 1985.

Kovels on Antiques and Collectibles (Beechwood, Ohio).
" 'Make-Up' a Collection," vol. 11, no. 6.
(February 15, 1985).

Schiffres, Manuel, Suzan Richmond, and Joan Goldwasser.
"Take a Powder."
Changing Times
(August 1988).

Catalogs

The American Perfumer (December 1920).
New York, N.Y.

Arts and Crafts, Art Nouveau and Art Deco.
Christie's East, New York (June 16, 1988).

Baird-North Catalog, 1917
Baird-North Co.
Providence, R.I.

Year Book 1926.
Baird-North Co.
Providence, R.I.

Elgin American Catalog, 1952–53: Exquisite Accessories.
Elgin American Watch Case Co.
Elgin, IL. September 1, 1952.

Your Bargain Book. Fall/Winter 1927–28.
F. H. Sadler Co.
New York Styles.

Holsman Company Catalog
Holsman Company
Chicago, IL.

Joseph Hagn Company Catalog.
Spring/Summer 1938.
Chicago, IL.

Montgomery Ward & Co.
Catalogue No. 109. Fall/Winter 1928–29.
Baltimore, MD.

Montgomery Ward & Co.
Catalogue No. 97, Golden Jubilee, 1872–1922.
Chicago, IL.

Pohlson Galleries (1920s).
The Pohlson Treasure Chest.
Pawtucket, RI.

Pohlson's Colonial Gifts.
Pohlson Galleries (1920s).
Pawtucket, RI.

Sears Roebuck Catalogues for 1897, 1908, 1923, 1927, 1928, 1930, 1935, and 1949.
Chicago, IL.

Gifts from The Shepard Stores (1923).
Shepard Stores.
Boston, MA.

Magazines and Newspapers

Arts & Antiques. May 1988.

Fortune. August 1930.

Glamour. November 1948.

Good Housekeeping. December 1928, December 1941.

Harper's Bazaar. December 1943.

McCall's Magazine. June 1929.

Metropolitan Home. March 1987.

Pictorial Review. October 1924, September 1925, April 1927, June 1928, January 1931, September 1931.

Redbook. December 1951, November 1954.

The Delineator. April 1919.

The Ladies' Home Journal. December 1921, March 1922, March 1924, December 1924, June 1925, April 1942.

Theatre Magazine. 1919, 1920, 1926, 1927, 1928.

Woman's Home Companion. December 1933.

Index

Note: Page numbers in *italic* indicate illustrations.

A. Bourjois & Co., plate 4
acorn-shaped compact, *49, 50, 84, 85*
AGME, *66, 141*
Alice in Wonderland compact, 14, plate 1
alligator compacts, *49, 50, 84, 85*
Alpacca, *144*
Alwyn, *113*
Amere, *63*
American Beauty, *63*
American Maid, *41*
Amita, *42*
Anna Pavlova, *133*
Annette, *133*
Annette Honeywell compact, *136*
appraiser, certified, 33
Armand, *111, 121*
Armed Forces emblems, 14, *59, 62*
Art Deco, 17, *54, 56, 149,* plates 15, 19
Art Nouveau, 17, *149,* plate 15
Artcraft, *67*
Arthur Murray Dancers compact, *64*
Asprey, 11, *160*
attribution, 18
automobiles, compacts for, *16,* 17
Avon, *136,* plate 1
B.B. Co., *116*
B.Co., *135*
BC, *134*
Baird-North, 17
bakelite, *135*
Bakst, Leon, 24
ball-shaped compacts, *160,* plates 6, 13
bar-brooch lipstick, plate 12
barometer/compacts, 17
basket motif/shape, *159*
basketweave compacts, *130, 134, 150*
Baume des sultanes, 3
beaded compact, *165*
Beauty-Full, plate 9
beetle-shaped compact, plate 4
belt chatelaine, plate 17. *See also* chatelaine
Bergen, Mrs. Edgar, 34
"Bird-in-Hand" compact, 25, *26,* 27
Black, Starr, and Frost, 11
blackbird compact, *110*
Blumpak, *72*
bolster-shaped compacts, *136, 150*
bolster-shaped vanity cases, *107, 118, 134, 157, 158, 165,* plates 2, 4, 20
Boston Shephard Store, 17
Boucheron, 11, 35
brass compacts, *111, 120, 123, 136, 155, 160*
Bree, plate 15
Britemode, *78*
Cambi, *141*
cane/compact, 6
"Cane Curiosa" (Dike), *170*
carryalls, 11, 27, *28, 29, 45, 73, 96–97, 102, 103, 146–147, 148, 216, 217*
carrying cases, *102, 108*
Carter, Ens. Jimmy, 14
Cartier, 11, 35
cartoon characters, 14
champlevé, *116, 117, 124, 155,* plates 6, 12, 19
Changing Times, 34
Chantrey, *149*
Charbert, plate 1
Charles of the Ritz, 12
Charlie McCarthy compact, 34, *213,* plate 1
chatelaine, 25
chatelaine compact, *24,* 25
chatelette, *24,* 25, *151,* plate 20
Chaumet, 11
Cheramy, *155*
Chicago Tribune, 34
child's cosmetics, *132, 133*
Christie's East Auction House, 33–34
Ciner, *76, 77*
clamshell compacts, *57, 140, 211, 212*
Cleopatra's needle, 14, *15*
clip-on compact, plate 13
cloisonné, *48, 54, 55, 56, 92, 116, 117, 118, 121, 128, 135, 144, 150, 155, 156, 158, 211, 213,* plates 6, 14, 19
clover-shaped compact, *110, 119*
coach-chatelette compact, *24,* 25
coin holders, *9,* 17, *24,* 25
Colgate & Co., *133*
collecting, tips on, 31–33
Colleen Moore, 12
Colt Purse Make-Up Kit, *121*
comb/whisk broom combination, *108*
combination compacts, 17, 34, 35, *54, 55, 56*
compacts: brief history of, 1–17; as hand mirror, *151,* plates 5, 19; shapes of, 14
compact/bracelet, 17, *154, 156,* plate 12
compact/camera combination, *137*
compact/canes, *170*
compact/cigarette cases, 8, *152*
compact/compasses, 17, *58*
compact/dance program, plate 17
compact/lipstick combination, *138–139, 168*
compact/music box, 12, *58*
compact/perfume container, plate 16
compact/thermometer, *58*
compact/watch, 12, *57, 63*

compact/watch/cane, *170*
"Compakit" vanity case, *44*
"Compliments of Van Raalte" compact, *142*
condition, as guide to value, 171
cookie-shaped compact, *135, 142, 150*
copper, use of, *120, 134,* plate 12
corduroy, use of, *95, 104*
cosmetic: derivation of, 1; laws against use of, 2–3
cosmetic bracelet, *156*
cosmetic containers: materials used in, 14, 201; styles of 8–11, *9, 10*
cosmetic sets, *133*
Coty, François Joseph de Spoturno, 19
Coty, 12, 19–24, *22, 23,* 34, *61, 63, 72, 82, 83, 88, 108, 109, 133, 134, 140,* plate 13
Council of Fashion Designers of America, 34
Crafters, *158*
Croco, *52*
D. F. B. Co., *117*
D. F. Briggs Co., *149, 166–167*
Dali, Salvador, 25, *26,* 27
damascene, use of, *42, 120, 143*
damask, use of, *90, 91, 104, 163,* plate 10
Daniel, *118, 143*
date, as guide to value, 171
decoration, as guide to value, 171
Delettrez, *75*
Deva-Dassey, *154*
Dike, Catherine, *170*
Divine, *111, 155*
Djer-Kiss, plate 1
Dorette, *50*
Dorothy Gray, *6, 7,* 12, *69, 82, 83, 100, 101, 136, 150, 152, 164*
double vanity, *211, 212*
dual-opening vanity case, plate 2
Dunhill, *169*
Dunhill Vanity, *56*
E. A. Bliss, Co., *123, 156*
E.A.M., *82, 83, 136, 149*
Edouardo, *132*
Edward's Bags, Ltd., *95*
egg-shaped vanity, *95, 113*
Elgin, 34
Elgin American, 8, *9,* 12, 25, *26,* 27, *40, 53, 57, 58, 66, 75, 92, 102, 107, 165, 215, 216,* plates 1, 13
Elgin National Watch Company, 12
Elizabeth Arden, 12, *69, 140*
embroidery, use of, *152, 164,* plate 13
"extension-gate top" vanity bag, *124*
Elmo, *75*
enamel, use of, *48, 53, 54, 55, 56, 59, 63, 65, 66, 71, 73, 96, 97, 110, 111, 112, 116, 135, 142,* 148, 155, plates 14, 15
envelope-shaped compacts, *52, 145, 148,* plate 5
Estée Lauder, 34, *163*
Evans, 8, 12, 13, *28, 29,* 34, *40, 41, 46, 48, 54, 55, 56, 57, 89, 105, 117, 118, 124, 128, 130, 141, 152, 155, 158, 163, 211,* plates 1, 6, 7, 15
Eve's Glossary (de Fontenoy), 3
Evening in Paris, 12, *75*
F. J. Co., *156*
Fabergé, 11
face powders, advertisements for, 218
fan-shaped compacts, *38, 45, 143, 150*
fans, compacts in, 17
Fifth Avenue, *146–147*
filigree, use of, *120, 122, 123, 125, 151, 156, 157,* plate 20
Fillkwik Co., *109*
flapjack compacts, 11, *68, 117, 141, 156*
flask/cigarette container, plate 8
Flato, *110, 148, 152, 155*
fleur-de-lis, *115,* plate 18
Fontenoy, Marquise de, 3
Foster & Bailey, plates 8, 12
Fouquet, Jean, 35
French ivory, *143, 157, 158,* plates 1, 2
Fuller, *75, 158*
G.L.B. Co., *117*
gadgetry compacts, 17
gemstones, *122, 123, 143. See also* jewels
Georg Jensen, *24, 145*
Girey, 34, *44*
Givenchy, *140*
Gone with the Wind (Mitchell), 14
Gorbachev, Raisa, 34
Graceline, *106*
Gucci, *142*
guilloche enamel, *110, 116*
Gwenda, *38, 141*
Hagn Merchandiser, *211, 212,* 213
halfmoon-shaped compacts, *158, 162,* plates 7, 15
hand mirrors, compacts shaped as, *4,* 14, *71, 72,* plate 19
hand-shaped compacts, *39*
harlequin-shaped compact, *69*
Harmony of Boston, *75*
Harriet Hubbard Ayers, *164*
hat-shaped compacts, *143, 150*
heart-shaped compacts, *40–41*
heart-shaped vanity case, *62*
Helena Rubinstein, 12
Henriette, 15, *160*
Hermès, 6, 11, *170*
Hoechst, *71*
Hollywood, *133*
horseshoe-shaped compacts, *49, 51, 52, 67, 136, 149, 158*
horseshoe-shaped vanity cases, *166–167,* plate 3
horseshoe-shaped vanity case/watch combination, *63*
Houbigant, 34, *109, 114*
Houppette, *121*
"ILYTG," 14
"I Like Ike" compact, plate 1
Illinois Watch Case Co., 12, *57, 63*
"Il Segreto di Susanna" (Wolf-Ferrari), 8
intaglio, plate 3
International Compact Collectors Club, 31
J. D. Mendes Co., *214*
Jet set, *164*
jewels, *122, 123, 125, 128, 141, 168,* plates 3, 10, 20
Jonteel, 12, *109*
K & K, 15, *45, 110, 154, 159, 162*
Kamra-Pak, 15, *44*
Kamra-Pak-style, *59, 60, 63*
Kigu, 15, *40, 112, 137, 152, 159, 160,* plate 1
Kreisler, *148*
kohl, 1
kohl-pots, 1, 2
kosmein, 1
La Dorine, *209*
La Faveur de Paris, *75*
La Mode, 34, *41, 55, 111, 113, 117, 141, 142, 156,* plates 6, 14
La Vedelte, *78*
Lablache advertisement, *214*
Ladies Home Journal, 214
Lady Esther, 12
Lady Vanity, *50*
Lalique, René, 24
Lamkin, *121*
Lampl, *55, 56,* plate 1
Langlois, *132, 150*
Larue, *51*
Lazell, *112*
Le Rage, *108*

leather, *49–52, 79, 82, 93, 149*
Lederer, *150*
Lee-Fran, *95*
Lentheric, *158*
Lesco Bond Street, *49*
lids, *122–125, 128, 129, 131, 135, 140–142, 152, 161, 162,* plates 5, 6, 14, 19
Limoges, *71*
Lin-Bren, *50, 76, 77, 90, 91, 103*
lip-blotter tissue case, *150*
lip-gloss container, plate 1
lipstick: compartment, *10*; concealed, *4*, 14, *121, 134, 157, 158,* plate 2; as opening device, plate 9; sliding, *82, 83, 125, 142, 145*
lipstick case, *4*, 13
lipstick sets, *133*
Little Lady, *132*
lizard compacts, *51, 76, 160,* plate 13
locket, *24, 111, 112, 154*
Lucien Lelong, *86–87*
Lucite, *74, 93, 113, 163,* plates 2, 4
Lucretia Vanderbilt, *148*
M.M.R., *146–147*
Ma Poudre, *89*
Maine Antique Digest, 35
Majestic, *76, 77, 106, 110, 134, 136*
Marathon, *40, 54, 55, 82, 83*
marcasite, plates 12, 20
Marcee, *51*
Marhill, *38, 45*
Marlowe Co., *167*
"marriage" between compacts, 32
Mary Dunhill, *164*
Mary Garden, *121*
Mascot, *56*
Maubousson, 11
Max Factor, *45*
Maxim, *74*
Maxley, *45*
May Fair, *117, 161*
Medana, *63*
Melba, *141, 163, 166–167*
Mello-Glo, *156*
mesh, *46, 118, 124–129, 207, 212, 213,* plate 16
Mickey and Minnie Mouse, 14, plate 1
micro-mosaic, *150, 155,* plate 11
minaudière, 11, 27, *28, 100, 101, 146–147,* plate 9
miniatures, *64, 68, 72, 138–139, 140, 141, 143, 150, 155,* plates 16, 19
Minois, *89*
Miref, *44, 65, 71, 162*
mirror, *4*, 32; diminishing, *129*; sliding, *141, 163*; swivel, *141, 152*
Mondaine, 34, *49, 51, 52, 82, 83, 112*
monogram, *9*, 28, *29, 57, 126, 153, 157, 166–168,* plate 11
Montgomery Ward, 17, *214*
mother-of-pearl, use of, *45, 62, 93, 152*
Motion Picture Actors' Home, 34
Mousse de fraises, 4
Nan Co-Ed, *52*
Napier, *140*
necessaire, 11, 17, *28, 29,* plate 8
nomenclature, 18
Norida, *132, 142, 210*
oblong-shaped compacts, *142,* plate 5
oblong vanity cases, *115, 136, 161*
octagonal compacts, *64, 134, 141,* 148, 149, 150, 155, 158, 161, plates 5, 19
octagonal compact/bracelet, *156*
octagonal vanity cases, *68, 82, 83, 117, 149,* plate 14
oval compacts, *117, 136, 141, 143, 157*
oval vanity bag, *124,* plate 20
Paris Fashion Co., *121*
parure, *70*
Pattie Duette, plate 20
perfume containers, *10,* 14, *152, 158,* plate 12
petit-point, *45, 46, 72, 93, 211,* plates 7, 19
pewter, *105,* 149
Picasso, Paloma, 35
Pilcher, *69*
pistol/compact, *69*
plastic, use of, *62, 72, 75, 94, 99, 111, 118, 142,* plate 2
Platé, *72,* plate 4
pli, 11, *121*
pochette, *48*
Pohlson, 17
Poudre d'amour, 3
powder bags, *75*
powder/lipstick cane, *170*
powder-puff container, *121*
Powder-Tier, *151*
powder-vial container, *143*
powder sifters, *140, 142, 143*
powderette, 11, *121*
Princess Pat, 12, *121*
provenance, 18
Puf-Kase, *121*
puff-kase, 11
purse-motif, *109, 116, 118, 123, 145, 148,* plate 5
Pygmalion, plate 1
Quinto, plate 7
R & G Co., *116, 117, 118, 144*
Reagan, Nancy, 34
Renard, *76, 77*
repoussé, *120, 131, 143, 145, 146, 149, 151,* plate 2
Rex Fifth Avenue, *38, 47, 62, 111, 142, 162*
rhinestones, use of, *48, 114, 134, 135, 142, 152, 156, 157, 161,* plates 4, 19
Richard Hudnut, 8, 12, 34, *53, 55, 76, 77, 82, 83, 121, 135, 148, 149, 165,* plates 6, 15
Richelieu, *157*
Rigaud, *111*
Ritz, 12
Robin Handbags, *104*
Roger & Gallet, *210*
Ronson, 8, *54, 55, 56*
Rosenfeld, *113*
Rowenta, plate 7
Rumpp, *10*
S & F., *131*
"Saint Genesius, Guide My Destiny" medallion, plate 6
Samaral, plate 1
Schildkraut, *38, 135*
screw-top compacts, *111, 146–147,* plate 2
screw-top perfume container, plate 13
Schuco miniature monkey, *138–139*
Sears, Roebuck, 17, *207, 208, 218*
Segal Key Company, 17, plate 13
shagreen, 35, plate 6
Shields, Inc., *158*
silhouettes, *111, 145, 149, 155,* plate 4
silk, use of, *100, 101, 136, 143, 152,* plate 13
Silvaray, plate 15
silver plate, *115, 131*
six-sided vanity case, *109*
Smith, Rosalynn, 14
snakeskin, use of, *50, 52, 117*
souvenir compacts, 15–17, 34, *64, 65, 66, 67, 68, 163*
sterling silver, use of, *4, 10, 24, 26,* 27, *28, 59, 64, 71, 82, 83, 109, 110, 116, 117, 119, 120, 121, 126–127, 129, 136, 140, 144, 145, 149, 155, 156, 160, 161, 164, 166–167,* plates 1, 4, 6, 12, 14, 19
Stratton of London, 12, 13 *38, 94, 140, 162, 165*
suede, use of, *48, 78, 80–81, 84, 85, 89, 107*
surrealism, 25
Suzuyo, *120*
tandem lipsticks, *148, 152,* plates 7, 12
Tangee, 12, *121*

tango-chains, 11, 34, *53, 82, 83, 116, 123, 135, 150,* plates 2, 12, 20
tassels, *94, 110, 118, 145;* jeweled, *122, 125;* lipstick in, *41, 122, 123,* plates 4, 14, 20
Terri, *114, 136, 148, 155*
Theatre magazine, *23, 209, 210*
thumbpieces, *124–127, 129, 140, 144, 146–147, 166–167,* plates 5, 16
Tiffany & Co., 11, *12,* 35, *145,* plate 16
Timepact, *63*
Tre-Jur, 12
triangular compacts, *110, 141, 165,* plate 7
triangular vanity cases, *117, 146–147, 155*
triple-tiered compact, 15
two-sided vanity case, plate 12
Van Cleef & Arpels, 11, 27, *28,* 35
Vani-Pak, *157*
vanity bag, 8, *10,* 18–*20, 21, 46, 124–129, 144, 168*
vanity box, 11, *79*
vanity/bracelet compact, 29–31; patent for, *30*
vanity cases, 5, 6, 8, *9, 42, 56, 62, 66, 108, 112, 141, 146–147, 149, 164, 166–167, 207, 208,* plate 19
vanity-case/compass combination, *58*
vanity clutch, 8, *10,* 11, *76, 77, 132*
vanity/hatpin, plate 18
vanity/pochette, 11, *46–48*
vanity pouch, 11, *46–48, 68*
vanity purse, 8, *48, 78, 80–81, 84–85, 88, 89, 90, 91, 95, 98*
vanity reticule, 11, *74, 84–87*
Vantine, plate 13
Venine, plate 4
vermeil compacts, *116, 117, 155,* plate 19
vermeil compact/bracelet, *156*
vermeil compact and lipstick set, plate 14
vermeil compact, lipstick, and comb set, plate 5
vermeil pli, *121*
vintage compacts, 32–34
Vitoge, *165*
Vogue Vanities, *160*
Volupté, 8, 12–13, 14, 15, 34, *39, 45, 48, 64, 73, 82, 83, 92, 103, 110, 113, 119, 134, 135, 136, 140, 141, 142, 154, 162, 164, 165,* plates 1, 13
WB, *169*
Wade Dade. *See* Whiting & Davis Company
Wadsworth, *38, 44, 52, 109, 114, 142, 150, 165,* plate 13
Wadsworth Watch Case Company, 12
Walters, Barbara
Warhol, Andy, 35
watch/compacts, 17. *See also* compact/watches
Webster Company, *28, 29*
Weltzunder, *60*
Whiting & Davis Company, 12, 13, 18–19, *20, 21, 124–127, 129, 144, 151,* plate 11
Wilardy, *90, 91, 99*
windshield wipers, on compact, 15, *169*
Wolf-Ferrari, Ermanno, 8
wood compacts, *59, 66, 136*
wood-marquetry compact, *150*
Woodbury, 12
Woodworth, 113, 140, 142, 163
Yardley, 12, 34, *113, 141, 146–147, 148, 152*
Zell Fifth Avenue, *43, 49, 59, 76, 77, 95, 106, 135, 159, 162, 168*
zippers, on compacts, *113, 136, 149,* plate 13

JAMES PRENDERGAST LIBRARY
3 1880 02171418